MRINAL K. DAS

The Encyclopedia of Aquarium Fishes in Color

David J. Coffey

MRINAL K. DAS

Photographs taken by Heather Angel MSC FRPS FIIP

The Encyclopedia of
Aquarium
Fishes in Color

Arco Publishing Company, Inc., *New York*

This book was designed and produced by
The Rainbird Publishing Group Limited
36 Park Street, London W1, England
for Arco Publishing Co. Inc.,
219 Park Avenue South, New York, N.Y. 10003

Designer: Alan Bartram
Illustrator: Christopher Sorrell

Library of Congress Cataloging in Publication Data

Coffey, D   J
   The encyclopedia of aquarium fishes in color.

   1. Aquarium fishes – Dictionaries. I. Title.
SF457.C6   1977   639°.34°03   76–54636
ISBN 0–668–04202–8

Filmset by Jolly & Barber Ltd, Rugby, England
Printed by Dai Nippon, Tokyo, Japan

Contents

Common names are fully cross-referred
in the encyclopedia

Introduction

Fish have been kept in captivity for many hundreds of years. Originally they were used to provide a readily available source of food but it was not long before they were also kept for the pleasure they gave in beauty of form and movement. Fish keeping became a hobby.

With the increasing urbanization of our society a relatively small tank in the corner of the sitting room may prove to be the best, if not the only, animal life the owners can accommodate. Since society now demands that the majority of western populations live in towns, keeping pet fish is just one of the ways of alleviating the unspoken displeasure one may have from this isolation from nature. As a result aquarists can now be counted in millions.

Scientific and technical advances have brought aquarism a very long way from the goldfish and glass bowl. To-day the facilities available to the aquarist are continually being added to. Indeed, I sometimes feel that the mass of elaborate electronic equipment which inhabits and surrounds many aquarists' tanks may, for some, become more demanding of the hobbyist's technical knowledge than it is of his understanding of the creatures he is trying to keep. Success demands a real understanding of the biological dependence of one living thing on another – ecology. Technology can never replace sound animal management. It has therefore been my intention when discussing the technology of aquarism to keep its importance at all times in perspective. Thus the belief is stressed that the simplest way is usually the best way. Unnecessary gadgetry often creates as many problems as it solves.

This book provides descriptions of coldwater, tropical and marine fish currently kept by aquarists, and contains illustrations of many in colour. It is therefore hoped that it will extend the hobby for the aquarist, by relating it to the science of biology. The aquarium should prove a starting point for, and then continue as an adjunct to, a full study of biology. In this way the hobby does not remain static, with limited horizons, but develops to embrace a whole range of biological pursuits, hopefully stimulating interest in behaviour, ecology and conservation.

The book is arranged in alphabetical order, according to the subject heading. Thus heaters or thermometers should be sought under those headings. Each species of fish is discussed under its scientific name. For example the Red Surgeonfish, *Acanthurus achilles*, is listed under its generic name *Acanthurus* together with all other members of the genus described. The family to which the genus belongs is also recorded but a family description will be found under a separate heading, e.g. Acanthuridae and this should be used in conjunction with the species description. At the end of each family description will be found a list of all the genera belonging to the family which are discussed here, to provide a complete cross reference. Acanthuridae therefore ends with the list of genera *Acanthurus, Naso, Paracanthurus* and *Zebrasoma*. Many of the species listed have been given symbols, for speed of reference, and the reader's attention is drawn to the key on page 42. Diseases have all been discussed under the one heading to simplify the reader's researches, but it is stressed that the whole subject should be read with care before any attempt is made to identify the problem, and before any action taken.

A book of this kind is the result of good team work. It would be impossible to quantify the importance of the individuals who have assisted. Without my wife, Jean's, interest and encouragement the task would have seemed much harder. A book of this kind owes a great deal to the visual sense. Heather Angel has, with painstaking professionalism, produced an excellent series of exciting photographs, and the Coral Bazaar, Walton-on-the-Hill, Tadworth, England very kindly allowed their fish to be photographed and were always willing to give advice. Rainbirds, who have produced this book, have been of endless assistance. Their patience, understanding and courtesy have made work a pleasure. Finally, to my mother and Mrs Sylvia Goble who deciphered my scribble and typed the manuscript goes my heartfelt thanks.

I would like to think that my own fascination with biological science and concern for conservation, as well as my interest in aquarism, is reflected in this book and that something of these enthusiasms will be passed on to the reader.

D.J.C.

Color Illustrations

Color Illustrations captions
Continued on page 41

2

3

4

5

6

7

8

9

11

13

15

16

17

18

19

21

23   24

25   26

27

28

29

30

31

32

33

34

35

36

37

38

39

41

43

44

45

46

47

48

49

50

52

53

56

57

58

59

60

61

62

63

64

65

66

67

68

69

71 72 ▽ 73

74

75

76

77

78

79

81   82   ▽83

84

85

86

87

88

90

91

92

93

94

95

96

97

98

99

100

101

102

104

103

105

106

107

108

112

113

114

115

116

117

118

119

121

122

123

124

125

126

127

128

129

▽ 131

▽ 132

133

135

134

136

137

138

140

141

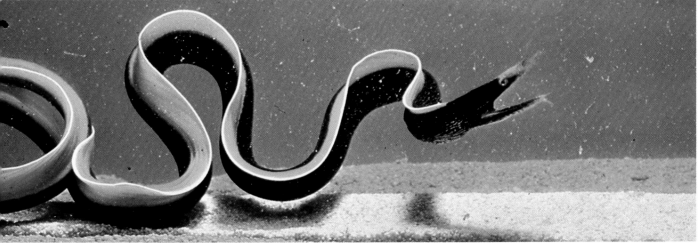

▽ 143

144

145

146

147

148

149

150

152

155

156

157

158

159

160

Key to symbols

⊕	Freshwater
Ψ	Marine
Ψ/⊕	Brackish
✂	Aggressive or solitary
◍	Shade preferred
◐	Semi-shade preferred
⊙	Bright light preferred
♂	Male
♀	Female

The colour illustrations are in **bold type**.

A

Abramites Anostomidae ⊕
– *microcephalus* NORMAN'S or MARBLED HEADSTANDER
15cm. (6in.)
As its popular names suggest, this fish of the lower Amazon swims with its head tilted downwards. It may grow to 15cm. long. There is little colour but blotches, bands and spots of dark grey and black on a background of light grey. The pectoral, caudal and anal fins are pale yellow. Its attitude would suggest it is a bottom feeder.

A fairly rare species; it is peaceful but has not been bred in captivity.

Abudefduf Pomacentridae Ψ
– *leucozona* ONE-SPOTTED DAMSELFISH 6cm. (2½in.)
A small damselfish from the Indo-Pacific. Its body is a greenish yellow, shading to a yellow cream belly with a pale bar on the middle of the sides. A circular spot decorates the dorsal fin. Recently placed in the genus *Plectroglyphidodon*.
– *melanopus* YELLOW-BACKED or BLUE AND GOLD
DAMSELFISH 7cm. (2½in.)
A species more popular in the USA than in the UK. It comes from the Indo-Pacific. Its most striking feature is the bright golden yellow of its body and the exaggerated points of its caudal fin.

It makes a good community member of the marine aquarium but prefers the company of its own species.

This species is sometimes wrongly called *A. xanthonotus*. Recently transferred to the genus *Paraglyphidodon*.
– *oxyodon* BLACK VELVET DAMSELFISH 15cm. (6in.) ✂
A fat dark blue-black body with a vertical yellow line dividing its body in half, and a horizontal neon blue stripe

above and below the eye, makes this one of the more striking and popular of the damselfishes. It is easy to feed providing live food is offered. It is very aggressive to members of its own species and can only be kept together in very large tanks with plenty of cover in the form of rock and coral hides. It is widely distributed in the Indo-Pacific. Recently placed in the genus *Paraglyphidodon*.
– *saxatilis* SERGEANT MAJOR DAMSELFISH 17cm. (7in.)
A popular and hardy fish, its yellowish green body is decorated with five dark vertical lines. There is, however, a good deal of colour variation and fading with emotion, and in the wild its body becomes dark blue in deep water. It is peaceful as a juvenile and easy to feed, but may become aggressive at maturity.
– *xanthonotus* see *A. melanopus*

Acanthodoras Doradidae ⊕ ◍
– *spinosissimus* TALKINGFISH, SPINY CATFISH
*c*18cm. (*c*7in.)
A well barbelled fish with a long dorsal fin which comes from the Amazon Basin. The brown body is decorated with a variety of white dots and patches. Grows to 18cm. in nature but somewhat less in captivity. Its popularity with aquarists is enhanced by its ability to produce loud noises with its pectoral spines, amplified by the gas bladder.

Acanthophthalmus Cobitidae ⊕ ◍
– *kuhli* COOLIE or STRIPED LOACH, LEOPARD EEL
8cm. (3in.)
This comes from the Malay Peninsula, Borneo, Sumatra and Java. The long slim rather eel-like body is golden yellow brown in colour carrying a number of wide dark vertical bars which are partly broken by a pale line. It has 6 barbels around the mouth. Dorsal fin is well towards the tail while the pelvic fins are more than half way down the body.

Active nocturnally, rather nervous, they are reasonable scavengers and prefer temperatures around 27–28°C. They have occasionally been bred in captivity. The mating involves a complicated and entwined embrace. These fish prefer a soft bottom for burrowing, as is typical of the genus. **1**
– *semicinctus* HALF-BANDED COOLIE LOACH 8cm. (3in.)
From the Malay Peninsula, very similar to *A. kuhli*, but is pinker, with less distinct bordering. Indeed all members of this genus are difficult to differentiate and are often sold as *A. kuhli*. However, it is slightly deeper in the body, with the pelvic and anal fins set a little more towards the head. Prefers to be kept only with its own species.

Acanthostracion Ostraciontidae Ψ
– *quadricornis* SCRAWLED COWFISH 45cm. (18in.)
A common species in the Caribbean and the Gulf of

Mexico, where it tends to live in rather deep water, up to 50–60 m. deep. It feeds on a wide variety of crustacea and plants.

The body is a pale greenish yellow or light brown with dark irregular lines on the head which break up into broken lines or dots along the body. A black line above the eye is distinctive. It gets its specific and common names from the two spines which protrude from above the eyes and a second pair slightly behind.

A fish which grows rather large in the aquarium but is kept quite commonly when young by aquarists. This fish has been recently classified in the genus *Lactophrys*.

Acanthuridae SURGEONFISHES, TANGS Ψ ⊙
This family of marine fish is widely distributed in the warmer seas and oceans. It includes many attractive and interesting species. In nature they usually congregate together and are found free swimming in shoals. Like the wrasses (Labridae) they use only their pectoral fins when swimming. Unfortunately for the marine aquarist they tend to grow rather large.

They get their common name from 2 very sharp scalpel-like blades which are on the tail just before the tail fin. Normally they are tucked back out of harm's way but if anything antagonizes the fish, the blades are flicked forward like stilettos and held erect and ready for trouble. In addition they are equipped with a vicious dorsal fin which also has the ability to inflict unpleasant wounds. They use these weapons in fights between themselves but may also attack other fish. In the aquarium, once settled, they are relatively peaceful but are likely to attack newly introduced fish with fatal consequences. Hence aquarists must take great care when introducing a new member. They approach their victim and with a swirling movement slash its side.

In captivity they prefer higher temperatures than many marine fish, usually around 27–28°C. They need large amounts of vegetable food in the form of algae, although in captivity, boiled lettuce or spinach can be substituted. They have rather small mouths. Any aquarist which scorns the armoury of the surgeonfish and puts a finger into the tank is likely to regret it, so be warned.

Surgeonfish are thought, in nature, to spawn in groups, mature adults simply shedding their eggs and sperms while performing a nuptial water ballet.
See *Acanthurus, Naso, Paracanthurus, Zebrasoma, Zanclus*.

Acanthurus Acanthuridae Ψ ⊙
– **achilles** ACHILLES TANG, RED SURGEONFISH 18cm. (7in.)
A lovely dark brown fish from the Pacific. An orange teardrop patch marks the area of the scalpel blades and there is also orange on the tail fin.

– **coeruleus** BLUE TANG c.30cm. (c.12in.)
Common in the Caribbean. The adult fish is coloured, as the common name suggests, in an extravaganza of blue. This colour is broken by horizontal dark lined patterns. The eye is a lovely mauve in some specimens. As in most surgeonfish the anal and dorsal fins are long based, low and rounded, accentuating the circular form of the body. In the young stage this fish is a bright yellow.

– **japonicus** PHILIPPINE TANG 18cm. (7in.)
A rather drab common name for a lovely fish which comes from the Rin Kin Islands and the Philippines. It has a compressed body rather deeper than is usual for the family. A deep browny orange near the head shades through bright orange to yellow, just before the tail. The caudal fin is a delicate almost transparent blue. Dark and white lines

Philippine Tang, *Acanthurus japonicus*.

border the dorsal and anal fins. The snout is adorned with a pink patch. **2**

– **leucosternon** LEMON BLUE or WHITE-BREASTED SURGEONFISH 30cm. (12in.)
From the Indian Ocean and the Indo-Australian Archipelago, this truly gorgeous fish is popular but difficult to keep due to its specialized algal diet. The body is a lovely pale blue wash. The dorsal fin is a bright daffodil yellow. The anal and pelvic fins are bluish white. There is a triangular area of dark purple on the face and a white crescent around its 'throat' from which one of this surgeonfish's common names, white-breasted, is derived. Dusky grey patterns decorate the tail.

– **lineatus** PYJAMA SURGEONFISH c.20cm. (c.8in.) ✂
Widely distributed from the shores of Africa to the Pacific,

this is a very attractive fish. It has yellow and bluish white lines running horizontally all over its body. Rather hardy, more aggressive than some and grows a little large for most tanks, it is of doubtful value to the smaller community tank unless small specimens are available. Like all surgeonfish it needs regular and plentiful supplies of green vegetation. Also easily adapted to dry flake foods.

– olivaceus ORANGE-SPOT SURGEONFISH   25cm. (10in.) An unattractive fish when adult. The body is a dull brown with a bright yellow orange patch behind the operculum. Young fish, however, make a pleasing exhibit being a bright orange yellow all over. Adults also develop a diffuse protuberance on the head.

This fish comes from the Indo-Australian Achipelago and the Pacific Ocean where it lives in fairly deep water, always close to rocks or coral. It feeds on microscopic organisms, waste organic matter and algae.

– sohal ROYAL SURGEONFISH   40cm. (16in.) An attractive fish though hardly royal in coloration, it comes from the Red Sea. Its body is striped horizontally with blue and black. The caudal fin, which elongates into streamers, is yellowish red and a similarly coloured patch decorates the pectoral fin base.

– xanthopterus EMPEROR TANG   50cm. (20in.) Also known as *Zebrasoma xanthurum* this fish gets its common name from the rich purple of its body colour, although this tends to fade as it matures to include grey overtones. The caudal and pectoral fins are a bright yellow. Widely distributed, it is found from the coastal waters of Africa to the east coast of America. The body is more elongated than many members of the family. For health adequate green food is essential. **3**

ACARA,
 BLACK see *Aequidens portalegrensis*
 BLUE see *Aequidens pulcher*
 BROWN see *Aequidens portalegrensis*
 GOLDEN see *Nannacara anomala*

Acaropsis Cichlidae ⊕
– nassa   20cm. (8in.) A cichlid native to the Amazon and Orinoco rivers, with a lovely green body and with typically flamboyant fins. Silver dots on the scales of the lower part of the body give a certain sheen. Dark vertical bands add interest, as do the large spots on the sides of the body. The fins are green with yellowish spots.

It breeds in the normal cichlid way – see *Cichlidae.*

Acclimatization to Tank

Although fish can adapt to a range of temperatures one of the important rules for the aquarist is *don't take a fish from water of one temperature and put it straight into water of a different temperature.* This will certainly subject the fish to stresses to which it cannot readily adapt.

Newly purchased fish will arrive in some kind of container. Unless supplied with a heater, the temperature will probably have dropped since removal from the original tank. It may have dropped several degrees below that of the tank to which the fish is to be introduced. By far the simplest and safest way of introducing it is to leave it in its travelling container – glass, plastic or plastic bag – and float the whole thing in the tank for which the fish is destined. Leave it there until the two temperatures – container and tank – are the same. This will take some time, depending on the size and heat conductivity of the travelling container. When satisfied, making sure to check with a thermometer, not your finger, very gently tilt the container and allow the fish to pass into the tank. Similarly, gradual mixing of water over a fairly long period will allow the fish to adapt to changes in pH, hardness, and salinity.

One further point of importance. It is extremely unwise to put a new fish into a tank containing a valuable collection. I always keep new fish in a quarantine tank for at least two weeks before introducing it to the main tank to make sure it is healthy. It is time and space consuming but well worth the extra effort if it prevents the introduction of disease. See *Adaptability, Hardness, pH, Temperature.*

ACHILLES TANG see *Acanthurus achilles*

Acoustico Lateralis System

This sensory system is found both in modern fish and in very primitive fish extinct since the Silurian epoch. It consists of the lateral line and the labyrinth.

The lateral line system is basically a line of pressure sensitive organs running from head to tail with a more branched system covering the head. These organs are used to detect vibrations in the water and changes in water currents and are used by fish living in streams and rivers in

Diagrammatic section of skin showing laterial line system.

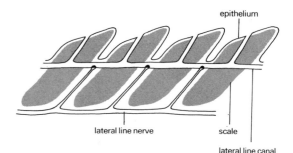

epithelium

lateral line nerve   scale

lateral line canal

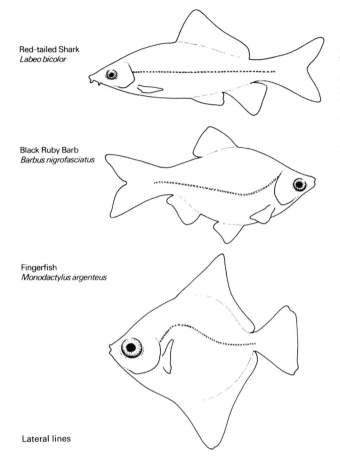

Red-tailed Shark
Labeo bicolor

Black Ruby Barb
Barbus nigrofasciatus

Fingerfish
Monodactylus argenteus

Lateral lines

which they can remain stationary for long periods by swimming against the flow of water just fast enough to prevent themselves being swept away by it. It is also of value for fish in the sea where tidal currents exist. The ability to sense vibrations gives fish a sixth sense of 'remote touch'. This sense guides sharks to injured fish from great distances and allows the blind cave fish, *Anoptichthys jordani*, to detect solid objects by their reflected vibrations caused by pressure waves generated as the fish swims.

The labyrinth is a system of semi-circular canals and otolith (bony) organs similar to those found in the inner ear of all vertebrates, including man. These organs, one on each side of the head, are concerned with balance and hearing. There has been considerable doubt as to fishes' ability to hear since the labyrinth has no spiral cochlea which is common in all other vertebrates. For a long time it was assumed that they were deaf, but detailed experimental work has proved beyond all doubt that they can hear and that the labyrinth is intimately concerned with this sense.

Acorus see under *Plants*

Actinopterygii see under *Classification*

Adaptability

The environment in which an animal lives does not always remain the same. It is constantly changing as day turns to night, winter to summer, or even as clouds cover the sun. Heavy rain washes soluble material from the land, altering the physical and chemical properties of the water in streams and rivers, while summer droughts concentrate salts in slow moving streams or stagnant pools.

In order to cope with these constant natural changes animals have evolved with the necessary ability to adapt to change. There are limits, of course, outside which they cannot survive, but within those limits they can adjust their bodily mechanism and live quite happily. Different species vary in the range of environmental conditions to which they can adapt. The more specialized animals have naturally narrower limits, and aquarists attempting to keep and breed them must be more knowledgeable and more diligent in controlling their environment.

Many of the rigid doctrines preached, which prophesy terrible consequences of even slight environmental variations in for example temperature, pH and hardness, are quite untrue. Indeed much experimental evidence exists to show that changes in the environment, far from being harmful, are beneficial to an animal's well being. It must be remembered, however, that in nature changes occur relatively slowly. They are not abrupt.

See *Acclimatization to Tank, Evolution, Hardness, pH, Temperature.*

ADDIS BUTTERFLYFISH see *Chaetodon rafflesii*

Adioryx diadema see *Holocentrus diadema*

Aeoliscus Centriscidae Ψ
– *strigatus* SHRIMPFISH 15cm (6in.)
A small fish from the Indo-Pacific and Red Sea. It is peaceful but a little delicate to keep. Not very colourful, greyish green with longitudinal stripes along back and sides, but amusing and interesting when seen swimming vertically with its head pointing downwards. Certainly a fish for collectors of the unusual. A feature of the genus is a mobile spine by the rear end of the dorsal fin and an entirely scaleless body protected by an outer armour of bone. It requires small live food, such as *Artemia mauplii*.

Aequidens Cichlidae ⊕
– *curviceps* FLAG BLUNTHEAD CICHLID 8cm. (3in.)
A popular fish among aquarists which comes from the Amazon region of Brazil.

The general body colour is greeny brown. Dorsally it is dark browny green which shades vertically to a green anterior lower half and a blue posterior. Several dark dots, almost bars, adorn its back. The tail fin has blue dots on a brown background. The dorsal fin is blue with a red border while the lovely anal fin is basically yellow. The pectorals and pelvics are clear but the pelvics have a blue anterior border.

Its popularity comes from its beauty, its small size and its unusually peaceful nature which makes it an ideal member of the community tank. In addition it extends its non-aggression pact with the other fish to include the plant life, so plants are unlikely to be uprooted. It breeds as described for cichlids – see *Cichlidae*.

– *latifrons* see *A. pulcher*

– *maroni* KEYHOLE CICHLID 9–14cm. (3–5in.)
A native of Guyana and Venezuela. A dark 'keyhole' shaped bar extends vertically down from the middle of the dorsal fin to the anal fin. A second vertical band runs through the eye. The body colour is beige, the fins are yellow in colour and there are green dots on the dorsal and anal fins.

A peaceful fish which lives in harmony in the community tank. Like many cichlids, it is easy to breed.

– *portalegrensis* BLACK or BROWN ACARA, PORT 25cm. (10in.), in captivity up to 12cm. (5in.)
A cichlid from Brazil and Bolivia. The body is a rich olive green colour which shades to a blue belly and head. A dark green band runs from the eye to an ocellated spot at the base of the tail. Running vertically from this band are 3 dark green bars. The elliptically shaped fins are a beige brown flecked with blue and yellow dots.

Gentle of nature and easy to breed it is a popular cichlid with aquarists. It does occasionally dig up plants.

– *pulcher* syn. *A. latifrons* BLUE ACARA, BLUE CICHLID 17cm. (7in.)
A medium sized cichlid from Trinidad, Panama, Venezuela and Columbia. In spite of its popular name the body colour is a greenish brown, with a blue shimmer on the flanks. Indistinct vertical bars adorn its body and midway along there is a large body spot. The lovely cichlid fins are a brownish orange with greenish markings. Has a temperature range from 22–29°C. but prefers temperatures around 27°C. for breeding. It breeds easily in captivity and

Keyhole Cichlid, *Aequidens maroni*. The dark head bar efficiently camouflages the eye.

is of gentle nature. Suitable, if rather large, for community life. Best kept with larger fish. **4**
– *tetramerus* SADDLE CICHLID 25cm. (10in.)
From the Amazon, this fish is greenish brown with a metallic sheen which shades to a pinkish grey belly. A horizontal bar runs from the eye to the tail, above which are dark vertical bars. A large round spot is positioned dorsally in the middle of the body while a second smaller dot embellishes the base of the tail. Spots and bars of darkened hue decorate the dorsal and anal fins. More aggressive as adults than other *Aequidens* species.

Aeration
A greater number of fish can be kept in an aerated tank than in an unaerated tank of the same size. It is a common misconception that as air bubbles through the water a gaseous exchange occurs. In fact very little exchange takes place in this way. The main action of the aeration process is to circulate the water, bringing deeper water containing carbon dioxide to the surface and thereby increasing the exchange which takes place there.

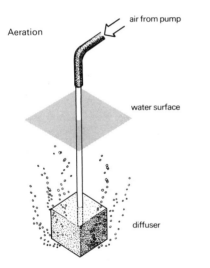

Aeration

air from pump

water surface

diffuser

A pump is used to force air down a tube. At the open end of the tube air escapes and bubbles its way up through the water. Greater circulation and agitation is attained if the air is passed through a diffuser, usually in the form of a porous stone, which breaks the air into fine bubbles.

Several types of air pump exist. The more expensive piston pumps are the best buy being long lasting, efficient and quiet running. Diaphragm pumps are cheaper but tend to be noisier. Technology is however reducing noise and increasing their efficiency and longevity.

The air pump may be used simply for aeration but is commonly coupled with a filter system. (See *Filtration*).

AFRICAN
  BANDED BARB see *Barbus fasciolatus*
  CLIMBING PERCH see *Ctenopoma*
  FEATHERBACK see *Notopterus afer*
  JEWELFISH see *Hemichromis bimaculatus*
  KNIFEFISH see *Xenomystus nigri*
  LEAFFISH see *Polycentropsis abbreviata*
  LUNGFISH see Protopteridae *Protopterus annectens*
  POMPANO see *Alectis crinitus*
  SNAKEHEAD see *Channa africana*
  TETRA see *Nannaethiops unitaeniatus*
AGASSIZ'S DWARF CICHLID see *Apistogramma agassizi*
Age see *Longevity*
Agnatha see *Classification*
AIRSHIPFISH, MALAYAN see *Sphaerichthys osphronemoides*
ALBINO LYRETAIL MOLLY see *Poecilia formosa*

Alectis Carangidae Ψ
– *ciliaris* TREADFIN or PENNANT TREVALLY
38cm. (15in.)
Young members of this species are particularly attractive. Their bodies are deep and their snouts short and rounded. What makes them so pleasing are the long trailing rays of the anterior part of both dorsal and anal fins. The species is widely distributed in the Indo-Pacific.
– *crinitus* AFRICAN POMPANO 90cm. (36in.)
In spite of its size this fish enjoys some popularity as an aquarium inhabitant, especially in the USA. It has a silver rather slender body with elongated anterior rays on both the dorsal and anal fins. When young, and therefore when it is popular as an aquarium fish, the body is deep and compressed with relatively very long anterior rays to the dorsal and anal fins. The body is also somewhat darker than the adult's.

A widely distributed fish found both in the Atlantic and the Indo-Pacific. It feeds on invertebrates.

Algal Growth see *Green Water*

Allopoecilia Poeciliidae ⊕
– *caucana* 4cm. (1½in.)
A native of the Cauca River and Panama, this small fish has a browny orange body with a blue tinting. The dorsal and caudal fins are a yellowish red, edged with black. Peaceful, well suited to a small fish community tank.

Alternanthera see under *Plants*
AMAZON
  LEAFFISH see *Monocirrhus polyacanthus*
  MOLLY see *Poecilia formosa*
  SWORDPLANT see under *Plants – Lagenandra*
  YELLOW DWARF CICHLID see *Apistogramma pertense*

Ambassis lala see *Chanda ranga*

Amblycirrhitus Cirrhitidae Ψ
– pinos REDSPOTTED HAWKFISH 9cm. (3½in.)
An attractive olive green fish which is found throughout the western tropical Atlantic, from Florida to the West Indies. The lower rays of the pectoral fin are long and give the fish a characteristic profile. Red spots decorate the anterior part of the body and spill onto the dorsal fin. A black line runs around the base of the tail and a dark spot is situated at the base of the dorsal fin. The pale grey base of the tail shades gradually to a light reddish brown.

In the aquarium it tends to stay motionless just above the bottom. It seems to appreciate plenty of coral hideouts and eats invertebrates.

Amphiprion Pomacentridae Ψ ⊙
CLOWNFISH, ANEMONEFISH
This distinctive genus, known popularly as Clownfish, contains some of the most attractive fish available to the marine aquarist. They are not the easiest of fish to keep but care, patience and diligent management should ensure success. The outstanding characteristic of the genus is its relationship with sea-anemones. All species live in continual proximity to this relatively static marine animal and return to the safety of its tentacles when danger threatens. How the two species – anemone and fish – communicate to prevent the poisoning of the fish is uncertain but it appears to be chemical in origin. Clownfish are not exclusively immune from attack by the anemone's tentacles. Other members of the family Pomacentridae can come within its clutches without provoking attack. However, if the Clownfish's mucus is removed it loses immunity from the anemone's tentacles and will be stung to death.

Some observers believe that the fish benefits not only from the safety of the poisonous tentacles but also from a cleansing action whereby the anemone removes parasites from the fish.

Clownfish come from the tropical waters of the Pacific, around the East Indies, and the Indian Ocean.

In captivity clownfish have spawned and several species are being successfully reared. There is parental care of the eggs. The problem of rearing is to provide the correct physical conditions for the parents at breeding time and sufficient quantities of suitable food for the fry. The small size of marine fish in captivity is at least in part due to space restriction. In nature when population explosions occur, individual space is obviously restricted, and this may bring into action a variety of physiological mechanisms which inhibit breeding, in an attempt to restore the population to suitable proportions consistent with food supply.

Finally one should mention that all anemones are not suitable. Beadlet, for example, found around the British coast, will kill them. Tropical anemones should be used preferably from the Stoichactinid family.
– akallopsisos YELLOW SHANK CLOWNFISH 10cm. (4in.)
This lovely pale orange fish has a white stripe running along its back from nose to tail. It comes from the Indian Ocean and Indonesia and is somewhat smaller than many members of the genus. Dependence on the anemone is marked and it only leaves this protection for the briefest of periods to obtain food. Consequently it would be foolish to purchase this fish without a suitable anemone. The preferred species of anemone is *Radianthus ritteri*.
– bicinctus ANEMONEFISH 13cm. (5in.)
Its range is restricted to the Red Sea. The body is a very attractive orange red decorated with two vertical white bars, a wide one just behind the eye and a second narrower one midway along the body. The white bars are edged with a generous border of dark brown.

This fish lives, in nature, in close association with anemones depending on the host's stinging ability for protection against predators. The anemone benefits from the association as well since the clownfish keeps it free from foreign objects and protects it from the gastronomic ambitions of some fishes. Anemonefish feed on the microscopic crustacea which pass close to their home anemone.
– clarki YELLOW TAILED CLOWNFISH 10cm. (4in.)
This fish is very widely distributed in marine waters throughout the Indian and Pacific oceans. The dark, almost black body is decorated with three white bands and it is finally adorned with a pale cream, almost white tail. There are many closely related species often confused with this fish. It is very hardy and dominant in a tank with other anemonefish.
– ephippium 15cm. (6 in.)
An attractive clownfish from the Indo-Pacific. This species appears to be less reliant on an association with sea anemones than most other members of the genus. It is often confused with a similar species, but much rarer import, *A. frenatum*. *A. ephippium* is bright orange-red. In the wild it develops a beautifying, black, heart-shaped patch on its flank, but sadly this usually fails to materialise as young fish mature in captivity. Occasionally there is a white cross-band behind the eye of young fish, which gradually disappears with age. **6**
– frenatum FIRE or TOMATO CLOWNFISH
13cm. (5in.) ✄
A smallish fish from the Pacific and Indian Ocean. Its body colour is usually a very bright red but it may be duller, fading to a reddish brown. There is a white band running around the head and usually, when young, there is a second,

small white band on the flank. Rather an aggressive fish with deep territorial inclinations, occasionally it will attack and damage other fish which invade its territory. Less dependent on the anemone than some of its generic cousins. **5**

– laticlavius see *A. polymnus*

– melanopus TEAK CLOWNFISH 10cm. (4in.)
It comes from the Indo-Pacific where it grows to only 10cm. A brownish body with a white head band, it is hardy, easily fed and not over dependent on anemones, although, in its natural habitat it is found in association with the anemone *Physobrachia douglasi*. The teak clownfish feeds on algae, crustacea and marine worms.

– ocellaris COMMON CLOWNFISH 8cm. (3in.)
It comes from the Pacific and eastern Indian Ocean and although named prosaically is none the less beautiful. It has an orange body decorated with wide, swirling white bands and a startling white head band, all of which are edged with black. It should be fed several times a day. **7**

– polymnus syn. *A. laticlavius* SADDLEBACK CLOWNFISH 5cm. (6in.)
From the Pacific Ocean, the Saddleback Clownfish is dark reddish brown, broken by a white saddle crossing the posterior half of the dorsal fin, and a white head band. The tip of the tail is also decorated with a white crescent.

Ampularia see under *Snails*

Anabantidae LABYRINTHFISHES
Previously this family included all the labyrinthfishes but further research by taxonomists has resulted in reclassification in the families Belontiidae, Osphronemidae

A Common Clownfish, *Amphiprion ocellaris,* swimming amongst the tentacles of a sea anemone.

and Helostomatidae. The remaining three genera, *Anabas, Ctenopoma* and *Sandelia*, are the climbing perches which belong in the Anabantidae. They make up a small group of freshwater fishes from Asia and Africa. Their interesting feature is an accessory respiratory organ above the gills which is greatly folded to give the popular name labyrinthfishes.

This allows them to survive in environments which would prove fatal to species with only the conventional gill breathing mechanism. Indeed they have come to rely on this method and will die if it is denied them. They can even leave the water, providing rain keeps the ground moist, and travel across land.

Members of the family are omnivorous, easy to feed but care should be taken to provide a varied diet. Most of the members of the family prefer temperatures of about 22°C. The climbing perch can survive temperatures close to freezing without trouble. See *Anabas, Ctenopoma*.

Anabas Anabantidae $\oplus$
– testudineus CLIMBING WALKING PERCH
10–25cm. (4–10in.)
A rather unpopular fish with aquarists since it is sluggish, very shy, pugnacious and can hardly claim great beauty. The body is browny grey above shading to yellow under-parts. The dorsal fin is grey, the caudal, anal and pectoral yellow. The female distinguishes herself from the male with a soft dorsal fin. In captivity it rarely grows longer than 10cm. It is widely distributed in south-east Asia, India, Sri Lanka, Malaya, South China and the Philippines.

In spite of a general lack of enthusiasm by aquarists this fish is interesting to keep. Its natural history is fascinating (see Anabantidae) and one of its methods of locomotion is unusual. It rests a great deal on the tank or river bottom but by utilizing its pectoral fins and operculum, it can creep along. It employs the same action to move across rain drenched land. One thing I have learnt from practical experience is to keep the tank covered since, despite its general sluggishness, it is a good jumper. A generously planted tank which affords plenty of cover is appreciated by the fish. It is omnivorous. It is reported not to make a nest and simply lays eggs which float to the surface there to lie without parental protection.

Anablepidae
A small family containing only a single genus, which in turn has only three species. They are of particular interest because of a unique adaptation of their eyes which allows them to see at the same time above and below the water surface. Members of this family live very close to the surface at all times. As they swim their eye is half in and half out of the water. A band of tissue divides the eye effectively into two separate parts. The cornea, lens and retina are functionally split and act as separate eyes. The upper 'eye', the part out of the water, is adapted to see in air while the lower 'eye' functions just like a normal fish eye.

Slim fish with blunt heads, rounded dorsal and caudal fins and, in males, a modified anal fin or gonopodium, used for internal fertilization. See *Anableps*.

Anableps Anablepidae $\Psi/\oplus$
– anableps FOUREYES 18cm. (7in.)
This fish is more commonly imported into the USA. than into the UK. It is worthy of discussion since it has some interesting adaptations. It comes from the north of South America, and Central America, where it is found in both fresh and brackish water.

The body is very elongated with a rounded caudal fin, and a posteriorly placed, small dorsal fin. The triangular pectoral fins are large and positioned just behind the operculum. The small pelvic fins are midway along the ventral side of the body. The anal fin is adapted into a gonopodium, in the male. A lovely yellow brown body is decorated with darker grey brown lines.

Foureyes are always found at the surface. Their eyes are specially adapted to life there, see Anablepidae. This fish can therefore keep a watery eye open for enemies from below while its 'dry' eye looks for flying insect food. In the aquarium it will take live food near the surface.

Foureyes produce a small number of live young. There are rarely more than four but they are large and are easily raised on live daphnia. The male's gonopodium may twist to the left or right and this modification corresponds to a similar situation in the female. Males with a left twist are restricted in their choice of partner to a female with a right-sided genital aperture, and vice versa.

A peaceful fish, well suited to a spacious aquarium with plenty of plant cover. It does well in a community tank.

Anaesthesia
Fish are difficult to handle out of water and therefore if any form of surgery is to be performed for treatment of a sick fish it is essential to anaesthetize it first. Many kinds of anaesthetics have been used for fish including most of those used for human beings. Marine and freshwater fish have all been successfully anaesthetized.

The usual practice is to put the fish into a special anaesthetic tank. This is usually a plastic tank which has similar water at the same temperature as the home tank but with the anaesthetic mixed in the water. It is usual to starve a fish for at least 24 hours before anaesthetizing it. This is essential as a fish may vomit under anaesthesia and this will block its gills causing asphyxiation. The transference should be completed with as much care as possible to avoid stress.

Most fish recover from anaesthetics within half an hour of being returned to their own tank.

Anaesthetics are also used by some shippers of fish in order to reduce oxygen consumption while in transit thus allowing some crowding of the fish.

Anatomy
Anatomy is the scientific study of structure. In addition to the usual structures fish have an important and characteristic feature in the swim or gas bladder. With a range of animals as varied as fish it is not surprising that their systems differ considerably. Pike are as different from sharks as horses are from tigers. These differences will be briefly indicated under the separate systems. See Acoustico Lateralis System, Blood System, Digestive System, Endocrine System, Eye, Fins, Gas Bladder, Muscular System, Nervous System, Reproductive System, Respiratory System, Skeleton, Skin, Smell, Touch, Urinary System.

ANEMONEFISH,
 see *Amphiprion bicinctus*
 MAROON see *Premnas biaculeatus*
ANGEL, BICOLOR see *Centropyge bicolor*
ANGELFISH see *Chaetodontidae, Centropyge, Euxiphipops, Holocanthus, Monodactylus, Pomacanthus, Pterophyllum, Pygoplites*
annelids see under *Marine Invertebrates*
ANGLERFISHES see *Antennariidae*

Anoptichthys Characidae ⊕
– jordani BLIND CAVE CHARACIN, BLIND TETRA 8cm. (3in.)
Blind cave characins come from underground pools near San Luis, Mexico. They are truly blind which in their environment of dark caves is no disadvantage. Other sensory systems have developed to compensate for the loss of sight. The body colour is a general translucent pink. Although some aquarists enjoy keeping these fish and

General anatomy

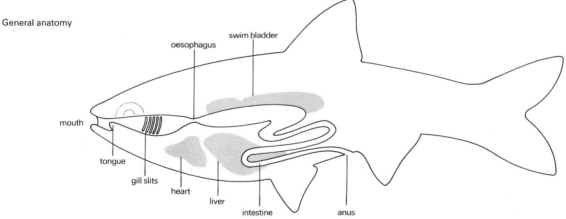

mouth

oesophagus

swim bladder

tongue

gill slits

heart

liver

intestine

anus

Anchor Worms see *Unwelcome Visitors*

Ancistrus Loricariidae ⊕
– cirrhosus VIEJA, BRISTLE-NOSED CATFISH
A catfish which is more popular and more common in the USA than in Europe. The body is dark brown with an irregular pattern of grey spots and patches. There are dark spots on the dorsal fin and a large black patch below the anterior dorsal fin.
 It is widely distributed in South America, being common in Brazil and Argentina.
– dolichoptera BLUE CHIN 15cm. (6in.)
Unspectacular but attractive, it has a greeny grey body peppered lightly with white dots. A number of extensions protrude from the head of the male, which give it an unusual appearance. The dorsal and caudal fins have white borders. From the Amazon and Guyana, it eats algae.

indeed they do well in a community tank they may seem out of place in an aquarium which has as its objective, aestheticism. They have frequently been bred in captivity, and are close relatives of *Astyanax mexicanus* from which species they probably originated.

Anostomidae
This family includes the headstanders of South America. They have rather elongated bodies, and terminal mouths. In general they are bottom feeders, as one might expect from their headstanding position. Some are carnivorous but most eat plants or minute organisms found on the floor of the aquarium. See *Abramites, Anostomus, Leporinus*.

Anostomus Anostomidae ⊕
– anostomus STRIPED ANOSTOMUS or HEADSTANDER 18cm. (7in.)

A slim streamlined fish which swims with its head down, the body at an angle of 45°. The lovely dark browny green body has three longitudinal yellow brown lines running from snout to the base of the tail. The fins are red sometimes paling towards the tips. A native of streams in Guyana and the Amazon Basin where they are bottom feeders. This headstander is a happy member of the community tank but is rather rare. **8**
– fasciolatus 23cm. (9in.)
Green general body colour shading to a yellow belly. The side has vertical bars of blue. A dark bar separates tail from body. Grows up to 23cm. in captivity. A native of the northern regions of South America.
– trimaculatus THREE-SPOTTED HEADSTANDER
20cm. (8in.)
This species has a rather long, rounded body, deeper at the front end. The body shades from a dark greenish brown above, through brownish yellow sides to a pale grey belly. The three spots which give it its popular and scientific names are situated along the side. It has an adipose fin. The somewhat tapered head supports a rounded snout.

From the Amazon, this is more popular in the USA than in Europe.

ANSORGE'S CHARACIN see *Neolebias ansorgei*

Antennariidae FROGFISHES, ANGLERFISHES Ψ
An interesting family of fish which have adapted to a slow moving, sedentary way of life, relying more on camouflage and cunning than the ability to move. They live among rocks or weed often close to the bottom and have evolved specially modified pectoral fins which enable them to crawl along.

They are chunky-bodied fish with scaleless skins which carry a number of projections. Distributed in all tropical and subtropical seas.

To compensate for their lack of agility they have developed a long projection or lure on their snout which dangles in front of the mouth and entices their prey to within snapping distance. See *Histrio*.

Anubias see under *Plants*.

Apeltes Gasterosteidae Ψ/⊕
– quadracus FOUR-SPINED STICKLEBACK 6cm. (2½in.)
Found on the eastern coast of North America from Virginia in the south, north to Newfoundland. A marine species that moves into rivers in the spring to spawn. The male produces an adhesive material from the kidneys and with this he prepares a nest which is attached to plants. One or more females lay eggs in the nest and the male circulates water through the nest to ensure adequate oxygenation.

Aphanius Cyprinodontidae Ψ/⊕
– dispar 8cm. (3in.) ⊙
The body colour is grey with silvery blue spots. The paired fins are golden yellow while the caudal fin is traversed by grey bands. The dorsal and anal fins are reticulated.

This attractive killy comes from the region of the Red Sea, Persian Gulf, and north-west India. Its peaceful nature makes it an ideal fish for the community tank, but it prefers brackish water conditions. In bright light, which it prefers, it spends its day in the middle to upper regions of the tank. A plant spawner. The eggs do not need to be dried to obtain successful hatching.
– fasciatus 6cm. (2½in.)
Native to the coastal regions of Italy, its attendant islands and the north coast of Africa, it prefers somewhat brackish water kept between 21–26°C. The body colour of the male is greenish blue. About a dozen vertical black bars adorn its side. Fins yellow, the dorsal with a black margin, and bands on the tail fin. In all other ways it resembles other members of the genus.
– iberus SPANISH LEBIA 5cm. (2in.) ⊙
The body of the male of this attractive blue killy is crossed by fifteen silver vertical bands. The female is green with dark irregular patches. It comes from Spain, Algeria and Morocco. Reaching 5cm. in length it has a peaceful approach to life preferring bright lighting conditions. In the latter it is of course rather atypical of the killifish. Will live in fresh water but like all members of this genus it prefers brackish conditions. Tends to keep towards the surface or middle of the aquarium and enjoys temperatures anywhere between 21–26°C. When it spawns it lays its eggs on plants. It does not require a dry period for successful hatching.
– sophiae 4cm. (1½in.)
The male of this species is olive brown with blue fins. The spots on the fins and body are white with a blue tinge. The female is rather drab.

It comes from Iraq, lives in brackish water and does better in the aquarium if a teaspoonful of salt is added for 4½ litres of fresh water. Enjoys temperatures around 24°C. although its tolerance is much greater.

Aphyocharax Characidae ⊕
– rubripinnis BLOODFIN, RED-FINNED TETRA 5cm. (2in.)
This delightful fish from La Plata Basin, Argentina, reaches 5cm. in captivity. Its silvery body is darker dorsally and gradually lightens towards the belly. The distinctive and captivating feature is the blood red fins. All except the pectorals, which are hyaline, are deep red at the base gradually becoming less intense towards the margins. They are unusual in having a tolerance to temperatures below 18°C. but do better in somewhat warmer water of 24–28°C.

Sexing is difficult since it requires both sexes for

comparison. The male is thinner with more brilliant fins but even these vary periodically.

The breeding behaviour is fascinating. After vigorous chasing a pair may jump out of the water and their bodies come in contact in mid air. As the female re-enters the water the eggs, non-adhesive, are scattered. Success is more likely if several fish are placed in the tank together. The young should be fed on infusoria and then daphnia. Looks at its best in groups. Suitable for the community tank. **9**

Aphyosemion Cyprinodontidae ⊕
– ***arnoldi*** ARNOLD'S LYRETAIL 6cm. (2½in.) ✖
A very popular if variably coloured fish from West Africa. The exotic streamers developed from the rays of the caudal fins are accentuated by flamboyant dorsal and anal fins. This species is somewhat aggressive. Breeds readily in captivity.
– ***australe*** LYRETAIL, CAMERONENSIS 6cm. (2½in.) ◍
Like all members of this genus *A. australe* comes from equatorial Africa where it lives in shaded ponds. It is an extremely beautiful fish, the male showing the extravagantly decorated fins of a real dandy. The tail fin is shaped with the classically elongated upper and lower borders giving the lyre shape for which the genus is justifiably known. The back of the male is a beige colour shading to silvery blue sides which are decorated with red dots roughly in longitudinal rows. The dorsal fin is broad based with red dots and a blue margin. The anal fin, also broad based, is orange brown at the base shading to blue before a dark brown band, It has a trailing elongation of the posterior border. The tail fin has a blue brown base with red dots outlined by a dark brown area. The wide upper and lower borders are orange with white trailing corners.

It is a smallish fish which the aquarist should keep in a shaded tank under subdued light at temperatures around 22°C. It prefers acid water and is basically carnivorous. A peaceful member of the community tank, it keeps to the lower third of the tank where it assumes a position with head higher than body. The female is a duller example of the same shape but without the appendicular flamboyance. She spawns in the plants, after a parallel swim and a tremble from the male, typical of the family. This has long been a favourite of the aquarist and from it has been developed the Golden Lyretail, often marketed as *A. australe hjerreseni.*
– ***beauforti*** see *A. gulare*
– ***bivittatum*** syn. *A. multicolor* TWO-STRIPED KILLY 5cm. (2in.) ◍
An unimaginative popular name for this jewel from West Africa. The male body is a lovely translucent pink shading to a deeper red on the head and a pale pink or yellow at the base of the tail. The dorsal fin is wide, pink and very pointed with a peppering of red and blue dots. The anal fin has a

blue base and is orange red. The lyre shaped tail is silver blue, edged with red, with a second band of red a short way from the upper and lower borders. The female has none of the fin spectacular but is quite attractive in her own right, with two dark horizontal lines on a silver-blue body. Once again this tantalizing beauty will not survive without care and diligent management by the aquarist. It likes, indeed needs, mature water kept around 22°C., well planted to provide shade. It thrives on a diet of live food.

A peaceful fish, it moves with quick spurts followed by periods of immobility. Not the easiest to breed, it is a plant spawner whose eggs hatch in 10–20 days. The young need small live food to start with. It is often known to the aquarist as *A. multicolor.*
– ***bualanum*** 5cm. (2in.)
This elegant little fish from Africa has the added advantage of hardiness and adaptability. Its yellow body is decorated with red dots and several transverse red lines along the body. The dorsal fin is pointed and the tail has elongated outer rays accentuated by dark lines.
– ***calliurum*** FLAG KILLY 6cm. (2½in.) ◍
A red speckled fish from Nigeria. The dark red back shades to a variable pattern of red dots. The throat is yellow. Pectoral, anal and dorsal fins have red bases, a brick red horizontal band followed by a wide orange border. The tail assumes the typical shape of the lyre but has a brick red horizontal band top and bottom and wide orange borders echoing the other median fins.

As well as beauty it offers peace and tolerance towards others which makes it a boon to the community tank keeper. Well shaded tanks containing mature acid water around 22°C. suit it well. It needs live food. A typical plant spawner whose eggs hatch in 10–20 days. It was originally wrongly called *A. elegans*, and is sometimes confused with *A. gardneri.*
– ***coeruleum*** see *A. sjoestedti*
– ***cognatum*** 3cm. (1¼in.) ◍
A small species from Zaïre. The male's lovely pale beige brown body, almost gold, is decorated with horizontal lines of red dots. The dorsal, tail and anal fins also carry the dots. The lyre tail is emphasized by the red upper and lower borders. A lovely little fish it makes an ideal member of the community tank. It stays nearer the bottom than the surface where it spends time in motionless contemplation until urged to move, often by the presence of live food, when it responds with a swift movement. Temperatures around 22°C. with shaded or subdued light create the best environment. A plant spawner, whose eggs hatch in 10–20 days; its fry require small live food.
– ***elegans*** see *A. calliurum*
– ***fallax*** see *A. gulare*
– ***filamentosum*** PLUMED LYRETAIL 5cm. (2in.)

A small slightly deeper bodied member of the genus. It is basically blue green in colour with a flamboyant speckling of red dots extending onto the fins. Red lines pass across the pelvic, anal and lower part of the tail fin. The female is the usual dull brown of the genus with clear rounded fins. It comes from Nigeria.

– *gardneri* GARDNER'S KILLY, STEEL-BLUE FUNDULUS 6cm. (2½in.) ◍✂

Like all members of this genus, this fish comes from tropical Africa. In a flamboyant genus this member stands alone in its glory. The blue body of the male is emblazoned with rich crimson markings which take the form of broken vertical bars, more in evidence in the posterior half of the body. These extend to decorate the tail fin. The margin of the tail fins has delicate pale yellow markings. The anal and dorsal fins have a blue green base. Some males have wide yellow borders to the anal and dorsal fins. Both types are found in equal proportion in natural populations. The female is less of a beauty with functional, rather plain fins.

Unfortunately it can be aggressive and should not be kept in a community tank. It is a difficult fish to breed, but when it does, it lays eggs in the bottom from where they hatch in 2–5 weeks. It requires temperatures of around 22°C, in shaded light. It will spend its time in the lower third of the tank.

When first introduced to the aquarist this was known as *A. calliurum*. It was, however, later sold as *A. nigerianum* until aquarist and ichthyologists got together to establish its correct identification. **10**

– *gulare* YELLOW GULARIS 6cm. (2½in.) ◍✂

A native of southern Nigeria. Male coloration is very attractive having a basic body colour of greenish-blue with plum coloured patches running horizontally from the operculum to the tail. The dots of the upper body spill onto the red dorsal fin. The tail too has red dots.

Its natural aggression is too much of a hazard for it to be kept in the community tank. In water at temperatures around 22°C. it spends its time in the bottom third of the tank, preferring subdued lighting. As befits a bottom dweller it lays its eggs in the bottom mud. Sometimes this fish is named *A. beauforti* or *A. fallax* by suppliers.

– *labarrei* 5cm. (2in.)

A lovely member of the genus from west Zaïre. The blue body is speckled with red dots. The fins are distinctive, having a basic green coloration with dark red edging. The tail has not the typical lyre shape but is square cut. It was first wrongly described by aquarists as a blue panchax.

– *multicolor* see *A. bivittatum*

– *nigerianum* see *A. gardneri*

– *sjoestedti* syn. *A. coeruleum* BLUE GULARIS 13cm. (5in.) ◍✂

Definitely not for the beginner, this species from Africa

requires careful and experienced handling.

The dorsal half of the male's body is a delicate translucent pink created from an interplay of yellow and red markings. The lower half is a reddish blue over a pink ground. The jaw and lower head can be bright blue. A yellow patch embellishes the side behind the operculum. The large dorsal fin carries a wide border of blue green. The tail fin is a glorious underplay of blue and red patterns, with long extensions to the outer rays forming wide trailers. Up to eight red bars run vertically across the hind part of the body.

Preferring mature water and shade it is unsuitable for the community tank and its aggressive tendencies are detrimental to the welfare of others. It enjoys temperatures around 22°C. A difficult fish to breed, it lays its eggs in the bottom cover, but rarely. A drying of the eggs as described in the family description is thought necessary for successful hatching.

– *spurelli* see *A. walkeri*

– *striatus* 5cm. (2in.) ◍✂

A fish from tropical Africa which has a silver blue body with horizontal dotted lines of brilliant red. The unpaired fins are a golden yellow with red decorations. The pelvic and pectoral fins have rich golden borders. It is aggressive and must be kept away from other species, which is a great pity but worth the effort. It lives close to the bottom in shaded pools where it lays its eggs and then dies, having an annual life span. The eggs may take many months to hatch. The aquarist must mimic nature and subject the eggs to an artificial dry season – see *Cyprinodontidae*. **11**

– *walkeri* 6cm. (2½in.) ✂

A lovely species from tropical Africa. The dazzling turquoise body is sparsely decorated with deep brown spots. The unpaired fins are a clear yellow, with brown patches which accentuate the beautiful body. Unfortunate tendency to aggression precludes its inclusion in the community tank. Temperatures around 22°C. It remains close to the bottom, where it lays its eggs. The fry emergence takes several weeks after being treated to a dry period by nature's rainless skies or the aquarist's peat mossed plastic bag, see *Cyprinodontidae*. They must be fed infusoria because of their small size. Often marketed as *A. spurelli*.

Apistogramma Cichlidae ⊕

– *agassizi* AGASSIZ'S DWARF CICHLID 8cm. (3in.)

The first of a number of members of the genus much favoured by aquarists since they are peaceful to the point of pacificism, attractive, small – hence dwarf cichlid – and easy on the plant life.

This particular fish is native to the Amazon Basin. The body is a basic mauve with a lovely metallic blue sheen caused by blue dots on the body scales. A dark bar behind the eye is surrounded by a diffuse yellow coloration. The belly is white with a very pale blue iridescence. The long dorsal fin has a purple base which gives way to a grey or a grey brown bar and finally a blue margin.

It grows about 8cm. in length and breeds freely in captivity laying cherry red eggs which produce a disproportionately large number of males. Usually males of this genus take little or no interest in the eggs after fertilization but defend their territories within which several females have their own territories. **12**

– cacatuoides COCKATOO DWARF CICHLID 6cm. (2½in.)
A beautiful fish having the unusual addition of a lyre shaped tail. The basic body colour is yellow grey but this is overshadowed completely by a wealth of gorgeous blue highlights. The belly, head and fins are a rich turquoise blue. The males have dorsal spines which distinguishes them from females, an elongated dorsal fin ending in a point and a blue spotted anal fin which is also pointed.

They are lovely, peaceful fish well suited to a community tank. They breed easily, often only the female performing parental duties.

– corumbae CORA'S CICHLID 6cm. (2½in.)
A dwarf cichlid from Brazil and Argentina. The yellowish brown body is transected by a number of vertical and horizontal bars. The unpaired fins are an attractive red with dark dots.

– pertense AMAZON YELLOW DWARF CICHLID 5cm. (2in.) ✄
A small smart fish, rather than a beauty, from the Amazon Basin. The body is a browny green shading to a silver belly. A dark horizontal stripe starts at the snout and continues through the eye to the tail. Several wide dark vertical bars adorn the side. In common with most cichlids these colours are variable and changeable. Two spots are included in the horizontal stripe and are less likely to fade. The head is diffused with green. Dorsal, tail and anal fins are yellowy grey, the dorsal with an orange border.

It is somewhat more aggressive than other members of the genus, but, with care, will breed in captivity.

– ramirezi see *Microgeophagus ramirezi*

Aplocheilichthys Cyprinodontidae ⊕
– macrophthalmus LAMP EYE 4cm. (1½in.)
A delightful fish from Nigeria and Dahomey. Sadly it is not the easiest of fish to keep. In its natural surroundings it lives in small streams in the thick forest regions. The body is moderately deep. It shades from a pale blue dorsally to a blue green below. A longitudinal pink line runs from the eye and below this is a pale brownish yellow line which parallels it. The caudal fin is rounded. The dorsal is narrow-based, lies two thirds of the way along the body, and is tall. The anal fin is large and rectangular. The pectoral fins are

transparent, and just caudal to these are the square-shaped pelvics.

Lamp eyes live in groups and make peaceful fish in the community tank. There is still doubt as to the most suitable water properties for these fish. For breeding they seem to do better in soft acid water, but they remain problem breeders and require a certain amount of diligence and care.

Aplocheilus Cyprinodontidae
– blocki MADRAS KILLY, GREEN PANCHAX 5cm. (2in.) ⊙
This fish is native to India. Its diminutive size is compensated for by its beauty. In the male an incandescent green body is decorated with rows of brilliant red dots interspersed with bright leaf green scales which also decorate the yellow fins. Sexes are easily distinguishable particularly by recognizing the flamboyant shape of the dorsal and anal fins in the male, and the less spectacular colouring of the female.

A peaceful fish for the community tank, it prefers the upper quarter of the tank. It does best at temperatures from 23–25°C. A plant spawner; the eggs hatch in 10–20 days and require infusoria. They are happy in bright light.

– dayi DAY'S PANCHAX, SRI LANKAN KILLIFISH 8cm. (3in.)
A rather large member of the genus from Sri Lanka and south India. The body is an olive green with each scale highlighted in yellow. The male has yellow fins. The dorsal and caudal fins have red dots on them, and the anal fin is patched with black. The pectorals are large and colourless. The female has rather rounded colourless fins.

A generally hardy fish which breeds well in the aquarium. The relatively large eggs do not need to be dried before hatching, as is the case with some cyprinodonts.

– lineatus MALABAR KILLY, LINEATUS 10cm. (4in.) ✄
A medium sized killy from India and Sri Lanka. The body is a dark greeny brown. Irregular dots of yellow brown adorn the side, running in horizontal rows from the operculum to the tail where they break up from their regular pattern to form a sparkle in the base of the caudal fin. The body colour is broken by about six vertical bands traversing the sides. The fins are yellow green with yellow and red dots and margins of red. The pelvic fins are elongated into beautiful appendages. The female has more pronounced vertical bars and a black dot at the base of her dorsal fin.

Aggressive, it can only be kept with larger fish. Tends to frequent the surface quarter of the tank and prefers temperatures of about 24°C. Very easy to breed, it is a plant spawner.

– panchax PANCHAX, BLUE PANCHAX 8cm. (3in.) ✄
A native of south-eastern Asia, in particular Malaysia, India and Burma, its usual adult length approaches 8cm.

Descriptions of this family are not easy. It is rather variable in colour, although the body is usually olive brown with blue dots and orange fins. In addition a black dot marks the base of the dorsal fin and blue marks the edge of the anal and tail fins. The male is identified by his pointed fins.

A fish which should be kept with larger fish well able to deflate its aggressive tendencies. Prefers temperatures of 23–25°C. Lays its eggs on plants from where they hatch in 10–20 days.

Apogon Apogonidae Ψ
– *lachneri* WHITE STAR CARDINALFISH 6cm. (2½in.)
A lovely red bodied fish from the Caribbean and the Gulf of Mexico. There is a black spot at the base of the second dorsal fin and behind that a white patch.
– *maculatus* FLAMEFISH 10cm. (4in.)
This is a delightful fish from the Caribbean and the Gulf of Mexico. It is naturally active at night and rests in shaded areas during the day. Its beautiful red body is broken by a black patch across the second dorsal fin and a black line running from the eye to the operculum. White parallel lines border its eye above and below.
– *nematopterus* PYJAMA CARDINAL 8cm. (3in.)
A small fish from the Indo-Australian Archipelago. The body is a lovely yellow green. Dark brownish red spots are scattered over the hind end of the body. The fins are particularly attractive being well spread with a dark band running vertically through the first dorsal fin, body, and pelvic fins. The posterior dorsal has a flamboyant elongation. Takes small live food including daphnia, and fish fry, and is quite easy to keep in captivity. **13**

Apogonidae CARDINALFISHES Ψ
Small, nocturnal reef living marine fish which tend to be territorial and live in small groups or alone. They are active swimmers though a little slow moving in the home aquarium. Common in many tropical or subtropical seas, particularly numerous in the warm, shallow, reef scattered waters of the Indo-Pacific. Their large eyes are often set against a basic body colour of red. They have two dorsal fins. Males tend to have relatively larger heads than females. The family are mouth brooders, the male taking charge of the eggs. See *Apogon*.

Aponogeton see *Plants*
APPLE SNAILS see *Snails – Ampullaria*
ARABIAN SNAPPER see *Lutjanus kasmira*
ARAWANA see *Osteoglossum bicirrhosum*
ARCHED CATFISH see *Corydoras arcuatus*
ARCHERFISH see *Toxotes jaculator*
ARGENTINE PEARLFISH see *Cynolebias bellotti, C. nigripinnis*

Argulus see *Unwelcome Visitors*
ARMOURED
CATFISH see *Doradidae*
CATFISH, COMMON see *Callichthys callichthys*
ARNOLD'S
CATFISH see *Otocinclus arnoldi*
CHARACIN see *Copella arnoldi*
LYRETAIL see *Aphyosemion arnoldi*

Art and Myth
Long before man evolved from his ape-like ancestors, fish may have provided an important item of food. Certainly fish feature in the earliest graphic recordings of man's activities. The ancient cave paintings and carvings of Palaeolithic man record his interest in, and dependence on, fish. From that time the art of many civilizations has depicted fish in various forms, and it is clear from this that fish were caught for food, and that a variety of methods, including spear, net, line and rod were all used. Greek, Roman, Egyptian, Assyrian, Aztec and Eskimo art are among the many that include pictorial representations of fishing. One famous Roman mosaic at Sousse, Tunisia, shows a great variety of fish and illustrates various methods the Romans used for catching them. An interesting Aztec illustration shows a combination of spearing and netting. Several fine examples of Assyrian wall carving show fish as part of the scenery. In particular a fragment depicting Ashurbaningal's triumph over Shamash-shum-ukin and his allies, has a fascinating frieze of fish.

Strangely, perhaps, the Celts of the iron age culture, which was widespread in Europe, are thought to have rejected fish as a food. It has been suggested that this followed naturally from their reverence for springs and rivers so catching and eating the occupants was to be abhorred. In addition the Salmon had an important place in Celtic mythology being one form in which their warrior heroes appeared. In ancient Egypt the fish was a symbol of religious significance since it was believed to guide the boat which carried the dead to sacred seas. Herodotus the historian records that fish were venerated by his people. Several Japanese gods took the form of fish and it is interesting that the Carp has been the symbol of the Samurai for many centuries, because of its power to withstand opposition and swim against the flow of the stream. The Buddhists too adopted the fish as a religious symbol.

It can, therefore, be seen that when the early Christians took the fish as their emblem it could in no way be called unique. It was merely another example of the readiness with which Christianity adopted the beliefs, symbols and customs of older religions and made them its own.
The fish can still be seen on the early Christian tombs in the catacombs in Rome.

With religious acceptance inevitably comes a culture of medicinal power. Fish have featured in cures for everything from bad teeth to hysteria and pregnancy to heart disease. The Tench seems to have been particularly venerated in medieval times, effecting a cure by simply being applied to the skin of the victim. The problems of childbirth were believed in mediaeval times to be easily and swiftly overcome if a Torpedofish, caught when the moon was in Libra and left for three days in the open, was introduced into the birth chamber.

Old wives' tales tell us fish is good for the brain. New wives extoll the virtues of codliver oil for its content of vitamins, those latest group of scientific gods which if taken in grossly excess proportions by perfectly healthy people reputedly cure all their ills. The cod's liver today, like a salmon's backbone in more ancient days, averts the evil eye.

The fish then is as attractive in Picasso's art today as it was in ancient times, and parts of its body are venerated by modern medicine as they were by pagan witches.

Ascellus see under *Food*
ASIAN SEAHORSE see under *Hippocampus kuda*
ASPIDISTRA, WATER see under *Plants – Acorus*

Aspredinidae BANJO or OBSTETRICAL CATFISHES ⊕
These are small catfishes, unarmoured except for a row of bony plates along the side, with a head out of proportion to the fine slender body. A number of species exist, all very similar in appearance. They are native to South America.

Some members of this family carry their eggs adherent to the spongy skin on the female's abdomen, but others are reported to simply lay them in the bottom cover. Since they are difficult to breed most aquarists will have little opportunity to confirm their breeding habits, but it is a challenge for those willing to accept it and good observations carefully recorded would add to ichthyologists' knowledge. See *Buncocephalus*.

Astronotus Cichlidae
– ocellatus MARBLED, OSCAR, PEACOCK-EYED, or VELVET CICHLID 30cm. (12in.)
Discreetly beautiful, this trimly shaped cichlid is sadly too large for the community tank when fully grown. A basic greenish grey body is decorated with rich reddish brown irregular patches. An ocellated spot adorns the tail base. The intensity of the dark markings varies considerably from time to time. It moves with a graceful gliding motion, reminiscent of the controlled actions of a ballet dancer. It has a large mouth into which small fish all too easily disappear.

It breeds in the cichlid manner, see *Cichlidae*. **14**

Astyanax Characidae ⊕
– bimaculatus TWO-SPOT ASTYANAX or TETRA 15cm. (6in.)
This is a larger aquarium fish from the eastern part of South America. In spite of its size it is a peaceful fish and fits well into larger community tanks. It gets its name from two black spots, one on its shoulder and the other on its tail. The body colour is a brassy yellow with reddish fins. Wide tolerance to temperature ranges. Breeds quite easily, preferring temperatures around 25°C. for success.
– mexicanus MEXICAN ASTYANAX or TETRA
8–10cm. (3–4in.)
Not as large as the Two-spot Astyanax, *A. bimaculatus*, and unusual in being the only characin from North America. It comes from Panama, Mexico and as far north as Texas.

The general body colour is silver with olive overtones above and yellow below. A faint broad band of blue extends from the operculum to the tail. This merges into a dark spot on the base of the tail which extends to the tail fin. The fins are often tinged with red.

It is hardy, breeds freely, and is peaceful, behaving well in a community collection, but its lack of colour and its large size have retarded its popularity. It adapts well to a wide range of temperatures and consumes large quantities of plants.

Atherinidae SILVERSIDES ⊕/Ψ ⊙
A large number of genera and species belong to this family which has a wide distribution in the coastal waters of both temperate and tropical regions. By far the majority are adapted to a marine environment, but some have adjusted to life in freshwater. They have two dorsal fins, the first being spinous, the second soft.

They like large, sunlit aquaria at temperatures of about 24°C. They are omnivorous and require plentiful supplies of both live food and algae.

In natural waters these fish are found in large shoals. They are oviparous, the eggs having short filaments which adhere to plants. See *Bedotia, Telmatherina*.

AUSTRALIAN
BLACK-LINED RAINBOWFISH see *Melanotaenia maccullochi*
LUNGFISH see *Ceratodontidae, Neoceratodus forsteri*
PINK-TAILED RAINBOWFISH see *Melanotaenia fluviatilis*
PURPLE-SPOTTED GUDGEON see *Mogurnda mogurnda*
RED SNAIL see *Snails – Bulinus*

Bacopa see *Plants*
Bacterial Diseases see *Disease*
BADGERFISH see *Lo vulpinus*

Badidae
The only member of this family – *Badis badis* – was, until recently, classified with the Nandidae. However the taxonomists have discovered similarities in skeletal structure and behaviour to the Anabantidae and it is therefore redesignated as a separate family. See *Badis*.

Badis Badidae
– *badis* BADIS 6cm. (2½in.) ⊕
A delightful fish from India. Its ability to change colour precludes description as it can rapidly pass through blues, greens, pinks and reds. Darker irregular lines are sometimes seen, more commonly in younger fish. The long dorsal fin is decorated with changing bars of colour.

Males have larger fins, larger bodies and are more hollow-bellied than females. For breeding the temperatures should be raised to 25–28°C.

The male prepares a shallow nest in the sand and then goes through a series of colour changes, presumably as a sexual signal to the female. When he stops they swim to the nest area, embrace over the nest and the eggs are laid and fertilized. The male protects the eggs which hatch in 48 hours.

Bagridae ⊕ ⫿
These are 'naked' catfish from Africa and Asia. They have no plates on the body to afford protection. Several long barbels embellish the mouth. Nocturnal, as are most catfish, and usually timid. See *Leiocassius, Mystus*.

BALA SHARK see *Balantiocheilus melanopterus*

Balantiocheilus Cyprinidae
– *melanopterus* BALA or TRICOLOR SHARK 36cm. (14in.)
A very striking fish indeed from south-east Asia. The body shape closely resembles that of the sharks. It is silver. The colour of the fins gives it its notable appearance. The dorsal fin is rather short based with a very tall anterior edge. It is yellow in colour with a wide black border. The anal and pelvic fins are of similar colour. The caudal fin is yellow at its base, shading to orange and again with a black border. The pectorals are clear.

For those with a suitably sized tank it makes an excellent member of the community. It is best suited in temperatures

around 25°C. Has not, as far as is known, bred in captivity.

Balinus see *Snails*

Balistapus Balistidae Ψ✕
– *undulatus* EMERALD or YELLOW-STRIPED EMERALD TRIGGERFISH 20cm. (8in.)
A small member of this family, what it lacks in length it makes up for in fury. A very aggressive piscine from the Indo-Pacific. A lovely emerald green body is liberally decorated with irregular yellow lines; yellow dots cover its head while lines surrounding its mouth suggest it is large. The tail is yellow. Pectoral, anal and dorsal fins are clear, with yellow rays. Eats greedily and grows rapidly. Its aggressive nature does not recommend it for a community tank. It will even attack fish four times its own size.

Balistes Balistidae Ψ
– *bursa* WHITE-LINED TRIGGERFISH 15cm. (6in.)
Like other members of the family it is distributed in the Indo-Pacific where it inhabits the coastal or shallow waters. Very similar to the Hawaiian Triggerfish, *Rhinecanthus aculeatus*, with which it is commonly confused. It can reach up to 30cm. in length in nature. It does not carry the dark stripes of *Rhinecanthus aculeatus* and can be distinguished by a large brown irregular spot close to the base of the tail. **15**
– *vetula* QUEEN TRIGGERFISH 61cm. (24in.)
This fish grows to some 61cm. in length, but captivity reduces this considerably. It is an extremely attractive fish indeed, being yellow in body with blue lines on the head and fins. The dorsal fin is large and flamboyant, extensions to the caudals enhance the beauty of the fish. It is found in the Caribbean and along the east coast of North America, and possibly more widely in the tropical regions of the Atlantic. Young fish grow rapidly and will soon outgrow the average home aquarium. A very hardy species.

Balistidae TRIGGERFISHES AND FILEFISHES Ψ
These rather personable fish live mainly in shallow marine waters of the Pacific. Characteristically they have very big heads but small mouths, indeed the greater proportion of their body consists of head. In spite of the small mouth, they are well equipped with vicious teeth and can inflict a most unpleasant wound on fish and finger alike.

They get their common name from an unusual mechanism which allows the first long spine of the dorsal fin to lock in an upright position. This enables them to fix themselves in a crevice between rocks ensuring predators will be unable to dislodge them. In addition the trigger can be activated when in open water and so making them difficult prey to swallow. They are unusual in having no ventral fin. Movement occurs by undulation of the dorsal and anal fins, stability being afforded by the pectorals.

They are easy to feed since they have large appetites and eat almost anything. They are not the best of community fish and most species should be kept alone.

Filefishes are sometimes grouped under a separate family, Monacanthidae.

See *Balistapus, Balistes, Balistoides, Cantherhines, Melichthys, Odonus, Oxymonacanthus, Pervagor, Pseudobalistes, Rhinecanthus.*

Balistoides Balistidae
– *niger* CLOWN TRIGGERFISH   50cm. (19in.)
The body of this magnificent fish from the Indo-Pacific is rather elongated and more ovoid in shape than most triggerfish. A beautiful sheeny brownish black with large rounded bluish white spots ventrally and fiery red lips. Dorsally there is a rectangular patch marbled with yellow. Easy to feed on the normal live foods. This is a highly prized species in any collection and is probably one of the most expensive fish available to the marine aquarist. **16**

BANDED
    BARB, AFRICAN see *Barbus fasciolatus*
    BUTTERFLYFISH see *Chaetodon striatus*
    CICHLID see *Cichlasoma severum*
    CLIMBING PERCH see *Ctenopoma fasciolatum*
    CYNOLEBIAS see *Cynolebias adloffi*
    EPIPLATYS see *Epiplatys fasciolatus*
    HUMBUG see *Dascyllus aruanus*
    JEWELFISH see *Hemichromis fasciatus*
    SEAPERCH see *Serranus scriba*
BANJO CATFISH see *Aspredinidae, Buncocephalus bicolor*
BANNERFISH, HUMPHEAD see *Heniochus varius*
BARBS see *Barbus, Esomus*
BARBER EEL see *Plotosus lineatus*

Barbus BARBS Cyprinidae ⊕
The genus *Barbus* is worthy of special note since it contains a great variety of fish popular with the aquarist. None is found in the American continent. They come mostly from Indonesia, Malaya, India and Sri Lanka, but a few are found in Africa. Barbs are active, attractive fish, with large shiny scales which reflect light as the fish move. Most of them have barbels around their mouths. They are peaceful, requiring temperatures around 20–26°C.

Most barbs are easily bred in captivity. Males are slimmer and with denser colours. They can be brought into spawning condition by raising the temperature a few degrees and providing a plentiful supply of live food. The female will swell with eggs when she is ripe. At this time she should be placed in a fresh tank with one or several males, plenty of dense vegetation to provide some security for the eggs. The male or males chase the female until excitement culminates in the inevitable result of mating and eggs are produced. Both parents, in captivity, attempt to consume the eggs; therefore, remove parents after egg laying is complete. The young are easily reared. See *Breeding* and *Cyprinidae.*

– *binotatus* SPOTTED BARB   *c*15cm. (*c*6in.)
A rather large, dull coloured barb from the Malayan region. Its body colour is silvery blue with a variable dark blue patch below the dorsal fin. Young fish have a number of spots on the body but these generally fade with age. Will breed providing it is given plenty of space.

– *callensis* MOROCCAN BARB   20cm. (8in.)
A large barb rarely kept by aquarists but noteworthy since it lives in hot springs and is said to tolerate temperatures as high as 60°C. It comes from Morocco, Algeria and southern Spain. Olive green back, shading through light brown to a silver belly. In aquaria it needs temperatures around 30°C. and is therefore unsuitable for the community tank.

– *callipterus* CONGO BARB   8cm. (3in.)
A yellow coloured fish native to the streams of West Africa. The tail and dorsal fins are red fading to pale pink at the edge. A difficult fish to breed in captivity.

– *chola* SWAMP BARB   15cm. (6in.)
A more streamlined form than its close relative *B. conchonius*. It can also be distinguished by a pair of barbels. The operculum is coloured violet with gold flecks and there is a dark blotch at the base of the dorsal fin. Anal and pelvic fins in the males are red. Breeds in aquaria.

– *conchonius* ROSY BARB   14cm. (5½in.)
One of the most familiar and popular fish of the aquarium. It comes from India and reaches over 11cm. in length. The body colour is silver with a greeny blue sheen. There is a dark spot just above the posterior extremity of the tail fin which is surrounded by a ragged gold border. During the breeding season the male develops a red underbelly calculated to excite the females and to this is added the red bases of the anal and pelvic fins. The dorsal, anal and pelvic fins have dark tips in the male which tend to fade a little out of the breeding season. It is a generous breeder spawning several times a year. **17**

– *cumingi* CUMING'S BARB   5cm. (2in.)
A delightful addition to the aquarist's armoury is this barb from Sri Lanka. It is small and dumpy and the body colour varies greatly as light strikes it. Silvery yellow with various overtones is the best description. Two vertical dark bars, one lying behind the operculum the second close to the tail are distinguishing features of this delightful fish. In the male the tips of the dorsal and pelvic fins are red.

Breed according to the common barb pattern. Easy to feed, peaceful by nature, they are splendid community members. **18**

– *dunckeri* DUNCKER'S BARB   30cm. (12in.)
A large Malayan barb of little merit for the aquarist although it is sometimes imported for the trade. Its body is a dull silver grey shading to a yellowish silvery belly. A large dark spot below the dorsal fin aids identification, although it fades with the passing years. The lower of the two pairs of barbels is relatively long.

Needs frequent water changes and is not easily bred.

– *everetti* CLOWN BARB   13cm. (5in.)
A delightful fish from Borneo and the Malayan Peninsula. Splendid of colour and shape it makes a striking exhibit in the community tank. The body colour is a brownish orange. There is a round mauve spot on the side with a number of similarly coloured wedge-shaped patches, one behind the operculum, one below the dorsal fin and one originating dorsally above the tail fin. The fins are a deep red. Two pairs of barbels adorn its mouth. Temperatures around 24°C. suit them best. Not the easiest fish to spawn although this can be induced if the temperature of a well planted aquarium is raised, the water well aerated, and a generous supply of live food is added.

– *fasciolatus* AFRICAN BANDED BARB   8cm. (3in.)
A rarely kept fish from Angola. It is a blue green fish with rather vague dark vertical bars. Has not been bred in captivity.

– *gelius* DWARF, GELI or GOLDEN BARB   4cm. (1½in.)
From Bengal and central India, this barb is uncharacteristic of the genus, smaller and slimmer than most and with unusual markings. The fins appear relatively more prominent than many barbs. The body colour is a dark olive dorsally, shading to a silver belly. Several irregular dark patches are present on the sides. The fins have a yellowish tinge.

Peaceful but shy, it makes a pleasing addition to the community tank. Does best at temperatures in the region of 22°C. Spawns with careful management but parents should be removed promptly or they quickly consume their young.

– *hexazona* SIX-BANDED or TIGER BARB   5.5cm. (2in.)
A brownish yellow fish from Sumatra, it is distinguished by six black vertical bars on the body. The first passes across the eye, the last must be aided by a little imagination to see it at the base of the tail. The anal, tail and dorsal fins are red in the male. The female has red only in her dorsal fin. Thrives best at temperatures around 27–30°C. A reluctant breeder in captivity. Regarded by some as a subspecies of *B. pentazana*.

– *lateristriga* 'T' or SPANNER BARB   8cm. (3in.)
Being large for the genus and without a great deal of colour it is not one of the most useful aquarium fishes. Native to the Malayan Peninsula and Indonesia, it reaches 8cm. in length in captivity. The distinctive feature is the arrangement of dark markings on the silvery-grey body.

Clown Barb, *Barbus everetti*. The caudal, anal and dorsal fins show damage to borders.

Striped Barbs, *Barbus lineatus*.

Two vertical bars, one behind the operculum and a second below the anterior origin of the dorsal fin, are joined by a horizontal bar which extends to the tail. Not easily bred in captivity. Enjoys plenty of live food.

– *lineatus*   STRIPED BARB   12cm. (4½in.)

An attractive fish from the Malayan Peninsula. The body colour is silver and several dark blue stripes run horizontally from the operculum. It likes temperatures between 21–26°C.

– *nigrofasciatus*   BLACK RUBY or PURPLE-HEADED BARB   5cm. (2in.)

For much of the time this fish is a rather ordinary dark green colour with darker vertical bands. In the breeding season the male develops a beautiful red coloration

Black Ruby or Purple-headed Barb, *Barbus nigrofasciatus*.

extending from the head to cover the anterior part of the body which produces a dramatic colour effect. A native of Sri Lanka. Easy to breed if provided with live food and temperatures close to 26°C. **20**

– *oligolepis*   CHECKERBOARD, ISLAND or BEAUTIFUL BARB
5cm. (2in.)
One of the more attractive members of this genus, it comes from Sumatra. The reddish brown body is set off, particularly in the male, by orange fins. The dorsal fin has a black border which distinguishes the species. The large barb scales each have a dark base and a reflective border giving the appearance of a checkerboard from which the fish derives one of its popular names. During breeding the male's colours intensify and the fins and body are infiltrated with black coloration. A small pair of barbels adorn its mouth. They breed like other barbs. The young are very small and require minute live food. **21**

– *pentazona*   FIVE-BANDED, BELTED or TIGER BARB
5cm. (2in.)
From the Malayan Peninsula, Borneo and Sumatra, this is one of several fish popularly known as Tiger Barbs. A

brownish red back shades to yellow underparts with five dark vertical bands across the body. Fins are all red. Breeds quite easily. Young are simple to rear at temperatures around 27°C.

– *phutunio*   DWARF or PYGMY BARB   4cm. (1½in.)
A small, spotted, silver bodied barb from the Indian subcontinent and Sri Lanka. The orange brown fins are darker in the male. A hardy happy fish which adds sparkle to the community tank, it breeds at temperatures in the region of 24°C.

– *sachsi* see under *Barbus schuberti*

– *schwanefeldi*   SCHWANFELD'S or TINFOIL BARB
35cm. (14in.)
In spite of its size, this species is commonly kept in captivity. Its lovely and highly reflective silver body shades to a cream belly. The head is broken by yellow highlights and the tail, anal and pelvic fins are a lovely orange. It comes from Sumatra, Borneo, Malaya and Thailand. If you buy one of these, take note of its adult size.

– *schuberti*   GOLDEN or SCHUBERT'S BARB   8cm. (3in.)
This delightful barb is well known to aquarists although it is not found in nature and is not recognized scientifically as a separate species. It is almost certainly a mutant from one of two species *B. semifasciolatus* or *B. sachsi*, the former being the most likely.

A rich golden yellow colour, darkening almost to orange, appears all along the upper third of the body. The fins are a rich orange brown colour. The length of the body is decorated with sparse irregular spots and blotches which vary with the individual. A larger spot is placed just anterior to the base of the tail. An easy fish to keep and to breed. **22**

– *semifasciolatus*   CHINA, HALF-BANDED or GREEN BARB
8cm. (3in.)
As one of the popular names suggests, this undistinguished barb comes from the rivers of southern China. Generally light brown in colour, several indefinite bands transverse its body and the fins have a yellow tinge. During the breeding season the males' colours intensify and are infiltrated with a red tinge. A rather drab barb in appearance, it has maintained a certain popularity as a result of its hardiness. It endures temperatures as low as 17°C. without harm, breeds readily, and is peaceful.

There is a probable colour mutation of this fish which is altogether more handsome, known as *B. schuberti* or Schubert's Barb, having a golden body colour.

– *terio*   TERI or ONE-SPOT BARB   9cm. (3½in.)
A plump barb from India. The male has a yellow body while the female is silver with clear fins. A diffuse orange covers the operculum. Above the anal fin there is a large body spot from which a line extends to a small spot at the base of the tail. The dorsal fin has an attractive if ostentatious pointed appearance.

During the mating season the male assumes an orange hue more intense on the anal and pelvic fins, but in captivity this display is all too frequently wasted for it is a poor captive breeder.

– tetrazona DAMSEL or TIGER BARB 8cm. (3in.) ✂
This is a real little beauty from Sumatra and Borneo. Its pinkish brown body shades to a silver belly. Vertical bands transverse the body through the eye in front of the dorsal fin, above the anal and at the base of the tail fins. The dorsal fin has a black base followed by consecutive bands of red, yellow and clear. The tail fin is clear with striking red borders. The body often appears flecked with gold.

It is very active, and somewhat aggressive, so is not a good candidate for the community tank. Kept in shoals, however, it makes a wonderful exhibit. Breeds in captivity but the adults are likely to eat their spawn and fry and so should be removed after spawning. A subspecies, *B. tetrazona partipentazona*, thought by some to be a separate species, is available, but is not so brightly coloured, having a silver body crossed by black bands and a red patch on the dorsal fin. It has a poor breeding record and is smaller, 4cm. (1½in.) **23**

– ticto TICTO or TWO-SPOT BARB 10cm. (4in.)
An attractive import from India and Sri Lanka. It is constantly active without being aggressive. The body is silver with greenish yellow tints and there is a diffuse spot which tries hard to be a stripe behind the pectoral fins and a further spot above the anal fin, the latter is surrounded by a golden margin. The fins are translucent, tinged with yellow except the dorsal in the male which has a wide border of red. The Ticto Barb breeds easily.

– titteya CHERRY BARB 4–5cm. (1½–2in.)
This fish is from Sri Lanka. Its coloration is variable. It has an attractive shape. The body is silver but in the male during the breeding season, assumes shades of pink or red which vary in intensity. A dark horizontal body line is bordered above by a wide band of gold. Fins are tinted red or orange.

It enjoys temperatures around 25°C. During its courtship display it often leaps out of the water and it is wise to cover the tank. **24**

– vittatus KOOLI BARB 6cm. (2½in.)
From India and Sri Lanka, this fish has a general body colour of silver, broken by dark spots on the body with a larger one near the base of the tail fin. All fins are clear except for the dorsal in which there is a dark band. Sex distinction is a problem for the aquarist except that the female is plumper when mature. Wide range of temperature adaptability from 18–27°C.

A good, if uncolourful, member for the community tank, it breeds reasonably well.

BARDIC PUFFER see *Canthigaster valentini*

BARRED
 CHANCHITO see *Cichlasoma festivum*
 CICHLID see *Cichlasoma festivum*
BATFISH see *Ephippidae, Platax*
BASS, SEA see *Serrandidae*
BEACONFISH see *Hemigrammus ocellifer*
BEAKED
 CORALFISH see *Chelmon rostratus*
 LEATHERJACKET *see Oxymonacanthus longirostris*
BEAKFISH see *Gomphosus varius*
BEAUTIFUL BARB see *Barbus oligolepis*
BEAUTY, ROCK see *Holocanthus tricolor*

Bedotia Atherinidae ⊕
– geayi MADAGASCAR RAINBOWFISH 10cm. (4in.)
Of unspectacular shape, this fish, is very variable in colour, from a blue green with an iridescent sheen to a pale yellow brown. The tail fin is tipped with red in mature males. Golden bases of the dorsal and anal fins add attraction. Breeds in captivity, preferring alkaline water, and the eggs hatch in 2–3 days.

Beetles see *Unwelcome Visitors*

Behaviour
Many areas of science are now so complex and require such expensive and technical apparatus that the amateur is virtually excluded from contributing. Behavioural science or ethology however, still makes considerable use of two cheap pieces of equipment – the pencil and paper. It is true that time lapse photography, tape recorders, television, event recorders and computers are employed in ethological research, but many experienced and competent behavioural scientists still rely heavily on observing an animal's behaviour and writing down these observations, as faithfully as possible, as they take place. Since fish are the most numerous of vertebrates, both in numbers of individuals and in numbers of species, the amount of work to be undertaken is immense. Here the amateur aquarist can be of tremendous help to science. By carefully and faithfully recording the behaviour of a species, describing in detail exactly what happens under what environmental conditions, the aquarist can provide the basic behavioural patterns, which are the bricks and mortar of ethology.

It is important that as much detail as possible is included. The exact time of day, the season of the year, the water temperature and other environmental conditions, such as the age and history of the fish being observed are basic requirements. For example, it is no good saying the male approached the female. It is necessary to know what sequence of events led up to the approach, whether she was approached from above or below, at right angles, head on or from the rear, whether his fins were spread or tucked, if his body was quivering, at what speed he approached. It is also necessary to know the concurrent behaviour and postures of the female. In this way a complete and detailed picture may be built up, and you may thus get the fullest enjoyment from your hobby.

Behaviour may be conveniently divided into types, examined under separate headings below.

FEEDING OR INGESTIVE BEHAVIOUR. The methods of obtaining and consuming food are related to the anatomy and physiology of the species. Since there are so many species of fish it is not surprising that there is a great variety of feeding behaviour. Some fish eat plants, some eat small microscopic animal life while others are predators, like the sharks and large cichlids. Others are parasites living attached to other fish. Some fish feed on the bottom, as the majority of catfish do, while others commonly feed close to the surface, even in some cases consuming insects out of water, as does the Archerfish, *Toxotes jaculator*. The Halfbeak, *Dermogenys pusillus* is so well adapted to surface feeding that it has evolved with a jaw structure which makes it physically impossible for it to feed from the bottom.

Some fish depend on olfaction or smell to identify and locate food. The eel, it has been found experimentally, can locate food in still water by detecting the concentration gradient, and lampreys, which are parasites on other fish, locate their victims by smell. Most species, however, rely on sight. An interesting fact about feeding by sight concerns the Archerfish which, when aiming his bullets of water at insects sitting on leaves out of water, must allow for the bending of the light rays due to the different refractive indices of water and air.

One of the most important factors affecting an animal's behaviour is the social relationship with other members of its species. Experiments with Goldfish, *Carassius auratus*, Zebrafish, *Brachydanio rerio*, Paradisefish, *Macropodus opercularis*, and Guppies, *Poecilia reticulatus*, have shown, for example, that each individual benefits from being kept in groups rather than in isolation. Pity the goldfish in its bowl. It was shown at the same time however that if the group became too large, if the population density increased beyond the optimum, then the disadvantages outweighed the benefits. This has been illustrated in one feeding experiment using the above species. Groups of four fish were compared to an equal number of isolated individuals in identical tanks. Live daphnia were fed daily. For the first three days of the experiment each fish in the groups ate more than those kept in isolation. At three days those in isolation were grouped while those which started in groups were isolated and the experiment continued as before. The newly grouped fish now consumed more daphnia. This continued until the fish were being fed 150 daphnia per fish

a day. At this point when the groups were getting a total of 600 daphnia at one time the advantage of grouping was lost. Undoubtedly this was due to a confusion effect. The large numbers of daphnia passing into view prevented the fish making the decision which daphnia to attack. When the 600 daphnia were fed at the rate of 150 four times daily the advantage of grouping was again evident.

LEARNING. In simple learning fish are as competent as other vertebrates but in more complex learning tasks, fish do less well than higher vertebrates. It has been shown that, given a choice between two levers, one of which supplies food and the other not, both the goldfish and the rat will soon learn to press only the lever which gives a reward. If the experiment is then reversed so that the lever which previously gave no reward now gives food, then both fish and rat soon learn to press the new lever. After repeated reversals, however, the rat makes fewer errors in adapting to the continual change, whereas the fish never learns and continues to make the same number of errors each time the lever is changed.

Goldfish, *Carassius auratus*, have been the subject of many studies on learning. They have, for example, been trained to pass through a hatch in a partition which divided their aquarium into two when a light flashed, to obtain a food reward. They very quickly learnt the light signal and would swim through for food quickly. An extension of these experiments showed that Goldfish can learn the trick by watching others. A partitioned tank was set up. A trained Goldfish was placed in the larger side and an untrained Goldfish placed in the narrow corridor able to see through the partition to its experienced colleague. The trained Goldfish was then put through its paces, while the untrained fish was left alone but able to swim up and down the corridor observing. After the trick had been repeated several times, the trained fish was removed and the untrained one placed in the larger partitioned area of the tank. It behaved as if it had been trained, by imitating its trained colleague.

Several variations on these experiments have been carried out and the ability of the Goldfish and other fishes to learn has been carefully studied. The inevitable conclusion one must come to is that although their learning ability is restricted, it exists and assists the fish in adapting to changes in its environment.

MIGRATION. Some species of fish, like some birds, undertake tremendous migrations. The story of the young Salmon's migration from the river of its birth to the sea, and the return to the same river when a mature adult for spawning, has always intrigued behavioural scientists. It seems that the fish are able to detect small chemical differences in the composition of the water and can in this way find their way back. In one experiment over 10,000 Salmon were recovered in their parent river and none was found in any other. The chemical composition of their home river must be learnt by the young early in life, because in experiments in which the young Salmon have been transferred at various stages to other rivers, they have returned not to the river in which they were experimentally placed and from which they migrated to the sea, but to the river in which they hatched.

The story of the Eel migration is even more mysterious. Eels breed in the Sargasso Sea and migrate, probably transported by the Gulf Stream, to the rivers of the north Atlantic in America and Europe. Crossing the Atlantic from the Sargasso Sea to Europe takes several years and the migration is over thousands of miles. What guides the elvers up the freshwater streams and how, when mature, they make their way downstream again and across the Atlantic to the Sargasso Sea is still under investigation.

REPRODUCTIVE AND PARENTAL BEHAVIOUR. This has been dealt with in other parts of the book, see *Breeding, Reproductive System*. Suffice to say that vision is a very important sense in reproduction. Most preliminary reproductive behaviour – courtship behaviour – depends on visual displays. Extensive and detailed studies of courtship and mating behaviour in the Guppy, see *Poecilia reticulatus* and the 3-Spined Stickleback, *Gasterosteus aculeatus*, have been undertaken over many years by behavioural scientists.

SCHOOLING. This is a well known characteristic of some species of fish when large numbers of a species swim together in a well defined group. Vision is the most important factor in fish which school, playing its role in both formation and maintenance. Smell and lateral line sensory systems do, however, have a lesser part to play. The importance of sight is well demonstrated by the common observation that schooling species disperse at night. It is known that hunger will cause a school to disperse, and attack by a predator causes the school to tighten its formation.

The development of schooling is interesting. At one time schooling was considered to be an instinctive behaviour pattern controlled by the genetic inheritance with which each fish was born. More recent studies have shown that fish reared in isolation approach one another but withdraw at once. Later the fish approach again and stay together for a while and then withdraw. Eventually they overcome the desire to withdraw and remain together. Schooling is therefore a combination, as is a great deal of behaviour, of instinctive behaviour, approaching, and learning behaviour, remaining.

One may question the advantages of schooling to a species. It acts as a protection against predation. Remembering the confusing effect large numbers of daphnia had on Goldfish, a similar effect is produced when

fish take the place of daphnia as the prey. Large numbers of fish confuse the predator and reduce his intake. Fewer of the species are killed. It is therefore adaptive for the species.

Schooling also facilitates reproduction since a school provides a wealth of mates. It also has a beneficial effect physiologically since experimental work has shown that individuals in a school use less oxygen than would be the case if the same number of fish were free swimming. A further advantage of grouping is the enhancement of learning which occurs. Finally large groups are at an advantage in searching for food.

SHELTER-SEEKING BEHAVIOUR. An important adaptive behaviour, common to many species, is to seek shelter from predation or attack. This does not apply to fast, free swimming species which rely on speed and agility to avoid enemies, but to small, slow moving species like for example many of the marine aquarists' coral-dwelling species.

Interesting behaviour which can be classified as shelter-seeking or maternal behaviour, has been studied in the mouth-brooding cichlid *Tilapia mossambica*. When the young brood are free swimming they may be alarmed, for example, by the approach of a predator. They all immediately swim towards the female. Experiments have shown that they swim towards the lower parts of a dummy, particularly dark areas and push into holes on the surfaces. Such activity in nature would increase the probability that they all found their way into the mouth of the mother.

Though most cichlid young seek shelter in the mother's mouth, some may be attracted by other dark places, such as her eyes or gills.

TERRITORIAL BEHAVIOUR. While some animals, including many species of fish, have an extensive range over which they roam, others restrict themselves to small territories which they defend, often with great ferocity. Some species, like many of the coral-dwelling species we keep in the marine aquarium permanently restrict themselves to a small territory or home range while others only so confine themselves at breeding seasons. Breeding territories are a valuable population control mechanism for the species since they ensure that only those which can find and defend a breeding area will breed. In this way overbreeding and overpopulation are controlled. The value of individual territories unrelated to reproductive behaviour has been the subject of studies on young Salmon. In the wild, young Salmon defend their territories by aggressive acts like chasing, nipping and aggressive displays. If a few of these fish are placed in an aquarium, one or two dominant fish control territories near the bottom while the remaining fish are left swimming aimlessly about in the middle water of the tank, and are attacked by those with territories if they dare approach. It has also been observed that the aggression by the territorial fish on the bottom is increased when little food is offered but diminishes when food is plentiful. Thus, it seems likely that, in the case of young Salmon, territorial behaviour regulates population dynamics to available food.

AGGRESSION. Fighting within a species, if extensive and uncontrolled, would be disastrous for the species. In general, acts of aggression are ritualized and little actual fighting takes place. Again the Three-spined Stickleback, *Gasterosteus aculeatus*, has been the subject of much study in this field. When defending a territory during the breeding season, the fish entrenched in the territory is usually dominant. If another male dares to enter his patch he will attack. Experimental work showed that a crude model hardly like a fish at all, would stimulate attack if it had a simulated red belly, and that if the model was presented in a head down position, then attack was even more readily provoked. Contrarily a perfectly shaped stickleback model without a red belly produced virtually no response at all. The fighting behaviour of the Siamese Fightingfish, *Betta splendens*, is well known. Marine aquarists are equally aware of the aggressive behaviour of some of the commonly kept coralfish.

Belonesox Poeciliidae ⊕
– belizanus DWARF PIKE, PIKE TOP MINNOW 20cm. (8in.)
A live-bearing fish from eastern Central America which is really for the specialist. The wickedly curved jaws are well endowed with teeth and its behaviour is reminiscent of the European Pike. A dark green or dirty brown body is highlighted with a metallic green sheen. A round spot resides on the base of its tail fin. The male grows to about 10cm.

A voracious feeder insisting on live delicacies. **25**

Belontia Belontiidae ⊕
– signata COMBTAIL 13cm. (5in.)

These fish are native to Sri Lanka. The appearance of the tail fin gives this fish its popular name. Adults are a rich reddish brown while younger fish have a blue underbelly. Dorsal and anal fins, which are also reddish brown, are pointed posterially. The anterior rays of the pelvic fins are elongated.

They should be kept in large tanks with species of similar size since they are aggressive to smaller fish. They are omnivorous but should have plenty of animal protein. Temperatures around 24°C. are most acceptable but should be raised for breeding to about 26°C. Their breeding habits are typical of the family – see *Belontiidae*.

Belontiidae
A family newly created to take many of the labyrinthfishes. The fish here classified were previously placed in the Anabantidae but were proved to have distinguishable anatomical features. It includes such popular aquarium species as the paradisefishes *(Macropodus)*, fightingfishes *(Betta)* and the gouramis *(Trichogaster)*.

They are distributed throughout Asia and are only found in freshwater. The accessory breathing organ which enables these species to breathe atmospheric air at the surface is situated above the gills in the gill chamber. They are commonly found in water with a low oxygen content. See *Belontia, Betta, Colisa, Macropodus, Sphaerichthys, Trichogaster, Trichopsis*.

BELTED
BARB see *Barbus pentazona*
SANDFISH see *Serranthus subligarius*
TRIGGERFISH see *Rhinecanthus rectangulus*
BENGAL DANIO see *Danio devario*
BENNETT'S BUTTERFLYFISH see *Chaetodon bennetti*

Betta Belontiidae ⊕
– brederi BREDER'S or MOUTH-BROODING FIGHTINGFISH
8cm. (3in.)
This fish from Java and Sumatra attains lengths of over 8cm. The general body colour is brown with a greenish tinge produced by a green dot on each scale. The fins are red.

The breeding behaviour is of interest since it incubates the eggs in its mouth. Observations suggest that while embracing the female, the male cups his anal fin and there catches the eggs and fertilizes them. The female then collects the eggs and spits them to the male who catches them in his mouth and there incubates them. Even more bizarre, some observers say that the pair throw the spawn back and forth to each other for a while until he accepts his task and the game is concluded.
– pugnax MALAYAN BETTA 8cm. (3in.)
Rather coarser and bulkier than *B. splendens* and without

the brilliant wrapping, it is brown with a blue tinge, resulting from a blue spot on each scale and comes from the island of Penang, west of the Malay Peninsula. Another pair who play with their spawn until the male is persuaded to start his mouth incubation. He doesn't attack the female after mating.

– *splendens* SIAMESE FIGHTINGFISH 6cm. (2½in.) ✂

There is no doubt that Siamese Fightingfish are aggressive and this behaviour has been well studied and documented by ethologists interested in aggressive behaviour. In nature such encounters would usually end with little or no physical damage to the participants but in the confines of the aquarium, where submission and retreat are impossible, physical damage may be considerable. Serious students interested in analysing the fighting behaviour commonly use a mirror which, when placed in the tank, will elicit appropriate reaction from the male fightingfish.

The wild species is native to streams and muddy ponds in south east Asia. It is a browny colour with dark bands. There are however individuals which are better endowed with colour. They adopt, particularly in the breeding season, a greenish blue sheen, patches of red, yellow and blue, and green dots pepper the body. The anal and tail fins become red or blue and may have green stripes.

From this basic species aquarists have developed the domesticated form which has certainly become one of the most popular and exotic of aquarium fish. The fins have been lengthened by selective breeding, looking rather like great lengths of fine silk. The colour varieties too are very vivid. Cambridge blue, Indigo, Crimson, Claret, and Emerald Green are accepted named varieties.

Apart from their feelings of aggression to their own species, which prevents more than one male being kept in each tank, they are pleasant, agreeable, hardy and undemanding inhabitants of the community aquarium. They prefer soft water with plenty of plants and temperatures around 24°C.

They breed according to the typical family pattern, except that both sexes spit the eggs into the little bubble nest. After mating, the female is discarded, indeed attacked and even killed, so she should be removed allowing the male to look after the nest. The young hatch in just a few hours and should be fed green water and small infusoria. After 2 or 3 days the male should also be removed or he will consume the brood. A further tip is not to introduce a male to an unripe female or her reluctance will be her undoing. **26**

BETTA,
  MALAYAN see *Betta pugnax*
  MARINE see *Calloplesiops altivelus*
BICOLOR ANGEL see *Centropyge bicolor*
BIG EYE see *Priacanthus arenatus*

BIGHEADED MOUTHBROODER see *Tilapia hendelotti macrocephala*
BIGSPOT KILLY see *Epiplatys macrostigma*
BIRDWRASSE see *Gomphosus varius*
BITTERLING see *Rhodeus amarus*
BLACK
  ACARA see *Aequidens portalegrensis*
  ANGELFISH see *Pomacanthus arcuatus*
  FLAG TETRA *Hyphessobrycon rosaceus*
  PHANTOM TETRA see *Megalamphodus megalopterus*
  RUBY BARB see *Barbus nigrofasciatus*
  SHARK see *Morulius chrysophekadion*
  TETRA see *Gymnocorymbus ternetzi*
  TRIGGERFISH see *Melichthys indicus, Odonus niger*
  VELVET DAMSELFISH see *Abudefduf oxyodon*
  WIDOW see *Gymnocorymbus ternetzi*
BLACK-BACKED BUTTERFLYFISH see *Chaetodon melanotus*
BLACK-BANDED
  LEPORINUS see *Leporinus fasciatus*
  SUNFISH see *Mesogonistus chaetodon*
BLACK-BARRED TRIGGERFISH see *Rhinecanthus aculeatus*
BLACK-BLOTCHED BUTTERFLYFISH see *Chaetodon ephippium*
BLACK-FINNED PEARLFISH see *Cynolebias nigripinnis*
BLACK-HEADED WIMPLEFISH see *Heniochus chrysostomus*
BLACK-LINE TETRA see *Hyphessobrycon scholzei*
BLACK-LINED RAINBOWFISH, AUSTRALIAN see *Melanotaenia maccullochi*
BLACK-SPOT GOATFISH see *Parupeneus pleurostigma*
BLACK-SPOTTED CATFISH see *Corydoras melanistius*
BLACK-WEDGE BUTTERFLYFISH see *Chaetodon falcula*
BLACK-WINGED HATCHETFISH see *Carnegiella marthae*
BLACKAMOOR see *Gymnocorymbus ternetzi*
BLACKCAP GRAMMA see *Gramma melacara*
BLACKJAW MOUTHBROODER see *Tilapia hendelotii macrocephala*
BLADDER, GAS see *Gas Bladder*
BLIND
  CAVE CHARACIN see *Anoptichthys jordani*
  TETRA see *Anoptichthys jordani*

Blood System

The arrangement of the circulatory or blood system is rather different from that found in land mammals with which most people are familiar. The heart, the pumping station for the blood circulation, is situated in most fish just behind the gill apparatus. It consists of a chamber, known as an auricle, into which the veins returning blood to the heart open and another chamber – a ventricle – which contracts rhythmically, forcing blood around the body, and finally there is a small bulb at the base of the artery which carries blood on its first stage of circulation to the gills.

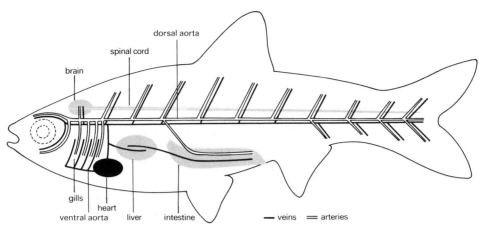

Blood system

From the heart the blood is pumped along a large vessel, the ventral aorta, which in turn gives off branches to the gills. These branches continually sub-divide until they attain the fine hair-like capillaries which ramify in the gill filaments. Here the blood gives up the carbon dioxide it collected on its last circulation and absorbs a fresh supply of oxygen. Replenished, this blood passes on to be collected up into larger vessels which eventually join the large dorsal aorta to transport the freshly oxygenated blood to the body tissue. This in turn gives off branch vessels which divide until they become again small capillaries carrying blood to the body cells. Here oxygen is released for biological combustion within the cells and carbon dioxide absorbed. The capillary vessels again re-unite into larger and larger veins carrying the de-oxygenated blood back to the heart. Vessels from the gut are slightly different. The veins collected together from the gut, go to the liver where they once again branch into smaller vessels, pass through the liver tissue and then re-unite yet again to pass into the heart. See also *Respiration, Gills, Oxygen.*

Blood Worms see under *Food*
BLOODFIN see *Aphyocharax rubripinnis*
BLOTCHEYE see *Myripistis murdjan*
BLOWFISH see *Tetraodon cutcutia*
BLUE
  ACARA see *Aequidens pulcher*
  ANGELFISH see *Holocanthus isabelita*
  BOXFISH see *Ostracion meleagris*
  CATFISH see *Corydoras nattereri*
  CHIN see *Ancistrus dolichoptera*
  CHROMIS see *Chromis cyanea*
  CICHLID see *Aequidens pulcher*
  DAMSELFISH, ELECTRIC see *Pomacentrus coeruleus*
  DAMSELFISH, SAFFRON see *Pomacentrus melanochir*
  DEVIL see *Pomacentrus melanochir*
  GAMBUSIA see *Gambusia punctata*

GOURAMI see *Trichogaster trichopterus sumatranus*
GULARIS see *Aphyosemion sjoestedti*
LEOPARD see *Corydoras paleatus*
LIMIA see *Poecilia melanogaster*
PANCHAX see *Aplocheilus panchax*
PETER see *Petrotilapia tridentiger*
PULLER see *Chromis caeruleus*
RIBBON EEL see *Rhinomuraena ambonensis*
RING ANGELFISH see *Pomacanthus annularis*
STREAK see *Labroides dimidiatus*
TANG see *Acanthurus coeruleus, Paracanthurus hepatus*
TETRA see *Mimagoniates microlepsis*
BLUE-BANDED
  BUTTERFLYFISH see *Chaetodon meyeri*
  HUSSAR see *Lutjanus kasmira*
  SEA PERCH see *Lutjanus kasmira*
BLUE-FIN KILLY see *Lucania goodei*
BLUE-GREEN
  CHROMIS see *Chromis caeruleus*
  FUNDULUS see *Nothobranchius orthonotus*
BLUE-LINE BUTTERFLYFISH see *Chaetodon trifasciatus*
BLUE-LINED
  GROUPER see *Cephalopholis boenack*
  TRIGGERFISH see *Pseudobalistes*
BLUE-SPOTTED
  BOXFISH see *Ostracion tuberculatus*
  CICHLID see *Herichthys cyanoguttatum*
BLUE-STRIPED GROUPER see *Cephalophilis boenack*
BLUE-TAILED DAMSELFISH see *Chromis cyanea*
BLUEHEAD WRASSE see *Thalassoma bifasciatum*
BLUNTHEAD
  CICHLID see *Tropheus moorei*
  CICHLID, FLAG see *Aequidens curviceps*
Blyxa see under *Plants*

Bodianus Labridae ♆
– axillaris CORAL HOGFISH 20cm. (8in.)

This fish from the Indo-Pacific has previously been known in the genus *Lepidaplois* either as *L. axillaris* or *L. albomaculatus*. The adult males are a rich purple colour anteriorly which ends abruptly midway along the body at a line which slopes forward at 45°. The posterior part of the body is a variable shade of orange, with faint longitudinal lines of different colour intensity. The young of this species are totally different having a black body covered with large white spots.

It is relatively easy for the beginner to keep and accepts a variety of food. **27**
– pulchellus CUBAN or SPOTFIN HOGFISH 23cm. (9in.)
From the West Indies, an incredibly beautiful fish with an elongated body. The basic body colour is red with a broad band of white running horizontally from below the snout back along the flank of the body. The dorsal and tail fins are decorated with bright yellow. It is uncommon but does well in the aquarium where greed readily overcomes its reluctance to eat. Usually found in water over 24m. deep.
– rufus SPANISH HOGFISH 61cm. (24in.)
An attractive hogfish from the western tropical Atlantic and the Caribbean to some south Atlantic islands. It is hardy and does well in the marine aquarium. It has a blue head and forebody with yellow underparts to the head and belly. In specimens from deep water, red replaces the blue. Feeds on crustaceans and molluscs. The young of this species are reputed to be 'cleaners'. A good community fish.

Bolbometapon Scaridae Ψ
– bicolor RED AND WHITE PARROTFISH 61cm. (24in.)
A white body which is decorated with a wide bar of red on the head passing through the eye in the juvenile stage. It also has red decoration on the tail and dorsal fin. A very attractive fish indeed from the Indo-Pacific region. It can reach 61cm. in length.

Boleophthalmus Periophthalmidae Ψ/⊕
– boddaerti GOGGLE-EYE, MUD-HOPPER 13cm. (5in.)
A greenish fish with several vertical bands and numerous dark spots, and dark fins. The first of its two dorsals is spiny. It comes from India and the Malayan Archipelago.

This species is fond of burying itself in the mud leaving its eyes exposed on the look out for food or danger. Its aquarium should therefore have a depth of mud which allows for such behaviour. Rarely imported.

As a rule, this group of fish does not venture out on land as do the closely related mud skippers, *Periophthalmus* species.

Bones see *Skeleton*

BONY TONGUES see *Osteoglossidae*

Hora's Clown Loaches, *Botia horae*.

Botia Cobitidae ⊕
– horae HORA'S CLOWN LOACH, MOUSE BOTIA 10cm. (4in.)
This fish is common in Thailand where it abounds in many of the rivers and larger streams. The body including the head is a pale brown with red tinged fins. Four faint lines cross the dorsal sides of the body, and a dark band runs from the snout to the tail dorsally which merges with a dark band across the base of the tail. It has a short dorsal fin and only eight branched rays which helps to identify it. **28**
– hymenophysa 15–30cm. (6–12in.)
A large fish which, like the rest of the genus, does not have the typical loach look. The body is compressed laterally, the head depressed and the tail fin is bifurcated. Barbels border the mouth. It is a native of Thailand, the Malayan Peninsula, Sumatra and Java.

A body colour of grey is adorned with dark brown stripes at various angles, oblique near the head becoming vertical at the tail. **29**
– macracanthas CLOWN LOACH, TIGER BOTIA
30cm. (12in.)
A really beautiful member of the genus which comes from Sumatra and Borneo. It has a lovely shaped body which looks well designed for an aquatic life. The body colour is a rich golden yellow. Three wide vertical grey to black stripes, which give it the popular name, pass, one through the eye, one just in front of the dorsal fin and the third just behind the dorsal fin. This third bar extends through the dorsal and anal fins. The tail and pelvics are orange while the pectorals are splashed with crimson red. Short barbels adorn the mouth. They like temperatures around 27°C. **30**

BOXFISH
see Ostraciodontidae, *Tetrosomus gibbosus*
BLUE see *Ostracion meleagris*
BLUE-SPOTTED see *Ostracion tuberculatus*
SPANGLED see *Ostracion meleagris*
SPINY see *Chilomycterus schoepfi*

Brachydanio Cyprinidae ⊕
– *albolineatus* PEARL or WHITE LINE DANIO 6cm. (2½in.)
The full beauty of this fish is seen in reflected light. Here its mother-of-pearl colouring will be fully displayed. It comes from East India, Thailand, Burma and Sumatra.

The general body colour is blue with reddish pink overtones. The ventral part of the body is tinted with a generous reddish purple. A red line commences below the dorsal and, gradually widening, extends to the top of the tail fin. Pelvic and anal fins have red bases. Small fine barbels are present.

Sexing is difficult and is based on size and conformation differences together with colour intensity variations. They breed easily and the non-adhesive eggs hatch within 3–4 days of laying. **31**
– *nigrofasciatus* SPOTTED or DWARF DANIO 4cm. (1½in.)
Native to Burma, the Dwarf Danio is similar to but smaller than the Zebrafish, *B. rerio*. It is less distinctive and certainly less popular. The horizontal stripes are present in the posterior half of the fish but anteriorly they break up into a series of blue black dots. These extend into the anal fin.

It is less hardy than the Zebrafish and not so easily bred. After the nuptial chase they assume a vertical stance and appear to clasp each other. At this point the eggs are dropped. The aquarist should take precautions to protect the eggs by trapping.
– *rerio* ZEBRAFISH or ZEBRA DANIO 5cm. (2in.)
Common as this fish is in private collections, it must be one of the most well loved of tropical fish.

Comes from India. It is very hardy and tolerates an exceptionally wide range of temperature conditions from 16°C. to over 30°C. In the aquarium it is active and tends to swim near to the water surface.

The body is quite streamlined and the blue black colour is separated by silver horizontal lines which extend from the gill covers to the very tips of the tail fin. The anal fin is similarly marked. Very fine colourless barbels are present.

Sexes can be differentiated by experienced aquarists. The female is of course fuller of form near to spawning but, in addition, is sometimes a paler blue than the male, especially on the tail fin.

A very easy fish to breed, some care must be taken to prevent the parents from eating the eggs. The female when near to spawning is placed in a tank where some form of trap is arranged which allows the eggs to fall through and prevents the fish from consuming them. At least two mature males must be placed with the female and these will chase the female enthusiastically as an inducement to spawn. The young should be fed infusoria, given plenty of growing room and must be given some live food. They seldom survive longer than 3 years.

A delightful fish, full of character and interest. **32**

Brachygobius Gobiidae ⊕
– *nunus* BUMBLEBEE or WASP GOBY, BUMBLEBEEFISH 4cm. (1½in.)
A native of India and south-east Asia. Has a yellow body with broad, vertical, dark brown or black bands. It is most at home and spends most of its time, close to the bottom of the aquarium. It eats live food and does best at temperatures between 25–28°C. Large scales and a squat appearance add to its attraction and charm. Does not breed with enthusiasm in captivity unless kept in slightly brackish water – one tablespoon of salt per 4½ litres.
– *xanthozona* BUMBLEBEE GOBY 4cm. (1½in.) ⊕/Ψ
A fish from south-east Asia, very similar to *B. nunus* but with a slightly more sleek outline, making it difficult to tell them apart, except by experts. This fish is small and dumpy with an undershot jaw. It prefers slightly salt water, as for *B. nunus*. Kept with its own kind it breeds easily in captivity. Spawning may be encouraged by placing a small flowerpot laid on its side in the aquarium. The male protects the eggs which hatch within five days.

BRAZILIAN SPOTTED CATFISH see *Plecostomus punctatus*
BREAM, GOVERNMENT see *Lutjanus sebae*
Breathing see *Respiration*
BREDER'S FIGHTINGFISH see *Betta brederi*

Breeding

Few aquarists can resist the temptation to indulge in breeding programmes for their piscine charges once they have firmly established their exhibition tanks. The pleasure to be gained from overcoming the many difficulties encountered in rearing young is indeed immense. In truth, some species are so easy to breed that avoidance of overpopulation is the main difficulty. These are, however, in the minority. Success in breeding most species depends on careful attention being paid to the environmental demands of the species concerned, good feeding, and not a little luck.

The diligent breeder will begin by delving as deeply as possible into the background of the species which he hopes to breed. Information concerning the principles of the reproductive system, the reproductive behaviour, whether it is live bearing or egg laying, are available in many species. The novice breeder would be well advised to begin with a species about which a good deal is known and which has proved itself in the breeding stakes.

As the germ cells – ova within the ovaries in females and spermatozoa in the testes of the males – begin to develop in the breeding season, external changes occur in the fish. The fish become more active and very often their colours heighten and intensify. In some species new colours become visible. The red underbelly develops for example in the Three-spined Stickleback, *Gasterosteus aculeatus*. The reproductive behaviour now becomes apparent. The male pays great attention to ripe females. Swimming and aquadancing displays are used to impress and encourage the female. Eventually the eggs in egg-laying species are passed to the outside via a tube – the oviduct. The male immediately discharges sperms into the water close to the eggs. This is essential for sperms cannot live for any length of time in water. A single sperm fertilizes each egg. See *Embryology*.

In live-bearers, notably Poeciliidae, the male actually introduces the sperms into the female using his organ of intromission, the gonopodium. The eggs are fertilized within the mother's body and are retained therein until ready for birth as small fish. At birth the offspring enter the world, usually tail first and rise to the surface to fill their gas bladders with a gulp of atmospheric air. With protection in the mother's body comes safety and fewer young are necessary to perpetuate the species. Egg-layers usually have to produce vast numbers of eggs in order to maintain the species since many eggs are lost to predators.

Species differ considerably in the amount of care afforded the young. It is essential that aquarists are acquainted with the parental behaviour of the species to be bred. Many fish take no interest in their offspring at all. Indeed, many consume their offspring either at egg or fry stage and the breeder then must prevent access if he is to rear a reasonable brood.

Some fish however conform more closely to the human concept of parental behaviour. The Cichlidae in general are good parents. The eggs are protected against predation and the young are herded and nurtured for some time. The male Three-spined Sticklebacks make excellent fathers while the female leaves as soon as she has deposited her eggs. The male again takes his parental duties seriously in the Centrarchidae, the freshwater Sunfishes. He lines a hollow which he has made at the bottom of the tank with sand. After the female has deposited her eggs there, he carefully guards and protects both the eggs and the young until they are old enough to take care of themselves. The bubble nests of the Osphronemidae are equally fascinating. The variations on the theme of parental care are numerous and are described more fully under the family and species headings.

Perhaps a note of philosophical caution is needed here. Fish should not be attributed human emotions. Their parental activities should not be confused with the human love for an offspring. For, as mentioned above, they may well eat their eggs and young.

For those who wish to indulge in special types of breeding, such as selective breeding, my feelings have been made clear elsewhere. In general the selection of arbitrary characteristics which amuse or please the human owner, as in for example the Celestial Goldfish, without reference to anatomical function or the welfare of the animal is, in my opinion, unforgivable. Man's assumption that he can improve on nature without incurring penalties is, I believe, a dangerous concept. Where it is necessary for greater production from domestic animals – high production dairy cattle, beef cattle with exaggerated muscle for prime meat, heavy-coated wool sheep and long-backed pigs – then a case can be made, even if not universally accepted, but to genetically alter animals for fashion I find abhorrent.

For those who wish to 'improve' a species by selective breeding by exaggerating one or other characteristic the method is to continually select those fish in any ordinary brood which show a greater tendency for the desired characteristic. For example if one wished to produce a fish with an enlarged dorsal fin one would select parent fish from the wild species which had slightly larger dorsal fins than the average. Since biological variation is always present this should be possible. Of the offspring a few specimens would again appear with larger fins. Again these would be used for breeding. Over many generations the dorsal fin could be enlarged. To hasten the process in breeding one can cross father to daughter or mother to son. A note of caution: such breeding programmes as well as producing larger numbers of fish with 'desirable' qualities may produce as many with undesirable ones and these, as part of the programme, must be destroyed. Such programmes are not for the sentimental. A touch of ruthlessness is essential. In addition such line or inbred animals become weaker, less robust and more susceptible to disease. Such activities should not be undertaken by anybody without an extensive knowledge of genetics and the problems involved since unintentional cruelty can so easily result.

A further method of breeding fish which produces variants from parent stock is found in hybridization. See *Hybridization*.

Successful breeding requires that the aquarist understands the environmental demands of the species at the breeding season, has a knowledge of reproductive physiology, acquires a basic background in genetics, appreciates the reproductive behavioural repertoire, provides correct conditions for the eggs and young and responds to the demands of fry for adequate and suitable food. To achieve success in breeding a species others find difficult, is reward indeed. See *Reproductive Systems, Genetics, Hybridization, Food and Feeding* (for fry feeding).

BRILLIANT RASBORA see *Rasbora einthoveni*
Brine Shrimps see under *Food*
BRISTLE-MOUTHED CATFISH see *Ancistrus dolichoptera*

BRISTLE-NOSE CATFISH see *Ancistrus cirrhosus*
BROAD-HEADED SLEEPER see *Dormitator latifrons*

Brochis Callichthyidae ⊕
– splendens EMERALD CATFISH 8cm. (3in.)
An attractive deep-bodied catfish closely related to the
genus *Corydoras* but differing from those species in having a
plate snout. The body colour is a mixture of metallic green
blue and yellow. It comes from South America. It requires
the same care as *Corydoras* species. *B. coeruleus* is a
synonym.

BRONZE CATFISH see *Corydoras aeneus*
BROWN
    ACARA see *Aequidens portalegrensis*
    RIVULUS see *Rivulus cylindraceus*
    SPIKE-TAILED PARADISEFISH see *Macropodus cupanus dayi*
BUENOS AIRES TETRA see *Hemigrammus caudovittatus*
BUFFALOFISH, KING see *Symphysodon discus*
BULLFISH
    see *Heniochus acuminatus*
    THREE-BANDED see *Heniochus chrysostomus*
BUMBLEBEE
    CATFISH see *Leiocassis siamensis*
    GOBY see *Brachygobius nunus, Brachygobius xanthozona*

Buncocephalus Aspredinidae
– bicolor BANJO or TWO-COLOURED CATFISH 15cm. (6in.)
In its natural surroundings, of the Amazon and its
tributaries. A dark grey body with dark spots. The fins are
dark grey brown. The dorsal fin is small-based and the
height is moderate. The anal fin is discrete and the tail
round. There are 6 barbels, some of fleshy consistency.
Prefers temperatures around 24°C. and plenty of hiding
places, behind rocks and weeds and in the sand. **33**

BURRFISH
    see *Chilomycterus schoepfi*
    STRIPED see *Chilomycterus schoepfi*
BUTTERFLY
    COD see *Pterois volitans*
    DWARF CICHLID see *Microgeophagus ramirezi*
BUTTERFLYFISH see *Chaetodon, Chaetodontidae, Chelmon,*
   Forcipiger, Megaprotodon, Pantodon, Parachaetodon,
   Pterois, Scatophagus

Cabomba see under *Plants*

Callichthyidae SMOOTH ARMOURED CATFISHES ⊕
The popular name comes from the two rows of overlapping
plates which protect each side. Members of the family come
from South America. There is an adipose fin which is
supported by a spine. The toothed or toothless mouth is
adorned with barbels.

    The presence of an accessory respiratory apparatus
allows the fish to utilize oxygen in atmospheric air which it
gulps in at the surface. The mechanism enables the fish to
live in stagnant, muddy and even polluted water which
would not support fish relying on conventional gill
absorption and in some species allows amphibious
excursions when the air is sufficiently humid. See *Brochis,
Callichthys, Corydoras, Catfish, Hoplosternum.*

Callichthys Callichthyidae ⊕
– callichthys COMMON ARMOURED CATFISH, THE HASSAR,
CASCARUDO 18cm. (7in.)
Not a very attractive fish. It has no fine line, the body colour
is brown with dark spots, and the two pairs of barbels fail to
enhance its somewhat grotesque appearance. A faint blue
tinge to the dorsal, anal and pectoral fins is there but not
very apparent.

    It comes from an area to the east of the Andes and grows
to 18cm. in length. It is adapted to a wide range of temperatures from 20–29°C. It is, of course, a scavenger
preferring animal products. It should not be kept with very

Common Armoured Catfish, *Callichthys callichthys*.

small fishes but is otherwise suitable for the community tank.

Aquarists who have successfully bred this rather difficult fish record that it makes a bubble nest and the male protects the young. **34**

Callionymidae DRAGONETS Ψ
A family whose members are usually, but not always, found in shallow inshore waters. Their bodies are elongated and depressed. They are adapted to bottom living with broad anterior pelvic fins and dorsally placed opercular openings. Many of the species lie buried in sand.

In most species the male is exotically and brilliantly coloured while the female is drab. Behaviourally, some exhibit complex courtship displays. There is an interesting field of observational research here, for the amateur aquarist. See *Synchiropus*.

Calloplesiops Plesiopidae Ψ
– altivelis MARINE BETTA, COMET 17cm. (6½in.)
A dark brown body with black longitudinal stripes is covered with bright pale blue spots. The upper jaw is short.

It comes from the Indo-Pacific. Occasionally imported into both the UK and US.

Callyodon Scaridae Ψ
– sordidus GREEN PARROTFISH 1–2m. (4ft)
Before it reaches full size this makes a colourful exhibit which is relatively easy to keep in health and happiness. It eats live food preferring crustacea and molluscs. It is basically green, complemented with a kaleidoscope of other hues.

CAMERONENSIS see *Aphyosemion australe*
Cancer see *Disease*

Canopy
Many fish are expert jumpers. Without a cover over the tank this activity all too often ends in desiccated tragedy. A sheet of glass covering the tank prevents injury and also reduces heat loss, retards evaporation and reduces corrosion to light fittings.

Since overhead lighting is both advantageous and aesthetic it is common practice to cover the tank in a specially designed canopy incorporating a light holder.

Cantherhines Balistidae Ψ ⊕
– pullus TAIL-LIGHT or ORANGE-SPOTTED FILEFISH
19cm. (7½in.)
An unusual fish from inshore waters of the tropical Atlantic, being particularly common from the west coast of North America, through the Gulf of Mexico to Brazil.

The body is a rich brown decorated with pale head stripes and a series of orange yellow spots with dark centres. Two white spots close to the tail are a constant feature. The dorsal fin is very high.

More common as an aquarium species in the USA than in the UK.

Tanks and tank covers

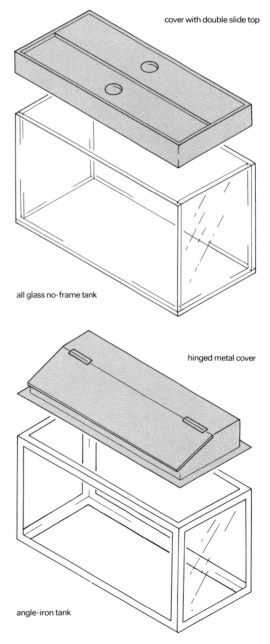

cover with double slide top

all glass no-frame tank

hinged metal cover

angle-iron tank

Canthigaster Tetraodontidae Ψ
– ***jactator*** 18cm. (7in.)
Navy blue body with white spots makes this a lovely and
startling fish, if rather severe in coloration. This is a little-
known species, but is occasionally imported for aquarists. It
comes from the Pacific, primarily Hawaii.
– ***margaritatus*** DIAMOND, DIAMOND-FLECKED or SHARP-
NOSED PUFFER 15cm. (6in.)
This marine member of the family is found from the Red
Sea to the Pacific. The reddish brown body with a beige
belly has a mottled effect produced by small green dots.
Easy fish to acclimatize and simple to feed.
– ***rostrata*** SHARPNOSE PUFFER 13cm. (5in.)
A pleasing fish which is quite commonly kept in the USA.
A brownish orange back shades to a pale yellow belly. The
lower part of the head is scattered with blue spots and blue
lines surround the eyes. Blue lines and bars also decorate the
caudal fin.
 Found widely distributed in the tropical Atlantic. It has a
catholic taste in both diet and habitat. It eats a wide variety
of both plant and animal life and may be found among
reefs, in weed or in rocky pools.
– ***valentini*** BARDIC PUFFER, MINSTREL PUFFERFISH
20cm. (8in.)
The Bardic Puffer is widely distributed throughout the
Indo-Pacific. The beige body is marked on the back with
four large black patches. With care this fish can be adjusted
to captivity where it is an indiscriminate feeder. Being found
in shallow water, it prefers warm water over 26°C.

CAPE FEAR SPATTERDOCK see *Plants – Nuphar*

Carangidae POMPANOS, JACKS or SCADS Ψ
A widely distributed family of fish found in tropical,
subtropical, and temperate waters throughout the oceans of
the world. Very few are kept as aquarium fish but small
members of the genus *Alectis* are imported, particularly into
the USA.
 Characterized by a steep forehead, a lateral row of spiky
scales, and a double dorsal fin. Just anterior to the anal fin
they carry two anal spines which may disappear with age.
The body shape varies from a disc shape in some genera to a
slender cylinder in others. See *Alectis*.

Carassius Cyprinidae ⊕
– ***auratus*** GOLDFISH 30cm. (12in.)
The common goldfishes, of bowl and pond fame, are all
decendants of the dull – even dreary – wild ancestral form,
the Crucian Carp or Wild Goldfish, see *Carassius carassius*.
The wild form was first domesticated by the Chinese over
one thousand years ago as a food crop. The fancy varieties
were incidental to the demands for food.

From the early Chinese forms have been bred a wide
variety of monstrosities. Some of these unfortunate breeds
are burdened with inherited deformities which can only be
described as cruel. These varieties come in several colours
including yellow, red, gold, black and speckled.
 The common gold variety, **35**, enjoys normal anatomical
structure. It is dark green when young and then becomes
almost black only to lighten again to the adult colouring of
rich metallic red gold.
 A popular and reasonably normal variety is the Comet
which is gold in body colour but has a slimmer body with
long exotically pointed fins, particularly the tail. It does well
in the aquarium when young. It comes in normal and calico
(small transparent scales) forms.
 The Shubunkin, **36**, is also relatively normal
anatomically. It too has an exotic tail which adds greatly to
its beauty. It is a calico variety which breeds very easily
under normal conditions. Several colour variations exist,
but the dark grey blue body with small black, and reddish
patches is attractive.
 Fantails are popular with many coldwater enthusiasts.
The body is shorter and deeper resembling an ovoid shape.
They have double tail and anal fins. Calico and normally
scaled varieties exist.
 Veiltails, **37**, were clearly developed by fanatical fantail
breeders. The body is almost spherical and the fins, particularly the tail, are as exaggerated as the Victorian
crinoline was an exaggerated skirt. Like the crinoline, it
must be admitted it has a grace and charm. There are
normal scaled and the de luxe calico forms. Care should
be taken to put only smooth rock in their tank or their
beautiful tails will soon be damaged. They do well and look
very graceful in a tank.
 To add confusion to the goldfish story there is the
popular black goldfish, the Telescopic-eyed Moor. Not
unlike a veiltail it should be a uniform black with no colour
break. It gets its name from the projecting eyes which stand
out remarkably. The Moor does well in aquaria but it is not
a variety for the beginner.
 The goldfish competes with the dog in its grotesque
varieties. Breeders have allowed their talents free reign to
produce fish of abnormal appearance and function. A good
example is the Celestial which has anatomically deformed
eyes which can only look upwards to gaze at the stars. An
ugly, slow, dull creature which is far from hardy and which
owes its burden to the eccentric egotism of man.
 Orandas, **39**, has a head covered in wart like protrusions, extending over the operculum. The body is a
mixture of red and silver grey. Its body is ovoid and it has
well developed fins with a long graceful tail.
 The Lionhead looks like a cross between a diseased
Oranda and a Fantail, and that is probably what it is. The

warty growths are extensive and large, it has no dorsal fin and the tail is like a Fantail's.

The hardy more normal goldfish make excellent inhabitants of the cold water tank however, and the aquarist should not be put off keeping them by the existence of the above freaks. **35, 36, 37, 38, 39.**

– carassius   CRUCIAN CARP or WILD GOLDFISH 30cm. (12in.)
This is a rather uninteresting fish being a dull olive green colour. It is eaten in parts of Asia. From this wild ancestral form which took readily to captivity and later domestication come the grotesque varieties of some domestic goldfish. In the wild state it is found throughout Europe and Asia.

Carassius hybrids   KOI CARP   30cm. (12in.)
These interesting cold water fish have been bred in Japan for many years. It was only after the Second World War that they were imported into Europe and America to any great extent. Their history is obscure. It is known that they originated from one or more species of *Carassius* and some authorities believe that the hybrid has been produced by using, at least in part, *C. auratus.*

As illustrated, the Koi is bred to be viewed from above. They are not strictly aquarium fish, but of more interest and value to the garden pond enthusiast. **40**

CARDINAL TETRA see *Cheirodon axelrodi*
CARDINAL, PYJAMA see *Apogon nematopterus*
CARDINALFISH,
  see *Apogonidae*
  WHITE STAR see *Apogon lachneri*
CARIBBEAN PRAWN see under *Marine Invertebrates*
CARMINE GOATFISH see *Parupeneus pleurostigma*

Carnegiella   Gasteropelecidae   ⊕
– marthae   BLACK-WINGED HATCHETFISH   4cm. (1½in.)
One of the smallest hatchetfishes kept in captivity, it is native to the Amazon and Orinoco rivers of South America. The basic body colour is silver but it is liberally sprinkled with black markings. The name comes from the black markings of the pectoral fins. The adipose fin is absent.

It is a hardy fish with a wide tolerance of temperatures, and will eat dried food.

– strigata   MARBLED or STRIPED HATCHETFISH 4·5cm. (1¾in.)
Native to Guyana and the Amazon Basin, this is a relatively colourful hatchetfish. The body is a dark olive or brown, delineated with a light horizontal stripe. The stripes which give this fish its popular name are brown or black. It is less hardy than its close relative *C. marthae* and it also has no adipose fin.

Marbled Hatchetfish, *Carnegiella strigata.*

Fish of this genus have been reported to flap their pectoral fins while 'flying' to prey on insects near the water's surface.

CARP,
  see *Cyprinidae*
  CRUCIAN see *Carassius carassius*
  KOI see *Carassius Hybrids*
  LIVEBEARING TOOTH see *Poecilidae*
CASCARUDO see *Callichthys callichthys*
CATALINA GOBY see *Lythrypnus dalli*

Catfish
Catfish were classified for many years by taxonomists in the single family Siluridae. More recent studies have made it necessary to divide them into different families but they all remain in the sub-order Siluroidea. Primitive fish, many have remained unchanged in anatomical form for millions of years being as well, if not better, adapted to the environments in which they find themselves today as the more specialized fish. They can certainly withstand environmental pollution and adverse physical conditions more effectively than some of the more recently evolved species. Catfish do not have scales but a number have large bony plates along the body. Most have broad flat heads with various numbers of barbels. A few families have developed sucker mouths which enable them to suck algae from rocks and plants, which is greatly to the liking of the aquarist. Generally they are hardy. Behaviourally most of them are nocturnal fish, hiding during the day under rocks and among the roots of plants. Most have little to offer in the way of a colourful appearance but there are a few exceptions. Catfish most favoured by the aquarist are the *Corydoras* species.

  See: *Acanthodoras, Ancistrus, Aspredinidae, Bagridae, Brochis, Buncocephalus, Callichthyidae, Callichthys, Corydoras, Doradidae, Etropiella, Farlowella, Hoplosternum, Kryptopterus, Leiocassis, Malapteruridae, Malapterus, Microglanis, Mochokidae, Mystus, Otocinclus, Pimelodella, Pimelodidae, Plecostomus, Plotosus, Schilbeidae, Siluridae, Sorubim, Synodontis*

Caulerpa see *Marine Plants*
CAVE CHARACIN, BLIND see *Anoptichthys jordani*
CELEBES RAINBOWFISH see *Telmatherina ladigesi*
CELESTIAL see *Carassius auratus*
Cellophane Plant see under *Plants – Echinodorus*

Centrarchidae FRESHWATER SUNFISH
This strictly North American family is composed of the North American Sunfish and Black Basses, the latter being closely related to the Sea Basses.

They are found mostly in sub-tropical and temperate climates although some species are tropical. Distinguished by the taxonomist by two smooth points on the operculum which are usually marked with a black spot. Strictly carnivorous most prefer live food in captivity although conditioning will change this. Daphnia and tubifex are quite suitable and readily accepted. Naturally found in hard to medium hard water but will adapt to other environments. All the species display intense parental care similar to the cichlids. The best colour is displayed by males during courtship. The males excavate nests in the sand with their tails. The female is induced to lay eggs in the prepared depression and these are vigorously protected. See *Elassoma, Mesogonistius*.

Centrechinus see under *Marine Invertebrates*

Centriscidae SHRIMPFISH, RAZORFISH
This family of marine fish includes interesting and unusual fish which live in underwater caverns, or hide away among the rocks on the sea bed and even make use of sea urchin spines for protection. They come from the Indo-Pacific region. Could be classed as a temporary territorial fish. See *Aeoliscus, Behaviour*.

Centropomidae GLASSFISHES $\Psi, \oplus/\Psi$
A family which has representative species from the east coast of Africa, in the Indian Ocean, throughout the Malayan Archipelago and into Australia. It is mainly a salt and brackish water family but a few are found in fresh water.

Notable is the very compressed transparent body which allows clear views of the internal skeleton. The organs of the body are contained in a small silver sac and the gas bladder is visible above the sac.

They prefer temperatures around 26°C. This family also contains, surprisingly, some large gamefish; the Snook, *Centropomis undecimalis*, which grows to 1·2m., and the Nile Perch, *Lates niloticus*, up to 2m. long and over 80kg. in weight are two examples. See *Chanda, Gymnochanda*.

Centropyge Chaetodontidae Ψ
– *acanthrops* PURPLE FIREBALL 8cm. (3in.)
A lovely small fish, from the coast of East Africa, which is a mixture of orange and mauve. The dorsal third of the body, including the dorsal fin and head are a rich firey orange and are clearly delineated from the rest of the body which is deep mauve, except for the orange tail. It is very suitable for the marine aquarist on a limited budget being reasonably easy to obtain cheaply. Hardy, easy to feed and attractive.
– *argi* CHERUBFISH 8cm. (3in.) ✂
A very small fish from the turquoise waters of the Carib-

bean. It has a rich, dark blue body with a yellow head. Hardy and easily fed, but needs algae in its diet. Sadly, the Cherubfish are a little aggressive towards each other.

– *bicolor*   BICOLOR ANGEL, ORIOLE ANGELFISH
11cm. (4½in.)
Another small member of the family which is suitable for the marine aquarist with limited space. The anterior body colour is yellow as is the tail fin. This is contrasted by a very rich blue eye mask and flank. It is native to the Pacific Ocean. **41**

– *bispinosus*   CORAL BEAUTY   13cm. (5in.)
From the Indo-Pacific. Colouring of the body consists of wine purple and yellowy orange. It is small, hardy and easy to feed, making it a much sought after fish. **42**

– *heraldi*   GOLDEN ANGELFISH   10cm. (4in.)
This is a reasonably new fish for the marine aquarist and comes from the tropical regions of the Pacific Ocean. The body shape and coloration is characteristic of the genus. The body and fins are a rich orange-yellow colour with a diffuse brown shading around the eye. Experience suggests that it does well in the aquarium, behaving in captivity like its generic cousins. **43**

– *vroliki*   PEARLY-SCALED ANGELFISH   13cm. (5in.)   ✂
This attractive member of the genus from the Pacific Ocean has characteristics which make identification fairly easy. The anterior three-quarters of the body is a pale pinkish silver, each scale being a composition of a pink base with a silver grey dot in the centre. The posterior quarter is dark brown. The dorsal, caudal and anal fins have a blue, sometimes almost purple, border. The base of the pectoral fins is rather an unusual orange in colour. The operculum has a dark border dorsally and an orange flash vertically. The eye is a rich orange and yellow.

In captivity these fish take a little time, but eventually settle well. Can be aggressive at times with their own and other species and will then inflict wounds by using the spine. This is a characteristic of the genus and is situated in front of the operculum.

Food of various kinds readily accepted but vegetable matter of some kind is essential, as for all the species of the genus. **44**

Cephalopholis   Serranidae   Ψ
– *argus*   JEWEL GROUPER, ROCK COD, GARRUPA
46cm. (18in.)   Ψ
Carnivorous with the usual grouper enthusiasm, this marine fish comes from the Indo-Pacific. It has a dark brown black body decorated with blue spots which vary in intensity with emotion. Not recommended for small aquaria. Will eat any fish it can swallow as it grows up.

– *boenack*   BLUE-LINED or BLUE-STRIPED GROUPER
30cm. (12in.)
From the Indo-Pacific the Blue-lined Grouper is peaceful, which is unusual for this family of marine fish. If given enough live food it will co-exist with other popular marines not too small in size. Beige body with dazzling bright blue horizontal lines over the whole body and extending into fins.

– *fulva*   CONEY   30cm. (12in.)
This species is quite commonly imported into the USA, but is less often seen in the UK. The body colour may be yellow or red. All have scattered blue spots on the body. The dorsal part of the caudal fin carries a very dark patch.

It is found along the east coast of America from Florida to Brazil. In captivity it soon settles down; it prefers a diet of crustacea.

Ceratodontidae   AUSTRALIAN LUNGFISH
This family has many similarities to the other lungfish families Protopteridae and Lepidosirenidae. Unlike them, however, it has one lung which is in communication with the gut. See *Neoceratodus*.

Ceratophyllum see *Plants*
Ceratopteris see under *Plants*
Cerise grouper see *Variola louti*

Chaetodon   Chaetodontidae   Ψ
– *auriga*   GOLDEN or THREADFIN BUTTERFLYFISH
23cm. (9in.)
A common and popular fish, for the marine aquarium, which comes from the Indo-Pacific. A white body is patterned with interlacing lines in black. The posterior part of the body is a lovely golden yellow. The eye is effectively lost by camouflaging patterns. A false 'eye' is positioned near the end of the dorsal fin. It feeds by browsing among rocks and caverns for algae; it also enjoys small live food and in captivity it will take proprietary live food. Like all members of this genus, it is not easy to keep. An inexperienced marine aquarist would be advised to get experience with cheaper fish before attempting to keep any of the genus. **45**

– *baronessa*   12cm. (4½in.)
This is an attractive fish from the eastern Indian Ocean, Indonesia and the Pacific Ocean, which is often called and imported under the name *C. triangulum*. It has the typical triangular shape of the genus. The body colour is a basic greenish blue. Blue chevron stripes decorate its sides. Brown bands decorate the head, one passing through the eye, one behind the eye and a third on the nostril to which are added red highlights. Above the eye is a reddish coloration. The pelvic fins are yellow and the dorsal and anal fins are edged with a chestnut brown and a thin rim of yellow green. From the base of the dorsal fin a darker brown fades to

the greenish blue of the body. The caudal fin is mainly transparent with a stripe of chestnut brown a little anterior to the edge. Bands of yellow cross the tail and pass onto the anal fin. Care and management of this fish is the same as for others of the genus. **46**

– *bennetti* BENNETT'S BUTTERFLYFISH 20cm. (8in.)
This fish is more popular in the USA than in Europe. It comes from the Indo-Pacific region and is most common on the eastern coast of India. The basic body colour is yellow and a dark vertical bar passes through and therefore conceals the eye. A false eye is situated near to the posterior of the body.

– *capistratus* FOUR-EYED BUTTERFLYFISH 15cm. (6in.)
The popular name comes from the realistic eye pattern on the tail. It comes from the Caribbean where it grows to 15cm. in length. It has a pattern of thin black bands on a silver body. Quite a hardy fish which prefers live food although it will take dry food under sufferance.

– *chrysurus* PEARLED or PEARL-SCALE BUTTERFLYFISH 15cm. (6in.)
This fish, from the Red Sea and Indo-Pacific, has the typical compressed body of the family with the subdued fin development. It has a dark grey body with light silver grey spots decorating its sides. A dark stripe passes through the eye. A crescent of orange precedes the tail which is mostly white with a dash of orange. It is hardy, easy to feed and peaceful by nature. **47**

– *collare* INDIAN BUTTERFLYFISH 18cm. (7in.)
A less common but gorgeous fish from the Indian sub-continental waters. Particularly common around Sri Lanka. It has a brown and mauve body with white decorations on the head and a red tail. Less hardy than some, it takes patience to get it acclimatized to captivity.

– *ephippium* BLACK-BLOTCHED BUTTERFLYFISH 30cm. (12 in.)
This species comes from the Indo-Pacific. It is quite frequently imported into the USA where it makes a very attractive exhibit but is difficult to keep. The body is a very pale lilac with a blue diffuse band running dorsally, and a number of pale blue longitudinal lines running ventrally. The lips, mouth and lower part of the head are yellow. A black line passes vertically through the eye. A large black patch covers the posterior dorsal quarter of the body. The black patch is bordered posteriorly with red. A small red patch decorates the base of the tail. A yellow border lines the anal fin. This small chaetodon is a very pleasing member of the group and is much sought after.

– *falcula* TEAR-DROP, SADDLED BLACK-WEDGE or BUTTERFLYFISH 20cm. (8in.)
This fish comes from the Indo-Pacific and the Red Sea but is particularly common around the coast of New Guinea. It is a lovely, if uncommon, fish for the marine aquarium. The

body is white and yellow with a definite yellow border and two brown saddle-like markings. These marks give it its common name. Hardy, easy to feed.

– *kleini* SUNSHOWER or WHITE-SPOTTED BUTTERFLYFISH 13cm. (5in.)
A very pleasant fish indeed from the Indian Ocean and Pacific. It is coloured brown, black and white with a liberal lacing of yellow. The colours are subdued. It settles well to captivity and has few feeding difficulties.

– *larvatus* RED SEA BUTTERFLYFISH 13cm. (5in.)
An attractive fish from the Red Sea area where it appears to be fairly common.

The body is a pale silvery blue which is crossed with a chevron pattern of yellow lines. The face is a deep rich yellow which ends just behind the eye. From the dorsal fin a dividing line runs down at 45° to end at the base of the anal fin. The patch dorso-posterior to this line is black. Difficult to keep on account of its natural food, which consists of coral-polyps. **48**

– *lunula* RACCOON, MOON or RED-STRIPED BUTTERFLYFISH 20cm. (8in.)
This butterflyfish comes from the Indo-Pacific. The body's colour is a combination of green, blue, black and yellow. An active, quite hardy, attractive species which is all too rarely available. **49**

– *melanotus* BLACK-BACKED BUTTERFLYFISH 18cm. (7in.)
From the Red Sea and Indo-Pacific, this fish has a white body with black bars running at an angle across it. Its fins are a pale yellow. A false 'eye' is placed on the tail fin. Hardy and, after some initial difficulties in persuading it to feed, accepts captivity. **50**

– *mesoleucos* 16cm. (6½in.)
A species which appears to be restricted to the Red Sea. Little is known of its natural history or behaviour.

Its decor distinguishes it. A white head coloration extends posteriorly to include the pelvic fins. A black vertical stripe passes through the eye. The remainder of the body is a greyish brown decorated with black vertical lines. A yellow crescent shaped band placed vertically divides the otherwise dark grey brown tail. **51**

– *meyeri* BLUE-BANDED BUTTERFLYFISH 15–25cm. (6–10in.)
A lovely blue butterflyfish from the Red Sea and Indo-Pacific. The delicate blue body is enhanced by an orange-yellow belly and fins and vertical black bands. It is difficult to keep in captivity but will be helped by a large tank and plenty of cover. Unfortunately relatively rare.

– *ocellatus* SPOTFIN BUTTERFLYFISH 20cm. (8in.)
A member of the genus which comes from the Caribbean. The body is silver. A black line passes vertically through the eye. The upper jaw is yellow. A flash of yellow behind the operculum passes onto the base of the pectoral fin. The

dorsal, caudal, anal, and pelvic fins are yellow. A dark somewhat indistinct line borders the posterior part of the dorsal and anal fins and the caudal. A black spot towards the middle of the base of the dorsal fin gives it its name.
– octofasciatus   EIGHT-BANDED BUTTERFLYFISH 10cm. (4in.)
A small fish which comes from the Indo-Pacific. A silver body with several dark vertical bars crossing its flank. The fins are often, but not always, yellow. It has a false 'eye'. Very little is known about their behaviour or natural history. They are rather difficult to keep and aquarists should obtain experience with other marine species before indulging a great deal of money. **52**
– rafflesii   LATTICED BUTTERFLYFISH   15cm. (6in.)
This fish comes from Indonesia and the Pacific. A lovely yellow body is decorated with an attractive interlaced pattern of dark lines. Relatively easy to adapt to captive conditions and easy to feed.
– semilarvatus   ADDIS BUTTERFLYFISH   23cm. (9in.)
From the Red Sea, this fish has a lovely golden yellow body decorated with numerous yellow brown vertical stripes. A dark blue brown triangular patch covers the eye. It has slightly protruding jaws. The dorsal and anal fins are beautifully curved. Some early difficulties in persuading it to feed in captivity are often encountered. Otherwise this is a hardy species.
– striatus   BANDED BUTTERFLYFISH   15cm. (6in.)   ✂
This rather aggressive fish comes from the West Indies where it grows to 15cm. in length. It has a silver white body with four dark vertical bars decorating the sides.
– triangulum   see *C. baronessa*
– trifasciatus   BLUE-LINE or RAINBOW BUTTERFLYFISH 15cm. (6in.)
From the Indo-Pacific. A rather elongated shape to the body is a variation of the normal body pattern. It has a yellow grey body decorated with horizontal blue lines, a dark band bordered with yellow, passes through the eye and the dark oval patch below the dorsal fin is an apology for a false 'eye'. The fins are a mixture of yellow, brown and black in distinctive patterns. Not the easiest fish to keep healthy. Providing an adequate food substitute for live coral seems to be the main problem.
– vagabundus   VAGABOND BUTTERFLYFISH   23cm. (9in.)
From the Indo-Pacific, a whitish grey body with indistinct lines crossing each other; a pale cream posterior end. It will settle quite well to captivity but needs to be fed small live food at first.

Chaetodontidae   BUTTERFLYFISHES and ANGELFISHES   Ψ
This is a very large and popular family of marine fish. Some authors put angelfishes into a separate family, the Pomacanthidae.

Their popular names come from the extravagance of colour with which nature has endowed them and which makes them some of the most beautiful fish in the world. The small fish are naturally prey for larger fish and midst all their beauty they commonly play down their eye by camouflaging it in a stripe or bar. In addition a dark spot at the other end confuses predators as to which end of the fish is which, and this provides a little more time to escape.

Timid by nature, they require plenty of rocky hiding places to give them security. Providing they feel secure they will reward owners with plenty of interesting activity. Some species are aggressive with their own kind. When this is the case they should be kept alone or in a large tank with plenty of rocks which will allow them to delineate and defend their own territory.

Butterflyfish have small mouths and feed on small organisms found in the reef. These include algae, crustacea, as well as live coral itself. On occasions they are difficult to wean onto available food in captivity.

Delightful fish, no marine aquarist can ignore them. Small, active, gorgeous and mostly peaceful they make ideal marine aquarium inhabitants. See *Centropyge, Chaetodon, Chaetodontoplus, Chelmon, Euxiphipops, Forcipiger, Heniochus, Holocanthus, Megaprotodon, Parachaetodon, Pomacanthus.*

Chaetodontoplus   Chaetodontidae   Ψ
– mesoleucus   18cm. (7in.)   ✂
Closely related to the genus *Pomacanthus*, this fish none-theless physically resembles the chaetodons.

Its rectangular shaped body shades from a very delicate pale yellow anterio-ventrally through pale grey to a wide posterior-dorsal area of dark blue grey. The whole body is decorated with a marbled effect. A dark wide band runs dorso-ventrally through the eye and the lips are marked with black. A pale pink very narrow border lines the margin of the dorsal and anal fins. The caudal fin is a bright orange.

This species is territorial and lives a solitary life apart from breeding periods, defending its domain against others of its kind. It is rather difficult to keep and the beginner is advised to avoid it. Prefers live food and demands a well kept, clean environment. **53**

Chain Sword Plants see under *Plants – Echinodorus*
CHAMELEON FISH see *Cichlasoma facetum*
CHANCHITO,
    see *Cichlasoma facetum*
    BARRED see *Cichlasoma festivum*
    CUTTER'S see *Cichlasoma cutteri*
    FLAG see *Cichlasoma festivum*
    GOLDEN see *Cichlasoma aureum*
    TWO-SPOT see *Cichlasoma bimaculatum*

ZEBRA see *Cichlasoma nigrofasciatum*

Chanda Centropomidae ⊕/Ψ
– *ranga* INDIAN GLASSFISH 5cm. (2in.)
A popular glassfish from Burma and Thailand. Its very compressed body is golden yellow divided by two vertical bars. The dorsal fin is deeply indented giving a double fin appearance. The dorsal and anal fins are golden brown edged with pale blue. Sometimes wrongly known as *Ambassis lala* as a result of confused classification by aquarists. The female is usually slightly duller, without the blue edging to the dorsal fin. Prefers slightly brackish water.
– *wolfi* GLASSFISH 23cm. (9in.)
A rather larger fish than *C. ranga* from Thailand, Malaya, Sumatra and Borneo. It has a clear silvery transparent body with a typical split dorsal fin.

Channa Channidae ⊕
– *africana* AFRICAN SNAKEHEAD 32cm. (12½in.)
Rather a large fish for the average aquarist, but has been kept by many enthusiasts. It comes from West Africa, south Nigeria and south Dahomey and can be distinguished from other species of the genus by the series of bands running along the back and sides. It also has a black line which starts at the snout, passes through the eye, and ends posterior to the head. Difficult to adapt to captivity, therefore not a fish for the beginner.
– *micropeltes* 100cm. (39½in.) ✂
A very large representative of this genus, members of which are commonly used for food. It comes from India, Burma, Thailand, Malaya and Indonesia. All members of the genus are large, carnivorous and aggressive fish.
　This fish is greeny yellow with two horizontal stripes, one

Indian Glassfish, *Chanda ranga*. The reason for the common name is clear: a large amount of internal detail may be seen.

from snout to tail through the eye and a second from the angle of the jaw to the lower base of the tail. The eye is yellow. It should not be kept in a small community tank.
– *orientalis* CHINESE SNAKEHEAD 30cm. (12in.) ✄
A long snake like fish native to south-east Asia. The olive green body is decorated with darker patches. Dorsal and anal fins are very long. Pelvic fins are absent. They have a well equipped set of teeth which they gluttonously use on their food and other fish as the mood takes them. They have a wide range of temperature adaptability from 18–29°C.

The eggs float to the surface and are left to take care of themselves.

Channidae SNAKEHEADS
A freshwater family with representatives in Asia and Africa. The wide, powerful head gives rise to the common name. The anal and dorsal fins are long based. These fish have accessory breathing organs in the dorsal part of the gill chamber. They can and do leave the water. See *Channa*.

Chaoborus see under *Food*
CHAPERS PANDRAX see *Epiplatys dageti monroviae*

Characidae ⊕
The characins, as they are popularly called, are a large family of fish living almost exclusively in the tropical regions of Africa and America. Aquarists have successfully kept upwards of 100 species in captivity. Most of the species are small, although some can reach over 30cm. (12in.) in length. They are relatively hardy and do well in temperatures between 21–24°C.

Characteristically characins have teeth and an adipose fin. Rarely do members of this family have neither although a few representatives have either the adipose fin or teeth but not both. This serves to distinguish members of this family from the carps and catfish. With two or three exceptions all characins have scales.

They are useful and common occupants of communal tanks since they are not very aggressive. In spite of teeth most species rarely fight; they may however use them for a little fin nibbling which can present problems and spoil some more treasured specimens.

Feeding characins is relatively simple. Although some are strictly vegetarian and others obligatory carnivores, most will accept a mixed diet and do well on it. Most species are fond of live food.

Characins are notoriously difficult to breed in captivity. This is a pity since this family contains some of the most popular and sought after fish for the aquarium. Males are usually smaller and more slender than females. In some cases there are colour differences between the sexes, and in some species the males possess a hook on the tips of the

median fins, usually the anal fin.

Some aquarists have found that by using soft water and raising the temperature to 28°C. success in breeding becomes easier. Plenty of weed, both submerged and floating, should be provided. Characins are egg layers, scattering their adhesive eggs, usually with some abandon, and are very likely to indulge themselves by eating the eggs, and if they escape, the young. See *Anoptichthys, Aphyocharax, Astyanax, Charax, Cheirodon, Curimatidae, Colossoma, Crenuchus, Ctenobrycon, Exodon, Glandulocauda, Gymnocorymbus, Hemigrammus Hyphessobrycon, Megalamphodus, Metynnis, Mimagoniates, Moenkhausia Mylossoma, Nematobrycon, Paracheirodon, Phenacogrammus, Phoxinopsis, Prionobrama, Pristella, Pseudocorynopoma, Rooseveltiella, Serrasalmus, Stevardia, Thayeria.*

Characidium Hemiodontidae ⊕
– *fasciatum* DARKER CHARACIN, TRITOLO 6cm. (2½in.)
A native of the Orinoco and La Plata rivers, it reaches some 6cm. in captivity. Like other members of the genus this fish is rather nervous, spending much of its time hiding among the rocks and plants. As bottom dwellers, they are rather unrewarding aquarium fish. They are, however, peaceful, easy to feed and adapt to a wide range of temperatures.

The back is a reddish brown, shading through yellow to white. A dark horizontal band runs from the snout to the tail. Vertical brown bars run around the body. There are dots on the dorsal and anal fins.

They breed according to the normal family pattern needing rather shallow water and plenty of weed to spawn. The young hatch in three days and need live food.
– *rachovi* 6cm. (2½in.)
Native to south-eastern Brazil and Paraguay. Its markings are not unlike those of *C. fasciatum*. The vertical brown bars are less apparent, however, as the body colour is generally darker.

CHARACIN,
    ANSORGE'S see *Neolebias ansorgei*
    ARNOLD'S see *Copella arnoldi*
    BLIND CAVE see *Anoptichthys jordani*
    DARKER see *Characidium fasciatum*
    OBLIQUE see *Thayeria boehlkei*
    SAILFIN see *Crenuchus spilurus*
    SERGEANT see *Prochilodus insignis*
    SPRAYING see *Copella arnoldi*
    SWORDTAIL see *Corynopoma riisei*

Charax Characidae ⊕
– *gibbosus* CHARAX, HUMP-BACKED HEADSTANDER
15cm. (6in.)

A native of Guyana and the Amazon Basin. This fish adopts a rather unusual position in the water. It swims with its head down and body pointing upwards at an angle of 40° to the horizontal. By an anatomical adaptation its head remains horizontal. Transparent orange brown in colour, it has a long anal fin with the adipose fin present.

The Charax has a rather inactive, slow moving, character, making it a good member of the community tank. It is easy to feed and enjoys temperatures around 24–26°C. It does breed in captivity.

CHECKERBOARD BARB see *Barbus oligolepis*

Cheilio Labridae Ψ
– inermis CIGAR WRASSE 40cm. (16in.) ✕
From the Red Sea and Indo-Pacific. A rather cigar shaped fish as the name suggests, with a variably greenish body. Its aggression towards members of its own species is renowned.

Cheirodon Characidae ⊕
– axelrodi CARDINAL TETRA 4cm. (1½in.)
This fish comes from Brazil. It competes with the Neon Tetra, *Paracheirodon innesi*, for beauty. The blue line is slightly less spectacular than with the Neon but this is compensated for by the increased amount of red coloration on the body, the whole body, apart from the blue line, being red. It favours soft very acid water. **54**

Chelmon Chaetodontidae Ψ
– rostratus COPPER-BANDED LONG-NOSED BUTTERFLYFISH, BEAKED CORALFISH 17cm. (6½in.)

Copper-banded Long-nosed Butterflyfish, *Chelmon rostratus*.

A very lovely fish from the Indo-Pacific. It has elongated jaws. Its silver blue body has six rich copper coloured vertical bands, one of which passes through the eye. They are lined with dark brown. A dark brown band is situated on the base of the body and there is a dark spot bordered with blue situated on the dorsal fin. Rather timid, it is difficult to acclimatize to captivity, but if provided with daphnia or brine shrimp at first it will later accept dry food.

CHERRY BARB see *Barbus titteya*
CHERUBFISH see *Centropyge argi*
Chilodonelliasis see *Disease*

Chilodus Curimatidae ⊕
– punctatus COMMON or SPOTTED HEADSTANDER
8cm. (3in.)
This fish, as the name implies, spends its day contemplating the beauty of the tank floor. It comes from Guyana. A very dark line runs from the snout to the tail. The body colour is a pleasing mottled mixture of blacks, browns, greens and greys, with a few ostentatious sequin like splashes of silver.

Peaceful and easily fed, it enjoys a temperature close to 24°C. It has rarely been bred in captivity. **55**

Chilomycterus Diodontidae Ψ
– schoepfi SPINY BOXFISH, STRIPED BURRFISH, BURRFISH
30cm. (12in.)
It comes from the western tropical Atlantic and Caribbean. It manages to frighten predators by forcing water through its gill openings which produces a disconcerting jerking movement. The greyish green body has horn like projections above the eyes. Eats most things. It is not aggressive but rather large for the home aquarist.

CHINA BARB see *Barbus semifasciolatus*
CHINESE
  PARADISEFISH see *Macropodus chinensis*
  SNAKEHEAD see *Channa orientalis*
Chironomus see under *Food*

Chlorine
Chlorine may be found in domestic water supplies. It is added by some water boards to kill harmful bacteria. Unfortunately chlorine is less well tolerated by fish than man. Chlorinated water should, therefore, be left to 'mature' for 2–3 days in the tank under aeration, or any other open container, before fish are put in it. During this time the chlorine will be dissipated into the air. See *Fluoridation, Water quality*.

Chlorophyll see *Photosynthesis*

CHOCOLATE
  CICHLID see *Astronotus ocellatus, Cichlasoma coryphaenoides*
  GOURAMI see *Sphaerichthys osphronemoides*
Chriopeops see *Lucania*
CHROMIDE
  GREEN see *Etroplus suratensis*
  ORANGE see *Etroplus maculatus*

Chromidotilapia Cichlidae
– guentheri GUNTHER'S CICHLID
A drab-looking fish from the west coast of Africa. A dark brown-purple body shades from dark back to light belly. The dorsal fin in contrast, has a yellow border which is

rather distinctive. The shape of the head, like *Geophagus jurupari* and its generic relatives, is rather grotesque.

This is one of the 'mouth brooding' cichlids (see *Cichlidae*). The male starves himself and accommodates the brood, from egg to free swimming fry, in his mouth. Temperatures of 25–26°C. are most likely to stimulate spawning. There is no need to remove the female during incubation. This species has a bad reputation for being rough on plants.

Chromileptes Serranidae Ψ
– altivelus PANTHERFISH 51cm. (20in.)
This delightful fish from the Indo-Pacific has a grey body with large spots scattered evenly over it. The fins are large

Pantherfish, *Chromileptes altivelus*.

and elegant. A gentle fish not noted for eating its tank mates and easily tamed. These are unusual characteristics for a grouper.

Chromis Pomacentridae Ψ
– *caeruleus* BLUE PULLER, BLUE GREEN CHROMIS
8cm. (3in.)
This fish from the Red Sea and Indo-Pacific has a longer more rectangular shaped body than its more commonly kept generic cousin *C. chromis* from the Mediterranean. It is extremely attractive, its body colour, including all its fins, being a pleasing mixture of blue green and mauve. In captivity it is hardy, easy to feed, and tolerant of its own and other species. **56**
– *chromis* see under *C. caeruleus*
– *cyanea* BLUE CHROMIS, BLUE-TAILED DAMSELFISH
13cm. (5in.) ✂
A very attractive blue fish with a black edged dorsal fin. It comes from the Caribbean, is territorial and defends with aggressive enthusiasm its own patch of rocks when protecting a nest. When not breeding clouds of this species school above the reef feeding on plankton.

Cichlasoma Cichlidae ⊕
– *aureum* GOLDEN CHANCHITO 20cm. (8in.) ✂
This fish, like other members of the genus, is native to Central America. Also and typical of the genus, it has a protruding mouth and several spines in the anal fin.

A golden brown body is highlighted with a blue green sheen. Several wide, rather irregular, vertical dark bars traverse the middle of the body, and there is a second smaller dark bar on the base of the tail. The green dorsal and anal fins are embellished with blue dots.

It is rather an aggressive fish, and care must be taken, when keeping several of this species in the same tank, to make sure there is plenty of space and many hiding places. It has catholic tastes in food but requires a percentage of plants in its diet.
– *bimaculatum* TWO-SPOT CHANCHITO or CICHLID
20cm. (8in.) ✂
A pugnacious character from northern South America. A bluish brown body which is sectioned by dark vertical bars, a horizontal stripe and two body spots. The dark bars may fade somewhat with age. Adopts a creamy yellow tinge to the belly during the breeding season.
– *biocellatum* JACK DEMPSEY 18cm. (7in.) ✂
With a name like Jack Dempsey one can expect an aggressive fish, and it is. It comes from the middle Amazon Basin, Rio Negro.

Its body colour, typical of cichlids, can change from a brownish black, to a superb metallic green. The basic body colour is dark brown with green dots on the scales. Several

V-shaped vertical bars can be seen on occasions, in particular at times of emotion. A dark body spot is visible midway along its body and an ocellated one on the tail base. Green dotted patterns extend to cover the unpaired fins which are large and flamboyant and a red line borders the dorsal fin.

Its breeding is typical of the cichlids (see *Cichlidae*). It is lethal to plants, biting and uprooting them.
– *coryphaenoides* CHOCOLATE CICHLID 20cm. (8in.) ✂
An aggressive fish from the Amazon Basin. Dark brown with bluish belly and vertical bars on the body. Its sides have a red tinge. Brown fins, the dorsal bordered with red, are poor competition for some of its more attractive cousins. Not the easiest fish to keep. It likes plenty of rock and plant cover and a good deal of live or high protein food.
– *cutteri* CUTTER'S CHANCHITO or CICHLID 13cm. (5in.)
A rather undistinguished native of Honduras. Its greenish body has a golden metallic iridescence on the anterior parts. The typical vertical bars and body spots adorn the sides. Unpaired fins are rich ruby red in the male, pinker in the female.
– *cyanoguttatum* BLUE-SPOTTED CICHLID, TEXAS CICHLID, FRESHWATER SHEEPSHEAD, RIO GRANDE PERCH 30cm. (12in.)
A large cichlid from Texas and North America. Good natured, if boisterous and tough. It is the only cichlid found in the USA where it inhabits the tributaries feeding the Rio Grande.

It is grey-blue and peppered with light silver blue spots.

It has a wide range of temperature adaptability but prefers 25–26°C. for breeding, which follows the normal cichlid pattern, see *Cichlidae*.
– *facetum* CHANCHITO, CHAMELEON FISH 30cm. (12in.)
A native of Argentina, Brazil and Paraguay. Its colour varies somewhat as the name suggests, but in general it is a rather uninteresting fish when compared to close relations. A yellow grey body is patterned with dark vertical bars transected by a horizontal line. Body spots occur on the side and base of the tail. Its colour and the intensity of the markings vary with the environment and its emotional state.

It is of historic interest since it was an early fish kept by aquarists – as long ago as the late nineteenth century.

The breeding habits are typical of the family, and it performs its reproductive tasks readily and without problems.
– *festivum* BARRED or FLAG CICHLID 15cm. (6in.)
A distinctive fish which comes from the Amazon and Guyana. The body colour varies from yellow to green with several dark vertical bars. It has an unusual dark band which runs from the mouth through the eye to the posterior point of the dorsal fin. A black spot with yellow rim is

Barred or Flag Cichlid, *Cichlasoma festivum.*

positioned at the base of the tail fin. The fins are yellowish brown with white spots. Sadly, age, emotion, and environment can, singly or in combination, fade the bars reducing an aquatic beauty to one of less distinction. It is peaceable by nature and may be kept in larger community tanks although it breeds best when the pairs are housed alone. **57**

– maculicauda   30cm. (12in.)   ⊕/Ψ
A native of fresh and brackish waters throughout Central America. Its greenish brown body fades to a pale green belly. Dark vertical bars transect its body and it has a very large black patch covering a considerable area of the tail fin base. The spinous dorsal and anal fins are rich green which fades to a golden colour in the soft parts of the fins. Usually peaceful, but don't take any chances with small fish.

– meeki   FIREMOUTH, RED-BREASTED CICHLID   15cm. (6in.)
A beautiful cichlid from Yucatan, Central America. The dark blue green body with darker bars, provides a contrast for the firey red belly and mouth. Flamboyant cichlid fins also carry the colour of fire and a distinctive irregular dark spot surrounded by yellow resides on the operculum.

A peaceful member of larger community collections, it breeds in captivity preferring temperatures around 27°C. and adopting the typical cichlid pattern. **58**

– nigrofasciatum   ZEBRA CHANCHITO, CONVICT CICHLID
10cm. (4in.)
Zebra is a more appropriate designation of this fish's coloration than the commonly known Zebrafish *Brachydanio rerio* which has horizontal stripes. The dark vertical bands which are of variable colour are separated by the bluish white basic body colour, and the markings closely resemble that of a Zebra. Dorsal, anal and tail fins are tinged with fluorescent green.

It comes from Guatemala, Central and South America. It is hardy and has been bred in captivity for many years. **59**

– severum   STRIPED, SEDATE or BANDED CICHLID, DEACON
20cm. (8in.)
Like many of the cichlids this has a tendency to change its colour with its emotional state. Just as you are about to show your prize collection to impress a friend it might lose the brilliant metallic green body colour it had two minutes before and degenerate into a dirty grey. Young fish have vertical bars but the distinctive posterior bar identifies this species. A dark spot on the posterior base of the dorsal fin is joined to a similar spot on the anal fin by a dark bar. Horizontally arranged rows of dots are present on the body of the male but absent in the female.

Reasonably peaceful, small species do well in a community tank. They are easy on the plant life except in the breeding season. Breeding is a little difficult but by no means impossible. Deacons come from the northern Amazon Basin. **60**

– tetracanthus   CUBAN CICHLID   20cm. (8in.)
A temperamental fish, native to the islands of Cuba and Barbados.

Its variably coloured greenish body supports three dark spots which are outlined by pale yellow surrounds. One is behind the eye, one mid body, and the third on the base of the tail fin. Various patterns of dots and lines enhance the beauty of the fins.

CICHLID see *Aequidens, Apistogramma, Astronotus, Cichlasoma, Crenicichla, Geophagus, Hemichromis, Herichthys, Labeotropheus, Microgeophagus, Nannacara, Nannochromis, Naru, Nyasa, Pelmatochromis, Tilapia, Xenocara.*

Cichlidae

The family Cichlidae consists of a large number of fascinating fish which come mainly from Central and South America, Africa, the island of Madagascar and a few species from the southern tip of India including Sri Lanka.

Structurally they are related to the Pomacentridae having spiny rays, only one nasal opening rather than the more common piscine pattern of two, and variations in the skeletal structure of the eye socket.

The family includes fishes of various sizes, from the larger species which attain lengths of 46cm. to the smaller, so-called dwarf, species which reach about 5cm. in length. They are beautiful fish, often of exotic colours which change with environmental and emotional variations. This is perhaps the most engaging but also frustrating feature. Extravagant fin development and body shape sometimes are combined with colour to produce some really exceptional fish.

Sadly for the aquarist many species are so aggressive that they cannot be included in a community collection. Their fascination and, in particular, their breeding behaviour however make them popular with aquarists.

Greedy fish, the majority are carnivorous and should be fed large quantities of live food.

A minor myth has grown up that cichlids would only thrive in soft acid water. All species of cichlids that live in rift valley lakes in East Africa (for instance lakes Malawi and Tanganyika) live in highly alkaline waters and should not be kept in soft and acid water. *Etroplus* species and many *Tilapia* also favour alkaline conditions. Most other species, especially those from South America, favour soft, acid water. See *Hardness* and *pH*. In addition mature – I dislike the term 'old' – water is favoured. Water temperatures at around 24°C. suit most cichlids for maintenance but when breeding they should have this raised to 28°C. Light should be subdued.

Cichlids may be described as anti-plant. They seem to take exception to the aquarist's attempts to beautify their surroundings with herbage. Plants are often attacked aggressively and uprooted. In fact this behaviour is most actively pursued around breeding time and it had been suggested that they naturally clear their breeding area of plants to give them clear views thus avoiding surprise attacks while rearing the family. The aquarist should therefore dispense with plants altogether or should plant tough well rooted plants well before introducing the fish into the tank.

Cichlids make good parents. They care for eggs and protect the young with a devotion that would put many higher animals, including man, to shame. Selecting breeding pairs has its problems for the aquarist. Initially there is the problem of sexing which in many cichlids is difficult from the external appearance. Males, however, have more pointed dorsal fins and are larger. I prefer to place several members of one species by themselves in a very large tank and allow them to form natural bonds. Pairing, incidentally, is often for life. Some aquarists place a pair in an aquarium one on each side of a glass partition. This tends to bring the participants to the brink of sexual enthusiasm before they meet, thus avoiding many of the fights which otherwise can ensue. Courting behaviour begins with a little showing off, a bit of strutting about. The body is dressed in its finest garb. The colours intensify. The fins are spread to show their beauty. The pair interlock jaws pushing and shoving for several minutes. If one shows weakness it can lead to a rapid demise at the hands of the other.

Having established a mating pair they should be housed in a large aquarium with a covering of gravel, perhaps a few well rooted plants, and subdued lighting. In addition, several pieces of flat smooth stone should be included on which eggs can be laid or an inverted flowerpot if the species is a cave breeder. The site for the deposition of the eggs is chosen by the pair and cleaned. A white tube or ovipositor is protruded from the female vent and a similar if sharper tube extended by the male. One at a time the eggs are laid and attached by the female to the prepared site. They are immediately fertilized by the male. This procedure is continued. The clutch contains several hundred eggs.

At temperatures of between 28°C. and 31°C. the eggs hatch in a very few days. During incubation the parents take turns in fanning the eggs. The reason for this is a matter of speculation. Many feel it is done to prevent particles of matter including fungal spores adhering to the eggs which would ultimately kill them. Others believe that it is to ensure circulation of water and therefore adequate oxygenation of the eggs. Experimental work with the sticklebacks, *Gasterosteus aculeatus*, who also fan their eggs, have shown that the intensity of fanning increases as the eggs get older and the demand for oxygen grows. However, definitive experimental work is needed before the answer is found. Like many facts in biology the answer may show that both reasons are valid since the eggs get both good oxygenation as well as cleanliness with water circulation.

Eggs which do develop fungal infections are eaten by the parents. Sadly some parents may become addicted and will consume the whole clutch of eggs. Make sure the fish are disturbed as little as possible during the critical stage while the eggs are developing. Adverse stimulation or too inquisitive a nature by the aquarist may also induce them to eat the eggs.

As the eggs are about to hatch the parents go into a rather strange routine. Collecting the ripe eggs or fry in their mouths they rush them to a depression in the sand. Here the mass of vibrating jelly, consisting of fry attached to their yolk sacs, are left in peace guarded by their parents for a few hours. Then off they go again. A new depression is found or dug and the parents shuttle the young there. A rest for a few hours and away again. This intriguing and fascinating activity is continued until the yolk sacs are absorbed and the fry are free swimming. The young then form a shoal with the parents in constant attendance and as they move about stragglers are collected in the mouth of a parent and popped back into the crowd.

The method of breeding described above applies to most of the Cichlidae. There is however a group of fish known as the 'mouth brooders' which have somewhat modified their approach. Having laid their eggs and fertilized them, one of the parents gathers up the eggs in its mouth and there they remain until they hatch, the yolk sac is absorbed and the fry are free swimming. Needless to say the parent so fully occupied cannot take food for the incubation period. In many species the female performs the task, in some species the job is delegated to the male, while in other species there are no hard and fast rules. The 'mouth brooding' modification can be seen as a simple evolutionary modification of the former behaviour.

Most cichlid fry are large and can be fed newly hatched brine shrimps or daphnia.

The sight of parental cichlids herding their brood is extremely rewarding. Many aquarists separate the parents from the young after 2–3 weeks without very much justification except their own convenience. I prefer them to be left together as long as the physical limitations of the tank allow.

When separation becomes inevitable keep the parents separated from each other by dividing the tank into two with a glass plate for a while, or they may engage in mortal combat which seems to be provoked by the loss of their young. See *Acaropsis, Aequidens, Apistogramma, Astronotus, Chromidotilapia, Cichlasoma, Crenicichla, Etroplus, Geophagus, Hemichromis, Hemihaplochromis, Julidochromis, Labeotropheus, Microgeophagus, Nannacara, Nyasa Cichlids, Pelmatochromis, Petrotilapia, Pseudotropheus, Pterophyllum, Symphysodon, Tilapia, Tropheus, Uaru.*

CIGAR WRASSE see *Cheilio inermis*
Circulatory System see *Blood System*

Cirrhitichthys Cirrhitidae
– aprinus SPOTTED HAWKFISH 13cm. (5in.)
An interesting, hardy fish which occasionally is offered for sale to aquarists. It comes from the Indo-Pacific where it is restricted to the central tropical regions.

The illustration here shows the typical white body with spots varying from a yellow to reddish brown, but there are several colour variations which are either local strains or due to diet. The pelvic fins alone are clear but the others are spotted.

Spotted Hawkfish adapt well to captivity. They are quite happy with the usual diet of brine shrimps and dried tubifex. They are rather sluggish spending a great deal of time motionless near the bottom. **61**

Cirrhitidae
Most members of the family come from the Indo-Pacific although one is found in the Atlantic Ocean. They live around rocks or coral into which they rush to hide if disturbed. The species is distinguished by a long body and three spines in front of the anal fin. See *Amblycirrhitus, Cirrhitichthys.*

Citharinidae
A large family of freshwater fish closely related to the

Characidae from Africa. Many are too large for most aquaria but a few of the smaller species have attained some popularity. The family is characterized by a compressed body, a large scaled adipose fin and an elongated dorsal fin. The head is usually broad and rounded and the mouth is ventrally placed. A simple method of distinguishing them from the characins is the lateral line which in Citharinidae runs in a straight line from the operculum to the caudal fin. See *Distichodus, Nannethiops, Neolebias.*

Clark's Degree see under *Hardness of Water*

Classification
Classification is an important part of any biological study since it allows man to understand the relationships which exist between one animal and another. Modern classification has developed since general acceptance of the theory of evolution which Charles Darwin propounded in the middle of the last century. See *Evolution*.

According to the theory all animals are related to one another since all evolved from common origins. Some 350 million years ago a group of fish gradually, over hundreds of thousands of years, left the water to become primitive amphibians. Primitive reptiles developed and these saw their greatness in the gigantic dinosaurs. Eventually environmental conditions prevailed with which the dinosaurs could not cope and small primitive creatures, more reptile than mammal, began to dominate the earth. From these creatures the wide variety of mammals we know today evolved. Many others such as the Sabre-toothed Tiger and the Mammoth, which found adverse conditions died out. From primitive reptiles also came the first bird-like reptiles and finally modern birds. All this time the fish groups, which had not left the water, were not idle. A few remained very similar over millions of years. The Coelacanth, *Latimeria chalumnae*, is an excellent and well known example which has hardly changed since the carboniferous period some 250–350 million years ago. Many new families, genera and species have however evolved, and certainly the class contains more species than any other group of vertebrates. Classification is a way of relating these various groups and indicating precisely their position in the evolution of animals.

How is an animal classified? Let us assume we are to classify the fish *Hyphessobrycon flammeus*. First, we perceive it is alive, therefore it is a plant or an animal. If an animal, it belongs to the life kingdom Animalia. Further study shows it to have a vertebral column. It is not therefore a crustacean, a coelenterate or any other primitive group but it must belong to the subphylum Vertebrata. The vertebrates are divided into the large groups of fish, amphibians, reptiles, birds and mammals. Now our animal is a fish belonging to what is sometimes called the super class Pisces. This large group is further sub-divided into two classes, Chondrichthyes, and Osteichthyes. In the class Chondrichthyes are placed the sharks and rays while Osteichthyes contain the bony fishes. The bony fishes – Osteichthyes – are further divided into two subclasses Crossopterygii (or Sarcopterygii) which are the lungfishes and Actinopterygii the higher bony fish. Subclasses are still very large groups and contain a great variety of bony fish. They are therefore grouped under some fifty orders. Our fish belong to one of these orders, Cypriniformes.

All members of each order have quite a lot in common and are quite closely related in evolutionary terms. However, they also have many differences and so once again they are divided into families; in our case Characidae. The members of each family have a great many features in common, but again it is convenient to divide them into smaller family units known as genera. Most genera contain a number of different types of fish all closely resembling each other both in looks and behavioural habits. Our fish belongs to the genus *Hyphessobrycon* which contains a few very closely related fish. The actual fish we wish to classify is given a specific name, which identifies it completely – *flammeus*. It is commonly known as a Red Tetra.

A species is a group of identical animals which behave and look alike and which breed together to produce offspring which resemble their parents closely. In captivity it is sometimes possible to breed from two closely related species to produce fertile hybrids but this rarely happens in nature, either because they are separated geographically or because natural behavioural patterns prevent their mating.

Our fish then – *Hyphessobrycon flammeus* – is classified as follows:

Kingdom	Animalia
Phylum	Chordata
Subphylum	Vertebrata
Super class	Pisces
Class	Osteichthyes
Subclass	Actinopterygii
Order	Cypriniformes
Family	Characidae
Genus	*Hyphessobrycon*
Species	*flammeus*

Under each separate family in the text will be found a list of genera belonging to that family dealt with in the book. In this way each fish can be completely classified and its relative position in the fish world identified.

When writing the name of an animal it is customary only to give its generic name a capital initial letter and its specific name a small initial letter. It would clearly be too exhausting to write all its classification each time.

CLEANER WRASSE see *Labroides dimidiatus*
CLERICAL SURGEONFISH see *Paracanthurus hepatus*
CLIMBING
   PERCH, AFRICAN see *Ctenopoma argentoventer*
   PERCH, BANDED see *Ctenopoma fasciolatum*
   PERCH, ORNATE see *Ctenopoma ansorgei*
   PERCH, SILVER-BELLIED see *Ctenopoma argentoventer*
   PERCH, STRIPED see *Ctenopoma fasciolatum*
   WALKING PERCH see *Anabas testudineus*
CLIMBINGFISH, DWARF see *Ctenopoma nanum*
CLOVER, WATER see under *Plants – Marsilea*
CLOWN
   BARB see *Barbus everetti*
   LOACH see *Botia macracanthus*
   LOACH, HORA'S see *Botia horae*
   TRIGGERFISH see *Balistoides niger*
   WRASSE see *Coris gaimardi*
CLOWNFISH see *Amphiprion*

Cobitidae LOACHES
This family is found in shallow, fast running streams throughout Asia and Europe. Nervous, rather shy fish, they spend a good deal of time in hiding. Many, however, can use their alimentary canal as a supplementary breathing organ by swallowing air at the surface. The oxygen is absorbed in the intestine and the surplus gases voided through the vent. They are closely related to Cyprinidae.

Loaches are best kept in a well planted aquarium with plenty of hiding places. They naturally eat insect larvae, worms and small crustaceans. In captivity they do well on prepared food, daphnia and some vegetable food. They are bottom feeders and have been used as scavengers, although a tendency to stir up the sediment creating cloudy water, has restricted their popularity.

Their breeding habits are not well known. They are oviparous but few species have bred in captivity. See *Acanthophthalmus, Botia, Misgurnus*.

Coccidiosis see Disease
COCKATOO DWARF CICHLID see *Apistogramma cacatuoides*
COD
   LUNAR-TAILED ROCK see *Variola louti*
   ROCK see *Cephalopholis argus*
Coelacanth see under *Classification*
Coelenterates see under *Marine Invertebrates*
Coldwater Fish see under *Establishing a Coldwater Tank*
COLDWATER HAPLOCHILUS see *Oryzias latipes*
Coldwater Tanks see *Establishing a Coldwater Tank*

Colisa Belontiidae ⊕
–fasciata GIANT GOURAMI 13cm. (5in.)
A native of India and the Malayan peninsula it is misnamed

since it is far from the largest of the gouramis.

It is found in rather muddy conditions very often and, like other gouramis, has been provided by nature with equipment to deal with such an environment. The pelvic fins have elongated to form two long mobile feelers. They can move in any direction and are often pointed forwards to 'see' what is just ahead.

The body colour is rich reddish brown, extending into the base of the dorsal fin and onto the tail. Blue vertical bars pointing obliquely forwards traverse the side. Blue forms the principal colour of anal and dorsal fins. Green patches decorate the head below the eye.

It prefers temperatures in the region of 24°C.; somewhat higher for breeding. Prolific egg producer, the female laying up to 1,000 eggs. **62**

– labiosa   THICK-LIPPED GOURAMI   8cm. (3in.)
The fish is similar to *C. fasciata* but it has thicker lips. A native of Burma. The mottled browny orange body is infiltrated from below by fingers of blue. The dorsal and anal fins have reddish margins. Males have red pelvic fins in contrast to the clear ones in the female. A hardy fish which does well in mixed tanks providing the other fishes are of similar size. Breeding behaviour typical of the family. **63**

– lalia   DWARF GOURAMI, LALIUS   5cm. (2in.)
A peaceful attractive member of the community tank. It comes from India. What it lacks in size it makes up for in colour being the most attractive of the genus. The reddish brown body is crossed by irregularly shaped blue bars. The body colour is continued into the unpaired fins which are patterned by blue dots and bars. The throat is a rich blue.

It thrives in a well planted tank and since it is rather timid, it likes the heavy algal growth that comes from bright sunshine.

The male makes a bubble nest and behaves with more chivalry towards the female than is common in this family. **64**

Colossoma   Characidae   ⊕
– nigripinnis   PACU   71cm. (28in.)
This fish comes from the Amazon. The young have spots which disappear as the animal attains maturity. Body colour is silver. The dorsal and anal fins are red in colour, intensified around the fin bases. Its length makes it rather a specialist fish although it is not an unfriendly creature. It is a vegetarian which relishes fruit such as bananas and melons, but will feed readily on prepared diets and live food. Has not bred in captivity.

COMBTAIL see *Belontia signata*
COMET see *Carassius auratus*
COMMON
   ARMOURED CATFISH see *Callichthys callichthys*

BATFISH see *Platax orbicularis*
CLOWNFISH see *Amphiprion ocellaris*
HATCHETFISH see *Gasteropelecus sternicla*
HEADSTANDER see *Chilodus punctatus*
KILLY see *Fundulus heteroclitus*
POND SNAIL see *Snails – Limnaea*

Community Tank
In a mixed aquarium, where several species of fish are asked to live together, harmony is the watchword. It is pointless to expect the very aggressive fish to live peacefully with shy retiring species. It is also pointless to expect large carnivorous species to live in a tank with very much smaller fish. Fast moving fish may upset smaller timid species.

In addition to giving consideration to the species of fishes which are to inhabit a tank, spare a thought for the layout. Make sure that suitable environments exist for each species you intend to include. For example those which like shelter should have plenty of rocky caves, or coral in marine species. Open water species should have room to spread. To ignore these simple principles creates psychological problems in the fish, is unkind and, predisposes them to disease.

Indications are given throughout the book under the family and species headings of the suitability of particular fish for inclusion in community tanks.

CONEY see *Cephalophis fulva*
Congential and Inherent Disease see *Disease*
CONGO
   BARB see *Barbus callipterus*
   GLASS CATFISH see *Eutropiellus debauwi*
   MOUTHBROODER see *Tilapia hendelotii dolloi*

Conservation
Aquarists keep fish for the aesthetic pleasure it gives within the home. There is no reason for their horizons to be wider than the frames of their tanks. It is, however, to be hoped that many, if not all, either begin with, or are stimulated to, take an interest in biology and natural history. Following such an interest comes concern for conservation. Far too many species have been made extinct by the thoughtless activities of man. The aim of aquarists must be to give to nature something in return for the pleasure received. We must not wantonly crop the rivers and seas of the world until the species of fish found there can no longer sustain adequate numbers, a situation which students of population dynamics have shown rapidly leads to extinction. We must learn to breed all our replacements in our tanks. This is an urgent need in the field of marine species. In addition we must learn and record as much information as possible in a scientific way in order that we increase the knowledge of the

species of fishes we keep. In this way we will build up comprehensive pictures of our fish and this, in turn, may assist scientists to conserve them in their wild environments. Conservation can only be achieved if we know what the species to be conserved needs to survive.

Constipation see *Disease*

CONVICT CICHLID see *Cichlasoma nigrofasciata*

COOLIE

    LOACH see *Acanthophthalmus kuhli*

    LOACH, HALF-BANDED see *Acanthophalmus semicinctus*

Copeina Lebiasinidae

– guttata RED-SPOTTED COPEINA 10–15cm. (4–6in.)
This fish is from the middle Amazon. It has an unfortunate tendency to pale its colours under some conditions but in full bloom is an attractive fish. The body colour is bluish green and the tail, anal and pelvic fins are yellow at the base grading to red tips. The dorsal fin is yellow and, particularly in the male, has a dark bar midway along its length. The male has several horizontal rows of red spots which clearly distinguish it. It is a fish that deserves more popularity.

A breeding pair makes a depression in the sand into which are deposited the eggs which are then fertilized by the male. The *Copeina* male drives away his spouse, and fans the eggs with his pectoral fins. When they hatch out in 48 hours he usually resists his urge to consume them, so can be left in the aquarium with young.

Slow moving, peaceful with a wide temperature tolerance, easily fed and easily bred, it makes a good community member and is a good fish for the beginner to cut his breeding teeth on.

Copella Lebiasinidae

– arnoldi ARNOLD'S or SPRAYING CHARACIN, SPRAYING SLAMET 8cm. (3in.)
Natives of the lower Amazon. The general body colour is greeny blue, being darker dorsally and shading down to a yellowish belly. The scales are lined giving a mottled effect. The fins are yellow with red bases and tips. The dorsal of the male has a white mark near the base. There is no adipose fin. The upper lobe of the male's tail fin is also very well developed.

This fish is a particular favourite, combining as it does elegance, beauty and interest. Most extraordinary are its breeding habits. It has evolved a very sophisticated and elegant method of protecting its eggs from predator assault. The pair which, it is hoped, will mate should be placed in a tank. The water should be slightly acid and at a temperature of 26–28°C. Place a sheet of glass with a roughened surface, and preferably painted blue or green, into the water, the top few centimetres being left above the surface of the water.

The male selects the spot, persuades the female towards the nuptial region and there they lock their bodies using fins, leaping at the same time from the water. Using mouth suction to hold onto a leaf, or the green painted glass, for a brief moment the female then deposits 5–12 eggs above the surface of the water. This is repeated until over 100 eggs lie above the waterline out of reach of hungry aquatic mouths. Aquatic eggs are not provided with a mechanism to prevent them from drying so being stranded, as these are, out of water would prove fatal unless they were kept moist. This the male does by rushing periodically to the surface and splashing them with water by lashing his tail. Having completed this burst of activity he retires to a hideout under a plant some distance away until the next watering time to avoid drawing predators' attention to the eggs' position. The embryos hatch in 36 hours and fall back into the water seeking shelter in the sand or pebbles on the bottom. After a few days they rise and begin swimming about in a shoal. They eat infusoria.

– nattereri 5cm. (2in.)
Native to the Amazon Basin. The body colour is silver grey with dark red spots along the side. The dorsal fin has a white mark and is pointed in the male. The upper lobe of the tail fin is elongated to a point.

It spawns in a normal characin way. The eggs are deposited on broad-leaved plants, below the surface, unlike *C. arnoldi*, from where they hatch in 24 hours.

COPPER-BANDED LONG-NOSED BUTTERFLYFISH see *Chelmon rostratus*

CORA'S CICHLID see *Apistogramma corumbae*

CORAL

    BEAUTY see *Centropyge bispinosus*

    HOGFISH see *Bodianus axillaris*

CORALFISH, BEAKED see *Chelmon rostratus*

Coris Labridae Ψ

– angulata TWO-SPOT WRASSE 1·2m (4ft)
A lovely fish which comes from the Indo-Pacific. As a juvenile its bright silver body is decorated with well differentiated black spots on the head and dorsal fin surrounded by a white border, and with a reflective red patch on the body below. As a young fish, a few centimetres long, it is hardy, easy to feed and reasonably common. **65**

– formosa SADDLE-BACK WRASSE 41cm. (16in.)
This fish, which comes from the Indo-Pacific, is often confused with a very similar species *C. gaimardi*. When young they are very difficult to distinguish. The body is basically red and there are three irregular white patches passing ventrically from the base of the dorsal fin. A further two white patches pass ventrally from the head. In this species, as opposed to *C. gaimardi*, the patches are larger

and descend further towards the ventral surface. The fins of *C. formosa* are darker, with irregular black patches. Like other members of the family, they bury themselves at night so it is essential to provide very fine soft sand.

Interesting and active fish, they make very good exhibits.

– *gaimardi* CLOWN or YELLOW-TAIL WRASSE 38cm. (15in.) Here is shown the variation between young and adult forms of the species so classical in the wrasses. The young fish is red, with wide black lines edging white patches on its back. The adult dispenses with the young pattern and would appear, to the uninitiated, to be a separate species, although it keeps the unusual red body colour. This fish which comes from the Indo-Pacific is very adaptable and takes to captivity well. It is peaceful and easy to feed. Like so many of the family it adopts unusual positions in the water. When young it closely resembles *C. formosa*, and this leads to difficulties of identification. **66**

Corydoras Callichthyidae ⊕
This is by far the best known genus of catfish. They are hardy, quite small and have a discreet coloration which is attractive. They are armoured as in *Callichthys callichthys*. In the wild, since they have accessory respiratory organs, they may leave the water and explore the countryside, providing the humidity is high. They are omnivorous and make excellent scavengers, clearing up food uneaten by other fish from the aquarium floor as well as other waste material. Corydoras can live in a wide range of temperatures from 18–29°C. They prefer soft mature water with a neutral or slightly alkaline pH of 7·2.

In general the genus is not easily bred, but *Corydoras aeneus* and *C. paleatus* are fairly prolific, while *C. hastatus*, *C. melanistius*, *C. rabunti* and *C. reticulatus* have performed occasionally. Males are fairly easily distinguished, having pointed dorsal and anal fins as opposed to the larger and more rounded shape of the female.

They can be brought into breeding condition by providing plenty of good, highly nutritious food; for example tubifex and earth worms. The participants should be placed in an aquarium furnished with mature soft water, a muddy bottom and plenty of cover. Lighting should be subdued. A rise in water temperature acts as an aphrodisiac. Most aquarists put several males into an aquarium with one female and so giving her the choice of suitor. Courting behaviour starts with the males swimming round her reluctant form, brushing her and prodding her until, after a while, she begins swimming with her suitors. They start to choose and clean sites for the deposition of eggs. One of the males now clings to the female pressing her against his belly by taking hold of her barbels with his pectoral fin. At the same time he releases his sperm. Now the female lays 3–5 eggs and holds them between her pelvic fins. The male

swims away and the female swims through the sperm cloud to a place where she deposits the eggs. Over a period of a few days the nuptial group will spawn several times, resting and eating between, and produce up to 300 eggs. To prevent the eggs being eaten the adults should be removed as soon as spawning is complete. The young hatch in about a week and should be fed infusoria.

– *aeneus* BRONZE CATFISH 7cm. (3in.)
A native of South America from Venezuela to the River Plate, Argentina, and including Trinidad. A soft golden yellow body is embellished by a copper coloured patch on the side of the head and a similarly coloured horizontal band dorsally. The barbels resemble a drooping moustache.

This is one of the two species of *Corydoras* which breed readily in captivity. **67**

– *arcuatus* ARCHED CATFISH 5cm. (2in.)
Found in the Amazon Basin, a pleasingly shaped fish which has a yellow brown body, blue mouth parts and a dark band which hugs the dorsal contour of the body, continuing to the ventral lobe of the tail fin.

– *hastatus* PYGMY or DWARF CATFISH 4cm. (1½in.)
This fish lives in the Amazon Basin. Its body shape is rather atypical of the genus being less domed and more compressed. A grey brown back changes abruptly to a silvery mauve ventral half. In the light portion a dark line runs from snout, through the eye to the tail, where it broadens to an ovoid spot. Active, hardy and easy to keep.

– *julii* LEOPARD CATFISH 6cm. (2½in.)
This species comes from South America in the region of the lower Amazon. This fish has distinctive markings. The general grey coloured body has a definite blue mauve sheen. Dark lines and patterns give it its popular name. These patterns continue into the tail fin. The other fins are clear, except the dorsal which carries a large black tip.

– *melanistius* BLACK-SPOTTED or GUYANA CATFISH 6cm. (2½in.)
A native of the Orinoco Basin, Venezuela. This is a poor mans *C. julii* with which it is often confused. Its body colour is a pale yellow beige and the pattern is an apology for the beautiful markings of *C. julii*. A dark mark near to the anterior attachment of the dorsal fin runs into the dorsal fin.

– *myersi* MYERS CATFISH *c.*5cm. (*c.*2in.)
From South America and one of the most attractive of the genus. The body has a metallic silver gold sheen pervaded by orange. A dark horizontal band runs from the anterior border of the dorsal fin to the base of the tail fin.

– *nattereri* BLUE or NATTERER'S CATFISH 7cm. (2½in.)
A native of eastern Brazil, this catfish has a pleasing coloration. The general body colour is orange with a blue sheen and a wide dark grey band parallels the dorsal contour from a point anterior to the dorsal fin to the base of the tail.

Blue Leopard or Peppered Catfish, *Corydoras paleatus*. The dull colouring of this bottom-living catfish is good camouflage.

– paleatus BLUE LEOPARD, PEPPERED CORYDORAS, PALEATUS OR PEPPERED CATFISH 8cm. (3in.)
A native of La Plata Basin in Brazil. A greenish body patched along its sides with dark blotches, with an overall peppering of black dots. Unpaired fins are adorned with spots while the pectoral and pelvic fins are clear.

An enthusiastic breeder even in the restricted environment of the aquarium.

– punctatus SPOTTED CATFISH 6cm. (2½in.)
A catfish found from the Orinoco in Venezuela to the northern tributaries of the Amazon. The brown body is decorated with dark spots and a bar extends from the head through the eye along the body. The tail fin is spotted but the other fins are clear.

– reticulatus RETICULATED CORYDORAS 8cm. (3in.)
Originating from the lower Amazon. The corydoras-shaped, pale orange brown body is overlaid with an irregular reticulated pattern of dark brown markings. A large spot embellishes the dorsal fin and dark bars decorate the tail. All the fins are clear.

– schultzei SCHULTZ'S CORYDORAS 7cm. (3in.)
This species comes from the Amazon. The basic yellow-silver colour of the body is enhanced by a blue green metallic sheen on the upper part of the back. The belly is golden and all fins are clear.

– spilurus PINK-THROATED CATFISH 6cm. (2½in.)
A dark grey back shades through light grey becoming pink on the underparts including the throat. Irregular dark patches and dots adorn the body. A dark line runs horizontally from the middle of the body to the tail. Apart from the tail fin, which is spotted, the fins are clear. **68**

– swartzi 5cm. (2in.)
A rather small member of the genus from Brazil and Surinam. Its shape is common to the corydoras pattern. The head and body are depressed and there are the typical barbels at the mouth. Along the side are rows of large overlapping scales. It is a grey silver colour with longitudinal black stripes along the sides and back. A recently imported, but now commonly available, species. **69**

Corynopoma see *Stevardia*

COSTIASIS see *Disease*
COWFISH,
   LONG-HORNED see *Lactoria cornuta*
   SCRAWLED see *Acanthostracion quadricornis*
Crabs see *Marine Invertebrates*

Crenicichla Cichlidae ⊕
– lepidota PIKE CICHLID 23cm. (9in.) ✂
Members of this genus are rather different in body shape from most of the cichlids. They are much slimmer in outline with generally less flamboyant fins than is usual. Very aggressive characters, they are unsuitable for the community tank and indeed are not popular with most aquarists. Plants are spared.

Found in the Amazon and northern parts of Argentina. It has a yellow brown body crossed by a horizontal line, above which run off vertical bars. These markings tend to fade with age. The fins are greenish brown speckled with dots.

For those who wish to keep them, they prefer temperatures between 21–26°C. and breed in accordance with cichlid principles, except that only the male assumes parental responsibility.

– saxatilis RING-TAILED PIKE CICHLID 41cm. (16in.)
A slender fish from South America including islands of the West Indies. The body colour is olive green which shades from the dark back through pale green to a yellow belly. A dark band often irregular or indistinct extends horizontally the length of the body. **70**

Crenuchus Characidae ⊕
– spilurus SAILFIN CHARACIN 6cm. (2½in.) ✂
These are rather large characins from the Amazon and Guyana and do not make good community members. The general body colour is brown shading to greeny yellow below with a horizontal gold band running the length of the body. The characteristically large dorsal and anal fin of the male is orange coloured and net like in appearance but does not develop until the third year; at this stage the male's fin display rivals that of *Betta* species. The tail and anal fins are red and have yellow spots.

Not much is known about breeding but reports of the male fanning the nest eggs after the female has deposited them on suitable surfaces, if true, reveals atypical characin behaviour.

CRESCENT PERCH see *Therapon jarbua*
CRIMSON-SPOTTED RAINBOWFISH see *Melanotaenia fluviatilis*
CROAKING
  DWARF GOURAMI see *Trichopsis pumilus*
  TETRA see *Glandulocauda inequalis*
CROSS-BANDED SNAPPER see *Lutjanus decussatus*
Crossopterygii see under *Classification*
CROWNED SOLDIERFISH see *Holocentrus diadema*
CRUCIAN CARP see *Carassius carassius*
Crustacea see under *Marine Invertebrates*
Cryptocoryne see under *Plants*

Ctenobrycon Characidae ⊕
– spilurus SILVER TETRA or KNIFEFISH 9cm. (3½in.)
A larger characin, from Guyana and Venezuela, this is a compressed bluish silver fish. There is a dark blotch or spot a little distance behind the operculum and a bar on the base of the tail fin. The male is distinguished from the female by the red colour on the anterior part of the anal fin. A peace-loving, omniverous fish.

A typical characin breeder preferring temperatures of 27°C., the female lays several hundred eggs which hatch in 2–4 days. The young eat algae or 'green water' infusoria and, later, small daphnia.

Ctenopoma Anabantidae ⊕
AFRICAN CLIMBING PERCHES
– ansorgei ORNATE CLIMBING PERCH 8cm. (3in.) ✂
All the species in this genus come from West Africa. Closely related to the genus *Anabas*, it is carnivorous, but though of evolutionary significance, rarely kept by aquarists. It is a mixture of blue and green. The anal fin is striped with yellow and blue. It lives in marshland or small streams and exists mainly on a diet of insects. It has attained some popularity as an aquarium fish but is quite aggressive towards other species. It adapts to captivity relatively easily and will take a wide variety of live food. Breeding is relatively easy as with other members of the genus.
– argentoventer SILVER-BELLIED CLIMBING PERCH 15cm. (6in.)
This particular species which is grey to olive green in colour with a vertical yellow band at the body centre, is native to the Niger River. This fish enjoys temperatures around 24°C.
– fasciolatum STRIPED or BANDED CLIMBING PERCH 9cm. (3½in.)
A smaller member of the genus which comes from Zaïre. A brownish fish with irregular gold coloured vertical bars. Carnivorous. The male builds a bubble nest. The young hatch after 24–30 hours at 26°C.
– nanum DWARF CLIMBING FISH 8cm. (3in.)
Another native of Cameroon and Zaïre. It has a brown body crossed by vertical bands.

CUBAN
  CICHLID see *Cichlasoma tetracanthus*
  HOGFISH see *Bodianus pulchellus*
  KILLY see *Cubanichthys cubensis*
  LIMIA see *Poecilia vittata*
  RIVULUS see *Rivulus cylindraceus*
CUBBYA see *Equetus accuminatus*
CUCHARON see *Sorubim lima*
Culex see under *Food*
CUMMING'S BARB see *Barbus cummingi*

Cubanichthys Cyprinodontidae ⊕
– cubensis CUBAN KILLY 8cm. (3in.)
As the scientific and popular names suggest, this fish comes from Cuba. An attractive yellow green fish, its sides are transected by several broken horizontal stripes running from the operculum to the tail. Between the stripes the body is reddish brown. The fins of both sexes are clear but the male carries a blue margin to the dorsal and anal fin. A peaceful community member which thrives well in temperatures between 21–26°C.

Basically a plant spawner, it has an unusual reported behaviour which distinguishes it from most other killifishes. Up to 12 eggs, when laid, are suspended by a thread attached to the female's body. After fertilization by the male the female moves into the plants where the thread snaps and the eggs adhere to the plants.

Curimatidae
A family of South American fish until recently classified as Characidae, but have now been proved to have distinguishable anatomical features. See *Chilodus, Prochilodus*.

CUTTER'S
  CHANCHITO see *Cichlasoma cutteri*
  CICHLID see *Cichlasoma cutteri*
Cyclochaetiasis see *Disease*
Cyclops see under *Food*

Cynolebias Cyprinodontidae ⊕
– adloffi BANDED CYNOLEBIAS 5cm. (2in.) ✂
In the wild this genus lives only for a year, buries the eggs in the mud at the bottom and then dies. The eggs lie dormant until after the dry season. The young fish emerge with the return of water to produce the next generation. In the aquarium, if no drought is simulated, the fish will live for two years.

An attractive native of south-eastern Brazil and Uruguay. The male is a gorgeous cerulean blue which is segmented by a number of dark vertical bars and the unpaired fins are a rich blue and peppered at the base with dark dots. The female is brown.

An aggressive species, they should be kept to themselves being no good for a community tank.

– *bellotti* ARGENTINE PEARLFISH, PAVITO
7cm. (3in.) ✂ ▥
Comes from the waters of Argentina. The male is a lovely deep turquoise with a dark blue back which is reflected in the margins of the dorsal and anal fins. The rounded tail is bordered by a dark reddish brown margin. Pale green dots cross the body in several vertical lines and break up to scatter over the unpaired fins. The female, completely different, is a light yellow green with dark brown broken vertical bars. The fins are decorated with dark brown lines.

This fish should be kept only with its own species. Does best in temperatures around 18–20°C. It prefers shade.

– *melanotaenia* FIGHTING GAUCHO 5cm. (2in.) ✂
A fish from Brazil. The male is a brownish red colour with two horizontal stripes. Yellow dots speckle the operculum and there are brown dots on the unpaired fins. The male's fins are pointed, in contrast to the conventional rounded contour of the female's.

The maintenance requirements are the same as those of other members of the genus.

– *nigripinnis* BLACK-FINNED or ARGENTINE PEARLFISH
5cm. (2in.)
A very attractive member of the genus from the La Plata Basin. The male has a very dark bluish purple body highlighted with paler blue spots. The dorsal and anal fins are quite large and wide-based, with the same coloration as the body, but with black borders. The female is smaller and brown with dark spots. They do best in temperatures around 21–22°C.

– *whitei* WHITE'S CYNOLEBIAS 8cm. (3in.)
This is another of the genus commonly imported. It comes from Brazil. Males tend to grow larger than the females. They are very easy to breed in captivity. Do best in temperatures in the region of 21–22°C. The male is blue in colour but the female is brown with dark spots.

Cypraea see *Marine Invertebrates*

Cyprinidae
Commonly known as carps, the Cyprinidae comprises the largest family of fish existing today. Widely distributed, its range extends, with the exception of Madagascar, throughout Africa, Europe, the Indian subcontinent, Asia and North America. It has no representatives living in Australia, New Zealand, or South America. Cyprinids range from the 1·8m. (6ft) *Barbus tor* of India to tiny rasboras less than 2cm. in length.

Not unlike Characins in general appearance, they can be distinguished by the absence of teeth in the jaws. The grinding function is undertaken by pharyngeal teeth in the throat. In addition there is no adipose fin. Barbels are a common feature.

A great many of the most attractive and popular aquarium fish belong to this great family. They are generally peaceful, as might be expected in toothless jawed animals, and easy to feed, being omnivorous.

Cyprinidae are egg layers. A pair ripe for breeding should be placed in a large tank filled with water to a depth of 20cm. and planted with thick leafy foliage plants. The temperature should be around 28°C. Spawning takes place soon after being placed in the tank.

Members of the genus *Barbus* perform a deal of prancing in and out of the plants until the female is moved to lay her eggs. These are attached to the plants, and immediately fertilized by the male. In captivity the parents are likely to eat the products of their labours so removal is essential. The eggs hatch in 2 to 3 days. The yolk sac is still present and provides food for the fry for a few days. They then require infusoria and algae, and later small daphnia etc.

Eggs of the genus *Brachydanio* are non-adhesive. The parents are rather too fond of *Brachydanio* eggs and for this reason shallow water and coarse gravel both lessen the time taken for the egg to sink and give them protection when they fall. Temperatures should be around 24°C. and the pH close to neutral or very slightly acid. A likely looking female if well fed on live food for a few days and then placed in a tank with a few ardent males will be induced to spawn. The eggs hatch in a few hours and are, like *Barbus* fry, still fed from their adherent yolk sac. This is absorbed in 2 to 3 days and then infusoria should be fed.

Many other Cyprinidae will breed in captivity although others have steadfastly refused to oblige. Some species have adhesive eggs, while others have not, and these simply gravitate to the bottom, if their parents don't eat them first.

Rasboras are slightly unusual in their approach to mating. After a small exhibition of aquabatics the female rubs herself against a leaf, turning upside down in so doing. The male, attracted by this activity approaches and, curling his body in a fleeting embrace, induces the female to deposit her eggs on the leaf. The act is repeated several times during 2–3 hours when up to 100 eggs may be deposited. The eggs hatch in about one day, and the young very soon require infusoria and later small daphnia.

The secret of breeding Cyprinidae is to choose mature healthy adults which should be separated; they should then be fed on good quality live food, before placing them in a clean shallow tank with as little disturbance as possible and then leaving them alone. See *Balantiocheilus, Barbus, Brachydanio, Carassius, Danio, Esomus, Gobio, Labeo, Leuciscus, Morulius, Notropis, Osteochilus, Phoxinus, Rasbora, Rhodeus, Scardinius, Tanichthys, Tinca.*

Cyprinodon Cyprinodontidae Ψ
– *variegatus* SHEEPSHEAD or PUSSY MINNOW Ψ/⊕⊙
8cm. (3in.)

A native of the eastern coast of the USA. The male is silver with blue highlights and orange underneath. Blue spots and dark vertical bars adorn its side. The dorsal fin is of light blue. The female is duller, olive green with cream underparts.

One of the species whose range of adaptability includes salt, brackish, and fresh water but, for best results, keep it in brackish water. It likes sun, temperatures in the region of 22°C. and peace.

The male defends a territory during the breeding season and induces, with a sexual tremble, the female to lay her eggs among the plants, after which he fertilizes them. The eggs hatch in 8–12 days in temperatures around 22°C. Small daphnia and newly hatched brine shrimp are taken by the fry.

Cyprinodontidae KILLIFISHES or EGG-LAYING TOOTHCARPS
This mainly freshwater family, popularly known as killifishes, are egg-laying toothcarps. They are widely distributed in tropical and sub-tropical regions. In America they are found from the north of the USA, throughout Central America and the islands of the Caribbean to the north-eastern mass of South America. In the old world they are found in southern Europe, most of Africa including Madagascar, the Indian sub-continent, southern China and the island area of south-east Asia. They are not found in Australasia.

Usually small fish, often of dazzling hue, they have elongated bodies with a dorsal fin placed well towards the tail. Their front ends are flattened large wide mouths.

Principally adapted by evolution to shallow stagnant pools or slow moving water, different species have a wide range of temperatures to which they adjust. Some can withstand relatively cold temperatures around 18°C. or less, while others do well at 36°C. However, most of the species kept by aquarists prefer temperatures near the lower end of the tropical range. Essentially they are shade lovers and aquarists would be well advised to accommodate this need by providing a heavily planted tank with subdued lighting. Many prefer hardish well filtered water (70–180ppm (DH4–10)), see *Hardness of Water*, which is slightly acid. A few species live in brackish water. Activity is not a strong point, perhaps understandably for those which live in warm, shady and shallow tropical pools. They spend much of their day idling, commonly assuming a head up position in the water. Occasionally, however, they are stimulated to sudden movement and are better leapers than one might expect, so keep the aquarium well covered.

Some species are aggressive, to other species as well as among themselves, so be wary of keeping them in a community tank. A general rule is to keep the size of killy at or below the size of the other fish in the tank.

The vast majority of cyprinodonts are carnivorous, and need a good supply of live food for health. Substitutes for their natural diet which includes mosquito larvae and bloodworms, can be tubifex, fruit flies, *Drosophila*, and chopped earthworms. In addition, modern frozen fish foods like frozen bloodworms and brine shrimps, *Artemia*, are excellent. Finely minced meat or pastes are also accepted.

Many species of this family will breed in captivity but require a little attention if success is to be assured. Basically they are egg layers but with interesting differences. The eggs have adhesive qualities derived from numerous hair-like protrusions from the thick shell. Many breed without conditioning but to ensure success the sexes should be separated for a few weeks and while in a state of celibacy fed well. On re-introducing the sexes to each other breeding behaviour is stimulated. Make sure there is plenty of plant cover, or the not very attractive substitute, a nylon mop. Spawning occurs when the male swims to a position alongside the ripe female and spreads wide his median fins. He hustles her, sometimes swimming a short distance ahead of her, and trembling. At this point, if she shows reluctance, he may indulge in some fin biting. Eventually swimming side by side the male wraps his anal fin, and occasionally his dorsal fin as well, around the female's body. Both bodies twist and tremble; a single egg is then produced and fertilized. In this way, by constantly repeating the performance, many eggs are laid over quite a long period. Some killifish attach the eggs to plants by the hair-like structures mentioned above. Others lay the eggs in the surface of the mud while another group bury them deep into the mud.

After 2 to 3 weeks of egg laying activity the adults should be removed. Most fry of the plant-attaching group of killies hatch in 1–3 weeks. Plenty of plant cover will offer fair protection to the early hatchers. The young are quite large and should be fed newly hatched brine shrimp, *Artemia naplin*, for a few days. For the smaller fry species infusoria is necessary. Feed the fry as frequently as possible, not less than 5 times each day. Later chopped bloodworms make excellent food. Some more sophisticated breeders remove the plants or the nylon mops and put them into separate prepared tanks every few days to avoid cannibalism by the parents or of the smaller fry by larger. Others remove the eggs by hand from the mops and hatch young in small glass vessels before returning them to larger tanks.

Many of the mud spawners can be bred in a similar way as long as low growing plants are provided or a nylon mop is allowed to sink to the bottom. These eggs usually take somewhat longer to hatch even under good conditions, in the region of 6–8 weeks and some considerably longer.

An adaptive mechanism, devised by some of the killifish living in ponds which dry out during dry seasons of the year, is of great interest. As the water evaporates the fish die but the eggs buried deep in the mud will withstand a considerable degree of desiccation, hatching when the rains come. The life cycle is therefore completed within one year. The eggs of these fish should be collected in a net by stirring up the bottom mud – most aquarists use sterile peat. They are then placed in sterile damp peat moss and kept for a few weeks in a somewhat dry condition. The peat should then be immersed in water and the eggs will hatch within a few hours. See *Aphanius, Aphyosemion, Aplocheilichthys, Aplocheilus, Chriopeops, Cubanichthys, Cynolebias, Cyprinodon, Epiplatys, Fundulus, Jordanella, Leptolucania, Nothobranchius, Pachypanchax, Pterolebias, Rivulus.*

D

DAMSEL BARB see *Barbus tetrazona*
DAMSELFISH see *Abudefduf, Chromis, Dascyllus, Eupomacentrus, Microspathodon, Pomacentridae, Pomacentrus.*

Danio Cyprinidae ⊕
– aequipinnatus GIANT DANIO 12cm. (4½in.)
It comes from India and Sri Lanka, and as its name implies, is one of the larger carps kept in the aquarium. It is a very common member of the community tank having all the right qualities; it is active, peaceable by nature, easily bred and long-lived.

General body coloration is blue with several horizontal

Giant Danio, *Danio aequipinnatus.*

yellow gold lines along the side, which extend into the base of the tail fin. Behind the operculum the horizontal line breaks up into rather indistinct vertical bars. The posterior underbelly is red, as are the pelvic, anal and dorsal fins during the breeding season.

Mature when 5cm. long; sexing is not easy. Females at breeding time have a swollen belly and the male has a greater density of colour. The golden stripes are somewhat more broken in the female and the lower jaw less pronounced than in the male. The male chases a ripe female in and out of the water plants until she lays her adhesive eggs and attaches them to the plants. There they are fertilized by the male. Giant Danios live happily at temperatures anywhere between 21–26°C. *D. malabarians* is a synonym. **71**
– devario BENGAL DANIO 10cm. (4in.)
A native of northern India. Much less commonly available from dealers than its well known cousin the Giant Danio, *D. aequipinnatus*, its body colour is green dorsally and becoming light silver below. The anterior part of the body has a bluish hue where blue green stripes extend from the centre of the body onto the tail fin. Anal and pelvic fins are clear with a hint of blue. Breeds like the Giant Danio.

DANIO see *Brachydanio, Danio*
Daphnia see under *Food*
DARKER CHARACIN see *Characidium fasciatum*

Dascyllus Pomacentridae Ψ
– aruanus BANDED HUMBUG or WHITE-TAILED DAMSELFISH 8cm. (3in.)
A small fish from the Red Sea, the Indian and the Pacific Oceans which lives in small rather loose social groups. It has the familiar black and white coloration so common in the family. This damselfish has three black stripes, the dorsal fin is black but there is no black marking on the tail fin. It

Banded Humbug or White-tailed Damselfish, *Dascyllus aruanus.*

spawns in captivity although the young have not to date been reared. It must be given plenty of rocky cover. **72**
– *marginatus* PRETTY DAMSELFISH 10cm. (4in.)
An interesting and attractive fish from the Red Sea. The body is a pleasing combination of beige, white and brown. When mature it can become aggressive in captivity.
– *melanurus* BLACK-TAILED or HUMBUG DAMSELFISH 10cm. (4in.)
A small fish which comes from the Indo-Pacific. Oval-shaped with a white body and broad vertical black stripes rather similar to *D. aruanus*, but it has a black tail. Rather more peaceful and accommodating than many damselfish.
– *reticulatus* RETICULATED DAMSELFISH 10cm. (4in.)
Rather a drab fish for the family, it comes from the Indo-Pacific. It needs plenty of rocky or coral shelter in the aquarium. It is easy to feed on standard small live food.

A Reticulated Damselfish, *Dascyllus reticulatus,* receiving the attentions of two Cleaner Wrasses, *Labroides dimidiatus.*

Blue, brown patterned body, with indistinct darker vertical bands. Rather similar to *D. marginatus*.
– *trimaculatus* DOMINO DAMSELFISH 14cm. (5½in.) ✕
A popular damselfish from the Red Sea and the Indo-Pacific. It has a deep black body broken by three small white spots, one on the head and one on each side of the body. It becomes aggressive as it matures and must be watched but it is easy to feed. Juveniles often live between the tentacles of giant sea anemones, like the clownfish.

DAWN TETRA see *Hyphessobrycon eos*
DAY'S
   PANCHAX see *Aplocheilus dayi*
   PARADISEFISH see *Macropodus cupanus dayi*

DEACON see *Cichlasoma severum*
DEER WRASSE see *Hemipteronotus taeniurus*
DEMON DEVILFISH see *Geophagus jurupari*
DEMPSEY, JACK see *Cichlasoma biocellatum*

Dendrochirus Scorpaenidae Ψ
– *brachypterus* DWARF or PYGMY LIONFISH 7cm. (6½in.)
Lives in the coral in the Red Sea and Indo-Pacific. It is smaller and somewhat less spectacular than its magnificent cousin *Pterois volitans* and the fins are less extravagant. It makes, however, a very suitable inhabitant of the marine aquarium. In spite of its small size it must be remembered that its dorsal spines are venomous.
– *zebra* ZEBRA LIONFISH 30cm. (12in.)
This is one of two members of this genus imported for the aquarist. When young they make suitable community fish providing they are well and carefully handled and given suitable conditions. They need plenty of space to swim and resonable cover. In common with other members of this genus and its relatives in the genus *Pterois*, the Zebra Lionfish has a striped body with exotic fin formation. The body is very dark indeed contrasted with the white thin bands which circle it. It comes from the Indo-Pacific.

Dermogenys Exocoetidae ⊕
– *pusillus* HALFBEAK 8cm. (3in.) ⊕/Ψ ✕
This fish is widely distributed throughout the Malay Peninsula, Thailand and Indonesia. It lives in both fresh and brackish water and is probably not averse to the sea from time to time. It is the body shape, rather than colour, which intrigues aquarists, the body being very slender and somewhat elongated. The body colour is a yellowy brown with vague suggestions of blue. Males have a bright red patch on the dorsal fin. It is a surface fish where it naturally consumes insects and their larvae. They prefer temperatures around 24°C.

   Live bearing, they produce up to 20 fry at a time, which are consumed if not protected. Young eat small daphnia from birth and fruit flies from the water surface.

   Not an easy fish for the hobbyist and therefore all the more challenging. The males are aggressive and tend to fight. The female, the larger fish, is prone to 'abortion' so very careful management is required. Gestation is up to 8 weeks.

DEVIL, BLUE see *Pomacentrus melanochir*
DEVILFISH
   DEMON see *Geophagus jurupari*
   EARTH-EATING see *Geophagus jurupari*
Diagramma albovittatus see *Plectorhynchus gaterinoides*
DIAMOND PUFFER see *Canthigaster margaritatus*
DIAMOND-FLECKED PUFFER see *Canthigaster margaritatus*

DIAMONDFISH, PSETTUS see *Monodactylus argenteus*
Didiplis see under *Plants*
Diet see *Nutrition*

Digestive System

The basic plan of the digestive system is similar to that of all other vertebrates. The mouth bordered by lips is supported by jaws often with teeth. The roof in addition has further 'teeth', and there are more on the tongue. This leads to the pharynx which has tooth pads on the gill arches and gill rakers guarding the bronchial openings. The gullet or oesophagus transports food from the pharynx to the stomach. From the pyloric end of the stomach opens the pyloric sphincter. This is followed by the first part of the small intestine, the duodenum, into which open the bile and pancreatic ducts. The small intestine continues, very often coiled, and passes into the shorter large intestine which opens to the exterior via the anus.

The purpose of this relatively long coiled small intestine is to provide a large surface area for the absorption of food. Sharks have approached the problem rather differently and have evolved the spiral valve which has the same effect, providing a large surface area, and the food is passed through a spiral arrangement rather like a horizontal helter-skelter.

As with any generalized discussion on fish, one must indicate some of the great varieties of modifications which have evolved depending on the type of fish being discussed. The mouths of predators are usually relatively large while suckerfish often develop tube like mouths for simply sucking in food or reaching into crevices in the rock.

Predatory fish have sharp, well developed pointed teeth to grasp and hold their prey, while fish which feed on microscopic plankton often have none. Fish which include snails, crabs, clams and other crustacea in their diet usually have large surface grinding teeth. The piranha and the barracuda have extremely well designed cutting teeth on which is based their infamous reputation. The teeth of many vegetable feeders are sometimes fused into sharp continuous ridges.

The stomach shows several interesting modifications. In some fish, notably the sturgeons, it is modified into a grinding organ rather like the gizzard of a chicken. Large fish which swallow smaller fish have, not surprisingly, a fish shaped stomach while omnivorous or mixed feeders have one shaped like a pig or man himself. Puffers use the stomach's elasticity by closing tight its entrance and exit and blowing it up to gigantic proportions when faced with danger.

As in land herbivores, like cattle and horses, the intestine of plant eating fish is often long and much folded. This is essential since the digestion of plant material, notably cellulose, is more difficult and complicated than animal material. Consequently carnivores like the pike have relatively short, less well folded, intestines.

The purpose of digestion is to break down food into simpler components which can be absorbed by the gut. Following absorption these simpler substances are transported, via the blood, to the cells of the body where they are either biologically burned to provide essential energy, stored as fat or used to build body tissues.

Passing down the digestive tract by wave like motions, produced by the muscular wall of the gut, it is subjected to a continuous deluge of digestive juices which break the complex chemical structure of the food into smaller and smaller units suitable for absorption. See *Food, Nutrition*.

Diodon Diodontidae
– hystrix PORCUPINEFISH 91cm. (36in.)
Small young specimens make delightful aquarium fish; however older fish are not suitable for the home aquarist unless he is prepared to keep them in a swimming pool since they use a lot of space. This fish is common in all tropical oceans. It feeds on crustaceans and molluscs and is easy to feed.

Porcupinefish, *Diodon hystrix.*

The body is a pale yellow ochre dorsally fading to a white belly. It is covered with numerous dark dots scattered between the spines.

Diodontidae PORCUPINEFISHES Ψ
A small family of marine fish which have the ability, like Tetraodontidae, to puff up to a very large size. In addition they are covered with sharp spines all over the body which makes them the most unattractive of prey. Small specimens are suitable for the community tank and can provide hours of viewing pleasure. They are also easy to feed. Their inflated and dried spiny skins are popularly sold as souvenirs in the tropics. See *Chilomycterus, Diodon*.

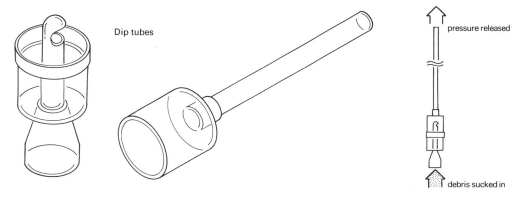

Dip tubes

pressure released

debris sucked in

Dip Tubes

These are simply glass tubes, preferably with wide ends which are used to remove small pieces of waste matter on the floor of the aquarium.

The finger is held over the top end and the tube then inserted into the water over the waste matter on the floor of the tank. The finger is then removed and as the water flows into the tube, to equalize the levels of water, the waste flows in with it. The finger is then replaced thus trapping the water and waste and the tube is removed.

DISCORD HATCHETFISH see *Thoracocharax stellatus*
Discosoma see under *Marine Invertebrates*
Discus see *Symphysodon discus*

Diseases

The study of disease is a complex undertaking requiring years of theoretical study, followed by years of experience. This is as true of fish disease as it is of illness in cattle, dogs or humans. Many animal enthusiasts believe, quite wrongly, that all one needs in order to treat disease is a list of symptoms which can be simply ticked off. If all symptoms are present, the disease is identified and the appropriate medicine can be administered. Sadly, perhaps, such a simplified view is very far from reality.

Any animal remains healthy as long as it is allowed to live in an environment to which it is adapted. Add to that environment any factor to which it can't adapt and it will begin to show symptoms of adaptation failure. In other words, it will become diseased.

A fish for example must have water as a basis of its environment. This must be at the correct temperature, pH and have the correct degree of hardness. Marine fish require a certain level of salinity. The water must have adequate oxygen dissolved in it and must be free from poisonous substances. It is essential that adequate quantities of food are available of the correct constitution. Light must be at an optimum. Psychological well-being is also an important adjunct to health. The environment should therefore be adjusted to the mental needs of the fish. It should have

adequate hiding places for those species which like them, large open areas for species that are fast and free-swimming, and be free from constant harassment by predators or more aggressive species. Scientific studies have shown that in any situation there is an optimum density of population for species. Under- and over-crowding, particularly the latter, are physically and psychologically detrimental to health. In addition, of course, the fish must be free from any inherited disease. If any one, or a combination, of these environmental requirements is not adequately met, then the animal will show symptoms of disease and, if no action is taken, it will either, depending on the severity of the fault, remain in poor health or die.

It is apparent, therefore, that if one's animals are to remain healthy, whether they are fish, fowl, cattle, or cats, good and diligent management is imperative.

Microscopic infectious disease organisms or germs are, of course, a further environmental problem with which the animal may have to deal. Some of these are so infectious that if they are present, disease will be inevitable. Others are less troublesome and will only affect the animal if it is concurrently weakened by other adverse environmental conditions. For example, bacterial gill disease, due to mixed myxo-bacteria, is more common in overcrowded salmon ponds. Experimentally it has been shown that disease will occur if there are more than 2 kilos of fish per $4\frac{1}{2}$ litres per minute flow and conversely that it can be successfully treated by simply reducing the density of fish without changing the water. In other words, the infectious disease organisms, myxo-bacteria, are there in the environment all the time. Both furunculosis and columnaris diseases are known to be similarly due to a combination of adverse environmental factors.

Disease prevention then should be aimed at by maintaining animals in optimum conditions and preventing the introduction of infectious organisms, like bacteria, protozoa, viruses and parasites. In those conditions where a combination of germ and environmental fault precipitate disease, removal or treatment of the germ will cure the symptoms. It is, however, also worth re-assessing one's management when disease strikes since it often implies environmental faults as well.

Finally there are diseases over which one has little control. Parts of the fish may cease to function correctly for a variety of reasons. When this happens the animal will exhibit symptoms of disease. For example, the kidneys may fail to remove the waste products due to either an acute inflammatory condition – acute nephritis – or as a result of senility. The well-known condition of sugar diabetes in man and other animals is the result of incorrect functioning of the pancreas. Failure of the circulatory system see *Blood System*, may be due to a variety of heart or blood vessel conditions. Hormone imbalance, see *Endocrine System*, causes considerable trouble. Sadly, fish are as commonly afflicted with cancer as other animals, the cause being just as obscure as it is in man.

Briefly, listed below are some of the commoner conditions which the aquarist may encounter. Significant advances in the treatment of fish diseases will only result if they are subjected to scientific study by those qualified to undertake the task. In view of the popularity of the pet fish hobby, such studies must continue with all haste. Empirical treatment, using proprietary drugs, dispensed by pet shop pharmacies, is not good enough for farm livestock or pet animals and it is not good enough for fish.

BACTERIAL DISEASES

Many diseases are either caused by these micro-organisms or are complicated and exacerbated by them. The study of bacteria, including the disease-causing types, is known as Bacteriology. It is a complex subject. In some cases, highly infectious, very specialized bacteria, may cause a specific disease. It is more common for bacteria of different kinds to attack parts of the body to produce what appears to be an identical condition. In addition, even within a species of bacteria, there are different strains, some of which are attacked by one antibiotic, some by another. Only careful laboratory examination by a qualified veterinary bacteriologist will be able to ascertain which bacteria is causing trouble and which antibiotic is likely to be effective. Undoubtedly, the most scientific approach to disease is to have the micro-organism identified and a sensitivity test carried out to be sure one uses the correct treatment.

Some of the more important, common diseases caused or complicated by bacteria include *Tail Rot* and *Fin Rot*, *Dropsy, Scale Disease, Skin Spots, Tuberculosis*. See under the separate headings below.

CANCER

Fishes are no more fortunate in escaping the horrors of cancer than man. A great many types of cancer afflict fish, affecting a variety of organs. Symptoms vary with the type of cancer and the organs affected. In recent years, there has been a great interest in fish cancer and several studies have been made. Treatment is rarely practical in fish but, with increasing interest from the veterinary profession, some successful treatments discovered in human and veterinary medicine will probably be tried in the future, no doubt including chemotherapy and radiation.

CHILODONELLIASIS

This condition produces a slimy skin and gills. The micro-organism responsible belongs to the genus *Chilodonella*. They are flattened leaf-shaped organisms. Fresh slime samples are essential for diagnosis. Treatment consists of a salt bath or immersion in methylene blue for several days. See *Cyclochaetiasis* for salt bath prescription, and *Ichthyophthiriasis* for methylene blue.

COCCIDIOSIS

Microscopic organisms which are all parasitic. They have, usually, ovoid cell bodies which live within the tissue cells of fish. Young coccidia enter cells, grow, divide and leave to spread into other cells of the body. When they reproduce they form two types of young cells, a large and a small. One of each kind unites to form a cyst (ovicyst) which usually leaves the fish in its faeces. Inside this cyst division occurs to form infective coccidia. When eaten accidentally by a fish, the process starts again. Many of these various species of coccidia live in the gut and other internal organs of the body. A few penetrate the blood system to damage the red blood cells, causing anaemia and weakness.

CONGENITAL AND INHERENT DISEASE

Some diseases are due to adverse environmental conditions while the fish is forming, see *Embryology*. Others are due to problems within the genes which control development, see *Genetics*.

CONSTIPATION

Although several causes are possible, poor feeding is by far the commonest, for example, very long periods with only dried food. Treatment includes gentle laxatives by mouth. Dried food soaked in liquid paraffin (mineral oil U.S.) is a simple cure. In very rare cases an enema may be necessary, but it should only be administered by a veterinary surgeon.

COSTIASIS

Costia necatrix, the cause of this complaint, is the most serious of the microscopic slimy skin parasites. It has four long hair-like protrusions or flagella. Once attached to the skin, it consumes skin cells. The slime cells in the skin produce excess slime due to the parasite's activities. It is a serious condition which attacks gills as well as skin and eventually causes death. *Costia necatrix* does not survive for long away from the fish and the removal of all fish to a hospital tank for 24 hours will be enough to clear the tank. The afflicted fish should be placed in a one per cent solution of salt for at least 40 minutes. Alternatively a solution of formalin (0·2ml. of formalin per 4 litres) for 20 minutes can be used.

CYCLOCHAETIASIS

This slimy skin condition is usually caused by the ciliate *Cyclochaeta domerguei*, a micro-organism which has a number of small hair-like projections known as cilia. It attaches itself to the fish's skin by a sucker and feeds on dead skin tissue. Afflicted fish produce large quantities of slime. It is a common parasite of goldfish, paradisefish and guppies. Several genera and species of similar types of parasite cause a similar condition, but treatment is identical.

The simplest home remedy is to bathe affected fish in a 2 per cent salt solution for half an hour every two days for three applications.

DROPSY

A swollen abdomen is not necessarily a symptom of dropsy since many widely differing conditions will cause such a swelling. In fish, the commonest cause of dropsy is a virus infection, see *Virus Diseases*, complicated by the bacteria *Aeromonas punctata*.

The fish's abdomen swells, and the contents are found to be diseased. The intestines are inflamed, the kidneys and liver are affected and there is a red or yellow tinged liquid in the peritoneal cavity. It usually only infects the one or two individual fish, normally only spreading from fish to fish with difficulty but it can become epidemic in certain circumstances.

Treatment is difficult but antibiotics have improved chances of success. Surgical drainage of the abdomen may be required and injections of antibiotics given. For valuable fish consult a veterinary surgeon interested in aquarism.

ENTERITIS and GASTRO-ENTERITIS

Enteritis describes an inflammation of the small intestine and gastritis an inflammation of the stomach. Gastro-enteritis a combination of both, is quite common. An afflicted fish becomes lethargic, goes off its food and shows fading colours. It is due to a variety of causes including bacterial infection, virus invasion, coccidia, incorrect feeding and metabolic disturbance. Starvation, injections of antibiotics or sulpha drugs and good nursing in optimum tank conditions are some of the treatments used.

EXOPHTHALMUS or POP EYE

This is merely describing a symptom and not the name of a specific disease. A great variety of conditions cause exophthalmus, including parasites, injury, bacterial infections of several kinds including tuberculosis, fungal conditions, hormonal disease, see *Endocrine System*, and viruses. Treatment obviously depends on cause. A specific diagnosis is therefore essential.

FIN ROT

This condition in freshwater fish is well described by the name. The fins, including the tail, become straggly and torn by the action of bacteria. It is also not uncommon for a fungus to join forces with the bacteria. Black Mollies are particularly susceptible to attack. Bacteria of great variety have been isolated from infected fish. It seems, therefore, that no specific bacteria is guilty of causing the disease. Neglected cases will spread to the body and kill the fish. The disease is more severe in marine fish.

Treatment consists of administering a suitable antibiotic in the feed and bathing the affected fish in a solution of antibiotic. In severe cases, surgical removal of infected areas of the fin may be necessary.

FUNGUS DISEASE OF SKIN

Fungal infections of fish are very common. They are due to a great variety of fungi belonging to the family Saprolegniaceae. Spores of many fungi are present in most tanks but can only gain entry to the fish tissue if it has a weakened resistance. Distinguishing different species of fungi is a job for the veterinary mycologist but fortunately identification is not really necessary in most cases since they all succumb readily to simple treatments. The disease appears as fine white threads on the skin or fins. Heavy growth in neglected cases resembles cotton wool. The fine fungal threads known as hyphae grow down into the skin and then on down between the muscle films causing death of the tissue. After the branching hyphae are well established, they begin to reproduce, forming large heads of spores at the end of the hyphae. These spores are able to move through the water to colonize and send out more vegetative hyphae on another damaged fish or on dead organic matter. Since fungi do not have to live on fish, but exist happily on dead matter, they are impossible to remove from a tank.

Preferably remove infected fish from the tank. In cases with small areas of infection, paint the afflicted part with a solution of iodine, a one per cent solution of mercurochrome or a one per cent solution of malachite green and then proceed as follows. Fish with more generalized infection can be placed in a tank containing methylene blue, as described for Ichthyopthiriasis, a solution of acriflavine or malachite green, see *Velvet Disease*, being careful to darken the tank. Attention should be given to removing the precipitating cause, since this is only a secondary infection. Check for faulty management and for any skin infections which allow the fungal spores to gain entry. It is worth noting that specific antibiotics used for mammalian fungal infections have been used but are expensive and probably have little advantage in fish until available for dosing by mouth. See *Skin Spots*.

GAS BLADDER DISEASES

Symptoms of tumbling may be seen in tropical fish which have been chilled. They roll over head first and spend time on the bottom, having failed to maintain their balance.

The gas bladder is also on occasion afflicted by coccidiosis, causing wasting and sometimes secondary skin disease, and by bacterial and viral inflammation. Treatment consists of the administration of appropriate antibiotics, therefore it is necessary to consult a veterinary surgeon.

GILL FLUKES

Gill flukes closely resemble skin flukes but are more difficult to clear. They produce signs of serious respiratory distress. The gill cover – operculum – opens wide and the mucous membranes can be seen to be pale in colour. Over 80 species belong to the gill fluke family Dactylogyridae, of which *Dactylogyrus fallox* is the most troublesome and difficult species to eradicate.

Unlike skin flukes, gill flukes produce eggs which are very resistant to chemicals designed to kill the mature flukes. It is therefore necessary to repeat treatment several times at intervals of a few days to ensure that all emerging worms are killed.

A favoured treatment is to place fish from the infected tank into a tank containing 1:2000 solution of ammonia for 20 minutes and then put them in a solution of one per cent methylene blue at the rate of 1 ml. for every 9 litres.

GILL ROT

A serious fungal infection of some coldwater species, including Carp, *Cyprinus carpio*, Tench, *Tinca tinca*, and Three-spined Sticklebacks, *Gasterosteus aculeatus*. The fungus produces typical threads or hyphae which grow into blood vessels in the gills to interfere with their function. Fish affected with this disease die rapidly of suffocation. Diagnosis is often difficult. Fortunately, it is very rare in aquarium fish. Treatment is by immersion in copper sulphate. Expert advice should be obtained before treatment is started.

ICHTHYOPHTHIRIASIS 'Ich', White Spot Disease

This is a very common condition of freshwater fish which is readily identified. Small white or grey spots appear all over the skin and fins. It is due to the protozoan organism, *Ichthyophthirius multifilius*. These unpleasant single-celled

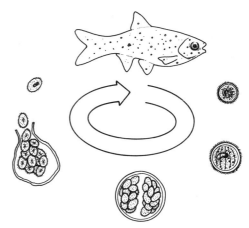

The life cycle of the white spot parasite.

organisms, which are covered in hair-like projections, penetrate the skin. The skin responds by producing large numbers of skin cells, giving the white appearance. Once inside the skin, the parasite feeds on red blood cells and skin cells of the fish. It reproduces here by simply dividing into two cells, then those two into four, and so on. When fully grown, these cells leave the skin for further reproduction. They fall to the bottom of the tank and there cover themselves in a jelly-like substance. Inside this protective jelly they divide again to form new young parasites. Each adult parasite which leaves our unfortunate fish can produce 1,500 young. These are soon swimming about the tank looking for a fish to infect. Fish in an infected tank are constantly re-invaded and gradually, if untreated, will die of the disease.

Young 'Ich' parasites soon die if they don't find a fish to infect. Therefore, if the fish are removed from an infected tank for treatment and the tank left empty of all fish, the parasites will soon die, and the tank will be 'clean' again.

'Ich' is one of those conditions which are related to environment. For example, tropical fish will be more susceptible to the disease if the water temperature is low, while coldwater fish will succumb more easily when it becomes too warm.

New fish should be quarantined, coldwater for 10 weeks, tropicals for 5 weeks, and should be treated with methylene blue. Since no drug will kill the parasite while in the skin, prolonged treatment, keeping the fish in a bath of methylene blue, is essential for prevention and cure. The colour will gradually fade in the tank and does little harm to plants, although I prefer to separate fish under treatment, placing them in a separate tank. One millilitre of 1 per cent methylene blue B.P. per 4½ litres, repeated in 3 days, is the correct solution. An alternative is 1 ml. of methylene green per 80 litres every 48 hours for 10 days. Other treatments, including some of the antibiotics, are effective but should only be used under veterinary supervision, in order to prevent a build-up of resistance. Coldwater fish are less likely to become infected than tropicals.

Marine fish afflicted with 'Ich' should be treated for somewhat longer periods – up to 3 weeks – using stronger concentrations of methylene blue (4ml. of 1 per cent methylene blue per 4½ litres). Diagnosis here is very important since other skin parasites, *Cryptocaryon irritans* for example, closely resemble 'Ich' which are not cured by methylene blue treatment. A microscopic examination of a skin scraping will confirm diagnosis.

LYMPHOCYSTIS

This is a rare condition in the aquarium, the only common freshwater aquarium fish known to succumb being the Paradisefish, *Macropodus opercularis*, although it is more common in various marine species.

Irregular growths of tissue slowly spread mostly on the fins. The viral damage to the skin opens the door to secondary skin bacteria and skin fungi, see *Fungus Disease of Skin*. However, death should never result if the fish are given good care; healing should soon occur.

POISONING

Various substances used in the normal home may dissolve in the fish tank, causing poisoning. Tobacco smoke, insecticides dispersed by aerosol, and paint fumes, are all likely to cause unfortunate symptoms and death.

In marine fish, special care must be taken to ensure that metals are not exposed to seawater, see *Tanks*, or corrosion will produce toxic salts in the tank.

POX DISEASE

A relatively widespread disease in fish of both coldwater and tropical species. It is evident as white spots caused by excessive growth and multiplication of skin cells as a result of virus activity. These spots grow and fuse to form large patches. After some time, the areas fall off, but re-infection occurs in a few weeks. The spots are not the typical mammalian pox lesions which are small blister-like swellings filled with fluid. Generally, the disease is not serious and, apart from retarding growth a little, spontaneous recovery is common. In severe cases, some damage to the skeleton may occur. There is no treatment.

ROUND WORMS *(Nematodes)*

Most species of roundworm live in the intestines of fishes. Some, however, live in other organs, including the muscles and the gas bladder. They cause wasting and lethargy, enteritis and anaemia. Early diagnosis is very important if treatment is to be successful, but sadly the condition is often not recognized until too late. Consult a veterinary surgeon, as cure, although possible, is not easy.

SCALE DISEASE

Although several conditions may cause this symptom, it is usually due to a specific bacteria. It can be contracted by one fish from another but the spread is slow, and requires some damage to the skin before the offending organism can gain entry. Siamese Fightingfish, *Betta splendens*, and members of the Poeciliidae are particularly prone to the disease.

Treatment is difficult, but antibiotics do produce cures in some cases. Prevention is the best cure. Prevent damage to the skin which can be caused by rough rocks or bad handling.

SKIN FLUKES

Skin flukes of freshwater fish are microscopic flat worms belonging mainly to two families, the Gyrodactylidae and the Dactylogyridae. There are many other species which attack marine fish. They are unpleasant parasites, armed with hooks which they force into the skin. Once attached, they consume the fish's body cells, causing damage and opening the body defences to secondary infection. They are able to inflict considerable damage resulting in death. Some flukes primarily attack the skin, while others concentrate their efforts on the gills. Victims of these infections show fading body colour with drooping, battered fins. The skin produces excessive slime and there are blood-stained ulcers where the parasite has attacked. The damage to the gills causes difficulty in obtaining sufficient oxygen. They gape in an attempt to breathe and the operculum is wide open. Afflicted fish are sluggish and tend to stay near the surface. Untreated infections commonly result in death. Diagnosis depends on a microscopic examination of the skin slime of afflicted fish.

These unpleasant parasites are commonly found on the Cyprinidae, Cyprinodontidae and the Characidae. Successful treatment depends on prompt recognition of disease, accurate diagnosis, and correct treatment. The safest and commonest treatment is methylene blue, see *Velvet Disease*, which may either be added to the home tank or added to a hospital tank. Other treatments include a 3 per cent salt solution for 20 minutes, a 1·2000 solution of ammonia for 10 minutes, particularly useful for coldwater species, and formaldehyde at the rate of 0·2ml. of formalin (40 per cent formaldehyde) to 4·5 litres. The latter treatment, which is unsuitable for coldwater species, should be given in a hospital tank for three days and then the solution should be re-made and again the fish left for three days. A one-hour bath at 1ml. of formalin per 4·5 litres is also effective and should also be repeated after three days.

SKIN SPOTS

Several species of fish have been found to have bacterial

infections of the skin which produce a variety of lesions. There may be white or red coloured spots, red patches, swellings and ulcers, all of which can have a secondary infection of fungus, see *Fungus Disease of Skin*. It seems that infection is commonest at the mating season, possibly as a result of hormonal changes taking place in the body.

Treatment includes identification of the offending bacteria, a sensitivity test and appropriate antibiotic therapy.

SLIMY SKIN

This is the name given to a skin condition which may be caused by a variety of infections. A grey slime covers the body which effectively dulls the body colour, and causes the fins to fold. See also *Cyclochaetiasis*, *Chilodonelliasis* and *Costiasis*.

SPOROZOANS

To this class of organisms, Sporozoa, belong a great variety of one-celled organisms. It includes the Coccidia – see *Coccidiosis*. A further large sub-class, Neosporidia, contains a large number of organisms which parasitize both freshwater and marine fish. They cause disease by damage to a great variety of tissue cells in the body. In the Goldfish, *Carassius auratus*, for example, some species cause damage to the cornea of the eye, see *Eye*, while others are found in the urinary and reproductive systems of the Three-spined Stickleback, *Gasterosteus aculeatus*. A further organism of the group is responsible for 'boil' disease in barbels, *Barbus* sp. Yet another causes a type of exophthalmus (pop eye) in aquarium fish. The list, while not endless, is certainly legion. Neon Tetra Disease frequently, but not exclusively seen in Neon Tetras, *Paracheirodon innesi*, falls into this group. It is characterized by a white discoloration on the blue fluorescent line in the early stages which spreads. Those which do not immediately succumb become emaciated and develop a cloudy film. White spots on muscle may also be seen.

Treatment of infected fish is difficult. The drug acetarsone, administered in the food, is coupled with potassium permanganate baths. Expert veterinary assistance is a great advantage in these cases. Tanks in which affected fish have been living should be disinfected with a 0·5 per cent solution of potassium permanganate for five days. Plants should be removed and burnt.

TAPE WORMS

Tapeworms, parasitic worms, living in the intestine, are, fortunately, rare in aquarium fishes, since they cause considerable harm when they are present.

A tapeworm consists of a head, or scolex, from which grow a number of segments. The segments are continually produced at the scolex end, and gradually, therefore, move away from the scolex as others form. Each segment is capable of producing eggs and sperms. The eggs become fertilized. When fully ripe, the segment is packed with eggs. These then break off and are passed out with the faeces. The egg must then be eaten by a so-called secondary host, which can be one of a great variety of other animals. If it is so eaten it develops into a cyst within that secondary host and then again has to await being eaten, along with its host, by another victim fish.

Fish afflicted show symptoms of swollen abdomen, lethargy, and sometimes refuse food. They may become infertile. Eventually death occurs.

Several treatments are possible. Consult your veterinary surgeon.

TUBERCULOSIS

This is a reasonably common disease affecting all fish. When afflicted they show a wide variety of symptoms, including apathy, lack of appetite, wasting, and sluggish movement. Other symptoms are exophthalmus, dropsy and rectal prolapse, or areas of ulceration and bleeding. An appearance similar to fin rot may appear. The skin may be pitted and scales may fall out. Body colours may fade. In species which are particularly susceptible, however, death may be the first indication of infection.

A post mortem examination, to reveal the typical tubercules of the disease, is essential for diagnosis, together with microscopic examination to identify the several species of offending bacteria which all belong to the genus *Mycobacterium*. Special staining techniques are required.

Tubercles occur in all parts of the body, penetrating even the skeletal system to cause twisted spines and misshapen head bones. The disease has been known to occur in epidemic proportions. Fortunately the bacteria causing the disease in fish do not cause tuberculosis in man, although reptiles and amphibians are not so lucky, probably because of their cold-blooded metabolism. A small mild ulcerating condition 'swimming pool ulcer', caused by one fish tubercle bacillus, does occasionally afflict man, but it is not serious.

Afflicted fish should be removed from the tank to arrest the spread of the disease. The treatment of tuberculosis in fish is more difficult than in man. Certainly, the first antibiotic used in human treatment, streptomycin, has not proved very effective. Some antibiotics have, however, been used with success. Some are administered by injection, others by the more convenient method of mixing with food.

TWIN WORM DISEASE

This is a small worm but it can be seen with the naked eye. Like some grotesque Siamese twin, it has two heads and two tails, forming an X shape. In fact they are two worms which join together with suckers as youngsters, an arrangement from which there is no divorce. Each worm is herma-phroditic (i.e. having both sexes in one body) and each fertilizes the other worm partner.

They are more common in coldwater species, where they are found in the gills, causing breathing difficulties. Treatment consists of bathing in methylene blue or formaldehyde.

VELVET or RUST DISEASE

Fish suffering from this disease are identified by the pale yellow dust which appears to cover the skin. It is due to a protozoan parasite known as *Oodinium limneticum*. This is a single-celled organism which belongs to a group of protozoa known as flagellates, having one or more long hair-like projections known as flagella. In this case there is one long flagellum which is used for swimming, and a smaller one tucked close to the cell body but also used to aid movement. The body is yellow because it contains a small amount of chlorophyll – the green pigment found in abundance in plants – which enables it, like plants, to photosynthesize its own food. While living free it is ovoid. When it finds a fish, it holds on with its long flagellum and sends out small finger-like projections into the skin or gills, giving the parasite a firm hold. Its body becomes pear-shaped. In this parasitic condition, it gets most of its food from the skin cells. When it has reached full size it becomes round and surrounds itself with a protective coat or cyst. Inside this coat it divides to produce over 250 new young cells. These grow flagella, become oval in shape and, bursting free from their protective coat, swim off to find more fish skin to infect. Adult fish are more able to withstand Velvet infection. It is young fish which are most vulnerable to the infection.

Fortunately, Velvet Disease readily succumbs to treatment. Methylene blue can be used in identical ways to that suggested for Ichthyophthiriasis. Afflicted fish are best put in a separate tank containing methylene blue for at least two weeks. Other treatments include malachite green – 4 drops of 1 per cent solution to every 16 litres of water, or acriflavine – 1mgm to every 40 litres of water, and solutions of copper sulphate. The latter treatment is not without its dangers since copper is very toxic to fish, and is therefore rarely advisable.

Oodinium pillularis closely resembles *O. limneticum*, but produces a grey powder rather than pale yellow, and the skin shreds off. Since the life cycle of the parasite is affected by temperature and light, these can be used in treating the condition. Afflicted fish should be placed in a 3 per cent salt bath for 20 minutes. They should then be placed in a clean well-aerated hospital tank which should be in darkness to help tranquilize the fish. The home tank in which the parasites remain should be brightly lit and the temperatures raised to 32°C. for 48 hours. The afflicted fish should be given a second salt water bath before returning to their home tank.

In marine fish a different species of *Oodinium* – *O. ocellatum* – is found. It is primarily a parasite of the gills although it will spread to the skin. It has a life-cycle identical to *O. limneticum* which causes Velvet Disease in freshwater fish.

The parasite causes small areas of inflammation on the gill tissue which eventually leads to small areas of dead tissue. This allows opportunist bacteria entry and the fish is soon faced with both a parasitic and a bacterial infection. The first symptoms of trouble are gasping as a result of lack of oxygen which inevitably follows the damage to the gills, see *Respiration*, and the consequential rising to the surface. The fish becomes weak and eventually dies.

Early treatment is essential if success is to be achieved since extensive damage to gills will soon cause suffocation. If treatment is commenced early enough it is usually successful. In order to make as much oxygen as possible available to the fish, the temperature should be lowered slowly, since cold water will hold more dissolved oxygen than warm. The tank should be kept dark for the tranquilizing effect produced. Methylene blue as described for Ichthyophthiriasis above is effective in most cases, treatment being continued for at least two weeks. The treatment is best carried out in a well-aerated clean hospital tank.

Copper sulphate at the rate of 1ml. of a 0·08 per cent solution per litre is most effective but below toxic levels for the fish. The fish again should be placed in a hospital tank with good aeration and they should be starved. Treatment should continue for 10 days at a temperature of 25–26°C. to speed up the life cycle of the parasite, after which the fish should be kept in clean salt water in a hospital tank for a further two weeks before returning to the main tank, which should have been unoccupied for the three-week period. Remember that living invertebrates are very susceptible to copper and will die in the concentration mentioned above for treatment.

VIRUS DISEASES

Viruses are very small particles, with a few exceptions, smaller than can be seen under a normal microscope, which live and multiply within cells of the body. They are on the border between living organisms and non-living chemicals. Some form crystals like chemicals, others multiply, which is a characteristic exclusive to living things. Viruses may be examined using the electron microscope. Some viruses are solely responsible for disease, others weaken the body tissues allowing secondary bacteria to invade and exacerbate the condition. A few of the more important diseases in which viruses are implicated alone or in combination with bacteria include Dropsy, Lymphocystis and Pox, see under separate headings. Undoubtedly, there are others and, as veterinary science focuses attention on the diseases of fish, more will be discovered and more solutions found.

Display see *Showing*

Distichodus Citharinidae ⊕
– *sexfasciatus* SIX-BARRED DISTICHODUS 25cm. (10in.)
One of the smaller members of this genus that is sometimes imported. As a young fish it makes an attractive member of a community tank. The deep body is a very lovely golden colour. Several dark bars cross the body vertically. All the fins are red except the pectorals which are clear. There is a small adipose fin.

They come from Zaïre.

Distribution
Why fish are often restricted to certain areas of the world and not spread evenly throughout all water, since ultimately, with the exception of some inland lakes, all water is connected, is a common question. The answer is simple with regard to freshwater fish. For example, a species living in a river in America cannot cross the Atlantic to a river in Europe even though the European waters may be perfectly suitable for their existence.

To understand the limitations of distribution one must appreciate the basic concept of evolution, see *Evolution*, concerning an animal's adaptation, by evolutionary processes, to the environment in which it finds itself. If a species evolves, for example, in warm salt water at a certain salinity, depending for food on a particular kind of algae only found in that area, its distribution is clearly restricted to that locality. A move to cold water would be as impossible as would a move to areas where its algal food is not to be found.

Marine fishes are thus kept to certain areas of the oceans. Fish living in the tropical seas of the Atlantic cannot move to similar areas in the Pacific Ocean since it would mean swimming around the bottom of South America through much colder water. Marine fish are further restricted to certain depths of ocean. Some fish are adapted to live close to the surface. Evolution has equipped others to medium depths while a further group, the bathypelagic fishes, with black or red coloration, wide mouths and small eyes live at greater depths. Finally a group of fish have become adapted to a stratum close to the ocean floor. Few of the fish which live in the surface layer are found in the really cold waters of the polar regions. Knowledge of those species living close to

the floor of the oceans – abyssal fishes – is still rather scant owing to the difficulties man has in reaching sufficient depths to study them. Some of these species which live close to the sea bottom, are restricted by submarine mountain ranges. Fish which live in enclosed waters, like the Mediterranean Sea, are equally restricted.

By far the greatest majority of species live close to the shores within the waters covering continental shelves. At the edge of all continental shelves, some 180m. (600ft) below the surface, there is a rapid falling away to the ocean floor over 6,100m. (20,000ft) below. As the shelf falls away, so the numbers of species decline.

Tropical seas, which can be divided into two main biological areas, the Atlantic and the Indo-Pacific, contain the greatest diversity of fish species. The Indo-Pacific extends from the east coast of Africa through the Indian Ocean to include Australia and on through the Pacific to the west coast of America. This vast area of water contains a great variety of species and genera, far greater than the Atlantic region.

Because of the extensive coast lines of the Indo-Pacific shore, some living species have been able to extend their distributions to include regions as far apart as the Red Sea and the islands of the south Pacific.

In the Atlantic some species of shore living fish are common to both the West African coast and the east coast of America, presumably having been able to cross the ocean at some time in history.

As we have seen, variations in water temperature act as an effective barrier to fish migrations. These temperature regions are also affected by water currents. The cold water current of Labrador meets the warm water of the Gulf Stream in the north Atlantic to produce sudden changes in temperature from cold to tropical. The fish species inhabiting respective areas are correspondingly different. The Gulf Stream carries warm water to the coasts of Europe and the British Isles maintaining warmer water than would otherwise be expected and again the variety and distribution of the species of fish respond to the environmental conditions.

Many apparent anomalies where the same species, or very closely related species, are found in two areas of water which are totally separated by land can be explained only if one examines prehistoric conditions. Some species, for example, common to the east and west coast of America had free range when Central America was under water, long before the isthmus of Panama restricted movement. Similarly some species of sub-Arctic fish common to the Atlantic and the Pacific are known to have had a continuous distribution along the north coasts of Europe to the north coasts of Asia in bygone eras when warmer climates existed in the Arctic Ocean.

The complex life histories of some fish affect their distribution. Fish such as the eel, *Anguilla anguilla*, and members of the salmon family, *Salmonidae*, spend some time in fresh water and some in the sea. The eel, for example, can be found struggling across the damp grass of an English meadow making for an isolated pond, or swimming in the tropical seas close to Bermuda in the western Atlantic. The Salmon, *Salmo salar*, can be found in the cold waters of the Icelandic coast or in fast running freshwater rivers of Europe or North America up which it travels to breed.

It can readily be seen that a great variety of factors influences the distribution of a fish species. Sometimes the story is lost in evolution, sometimes in geological changes. It may be affected by the temperature of the water by the depth of the ocean, by currents and by salinity. The ability of the species to adapt to environmental changes like salinity may in some cases restrict its distribution or in others permit wide areas of colonization.

DOLLARFISH
  see *Metynnis*
  SILVER see *Mylossoma argenteum*
Domestication see *History of Domestication*
DOMINO DAMSELFISH see *Dascyllus trimaculatus*

Doradidae   ARMOURED CATFISH
A group of Armoured Catfish from Brazil. They charac-teristically have the ability to make short grunting noises by a special mechanism which includes the gas bladder. A series of plates along the side of these fish are all armed with a spine. In some species there are additional lines of plates above and below the main one. The pectoral fins are also armed with spines on their inner aspect, which they can clap against their sides to capture the enemy or prey, so watch your fingers which can be badly mangled. They are also excellent scavengers. An adipose fin is present but without a spine. They build nests and both parents take an interest in the eggs' welfare. Temperatures in the region of 27°C. suit them best. They are not well suited to the community tank. See *Acanthodoras*, *Doras*.

Doras   Doradidae   ⊕
– asterifrons   11cm. (4½in.)
A grotesque looking fish from central and eastern Brazil. It is endowed with an extravagance of barbels and some exotic brown markings. A nocturnal species that will spend all day buried in the sand or under cover, foraging at night.

Dormitator   Eleotridae   Ψ/⊕
– latifrons   BROAD-HEADED SLEEPER   25cm. (10in.)
A native of the west coast of the Americas from California

to Ecuador. Its natural environment is brackish water. The general body colour is brown with several rows of orange brown spots along its sides. The fins are green and the dorsal and anal fins are decorated with red spots. It has a large head in relation to body size. All sleepers are ravenous feeders.
– maculatus   SPOTTED or FAT SLEEPER, SPOTTED GOBY
25cm. (10in.)
A native of the eastern coast of the Americas from Virginia to Brazil. It lives there in both brackish and fresh water.

A grey body is patterned with dark horizontal stripes. It has two dorsal fins and an attractively rounded tail edged with blue. Clear fins are spotted with blue and a blue spot is placed behind the operculum.

Suitable, if a little large for the community tank, but rather timid.

Breeding is very rare in captivity. Eggs are attached to stones cleaned by the fish. It adapts to water anywhere between 18–30°C.

DOTTY BACKS see *Pseudochromidae*
DRAGONETS see *Callionymidae*
DRAGONFISH see *Pseudocorynopoma doriae*
DRAGONFLY LARVAE see under *Unwelcome Visitors –*
  Odonata
DRAGON WRASSE see *Hemipteronotus taeniurus*
Dropsy see *Disease*
Duckweed
  see under *Plants – Lemna*
  Three-pointed see under *Lemna*
DUNCKER'S BARB see *Barbus dunckeri*
DWARF
  BARB see *Barbus gelius*, *Barbus phutunio*
  CATFISH see *Corydoras hastatus*
  CICHLID, AGASSIZ'S see *Apistogramma agassizi*
  CICHLID, AMAZON YELLOW see *Apistogramma pertense*
  CICHLID, BUTTERFLY see *Microgeophagus ramirezi*
  CICHLID, COCKATOO see *Apistogramma cacatuoides*
  CICHLID, LATTICE see *Nannacara taenia*
  CLIMBINGFISH see *Ctenopoma nanum*
  DANIO see *Brachydanio nigrofasciatus*
  FLAG GROUPER see *Pseudochromis gutmanni*
  GOURAMI see *Colisa lalia*
  GOURAMI, CROAKING see *Trichopsis pumilus*
  GROUPERS see *Pseudochromidae*
  GROUPER, YELLOW see *Pseudochromis flavescens*
  LIONFISH see *Dendrochromis brachypterus*
  MINNOW see *Heterandria formosa*
  PANTHERFISH see *Pseudochromis punctatus*
  PENCILFISH see *Nannostomus marginatus*
  PIKE see *Belonesox belizanus*
  RUSH, JAPANESE see under *Plants – Acorus*

SEAHORSE see *Hippocampus zosterae*
SUCKING CATFISH see *Otocinclus affinis*
SUNFISH see *Elassoma evergladei*
SWORD PLANT see under *Plants – Lagenandra*

EARTHEATER,
    MOTHER OF PEARL see *Geophagus brasiliensis*
    POINTED-HEAD see *Geophagus acuticeps*
EARTH-EATING DEVILFISH see *Geophagus jurupari*
Earthworm see under *Food*

Echidna Muraenidae Ψ
– zebra ZEBRA MORAY EEL 1·2m. (4ft)
As the name suggests, the body is marked with zebra-like
patterns of deep purple, black and white. It is a startling, if
uncolourful fish. It comes from the Indo-Pacific and Red
Sea. Beware of its teeth, though these are not as formidable
as other morays'. They are carnivorous and should be fed
on pieces of fish or meat.

Echinoderms see under *Marine Invertebrates*
Echinodorus see under *Plants*

Ecology
Ecology is the study of a total environment. The relationship of all species of animal and plant in a given area with
their physical surroundings. An understanding of ecological principles is essential to an aquarist's success since
the aquarium itself constitutes a small ecological unit.

EEL,
    BARBER see *Plotosus lineatus*
    BLUE RIBBON see *Rhinomuraena ambonensis*
    GYMNOTID see *Gymnotidae*
    LEOPARD see *Acanthophthalmus kuhli*
    MORAY see *Muraenidae*
    SPINY see *Macrognathus aculeatus, Mastacembelidae*
    ZEBRA MORAY see *Echidna zebra*
EGG-LAYING TOOTHCARPS see *Cyprinodontidae*
Egg Yolk see under *Food*
EGYPTIAN MOUTH-BROODER see *Hemihaplochromis multicolor*
EIGHT-BANDED BUTTERFLYFISH see *Chaetodon octofasciatus*
EINTHOVEN'S RASBORA see *Rasbora einthoveni*

Elassoma Centrarchidae
– evergladei PYGMY or DWARF SUNFISH, PYGMY PERCH
2·5cm. (1in.)
As the specific name suggests it comes from the Everglades
in Florida and as far north as the Carolinas.

An attractive little fish, the male has a fine anal fin
and excels himself with his dorsal which is large and of
flamboyant shape. The tail fin is rounded. Out of the
breeding season the body is dark green with metallic flashes
and dark vertical bars. At breeding time a velvet black coat
is donned which is covered in green and gold sequins, and
the vertical bars become a rich sea green. The female has a
drab green brown body with a few spots of black and only
the merest touch of rouge on her body. Temperatures
anywhere between 6°C. and 28°C. are tolerated.

The male builds a plant nest near the bottom and then
performs a fish's equivalent of a belly dance before the
female until she deposits her eggs in the nest, whereupon he
dashes over to fertilize them. She repeats this performance
several times a day for a week. The young hatch in about 48
hours. Parents may consume young in captivity and so are
best removed.

ELEGANT RASBORA see *Rasbora lateristriata*
Eleocharis see under *Plants*
ELECTRIC
    BLUE DAMSELFISH see *Pomacentrus coeruleus*
    CATFISH see *Malapterurus eletricus*

Electrophoridae
Some Taxonomists choose to separate the Electric Eel,
Electrophorus electricus, into this separate family on its
own. It is more common to include it with the Knifefish. See
Gymnotidae.

Eleotridae SLEEPERS
The characteristics of this family are identical with the
family Gobiidae except that the pelvic fins are quite separate
and do not form a sucker device. They have been classified
under Gobiidae rather than being placed in a separate
family. Most members of the family are found in sea or
brackish environments but a few live in fresh water. They
have eyes which appear opaque in some lights and are
nocturnal, resting during daylight hours among the plants.
This gives them their popular name – Sleepers.

All species are carnivorous and like a large volume of live
food. Temperatures between 21–26°C. suit them best.
Sexing is extremely difficult. See *Dormitator, Hypseleotris,
Mogurnda, Oxyeleotris*.

ELEPHANTFISH see *Mormyridae*
Elodea see under *Plants*

Embryology

Embryology is the study of an animal's development from the moment it is conceived by union of a sperm to an egg until it becomes an independent individual by either hatching or emerging from the protection of its parent's body. Many fish, when they hatch, are still fed from the yolk sac to which they remain attached. Technically this is not a free-living individual and may still be included in an embryological study.

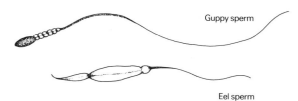

Guppy sperm

Eel sperm

In egg laying species millions of sperms are shed by the male at mating. Large numbers surround each egg in an attempt to penetrate and enter. Only one is successful. The sperm head enters leaving its tail outside and the egg becomes totally impervious to other sperms. The shell hardens in those fish where external fertilization occurs. Entry of the sperm is soon followed by the union of its nucleus with that of the egg. It is here that the chromosomes from the male unite with chromosomes from the female bringing a variety of characteristics to the new fish. The characters are carried in genes which, strung together like beads, make up the chromosome, see *Genetics*. The egg now contains a cell with a nucleus consisting of chromosomal elements from both parents and a large mass of yolk. The

cell divides, first into two cells, then into four, and so on. The mass of cells produced after several cell divisions form themselves into a layer or curved plate of cells which lies on the yolk. This stage is reached in less than six hours. There follows a turning under of the rim of this disc. Continued growth of the rim produces two layers of cells. At the same time the head end and the tail end are established. The next stage is an elongation of the two-layered disc and the minute fish begins to take shape. The primitive internal organs are already being formed. A layer of cells now grows around the yolk forming a yolk sac. There appears within 24 hours a small fold running along the midline of the small fish – the neural plate – which is the beginning of the central nervous system, see *Nervous System*. This gradually turns into a tube. Soon the primitive body segments – somites – represented in adult fish by the muscle blocks, see *Muscles*, differentiate. The brain and eyes are now very apparent. After a few days the heart is formed and it can be seen beating. The pectoral fins begin to appear. The next stage is for the tiny half-formed fish to start moving. This naturally has had to await adequate muscle development. Following the beginnings of movement, the heart can be seen not just beating but actually pumping blood around the young body. The fish baby, now easily recognized as a fish, lies on its balloon of yolk within the shell. The urinary system forms and the liver takes shape. Soon the fins, eyes and mouth can be seen moving. The gas bladder, as an off-shoot of the newly formed food tube or oesophagus, appears. Many fish hatch at this point, still with a large yolk sac, on which they are to feed for a few days, attached. Development continues and the gas bladder grows. Gradually the yolk sac disappears as its food supply is used up and the small fish becomes a free-living individual.

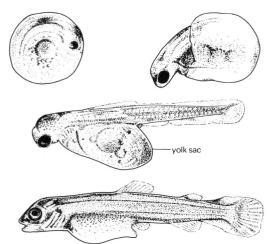

Development of egg into fry showing reabsorbtion of the yolk sac.

yolk sac

EMERALD
    CATFISH see *Brochis splendens*
    FILEFISH see *Oxymonacanthus longirostris*
    TRIGGERFISH see *Balistapus undulatus*
EMPEROR
    TRIGGERFISH, YELLOW-STRIPED see *Balistapus undulatus*
    ANGELFISH see *Pomacanthus imperator*
    SNAPPER see *Lutjanus sebae*
    TANG see *Acanthurus xanthopterus*
    TETRA see *Nematobrycon palmeri*
Enchytraeus see under *Food*

Endocrine System

The body's various activities are under the control of both the central nervous, see *Nervous System*, and the endocrine systems.

    The endocrine system of fish includes a number of so

called endocrine glands which discharge their chemical secretions – hormones – into the blood stream.

The endocrine glands and the nervous system interact in a complex way. For example, spring, in some species, will be appreciated by the sensory systems which will inform the brain via the appropriate nerves. The brain is in close communication with the master endocrine gland, the pituitary, which, in turn, controls the other glands with its blood-borne secretions. The pituitary, aware that it is spring, tells the testes and ovaries to get ready for action. When the action has occurred messages are relayed to the pituitary via the brain and nerves. The pituitary tells the testes and ovaries to shut down for the time being and it may instruct the other glands to assist the body in taking care of the young. For example, the skin secretions of the Discus, *Symphysodon discus*, which provide food for the young, are probably under endocrine control.

This complex inter-relationship between the environment, the nervous system and the endocrine system is fascinating. A considerable amount of work still needs to be done before anything approaching a full understanding is attained.

Enteritis see under *Disease*

Ephippidae SPADEFISHES, BATFISHES
A small family of tropical and warm water fishes with very laterally compressed bodies. They live among reefs and feed on molluscs. Until recently, spadefishes and batfishes were placed in separate families Ephippidae and Platacidae respectively. The former have separate spiny dorsal fins while the latter have large elongated dorsal and anal fins giving them a lovely and unmistakable appearance. Young batfishes and spadefishes mimic floating leaves or unpleasant tasting invertebrates as a camouflage. Several species of batfish have been described here, but some authorities believe them to be variants of the same species. See *Platax*.

Epinephelus Serranidae Ψ ✕
– ***flavocaeruleus*** POWDER BLUE GROUPER 50cm. (20in.)
One of the most beautiful of this family with a texture and delicacy of colour, as suggested by the name, that seems wasted on the creatures of the deep. It comes from the Indian and Pacific oceans. Some other members of this genus grow to over 3m. (10ft) in length and are aggressive towards man so be a little careful when purchasing young specimens.

Epiplatys Cyprinodontidae ⊕
– ***dageti monroviae*** REDJAW or FIREMOUTH KILLY, CHAPERS PANCHAX 5cm. (2in.)

A native to West Africa with a general body colour of greeny brown in the male attained by mottled green and brown patches on each scale. The lower half of the body is coloured blue. Vertical dark bars traverse the body. The fins are beige in colour with a variety of dark dots and patches and the anal and tail fins are attractively marked with dark borders. The male is more beautiful than the female, and has a red lower lip and throat, which extends to the fin colour and the pointed elongation of the lower border of the tail fin.

A peaceful member of the community tank, the fish inhabits the upper quarter of the water. Temperatures around 24°C. suit. A typical plant spawner of the family, see *Cyprinodontidae*.

This species is often confused with *E. chaperi*, which is very similar, but without the red mouth and throat. **73**
– ***fasciolatus*** STRIPED PANCHAX or BANDED EPIPLATYS 8cm. (3in.)
A West African cyprinodont with a lovely body shape. The brownish body flecked with red is transected vertically with 10 dark bars and horizontally by a line from the operculum to the tail. The greenish yellow fins are spotted with red dots and the tail and pelvic fins are bordered in red. The female has a more washed out look to her colours and is without borders to the fins.

Lives happily in a community tank kept at temperatures around 21–26°C. where it frequents the upper water regions. A typical plant spawner.

– ***longiventralis*** 6cm. (2½in.) ⊙
An unspectacular cyprinodont from the Niger delta, West Africa. A dark back shades through green sides to a yellow belly. Often has red flecking on the unpaired fins and vertical bars on the body. Sexually distinguished by the shape of fins, in the male the dorsal and anal fins are pointed, whereas in the female they are rounded.

A relatively small fish, it makes a peaceful, if uncolourful, addition to the community tank where it inhabits the surface quarter. Likes temperatures around 21–23°C. and bright lights. A plant spawner, its eggs develop in 10–20 days.
– ***macrostigma*** BIGSPOT KILLY 5cm. (2in.) ◍
This is a smallish fish from Zaïre. Its brown back shades to a blue belly. It gets its popular name from the deep red proportionately large spots on its sides which also spill over to adorn the greenish blue fins. The dorsal and tail fins are bordered with red.

A peaceful, hesitant fish which is well suited to the aquarium tank kept at temperatures around 24°C., as long as plenty of shade or secluded lighting is provided. **74**
– ***sexfasciatus*** SIX BANDED PANCHAX 10cm. (4in.)
Rather similar to *E. fasciolatus*, this species also comes from

West Africa, and makes a drab but peaceful inhabitant of the community tank. Prefers water near the surface preferably around 21–23°C. A plant spawner whose eggs hatch in 10–14 days.

The male can be described as having green back shading to a yellow belly with several, usually six or seven, blue black vertically placed bands on the side. The fins are light brown with dark margins and the pelvic fins are long and pointed. The female is dowdy.

Equetus Sciaenidae Ψ
– *acuminatus* CUBBYU 23cm. (9in.)
An attractive fish from the western Atlantic and Caribbean. It is found off the coast of Florida, as far south as the east coast of Brazil.

A bright silvery body is distinctively marked with very dark brown longitudinal lines. The body is deep. The dorsal fin is double with a short based first portion, somewhat elongated. The second part has a very long base. The anal fin is small and triangular.

A fairly common import into the USA. It lives in and around reefs and this kind of environment should be provided in the aquarium.
– *lanceolatus* JACKKNIFEFISH 23cm. (9in.)
A really remarkable fish from the Caribbean, the coast of Florida and the tropical western Atlantic from South Carolina to Brazil. Sadly this fish is all too rarely found on sale in the UK but is often available in the USA.

The body domes dorsally about one third of the way along its length. From this high point a very tall, short-based dorsal fin rises, giving a very unusual and very elegant shape to the body. The body is coloured a light beige. A dark brown band starts at the base of the dorsal fin and passes backwards, gradually narrowing as it goes, and continues onto the rounded caudal fin. Also from the base of the dorsal fin it passes up the fin to the tip, narrowing as it goes. This dark band is bordered on both sides by pale edges. A second dark brown band passes from a point just anterior to the dorsal fin across the body and onto the long pelvic fins. Finally a third band passes vertically through the eye. The dorsal and anal fins are beige like the body. The head has yellow highlights.

Esomus Cyprinidae ⊕
– *dandica* FLYING BARB 10cm. (4in.)
The popular name is no misnomer; this fish will jump out of water with an ease which has surprised many aquarists, so be warned and keep the tank covered. However, it really isn't a barb. It is one of the larger fish for a community tank, but gets on well in spite of this apparent handicap. It has two pairs of barbels, the lower of which reaches backwards to the pelvic fins. A dark band, bordered above by a gold

line, separates a greenish back from silvery sides, and there is a small red spot at the base of the tail. It comes from India, Sri Lanka and Burma.

They are prolific breeders, best accommodated for this purpose in a tank with only a few inches of water. The bottom cover should be marbles or large stones to conceal the dropped eggs. Temperatures around 27°C. are preferred. Breeding begins when the male unceremoniously nudges the side of a chosen female. She returns the compliment to stimulate release of his spermatozoa for fertilization. Inclined to infanticide, so remove parents after egg laying is complete. The eggs hatch in 24–48 hours but the fry are difficult to raise. A constant supply of very small live food is one of the essentials for their success.
– *malayensis* STRIPED FLYING BARB 8cm. (3in.)
Probably more suitable for the aquarium than *E. dandica* because of its smaller size, this fish is not unlike its close cousin. It can be distinguished by a less distinctive side band and larger, deeper red coloured spot on the base of the tail, and the presence of a black spot at the base of the anal fin. It behaves very much as does *E. dandica* but is the more attractive of the two.

Establishing a Coldwater Tank
The principles for establishing a coldwater tank are identical to those for establishing a freshwater tropical tank except that no heating is required. In addition, care should be taken to ensure that cold water plants or plants adapted to cold water conditions are used – see *Plants*.

Sadly the goldfish *Carassius auratus*, one of the most popular fish kept as a pet, is all too often kept in a round bowl. Since fish use dissolved oxygen for respiration (see *Respiration*) and this oxygen is dissolved at the surface, it is important that as large a surface area as possible relative to the volume of water, is available. The goldfish bowl clearly does not provide adequate surface area when filled since the large volume has only a very small surface where oxygen can be dissolved from the air and carbon dioxide given off. In addition the bowl affords no cover for the fish which is exposed on all sides to light from which it cannot escape. This lack of security may well create feelings of psychological insecurity in the fish which are clearly detrimental to its welfare. Do not keep fish in a bowl.

There are several other fish commonly kept in cold water aquaria, and descriptions will be found under the appropriate headings. These are: the Domestic Goldfish, *Carassius auratus*, the Crecian Carp, *Carassius carassius*, the Three-spined Stickleback, *Gasterosteus aculeatus*, the Gudgeon, *Gobio fluviatilis*, the Golden Orfe or Ide, *Leuciscus idus*, the Minnow, *Phoxinus phoxinus*, the Bitterling, *Rhodeus amarus*, the Golden Rudd, *Scardinus orythrophthalmus*, and the Golden Tench, *Tinca tinca*.

Establishing a Tropical Freshwater Tank

Having decided upon the type and size of tank you want, see *Tanks*, and settled where, see *Positioning the Tank*, and on what it should be sited, see *Stands*, then comes the moment which is one of the best moments in the aquarist's life – establishing a new tank. There is a great feeling of creativity and a sense of achievement in designing and working out an aesthetic combination of sand, rock, plant and, of course, fish.

The tank should be thoroughly rinsed out if new and disinfected as well if it has housed fish previously. It should then be placed empty in its permanent position. To carry a full tank around is fraught with danger. It can split the glass, damage the fish, and most important break your back, since anything but the smallest tank is almost impossible to lift. Having settled it in position, put in the under gravel filter plate, if one is to be used. Next, in the kitchen, pour some gravel, obtainable from all dealers, into a bucket, until it is about one-third full. Then fill the bucket two-thirds full of warm water. Now plunge your hand among the gravel and churn it round and round. The water will probably become very dirty. Empty the water and repeat until the water in the bucket stays clear. This can be a long tedious job, since 10–15 water changes are sometimes necessary. People with delicate skin should protect their hands with rubber gloves, because the process is hard on skin and nails. Gravel which has been used previously should be washed clean, using no soap or detergent, and then boiled to sterilize it. When satisfied that the gravel or sand is clean and sterile place it in the tank. Keep repeating this process until it covers the bottom evenly to a depth of about 5cm.

The next step, adding rocks, brings out the artist in you. Great care should be taken to ensure safe rocks are used. They should not, for example, contain calcium in the form of limestone or marble, since this will dissolve in the water. Hard rock which has been weathered is the most suitable. This should again be washed and, if any doubt remains about its sterility, boiled for ten minutes. The artistic arrangement of rocks in the tank will do much to enhance the appearance of your exhibit. It is by far the best to use rocks to create different levels in the gravel. To provide a terrace or step, build a wall of rocks and bank the sand or gravel up behind it. Depending on the size of the tank two or three levels can be prepared. Straight lines are usually less attractive than curves or waves. One arrangement is to bring the rock wall out towards the ends of the tank. The original 5cm. of level gravel is now arranged in steps, shallow at the front of the tank in the centre and getting higher behind rock walls towards the back and sides.

Next, the tank must be filled with water. Fill coldwater tanks with cold water, tropical tanks with water at about

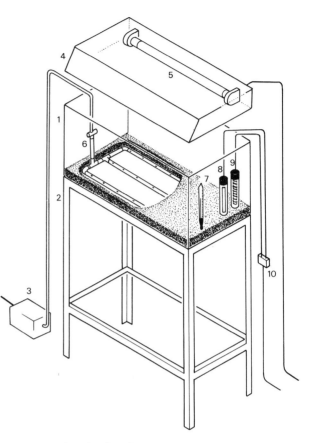

Aquarium layout

1. Tank
2. Tank stand
3. Air pump
4. Tank cover
5. Light
6. Internal filter and aerator
7. Thermometer
8. Thermostat
9. Heater
10. Connecting strip

27°C. Tap water may be used, see *Chlorine*. It should not be poured straight in from a jug but use should be made of a cup and saucer. The saucer is placed on the sand and the cup on the saucer. The water is slowly poured into the cup which overflows gently into the saucer which overflows even more gently into the tank. In this way churning of the sand and destruction of your layout will be avoided. When the tank is filled to within an inch or two of the top take out the cup and saucer.

Plants are now introduced, see *Planting*. The heater, see *Heating*, thermostat, thermometer, see *Thermometers*, where appropriate are added and the aerator and filter, see

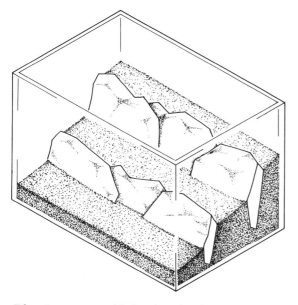

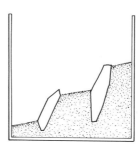

Banked gravel

Filtration, are assembled and put in place. Top up the water, if necessary.

Then follows a frustrating but essential period of waiting. The tank should be allowed to stand in that condition for at least four days. This will ensure that the water matures, chlorine is voided and the plants take root. It also allows the water temperature to stabilize and checks to be made on the efficiency of the electrical apparatus.

After this waiting period you can introduce your fish, see *Acclimatization to Tank*.

Establishing a Tropical Marine Aquarium

The beauty of marine or coral fish commonly kept by aquarists is truly magnificent. Many a person indifferent to the delights of freshwater tropicals has been captivated by their salt water cousins. However, a strong word of caution. Do not embark on the difficult path of the marine aquarist until competence has been gained in the freshwater field. To ignore this advice is to court disaster. It may well incur considerable expense and the death of your delicate marine dependants.

Currently, very few species of marine fish breed in captivity. The notable exception being, of course, the sea horses. This means that virtually every fish introduced into captivity is taken from natural waters. Such harvest rightly gives concern to conservationists. It is up to the marine aquarists to offer something for the pleasure he receives. Ideally, this would be to breed his own supplies of marine fish, and this must be the goal to which all should direct their efforts. Until this reality is achieved the fish in captivity should be treated with the utmost respect and the greatest possible care should be taken to prolong their lives. Their habits and life requirements should be carefully observed

until we can confidently, not only manage our aquaria with a minimum of disease, but replace our fish at the end of their lives by others bred in our own aquaria.

In any of the many fields of biology, and keeping tropical fish is included, there are so-called experts who confound the beginner with an excess of technology, absolute rules and taboos in an attempt to obscure their own lack of understanding and competence. The marine fish hobby is a new and exciting pastime where few really knowledgeable people exist. Indeed a great deal of work still needs to be done before even a basic understanding can confidently be claimed. There are however a surfeit of experts only too willing to pronounce absolute do's and don'ts. Like all biological systems nothing in the aquarium is static. It is in a state of dynamism with constant change and adaptation. The amazing fact to be learned about all forms of life is not how little they will put up with, but how much, see *Adaptability*. The technocratic aquarists referred to above remind me of their counterparts in the musical recording and reproduction field where the quality of the sound becomes more important than the music. Surrounded by an excess of mechanical devices of doubtful value, they become so obsessed with their knob twiddling and testing that they forget to look at the beauty of their fish.

For almost every book one reads where absolute rules are laid down there are other experts who dictate exactly the opposite. Many, finding something works, assume it is the only way, instead of realising that it is just one way. For example some experts get excited about a build up of nitrate which results from protein metabolism. Levels of over 100 parts per litre cause them distress accompanied by furious water changing activities. Other experts will not worry overmuch at levels in excess of ten times that amount. The fish will soon let you know if the level is uncomfortable by their behaviour.

The answer then is trial and error, added to which there should be a large helping of common sense. There are a few general principles and guidelines which will short-circuit some of the pitfalls for the new marine aquarist. However, they are guides not rules, and must be adapted to particular circumstances.

It should be stressed that metal is rapidly corroded by salt water and that dissolved metals can be fatal to fish. Unprotected metal should not be exposed to the water in a marine aquarium. With the growth of the hobby many commercially-produced tanks of excellent quality are available and it is as well to discuss your needs with a competent dealer. Where plate glass is used with protected metal frames, it is as well to check the sealing substance and, if in doubt, re-seal.

The size of tank is a matter of available room space, finance and personal preference, remembering that tank size dictates the number of occupants. The rule, as with freshwater, is the bigger the better. Certainly a tank of less than 90 litres (20 gallons UK) capacity is hardly worth the bother. This is achieved by tank dimensions of, for example, 76cm. × 38cm × 38cm. or 91cm. × 30cm. × 38cm. (30in. × 15in. × 15in. or 36in. × 12in. × 15in.).

Before setting up the tank, thoroughly clean in strong salt water and rinse several times in fresh water. If the tank is not new, exposure to several hours of good sunlight has a strong sterilizing effect.

Siting the tank is, if anything, more important for the well being of marine fish than freshwater, see *Siting the Tank*. Keep out of draughts which cause sudden chilling of the tank and away from intense sunlight; these are the two basic principles.

Before adding anything to the tank it is as well to consider briefly the subject of filtration, see also *Filtration*. Technical aids should be kept to a minimum and are only justified when their value can be truly demonstrated. The amount of sea water available to dilute poisonous substances in the ocean is truly tremendous, and the length of fish per volume of available water is infinitesimal. In the aquarium where such a buffer is not available the toxic substances build up. Carbon dioxide and other waste products of human existence on earth are mostly lost in the vastness of the environment. In a hot and stuffy spaceship, the air available is so limited that, were it not for filtration and plentiful canned supplies of oxygen, the occupants would rapidly die. It is therefore true that, unless you are prepared to have a vast tank with only one or two small fish, the build up of toxic substances will rapidly prove a problem. It would theoretically be possible to dispense with filtration if water was very frequently changed. This

however presents its own problems and is impractical so most of us are forced to accept some form of filtration in our marine tanks.

It is probably impossible to over-filter the tank. A complete cycle of all water every hour is desirable. This means larger filters than commonly used in freshwater systems. There are so many different filter systems with varying modifications that it would be impossible to evaluate all of them. Again, consultation with a competent dealer will help you to choose from those currently available. Some people prefer only outside filters, some an under-gravel filter, and others a combination of the two, see *Filtration*. My preference is for the latter of the two.

It should be placed into the clean tank which has been correctly positioned in the room. Onto this is placed a thin layer of up to 12·7mm. of 4–6mm. diameter gravel. This diameter is not absolute but should be large enough not to fall through the holes in the filter plate. Onto this place finer coral sand. Some fish, notably Wrasses, bury themselves in the sand at night and sharper sand could damage their skins. In addition some of the invertebrate members of a mixed species tank filter the sand and prefer not to gulp in a mouthful of needles. Some experienced marine aquarists layer the under-gravel filter plate with nylon fibre before covering it with gravel or sand. In my opinion this is unnecessary and it rapidly becomes dirty. Cleaning requires the removal of all the sand, a time-consuming and, I feel, pointless task. In freshwater tanks it is customary to terrace the sand using rocks. The under-gravel filter is less efficient in such circumstances but it is common practice in marine tanks to keep the gravel or sand level, or nearly so, perhaps allowing just a slight slope down to the front of the tank.

Before continuing with the mechanics of tank assembly it is worth mentioning that many different substances as well as gravel and sand are used as bottom cover. Anything from black basalt to coloured plastic chips are employed and it is up to the aquarist to experiment to find the medium which is pleasing and best suits the purpose for which it is required.

Now is the time to add the water. If you live near clean relatively, pure sea water, then use it. If not, then use the synthetic substitute. I would not fill a marine tank in the south of England with the diluted sewerage which surrounds that part of our coast.

For the sake of completeness one of the better known salt water formulae is included but there are endless variations and modifications with which the technically-minded can experiment.

Wiedermann-Kramer Formula
In 100 litres of distilled water:
2765 grams sodium chloride (NaCl)
706 grams magnesium sulphate crystals ($MgSO_4$ $7H_2O$)

558 grams magnesium chloride crystals ($MgCl_2\,6H_2O$)
154 grams calcium chloride crystals ($CaCl_2\,6H_2O$)
69·7 grams potassium chloride (KCl)
25 grams sodium bicarbonate ($NaHCO_3$)
10 grams sodium bromide ($NaBr$)
3·5 grams sodium carbonate (Na_2CO_3)
2·6 grams boric acid (H_3BO_3)
1·5 grams strontium chloride ($SrCl_2$)
0·01 grams potassium iodate (KIO_3)

The potassium chloride (KCl) should be dissolved separately with some of the 100 litres as should the calcium chloride ($CaCl_2\,6H_2O$), and they should be added after the other substances have been dissolved. Most of us are, however, not inclined to make our own solution and simply add packets of commercially available sea salts to dechlorinated tap water.

On the levelled gravel or coral sand is placed a sheet of clean plastic. On top place a clean plate or saucer and, finally, on the plate, a cup in just the same way as for filling the freshwater tank. The natural or synthetic salt water previously prepared is now added. Some prefer to place the undissolved salts in the cup and simply fill with distilled or tap water. Either way is quite acceptable but I prefer the former. I once read that one should not use distilled water as it is dead – this is not so. It is, however, more expensive and quite unnecessary. The tap water used should preferably not be too hard. The tank should not be completely filled as room must be left for the rocks and coral decoration.

Since it is rare to use plants in the marine aquarium, we must rely on a combination of rocks, coral and bottom cover for decoration. The rocks should be of the hard insoluble kind. Many marine aquarists experiment freely with rocks to obtain some enchanting effects. Black basalt and pure slate are possibilities and contrast well with white coral. The basic purpose of rock and coral is however, not to decorate the tank but to provide hiding places and thereby psychological security for its inmates. Caves and tunnels in my opinion should abound, since they are equally as important as cleanliness for fish welfare. Further decorative effects can certainly be obtained using coral and large shells. The waters surrounding the Bahama Islands abound in large shellfish known as Conch. Their shells are exotic of shape and colour and add considerably to the beauty of the marine tank. It is important that coral and shells are thoroughly cleaned and purified before placing them in the tank, for even small amounts of dead organic tissue if left will decay and putrefy, causing severe problems. Coral and shells should be washed thoroughly, however well the dealer's label claims they have been prepared, and then placed in a bath of strong bleach for up to two days. They should then be placed in several changes of clean

water over several more days then boiled and finally washed again in several changes of fresh water. Any dead tissue surviving that treatment is harmless to the tank. Before putting it in the aquarium soak well in clean salt water.

Now top up the tank. If natural or prepared synthetic salt water was used, use that for topping up but if a packet of commercially-available salts for use in a set amount of water, usually for use in quantities of 20 gallons, top up with tap or distilled water.

The under-gravel filter is next connected to the air pump. There are normally two air lifts to the filter and the air lines must be adjusted to ensure both are functioning. This is done quite simply by altering the clip provided.

Some aquarists use an external filter in conjunction with an under-gravel filter and it should now be assembled. In place of the normal charcoal used in freshwater filters, see *Filtration*, it is essential to use marine charcoal or one of the ion exchange resins commercially available. Internal filters can be used but are not recommended.

The next step is to install the heating. Some aquarists still prefer to use separate heater and thermostat units but the combined units are quite acceptable and, in my opinion, preferable. Although some units are advertised as totally submersible keep the top out of water as salt water is notoriously efficient at creeping in where it is not wanted. Put the thermometer in place.

The marine aquarium should be covered with a sheet of glass or plastic before the canopy is added. Many of the marine fish are excellent jumpers and could damage themselves against the hot bulbs but more important, the salt water can attack the metal of the canopy or bulbs, forming toxic substances which can kill the fish if they drop into the tank. The canopy should be painted carefully on the inside with non-toxic gloss paint. Any corrosion can result in electrical shorts and dangerous conditions for the aquarist.

The tank is now ready; all its parts are switched on. The heater is heating, the filters filtering and the rocks are stationary and firm. In this state, it should be left for at least three days to settle down. At the end of this time the temperature, pH, and specific gravity can be checked and if all is well, the first one or two hardy fish may be introduced. A note on lighting the tank is appropriate here. Too little is known on this subject as the diverse opinions show. Algae are, however, important components of the marine biosystem and, most aquarists agree, should be encouraged. Adequate light is therefore essential. Conversely, others dictate a minimum of illumination to prevent algae formation. Combinations of fluorescent, coloured if preferred, and tungsten lighting are satisfactory. So much depends on the position of the aquarium, the amount of natural light, state of the aquarium, and length of time that the light is to be used, that hard and fast rules are impossible. Experience and on the spot advice from a competent dealer or fellow enthusiast is invaluable. A rough guide is to provide 80 watts of light for the average 90-litre tank.

With a couple of very small hardy and preferably inexpensive fish in the tank it should be left to mature. A minimum of four weeks should pass before further fish are added. For the technocrats, regular testing with a nitrite kit will indicate the level of maturation. The nitrogenous waste of decaying organic material both uneaten protein and excretory products are broken down by bacteria to ammonium compounds. These are converted by another kind of bacteria to nitrites. Both ammonia and nitrite are poisonous. The nitrites are finally converted to nitrates which are, in this form, utilized by small living organisms including algae and converted into proteins by them. These are then available again as food for fish. The nitrite tests indicates the efficiency and level of bacteria involved in this cycle and is therefore a useful indicator to the maturation of the tank.

Personally I distrust scientific tests and use them only as a guide. If the fish look right and the water smells right, I would be prepared to back my judgment and experience and increase the complement of fishes. Remember here that overcrowding is a serious crime for the aquarist and no amount of gadgetry or technical toys will alleviate the inevitable result – failure. I would allow 15·75 litres (3½ Imp. gallons) for each fish.

To conclude, one can theoretically improve one's marine system by the inclusion of power filters, ozonizers, protein skimmers, ultraviolet sterilizers and several electronically-operated tests for pH, temperature, hardness, and nitrite levels. Some of these are discussed more fully under separate headings – see *Maintaining the Marine Aquarium, Ozonizers, Power Filters, Protein Skimmers, Ultra violet Sterilizers.*

Ethology see *Behaviour*

Etroplus Cichlidae ⊕
– maculatus ORANGE CHROMIDE 8cm. (3in.)
An unusual cichlid in that it is one of few that come from India and Sri Lanka. At its best in the breeding season when it is really beautiful. The basic orange-beige colour gives way to a rich leaf green on the side. The body is adorned with horizontal rows of red dots. Indistinct vertical bars cross the body and a large dark, sometimes blue body spot occurs midway along the body. The fins in general reflect the beige body colour interspersed with a little added red, sometimes with a tendency to yellow. Dark shading and dots enhance their beauty. Blue highlights in the eye give it a wistful look. Small, this is a peaceful creature suitable for community life. Its popularity is limited due to its delicate nature, which is a pity for such a lovely fish.

It breeds at high temperatures around 27°C. but is rather reluctant. The pattern of breeding is typically cichlid. The dark eggs are attached to a stone by a fine filament. The young feed on a mucus secreted by the skin of the adults. **75**
– suratensis GREEN CHROMIDE 30cm. (12in.) ⊕/Ψ
To get the best colour from this fish it is advisable to keep it in slightly salt water although it is found naturally in both brackish and fresh water in India and Sri Lanka. The green body is decorated with a variety of vertical bars and dots of several hues. The fins are slate grey.

Eupomacentrus Pomacentridae Ψ
– planifrons YELLOW DAMSELFISH 13cm. (5in.)
A fish which is commonly kept by aquarists in the USA. The young are a very bright yellow with three black spots on each side, one large one below the dorsal spine, one situated dorsally on the caudal fin, and one at the base of the pectoral fin. The adult gradually looses the brilliance of its colour to become a brownish orange, and with this change the spots tend to fade.

It comes from southern Florida and the Caribbean. In captivity it has proved reasonably successful after a little early reluctance. It seems to do well on small crustacea.

EURASIAN CATFISH see Siluridae
EUROPEAN SEAHORSE see *Hippocampus rambulosus*

Eutropiellus Schilbeidae ⊕
– debauwi CONGO GLASS CATFISH 8cm. (3in.)
Although classified in a different family it bears a very close resemblance to the Glass Catfish *(Kryptopterus bicirrhis)* of India. Its body colour is a lovely sky blue with a dark dorsal band running horizontally, a similar middle band and a fainter vertical band. Three short pairs of barbels surround its mouth. The dorsal fin is set just behind the operculum. The anal fin is very long. The female is fatter than the male, and her colouring is not so bright and well defined.

Behaviourally they are group fish which form very active and attractive shoals. They prefer live food but are omnivorous. No records exist of their having bred in captivity, although sexual differentiation is fairly simple.

Euxiphipops Chaetodontidae Ψ
– navarchus MAJESTIC ANGELFISH 30cm. (12in.)
A gorgeous fish which has a kaleidoscopic mixture of orange and yellow and blue with black markings. It comes from the Pacific region.
– sexstriatus SIX-BARRED ANGELFISH 50cm. (20in.)
An interesting and beautiful fish from the Indo-Pacific. The

body scales are creamy brown with a central blue grey patch. The head, as far back as the operculum, is a dark grey black. There follows a variable number, though usually six, of vertical dark bars. The posterior part of the dorsal and anal fins and the caudal fin are black with blue dots. A white vertical bar descends just behind the eye three-quarters of the depth of the body. The body is triangular in shape when viewed laterally. Does well in captivity, although large. **76**

–xanthometopon   YELLOW-FACED ANGELFISH
30cm. (12in.)
This lovely species is found in the Indo-Australian Archipelago and the Pacific Ocean. A chequered career has seen it classified in the *Holocanthus* genus and as a *Heteropyge* but taxonomists currently place it in the genus *Euxiphipops*.

Each of the body scales is a rich dark green-brown bordered by a bright yellow gold. A patch around the eye, the pectoral fins and a diffuse area anterior to the pelvic fins are coloured gold. From the jaws as far back as the operculum is covered with a network of blue on yellow giving a gaudy, almost unreal, appearance. The pelvic fins are rather elongated and their leading edges are blue. The anal fin is also bordered with blue.

It takes well to captivity but likes space and is better kept alone. Takes almost any live food and algae. **77**

Evolution
In the middle of the last century Charles Darwin rocked scientific thinking and outraged religious philosophy with the theory of evolution published in his great work *The Origin of Species*. Since then it has become accepted by the majority of thinking people prepared to examine the evidence, that all the great variety of animals alive today, and those which are now extinct, evolved gradually over many millions of years. The converse hypothesis that each species was created separately is now regarded as untenable.

The basic concept of evolution which must be understood is that, in order to survive, an individual must be suited to the environment in which it finds itself. A committed freshwater fish suddenly finding itself in salt water will die, since it has not the necessary mechanisms to deal with salt. For a species to survive, the individual must meet a fish of the opposite sex, after it has reached maturity, and mate to produce live offspring which again are fitted to the environment into which they hatch or are born.

Evolution is a very gradual process. A slight change in the environment, for example, a small change of climate or a slight variation in salinity will not necessarily kill the fish which live there. However, since individuals within a species differ in their ability to stand cold or heat or salt, some will find themselves better able to adapt to the change than

others. In addition small changes or mutations which occur in the genes, see *Genetics*, will, over many hundreds of thousands of years, slightly modify some members of the species, enabling them to better adapt to the new environment. The effect is to gradually change the species until it is composed of individuals better adapted to the new environmental conditions. This process has been continuing for hundreds of millions of years.

Fish were the first vertebrates to appear on earth. They evolved from simpler invertebrate forms probably some 500 million years ago. Four hundred million years ago, in Silurian times, the two great fish groups, Agnatha the jawless fish, and Gnathostomata the jawed fish, were already well established. The jawless fish didn't stop suspended in evolution, they went on evolving. Many types, unable to adapt to the great variety of environmental changes they encountered, became extinct. Others survived and developed into the lampreys and hagfishes alive today.

The jawed fishes, Gnathostomata, were more successful. They spread wide like the branches of a tree. Very early in fish evolution the two main trunks, the bony fishes, Osteichthyes, and the cartilaginous fishes, Chondrichthyes, separated. The former developed into the great range of bony fishes we know today, and sent off great branches which were to evolve into amphibians, reptiles, mammals and birds. The Chondrichthyes evolved into the sharks and rays.

On their way through time species on many branches died out, unable to adapt to changes in environment.

It is important to remember that the amphibians, reptiles, birds and mammals developed from branches of the evolutionary tree. Fish didn't stop evolving as soon as the first amphibian emerged, but continued the evolutionary process in the water and are still, today, evolving. It is difficult to be exact about time, but it has been said that for a new species to become a definite entity can take up to one million years. Thus, some of the latest fish species to evolve are probably no older than some of the newest species of mammal.

As we have seen in genetics, see *Genetics*, the genes are responsible for passing on the characteristics of the parents to the offspring, half coming from the male and half from the female. Most of the time the gene faithfully reproduces in the offspring the characters of the parents. However, the essential element of evolution is change. This is achieved by small variations in the genes called mutations. As a result of a mutation the offspring may have slightly longer legs than either parent, slightly shorter tail, marginally smaller ears, fractionally darker body colour. If these changes better adapt the individual to its environment then it and its descendants will become the dominant form and the older less successful type will gradually, over many generations, be replaced. A slight change will become established. Conversely, and this is as likely as the alternative, the mutation may make the animal less successful, in which case the mutation will be lost since any animals which carry its effects will not survive.

Evolution then, rarely if ever, takes place with large dramatic changes. Essentially it results from a combination of minute variations over millions of years.

Evorthodus Gobiidae ⊕
– breviceps

This typical member of the family of freshwater gobies from Trinidad and Surinam is a scavenger. They have an unusual head action when feeding which makes them look as if they are craning their neck for food and they swim in a series of leaps. The male has an elongated anterior posture of the dorsal fin. They are useful members of a community tank being peaceful and, although scavengers, they do not stir up the sediment at the bottom. They prefer temperatures between 21–24°C. Have not bred in captivity.

Excretion see *Osmoregulation and Excretion*

Exocoetidae FLYINGFISHES, HALFBEAKS

The flyingfishes and halfbeaks were previously classified in two separate families, the halfbeaks in Hemirhamphidae and the flyingfishes in Exocoetidae. The great majority of halfbeaks are found in marine habitats although a few are found in fresh water. The latter are confined to south-east Asia and Indonesia. Their name comes from the unusual anatomical construction of the jaws, the lower jaw is much longer than the upper jaw and is prolonged into a slender 'beak'. The marine species lay eggs while most of the few species which live in freshwater bear live young.

Flyingfish are included in this family, but for obvious reasons they are not suitable aquarium fishes. See *Dermogenys*.

Exodon Characidae ⊕
– paradoxus EXODON 13cm. (5in.) ✂

A medium sized, rarely seen, characin coming from the Amazon. It has a greenish-grey body with purple highlights. There are very large round black spots, which characterize this fish, one on the shoulder and one on the tail. With the exception of the tail fin which is red, the fins are yellow. Like the Siamese Fightingfish, *Betta splendens*, one individual makes a happy addition to the community tank, since its swimming movements are particularly graceful, but they fight endlessly among themselves and many also nip the fins and scales of other fishes. Has seldom bred in captivity.

Exophthalmus see *Disease*

Eye

The importance of the eye to fish varies considerably with the species. Those which have evolved in environments where plenty of light can penetrate are usually reasonably reliant on sight. Many fish hunt by sight. In contrast, some fish living in caves where total darkness prevails, have no functional eyes at all.

Where vision is used by the fish, the eye appears as a relatively large organ. It is controlled in orbit by six muscles which allow considerable rotation. In general, eye movements are co-ordinated but some species are capable of independent chameleon-like eye movements.

The eye itself can be compared to a photographic camera. Light passes through the clear area at the front of the eye, the cornea. It is focused by the lens which is a spherical structure just behind the cornea, and like the camera the picture is finally received by a flat tissue at the back of the eye known as the retina. The retina, having received its picture, informs the brain about the information it has obtained, sending a message along the optic or sight nerve.

The retina has two different kinds of light receivers – the rods and cones. The rods are for seeing in the dark whilst cones are used for day vision. Many mammals, like some of the elasmobranchs or cartilaginous fish, have few cones and are therefore most suited to night vision. Most teleost or boney fish are equipped with a proportion of both rods and cones, and can see reasonably well in all situations.

Deep sea fish living at depths of 400–2,000 metres, where sunlight does not penetrate, have very large eyes indeed. Some of these deep sea fish possess the largest eyes known in vertebrates. They have special modifications with a large pupil and an enormous lens, together with a very unusual elongated shape to the eye. The large lens concentrates the little available light on a specially enlarged and modified area of the retina.

Fish like Mudskippers, *Periophthalmus barbarus*, which

Section through the eye

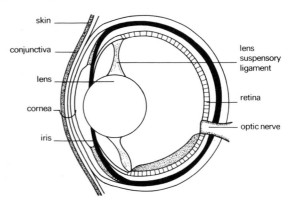

skin
conjunctiva
lens
cornea
iris
lens suspensory ligament
retina
optic nerve

live a good deal of the time out of water, also have specially modified eyes enabling them to see both under water and on land. Burrowing fish like some Indian members of the Gobiidae have small modified eyes. Another species has developed a transparent skin which completely covers and protects the eye but allows sufficient light through for the eye to have a function.

EYE-SPOT RASBORA see *Rasbora dorsiocellata*

FALSE FEATHERBACK see *Xenomystus nigri*
FANTAIL see *Carassius auratus*
FANTAILED FILEFISH see *Pervagor spilosoma*

Farlowella Loricariidae ⊕
– acus NEEDLEFISH or LONG-BODIED CATFISH 17cm. (6½in.)
A very attractive fish from Brazil. It has a long slim body and a long snout. The dorsal body is beige, the belly white, and between runs a wide dark brown band from snout through eye to tail. The fins are large and decorative being spotted with brown dots. The tail fin is very attractive, the outer rays being extended.

FAT SLEEPER see *Dormitator maculatus*
FEATHERBACK,
    AFRICAN see *Notopterus afer*
    FALSE see *Xenomystus nigri*
FEATHERFIN
    SEE *Heniochus acuminatus*
    TETRA see *Hemigrammus unilineatus*

FEATHERTAIL TETRA see *Phenacogrammus interruptus*
Feeding see *Food*
Feeding Behaviour see under *Behaviour*
Feeding Fry see *Food*

Feeding Rings
Simply a small floating ring into which the food is placed. The food being so contained is stopped from spreading over the surface. I think they are superfluous, if not bad in principle, since they concentrate the fish in a small area increasing aggression and preventing the weaker fish from eating.

FERN
    FLOATING see under *Plants – Ceratopteris*
    INDIAN see under *Plants – Ceratopteris*
    SUMATRA see under *Plants – Ceratopteris*
FIGHTING GAUCHO see *Cynolebias melanotaenia*
FIGURE 8 PUFFER see *Tetraodon steinachneri*
FILEFISH
    see Balistidae
    EMERALD see *Oxymonacanthus longirostris*
    FANTAILED see *Pervager spilosoma*
    TAIL-LIGHT see *Cantherhines pullus*
Filters see *Power filters*

Filtration
The purpose of filtration is to remove particles of suspended waste matter, to allow for bacterial decomposition of waste materials and to absorb toxic substances dissolved in the water. In practice these objectives are not entirely realized and many dissolved toxic substances cannot be removed by commercially available apparatuses. They are however of considerable value in maintaining a relatively sweet, clear environment for the fish.

Many different types of filter systems exist with almost

Basic feeding ring

Floating feeding ring

Worm feeder

water surface

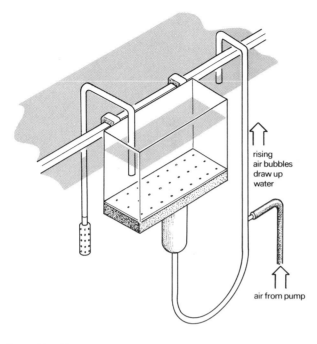

External box filter

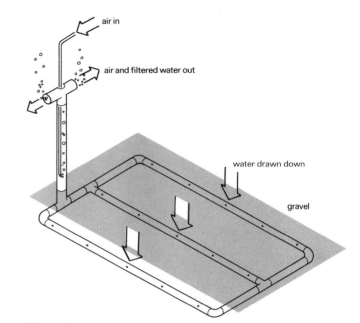

air in

air and filtered water out

rising
air bubbles
draw up
water

air from pump

water drawn down

gravel

Internal filter and aerator.

infinite modifications possible. There are two main types, the box and the under-gravel filter. Box filters are used in several different ways but the principle remains the same. A plastic box with a perforated bottom is filled with various filtering layers. At the bottom is a layer of small stones, then comes a layer of activated charcoal followed by a layer of sand and finally a layer of glass wool. Water from the aquarium is siphoned or pumped into the top of the box. It passes down through the various layers which remove small particles. Charcoal deals with dissolved toxic substances. The water having percolated through the layers arrives at the bottom of the box in a cleaned and purified state. It now either drops back by gravity or is pumped back into the tank by the air pump, using an air lift which, at the same time, aerates the water.

The principle of the air lift is simple. A long wide, open-ended tube curved over at the top has a smaller tube leading from the air pump joined to it a few centimetres above the bottom. This is placed in water which rises up the main tube finding its own level. Air, now pumped in through the smaller tube, bubbles into the main tube lowering the specific gravity of the water in the large tube thereby causing it to rise and spill out of the curved end. As it does so it aerates the water as well.

Commercially, the so-called internal box filters are clipped to hang inside the tank. An air lift raises water from the bottom of the tank to spill into the top of the box. The water percolates through and back into the tank. External box filters are situated, as the name suggests, outside the tank. These are larger and therefore more efficient. Water siphoned or pumped from the tank drops into the top of the box. As it percolates through it is cleaned. When it reaches the bottom it runs into a separate container where an air lift is placed which returns the water, now clean and aerated, to the tank.

Filters become dirty and must be changed regularly. Charcoal can be easily revitalized but not totally reactivated by baking it in the oven which dispels the absorbed toxins. Under-gravel filters are a newer modification which use the gravel of the tank itself as a filter medium. The under-gravel filter consists of a sheet of plastic, slightly convex, which is perforated. It should fit the tank as closely as possible to avoid pockets of waste material accumulating. An air lift is attached to the apparatus, drawing water and waste down through the gravel and returning purified water to the water surface. The waste which remains in the gravel is broken-down biologically by aerobic bacteria.

Aquarists disagree as to the value of both aeration and filtration. There is no doubt that aeration allows more fish to be kept in a tank. Some fish however dislike fast moving water while others prefer it.

FINGERFISH see *Monodactylidae, Monodactylus argenteus*
Fin Rot see *Disease*

Fins

Fins can be conveniently divided into two types, the median or unpaired and the paired. The median fins are those in the midline of the body and consist of the dorsal fin, the caudal or tail fin and the anal fin. In some fish, the trouts, characins, and catfishes there is also a fatty, so-called, adipose fin which rarely has rays.

There are two sets of paired fins, the pectorals and pelvics which correspond respectively to the front and hind legs of land animals.

The pectorals are always situated just behind the head but the position of the pelvics varies considerably in different groups of fishes.

Fins have a variety of functions. Primarily they are organs of stability preventing the fish from rolling and pitching. In addition they assist the fish in turning and stopping, adding manoeuvrability to movement. Finally in some species, fins have become important organs for locomotion.

The dorsal fin is retained by many sharks for its primary function, acting like a keel for stabilization. In some ray fishes which have become flattened or depressed, the dorsal fin has disappeared. In bony fish it is rarely totally absent but may become reduced to minute proportions. It may be grossly enlarged as in the Sailfin, *Poecilia latipinna*, and some of the ornamental Goldfish, *Carassius auratus*. It is elongated in the Ribbonfish, *Lepidopus caudatus*, and in this species is mainly used for swimming, by producing wave motions. There may be more than one dorsal fin as in some of our commoner food fishes, including the cod, *Gadus morhua*, and haddock, *Melanogrammus aeglefinus*, the cod carrying three. Some species have dorsal fins with modified spines assisting in defence. Where present, the adipose fin is a second dorsal. It is a small protrusion of fatty tissue without any supporting structure. Some of the catfish have adipose fins reaching relatively large proportions.

The dorsal fin of most fish can be erected or lowered by activating the relevant musculature; when swimming at speed they are lowered, in some cases folded in grooves in the body to maintain the streamlining of the body.

The anal fin like the dorsal fin is very variable in size and structure. It may be absent altogether, greatly enlarged, divided into two or modified to form an organ of copulation.

Technically the skeletal support for the caudal or tail fin divides the tails of living fishes into two types. A third form, known from fossil remains, the more primitive protocercal tail being probably extinct. The heterocercal tail characterized by the sharks is produced by an upbending of the vertebral column and the two lobes of the caudal fin are very different in size. The upper lobe is greatly enlarged while the lower is very small, producing an asymmetrical

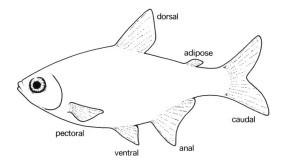

Fin arrangement on a carachin

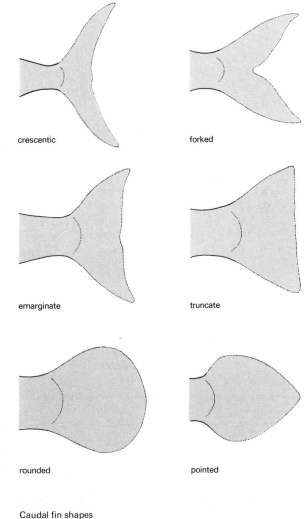

Caudal fin shapes

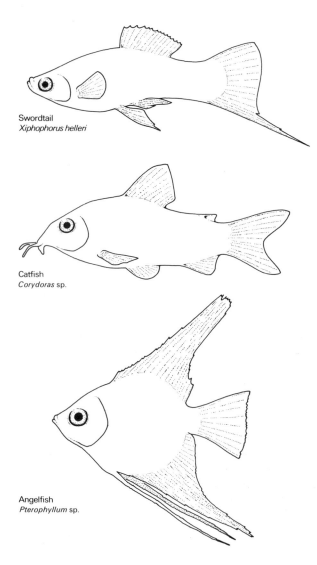

Swordtail
Xiphophorus helleri

Catfish
Corydoras sp.

Angelfish
Pterophyllum sp.

Fin arrangements

tail fin. The homocercal fin, common to most of the bony fishes appears superficially symmetrical. In reality however the bony structure reveals that it is a modified form of the heterocercal tail which has been adapted by evolution. The variations in this type of symmetrical tail are as varied as the other median fins. It may be absent altogether or adopt one of the several recognized shapes: crescentic, forked, emarginate, truncate, rounded and pointed. Each of these shapes is specifically adapted for a certain purpose. For example, crescentic tail fins assist fast swimming, while round or pointed fins are usually found on slow swimmers.

The pectorals are less commonly modified in size, shape or position than other fins. Rarely are they absent, usually

they are small and spatula shaped, positioned just behind the head. The classic example of gross enlargement is seen in the flyingfishes, *Exocoetidae*, which use them to glide once they leave the water following great exertions of the tail which provides the initial impetus for the flight. Various other more grotesque modifications allow Mudskippers, *Periophthalmus*, to amble on land and Frogfishes, *Antennarius*, to crawl on the sea bed.

Pelvic fins are not so constant in position as the pectorals. They can be anywhere from just in front of the pectorals to immediately anterior to the anal fin. In some fish like the eels, *Anguilla*, they are totally absent, while in others they are greatly reduced. In male sharks or rays, they are modified to form claspers used to grip the female during copulation. See also *Locomotion, Skeleton*.

FIRE
    CLOWNFISH see *Amphiprion frenatum*
    KILLY see *Nothobranchius rachovii*
FIREBALL, PURPLE see *Centropyge acanthrops*
FIREFISH
    see *Ptereleotris splendidum*
    RED see *Pterois volitans*
FIREMOUTH
    see *Cichlasoma meeki*
    KILLY see *Epiplatys dageti monroviae*

Fish – What is a fish?
Fish are cold-blooded animals which have a backbone – the vertebrae. They are, with rare exceptions, totally dependent on water in which they eat, drink, sleep and breed.

There are more species of fish on earth than any other type of vertebrate. Some 25,000 different species are thought to exist, compared to *c*.8000 birds and *c*.4000 mammals. Different species vary in size from less than 1·3cm. ($\frac{1}{2}$in.) to some of the larger sharks which are well over 18 metres (60ft) in length and weigh over 25 tonnes.

As a result of their long evolutionary history they have managed to adapt to life in a very wide range of environmental conditions. Fish are found in hot springs where the water is more than 38°C. and in arctic and antarctic water below freezing. Some live in dark, still, cold waters so deep in the oceans that they remain unexplored by man while others frolic in fast flowing sunlit mountain streams several thousand metres above sea level. Some live in salt water, some in fresh water. Others trapped thousands of years ago in inland waterways and lakes have been forced to adapt to extremely salty water.

While most fish are 'fish shaped', others have become flattened, elongated, tall, short, squat and even square. Others are so grotesque that they defy description.

From this vast range of animals grouped under the

general name fish, aquarists keep but a very small sample. See also *Protopterus annectens, Periophthalmus barbarus, Classification, Distribution, Evolution* and *Skeleton*.

FIVE-BANDED BARB see *Barbus pentazona*
FIVE-SPOTTED CICHLID see *Pelmatochromis ansorgii*
FLAG
    BLUNTHEAD CICHLID see *Aequidens curviceps*
    CHANCHITO see *Cichlasoma festivum*
    CICHLID see *Cichlasoma festivum*
    GROUPER, DWARF see *Pseudochromis gutmanni*
    KILLY see *Aphyosemion calliurum*
    TETRA, BLACK see *Hyphessobrycon rosaceus*
FLAG-STRIPED TETRA see *Hyphessobrycon heterorhabdus*
FLAG-TAILED PROCHILODUS see *Prochilodus insignis*
FLAGFISH see *Jordanella floridae*
FLAMEFISH see *Apogon maculatus, Hyphessobrycon flammeus*
Flea, Water see under *Food*
FLOATING FERN see under *Plants – Ceratopteris*
FLORIDA FLAGFISH see *Jordanella floridae*
FLUKES,
    GILL see under *Disease*
    SKIN see under *Disease*

Fluoridation

In an attempt to prevent tooth decay in the human population it has become the practice in some countries to add the element fluorine as a fluoride to public water supplies. Naturally this has concerned aquarists, fish farmers, anglers and others who are worried about the toxic effects of the substance. The main commercial concern has been the danger of polluting the rivers and river estuaries and, to this end, experimental work has been carried out with Rainbow Trout, *Salmo gairdneri*, and Carp, *Cyprinus carpio*. The eggs of both species are more resistant to toxic concentrations than adult fish.

In experiments using very high levels of fluoride (over 70 parts per million) a high proportion, but not all, of the fish died, but when water containing only one part per million was used in their tanks, that is the amount used to fluoridate public water, the loss was so small that it could be ignored. There are different effects depending on the hardness of the water. A combination of soft water and high concentrations of fluoride prove more toxic than hard water with the same amount of fluoride. However, again at levels normally found in public water supplies, the losses are minute.

Experimental work, using primarily the Rainbow Trout, shows that aquarists need have little concern for water supplies to which fluoride is added. Certainly no evidence from aquarists has been presented which would suggest dangers from fluoridation. Fluorine remains another chemical component of water which may affect very

sensitive fish or be a factor in the breeding success of some fish under captive conditions. Clearly we need more experimental work on the subject.

FLYING
    BARB see *Esomus dandica*
    BARB, STRIPED see *Esomus malayensis*
    HATCHETFISHES see *Gasteropelecidae*
FLYINGFISHES see *Exocoetidae*
Foam Removers see *Protein Skimmer*

Food

One of the most difficult problems which a veterinary surgeon has to deal with is overfeeding. Many pets are fed until obesity threatens their very life. There seems to be among the general public a concept that good feeding means overfeeding. Sadly this is equally true of many aquarists, particularly beginners. Unlike pet dogs and cats, however, which all too often consume all the food offered, pet fish leave what they don't want and it falls to the bottom, there to decompose, producing a variety of toxins which rapidly adversely affect the health and well-being of the fish. The fish become lethargic at first and if overfeeding is continued pollution may become so bad that the captive inmates die.

Like most higher animals kept in captivity, fish soon get to know the hand that feeds them. When the owner approaches the tank a begging routine is commenced which fools beginners into believing the fish are hungry. Food is poured in every time the tank is passed. Result – disaster. Don't be fooled by their antics. Harden your heart for healthy fish. Scavengers in the form of either catfish or snails are not able to deal with the amounts of food some people pile into the tank.

The best indication of trouble is the lassitude of the fish, but other signs are a darkening of the gravel and occasional escape in the form of a bubble of the poisonous gases trapped there.

To correct a sour tank, provide aeration and change at least half of the water and, above all, stop overfeeding. Fish should only be given, each day, that amount of food which they will eat in five minutes. So put in a little and wait to see that it is eaten, if so, add more, but stop when they stop. Better by far to underfeed than to overfeed.

As for all animals the basic food constituents are proteins, fats and carbohydrates with minerals and vitamins. Many prepared foods are available now, which claim to provide a balanced diet. As a scientist I am sceptical that scientists can be certain that all of the nutritional requirements are present in the correct quantities, and I am equally sceptical about manufacturers' ability to formulate the food with accuracy. It is therefore my habit to provide all animals, including fish, with a naturally varied diet. Certainly the proprietary foods can provide a basis of any fish diet, but it should be supplemented with live food, freeze-dried live food and fresh vegetable matter, according to the particular fish's requirements, as frequently as possible.

Finely minced cooked meat, fish and shellfish, are very acceptable foods and can be given occasionally in very small quantities. Hard-boiled egg yolk is useful in a variety of situations, but should be given in very sparing quantities.

Traditional live foods keep the fish in good health and should be included in any well-balanced diet, since they not only have nutrient value but the fish enjoy catching them, so gaining psychological benefits as well. The commoner live foods include:

Algae. This is used as a food for some fish but must be kept under control. See also *Green Water*.

Asellus, Water Hog Louse. Rather resembles a wood louse. Lives among the plants in streams.

Chaoborus larvae, Glass or Ghost Worm. This is the larva of the Plumed Gnat. It closely resembles *Chironomus* larvae except that it is transparent. It has one advantage over all other live food in that it can be found in winter.

Chironomus larvae, Blood Worms. These are the larvae of the midge. They are about 2·5cm. (1in.) in length and are bright red in colour. Take care not to feed them to fish which swallow whole or they may damage the fish with their mandibles before they die.

Culex larvae, Gnat Larvae. This popular form of live food is found during the summer in most stagnant pools. They are even found in buckets of water left outside, and this is a useful way of obtaining them. Rinse in clean water before feeding.

Cyclops. These crustaceans are found in stagnant pools. They can be cultivated by placing a few in a container filled with rain water to which has been added a little rotting leaf mould and animal manure. The container should be stood in the sun.

Daphnia, Water Flea. Though popularly known as the water flea, because of its jerky movements, it is not a flea. It provides roughage in the diet as well as nutrient. Remember the golden rule, only a few at a time.

They can be collected from stagnant pools. Take care when transporting them, however, or they will die due to insufficient oxygen or physical trauma from the journey. They can equally well be cultivated in the same way as *Cyclops*. They should be washed before feeding.

Dried daphnia is available and fish like it, but it is an inferior food. Quick frozen foods including daphnia, tubifex and mosquito larvae are very useful since they are always available and retain their nutritional value very well indeed.

Drosophila melanogaster, Fruit Fly. A small fly, popular

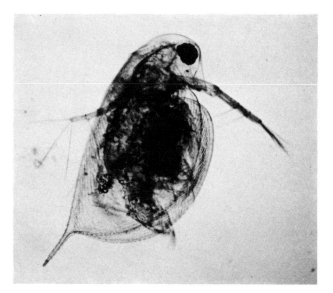

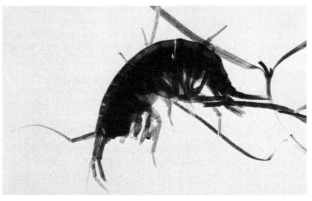

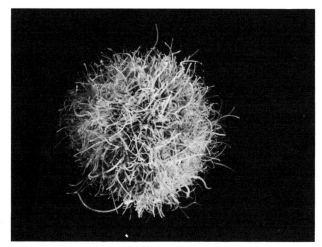

Top to bottom: Water Flea, *Daphnia* sp. ×100; Freshwater Shrimp, *Gammarus* sp. ×15; Mud Worms, *Tubifex* sp. ×2.

with geneticists, which makes an excellent food for the surface insect feeder.

Enchytraeus, White Worm. A genus which includes the close relative, the Grindal Worm, is popular with some aquarists. They should be fed sparingly. White worms are pale yellow and grow to about 13mm. ($\frac{1}{2}$in.). They can be fed whole or mashed. Cultivation is easy. Place a few worms in a box of moist sterile soil and add waste vegetable scraps or bread. Keep warm, moist and fed, and there will be a constant crop.

Gammarus, Freshwater Shrimp. It lives among the plants at the side of streams. Take care when transporting. It can be cultivated in stagnant rainwater, to which has been added animal manure, in a similar way to cyclops and daphnia.

Lumbricus, Earthworm. This is one of several genera to which the commonly found earthworms belong. These are excellent as live food. Small ones can be fed to larger fish or they can be mashed for smaller fish.

Tubifex, Mud Worms. These are found in waters which contain large quantities of organic material. One of their favourite sites is near sewage outflows and for reasons of contamination may be of doubtful value. Most dealers sell tubifex which has been cleansed. They will live out of water for a long time but are best kept in a constant stream of running water. They should be placed in a floating feeding basket for feeding.

Food for Breeding

Animals only breed if conditions are to their liking. Wild animals are, to a large extent, able to choose their own conditions. In the aquarium, it is up to the aquarist to provide conditions as near perfect as is humanly possible. Part of this routine includes correct food. Most fish will be helped into a breeding mood if they are given a suitable feast of live food for several days.

Feeding is an important skill which has to be learned if success is to be achieved. No hard and fast rules apply. Each tank, each fish, each day of the year is different from all others. It is up to the aquarist to judge the particular requirements for each day. Too little food and the fish starve or are weakened and unable to resist illness. Too much and they become sick and die due to toxins in the polluted tank. Experience cannot be bought from even the most helpful dealer.

Food for Fish Fry

Fish fry are tiny and need very small particles of food. The fry of live bearers are relatively large and may be fed on finely powdered dry food or small daphnia. The fry of egg layers when first hatched are truly minute and need very fine food on which to feed when the yolk sac is exhausted.

Brine Shrimps. These tiny crustaceans are shrimps from

saltlakes which are hatched from the eggs. The eggs are supplied by dealers in their dried state.

Infusoria. This is a useful food for the very small fry. It consists of very small living organisms, microscopic in size, which multiply in water containing decomposed vegetable matter. By placing some vegetables in water and leaving them to stand, you will produce the necessary culture in a few days. This can be poured direct into the tank. Needless to say, the commercial firms have jumped into the act and produce bottles of instant food for fry.

Egg Yolk (hard boiled). This, in really minute quantities, is a useful food for very small fry. It does, however, all too readily cloud water, so be careful.

Forcipiger Chaetodontidae Ψ
– flavissimus YELLOW LONG-NOSED BUTTERFLYFISH
15cm. (6in.)
This fish has a wide distribution but is common in the Pacific. It is a delightful creature with a yellow body and a brown triangular patch on the head. A dark 'eye' spot is situated on the anal fin. The jaws are elongated. It feeds off algae on the rocks but should be fed brine shrimps in addition. A closely related species, *F. longirostris*, is very similar in appearance and is easily mistaken for this. **78**

FOUR-EYED
    BUTTERFLYFISH see *Chaetodon capistratus*
    FISH see *Anableps anableps*
FOUREYES see *Anableps anableps*
FOUR-SPINED STICKLEBACK see *Apeltes quadracus*
FOXFACE see *Lo vulpinus*
FRENCH ANGELFISH see *Pomacanthus paru*
FRESHWATER
    SHEEPSHEAD see *Cichlasoma cyanoguttatum*
    SHRIMP see under *Food*
    SUNFISH see *Centrarchidae*
    TANK see *Establishing a Tropical Freshwater Tank*
    TETRAODON see *Tetraodon fluviatilis*
Fry, Feeding see *Food*
FULLEBORN'S CICHLID see *Labeotropheus fuelleborni*

Fundulus Cyprinodontidae ⊕
– chrysotus GOLDEN or GOLDEAR KILLY
8cm. (3in.) ⊕/Ψ ✂
This killy comes from Florida and the Carolinas. It lives in brackish water naturally but will live in fresh water. An aggressive fish at spawning time, it can only be kept with larger species in a community tank. It occupies the middle layer of the tank. Shade is not obligatory. Temperatures around 21–22°C. suit it best. A general body colour of blue green is peppered with red dots. In some specimens black dots accompany the red. The median and pelvic fins are pale

red and a green patch adorns the operculum. The female is brown with darker patches on her flanks. Eggs are deposited among the plants and hatch in about 8–15 days.

– dispar STARHEAD MINNOW   6cm. (2½in.) ✂

One of the less attractive killies from the south of the USA, the male having a basic body colour of blue green which is broken by rows of dark brown dots and vertical bars. The fins are pale yellow with dots on the medians. The female shows paler, less intense body colour without the vertical bars but with horizontal stripes. It is generally peaceful but, being liable to aggression, should be kept with larger fish only, in temperatures around 21–22°C.

– heteroclitus COMMON or ZEBRA KILLY, MUMMICHOG   15cm. (6in.)   ⊕/Ψ ✂

Widespread in the USA, this has an orange brown body transected vertically by some 12 blue bars. The unpaired fins are decorated with a number of blue dots. In addition, the dorsal has a margin of red. The female is duller and darker; vertical markings are either indistinct or absent. It lives in fresh, salt or brackish water naturally, although slightly salt water is recommended for the aquarist's use. An aggressive character restricts its social colleagues of the community tank only to large fish. Temperatures around 19–20°C. suit it admirably. Eggs laid on the bottom of the tank, hatch in about 10–12 days.

– notti NOTTS KILLY or STARHEAD MINNOW   6cm. (2½in.)   ⊕/Ψ

From the Mississippi eastwards to North Carolina and Florida. A grey brown back shades to a silver belly. Six broken horizontal bars decorate the side which in turn are crossed by several dark vertical bands. The unpaired fins are reddish brown with dark spots. Female duller. A peaceful nature makes it suitable for the community tank. Brackish water in the region of 21–22°C. suits it best. Tends to keep close to the surface of the tank. Spawns on plants from which eggs hatch in 10–20 days.

– pallidus TEXAS KILLY   15cm. (6in.)   ⊕/Ψ

A brackish water killy from Florida, Texas and Mexico. The body colour is an attractive olive green which shades to yellow on the belly. The sides are transected by numerous dark vertical lines. Green dots adorn the sides of the body and the fins. Female less attractive with less definite markings. Eggs are deposited among the plants where they hatch in 10–20 days.

– sciadicus   8cm. (3in.)   ⊕ ✂

Widespread in the southern half of the USA. An attractive pale green body with a silver belly is broken by a dark patch beside the pectoral fin from which a blue line passes to the tail. The fins are red with a dark brown edge. The female is duller with less distinctive markings. It is one of the smaller killies, but is so aggressive that it is unsuited to the community tank. It prefers fresh water at temperatures of

22–24°C. A plant spawner, its eggs emerge in 8–10 days. It prefers bright light, unlike many of its cousins.

FUNDULLUS see *Aphyosemion, Nothobranchius*
Fungus Disease see under *Disease*

G

Gambusia   Poeciliidae   ⊕

– affinis TEXAS GAMBUSIA or MOSQUITOFISH   6cm. (2½in.) ✂

Two subspecies exist, the eastern and western forms. The former is native to Florida, Georgia and the Carolinas, while the latter resides across geographical barriers in Mississippi, Alabama, Texas and Mexico. The eastern form is known as *G. affinis holbrooki*, while the western representative is *G. affinis affinis*. There are slight anatomical differences which microscopic examination can identify. They have basically a silver grey body with metallic blue overtones. Selective breeding by fanciers has produced speckled varieties of both subspecies, and it is these variants of the wild form which are usually kept by aquarists.

They are hardy, omnivorous, and to say they are easy to breed is an understatement. The pugnacity, fin biting and physical drabness seen in this live-bearing species is reflected in other members of the genus which, as a result, have become less popular with aquarists.

– punctata BLUE or SPOTTED GAMBUSIA   ♂ 4cm. (1½in.)   ♀ 7cm. (3in.)

A native of Cuba. Blue in this case is a euphemism for dirty silver which, under conditions rarely found in the aquarium or nature, is said to have a blue sheen. Brown dots, looking similar to the beginnings of an infection, may be evident on its sides. The unpaired fins have a trace of blue and the dorsal in some specimens runs to a flash of yellow. A striking blue eye somewhat redeems this fish.

Gammarus see under *Food*
GANTER'S GOURAMI see *Trichogaster trichopterus*
GARDNER'S KILLY see *Aphyosemion gardneri*
GARRUPA see *Cephalopholis argus*

Gas Bladder

The gas or swim bladder may be seen in many of the higher fishes when dissected as a white balloon-like structure. The gas bladder has a great variety of functions, many of them quite unrelated, in different species of fish.

It is possible that it originally evolved as an organ of respiration. The gas bladder develops as a pouch of the oesophagus (gullet). The pouch enlarges during the fish's development until, as an adult, it remains connected only by a narrow tube. Even this tube may disappear in some fish. In most fish it develops from the roof of the oesophagus but in the lungfish, Ceratoditidae, Lepidosirenidae and Protopteridae, where it has evolved into a respiratory organ, it develops from the ventral regions. When its function is respiratory, as in the Lungfish, Gar-pike, *Lepisosoteus*, and Bowfin, *Amia*, the surface area is increased by folding as in true mammalian lungs and fish gills, and a rich blood supply provided. In many fish it is a single structure but in lungfish and to a lesser extent in Bowfins, Gar-pikes and Bichirs, *Polypterus,* it takes the form of two pouches reminding one of the two-pouch system in mammalian lungs.

A further function for the gas bladder is as an hydrostatic organ. By varying the amount of gas in its gas bladder the fish can remain indefinitely at any depth it chooses without expending energy in so doing. In fish where the connection with the oesophagus remains, the fish fills the bladder by swallowing air which is taken in at the water surface and emptying it by expelling bubbles through the mouth. When the connection is closed and the pouch is truly sealed, gas is actively pumped in by the gas gland, which is situated towards the front of the pouch. Gases are removed by another structure – the opum. This process is far from instantaneous and deep sea fish dragged rapidly to the surface during commercial fishing activities, would often be unable to return to the deep because of damage to the gas bladder, even supposing they escaped the fisherman's knife.

In some fish, notably herrings, *Clupeidae*, mormyrids, characins, gymnotids, cyprinids and catfishes, there are varying degrees of connection with the ear. In these species the gas bladder does duty as an extra organ of hearing, accentuating the sound waves.

Finally, a few species of fish produce sounds by expelling air in a controlled way through the pneumatic duct or tube which connects the gas bladder to the oesophagus. For Gas Bladder Disease see under *Disease*. See *Hearing, Respiration, Sound.*

Gasteropelecidae   HATCHETFISHES

These are an unusual and interesting group of fish but it must be said at once that they are not a suitable species for the novice. They have unusual behaviour which makes some of them unsuitable for the community tank, are short lived in captivity and have rarely bred. They are all quite small with large bulbous bellies but compressed markedly when viewed from the front. Hatchetfishes stay close to the surface and can ride on the water surface and are said to

actually leave the water and fly, using their pectoral fins as wings which they flap. This is in contrast to the true marine flyingfish, *Exocoetus*, which only glide having left the water by powerful thrusting with the tail.

In one of the few observed spawnings the pair made several jumps out of the water but spawned while swimming head to tail. The eggs were scattered in the floating plants. There are no external sexual differences to facilitate identification.

Their natural food consists of live surface insects. It may be that daphnia, the usual substitute, do not entirely fulfil the nutritional requirements and this may be one of the factors which makes them difficult to keep although the reasons are probably far more subtle and relate to a diversity of factors including their difficulty in adapting to a closed environment, perhaps with insufficient 'flying' space. See *Carnegiella, Gasteropelecus, Thoracocharax.*

This head-on shot of a Silver Hatchetfish, *Gasteroplecus levis*, shows this family's unusual shape.

Gasteropelecus Gasteropelecidae ⊕
– ***levis*** SILVER HATCHETFISH 6cm. (2½in.)
The Silver Hatchetfish is native to Guyana and the Amazon
Basin. The body is olive above and silver below separated
by a dark horizontal band which is bordered by pale grey
lines. The fins are hyaline, the dorsal having dark colouring

Silver Hatchetfish, *Gasteroplecus levis*.

at the base. It closely resembles *G. sternicla* which is more
commonly imported.

Enjoying temperatures around 23°C., they spend a great
deal of time near the water surface. They are not easy to
keep in captivity and seldom live longer than a year.
– ***sternicla*** COMMON HATCHETFISH 6cm. (2½in.)
The most commonly imported hatchetfish which comes
from the upper Amazon Basin and Guyana. The deep body
is coloured yellow with silver overtones. A longitudinal
dark line divides the body. All of the fins are transparent.
Spends its day near to the surface, where it hangs
motionless. Makes a fair community member and may live
several years in captivity.

Gasterosteidae STICKLEBACKS
The main justification for including this family in a book for
the aquarist is that the scientific studies of sticklebacks by
behaviourists have contributed a great deal to our
understanding of mating behaviour and aggression. In
addition one may speculate that a number of aquarists were
originally stimulated to take an interest in fish as a result of
an afternoon spent with net and jam jar at the local stream.

They are found in temperate and subarctic climates of the
northern hemisphere. The family is characterized by having
a number of spines along the back in front of the dorsal fin.
See *Apeltes, Gasterosteus*.

Gasterosteus Gasterosteidae ⊕
– ***aculeatus*** THREE-SPINED STICKLEBACK 8cm. (3in.) ✂
A small silver fish, a native of temperate regions of Europe,
which has three rigid free spines in front of its dorsal spine.
Dorsal and anal fins are set well back and the tail fin is
triangular. During the breeding season the male adopts a
brilliant red colouring on the belly. With the appearance of
the red belly, the male establishes a territory and becomes
aggressive to all other males. Some interesting experiments
have shown that the aggression is primarily stimulated by
the red belly. Models bearing little resemblance to a fish let
alone a male stickleback elicit aggression providing the
under part is red. Models of male sticklebacks without the
red belly produced much less effect, showing that it is
primarily, though not exclusively, the red that sends the
male stickleback into a fighting mood. When they are
warning other male sticklebacks off their patch they assume
a head down posture and, if the model is so positioned as to
challenge the fish's right to his patch, then he becomes even
more aggressive.

Having established a territory he makes a nest in the
sand. Using plants as anchors he constructs a tunnel. When
a fecund female stickleback appears full of eggs he performs
a downward zig zag dance towards the nest. This is
repeated. If she accepts his offer she burrows into the
tunnel. The male trembles and she deposits her eggs which
the male fertilizes. The female, task complete, goes off while
the male's paternal instincts demand that he remains with
their offspring to guard and fan them with his tail to keep
them well oxygenated. To do this he takes up a position in
front of the nest pointing towards it and moves his tail as if
to swim forwards. At the same time his pectoral fins are
mobilized to stop forward movement. As a result the stream
of water passes across the eggs. Four days later the fry hatch
and are protected by the male for a few days with gradually
dwindling enthusiasm. **79**

Gastro-enteritis see under *Disease*
GELI BARB see *Barbus gelius*

Genetics
Genetics is the study of inheritance, the way in which
characteristics of the parents are passed on to the offspring.

Briefly, each characteristic, whether it is a red fin, black
body spot or coloured eye, is developed in the individual on
the instructions of a microscopic part of a tiny chain of
protein contained in the nucleus of the fertilized egg. The
chain is a chromosome and the tiny part a gene. The
chromosome is, in fact, composed of two parallel strands,
the chromatids. Each new individual receives one chromatid
from each parent. A characteristic from one parent may be
dominant over the other. To take a simple and imaginary

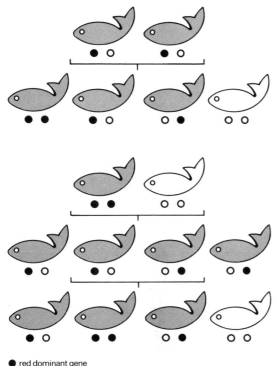

● red dominant gene
○ blue recessive gene

If one now wishes to breed a pure line of reds or a pure line of blues it would be necessary to use parents with RR chromosomes for red and bb for blue. The bb are easily indentified just because they are blue. The RR are much more difficult because to look at they are exactly like the Rb as a result of the dominant R gene. Only by extensive breeding programmes can you be sure your lines are pure and being bred from pure RR parents.

This simple type of inherited pattern is known as Mendelian inheritance after the monk Mendel who first studied the phenomenon scientifically. Actual examples may be seen when Golden Guppies, *Poecilia reticulata,* – a recessive character produced by loss of pigment in the skin – are crossed with a wild type of guppy. The offspring of this mating all look like the wild parent, but if two of these – brother and sister – are crossed then their offspring will be three quarters wild type and one quarter golden. Remember, to get a golden colour both genes, one of each chromatid must be golden.

This is a very simplified look at genetics since many characteristics do not follow the simple pattern illustrated here. Some are due to several genes all acting together and this produces a great number of complications. For example, if an albino guppy – white with pink eyes – is crossed with a wild type, all the offspring look like the wild type. If two of these young are mated together however, instead of wild look to albino being in the ratio 3:1, there are many more wild types than albinos. This is explained by the fact that the gene of albinism often causes death of the embryo so reducing the expected 3:1 result.

Further complications arise from linked genes, cross over effects where part of each chromatid crosses to its partner, and a variety of other manifestations.

Work on fish genetics has been carried out by a number of ichthyologists. The genetics of the black spot in the dorsal fin and its relationship with the gene determining sex has been studied in the Golden Guppy. Inherited sexuality has also been examined in the Platy, *Xiphophorus maculatus.* Indeed there has been extensive work on the latter species and its genetic relationship with the Swordtail, *Xiphophorus helleri.* Similar studies on hybridization have been carried out with several members of the Cyprinodontidae and with species of *Poecilia.* Indeed tropical fish have taught geneticists a great deal about many aspects of their fascinating subject. Those particularly interested in the subject, such as breeders seeking new varieties, should consult textbooks dealing in detail with fish genetics.

Geophagus Cichlidae ⊕
– acuticeps POINTED-HEAD EARTHEATER
30cm. (12in.) ✂
This member of the eartheater genus comes from the

example, if a fish occurred in two colours, red and blue, red might be dominant. This means that if the young fish had received a gene carrying red body colour in its instructions from one parent then it would be red, even if it also received a gene carrying blue instructions from the other parent. When sperms or eggs are formed, each chromosome contained in the normal body cells, which have a fixed number of chromosomes, splits into its two chromatids. One chromatid goes to one sperm or egg, the other goes to a second. The male sperms unite with eggs from a female at mating. The two chromatids, one from each parent, unite to form the normal number of chromosomes, with one gene relating to each characteristic from each parent. To take our imaginary example – the colour of the new individual will depend on the type of body colour genes it receives.

As each parent has two genes itself, let us assume that one is instructing red body and one blue in each parent. Now since both have one red gene both parents will be red because it is dominant. When they split to form sperms and eggs however half will carry red instructions only and the other half blue only. When they re-combine, i.e. when sperms fertilize the eggs at mating the various combinations are seen in the diagram. Three out of four will be red since they have at least one dominant red gene. Only one in four will be blue which have only blue instruction genes.

Amazon Basin. It has a greenish body shading to a silver belly. A number of vertical lines extend from the back to disappear midway to the belly. Rich blue dots are scattered over the side. The fins are green.

As with all members of this genus it has a rather unusually shaped head for a cichlid. The long curved upper part of the head with highly placed eyes gives it a strange, almost sinister, appearance. Of doubtful character they are not suitable for community life, and they damage the plants, by disturbing the roots.

– brasiliensis RED-FINNED CICHLID or MOTHER-OF-PEARL EARTHEATER 28cm. (11in.) ⊕/Ψ
A fresh and brackish water member from Brazil. It gets one of its names from the mother-of-pearl dots on the operculum. The yellow body is decorated with horizontal lines of dots. Young fish have a variety of lines, bars, dots and patches on the body which fade with maturity. The dorsal fin, as with other members of the genus, is particularly grand being tall throughout its length. All unpaired fins are yellow or brown with red, silver or yellow dots.

– jurupari DEMON or EARTHEATING DEVILFISH 25cm. (10in.)
This species is relatively peaceful as cichlids go and is kind to the plants. Its body is a brownish yellow with a blue tint but, like all cichlids, this is variable. It comes from Guyana and north-eastern Brazil.

Unlike most other members of the genus it mouth broods for part of the hatching. After laying the eggs they are left in the depression for up to 48 hours then the female collects them into her mouth and keeps them there until the fry are free swimming. As the name implies fish in this genus busy themselves sifting gravel through their mouths apparently searching for food. **80**

GHOST
    CATFISH see *Kryptopterus bicirrhis*
    WORM see under *Food*
GIANT
    DANIO see *Danio aequipinnatus*
    GOURAMI see *Colisa fasciata*
    SAGITTARIA see under *Plants*
    SAILFIN MOLLY see *Poecilia velifera*
    SEAHORSE see *Hippocampus erectus*
GILL
    FLUKES see *Disease*
    ROT see *Disease*

Girardinus Poeciliidae ⊕
– falcatas YELLOWBELLY ♂5cm. (2in.); ♀8cm. (3in.)
A fish from Cuba with a body colour of a metallic browny yellow. The distinguishing coloration is an intensified golden colour on the belly; which provides the excuse for its popular name. The fins are clear giving an unfinished appearance. The male's gonopodium has a double pointed end, the larger being hooked.

– metallicus GIRARDINUS ♂5cm. (2in.); ♀9cm. (3½in.)
From Cuba and Costa Rica. The basic dark green body is divided along the side by over 12 vertical bars shaped like badly written V's. These are silver grey in colour. The eyes and operculum are speckled with metallic blue green dots. A dark green spot adorns the base of the dorsal fin. The male's gonopodium or intromissive organ has two ends, the larger of which is hooked.

A good community fish, if somewhat unspectacular, it is hardy, omnivorous, greedy and accommodating about water temperature, accepting anything from 22–29°C. It breeds in captivity.

Glandulocauda Characidae ⊕
– inequalis CROAKING TETRA 6cm. (2½in.)
This fish, like several others, utilizes atmospheric oxygen. It has accessory breathing organs, see *Respiration*, which are filled with air as the fish comes to the surface and gulps. It is here that the characteristic noise is made from which it derives its common name. The body colour is a pleasant dull blue sheen with silvery highlights. The tail fin colours are very variable in shades of yellow to green. The dorsal and anal fins are barred brown and grey. Males are generally larger than females and have wider pelvic fins and the first outer rays of the lower caudal fin are somewhat thickened. It is a native of Uruguay.

Fertilization is internal in this species, the male has a gonopodium, and the female deposits eggs under leaves. It is not particularly easy to breed but when hatched the young do well on small infusoria and later daphnia. Non aggressive with a fairly wide range of temperature tolerance (19–24°C.).

GLASS
    CATFISH see *Kryptopterus bicirrhis*
    CATFISH, CONGO see *Eutropiellus debauwi*
    TETRA see *Moenkhausia oligolepsis*
    WORM see under *Food*
GLASSFISH see *Centropomidae, Chanda*
GLOBEFISH see *Tetraodon cutcutia*
GLOWLIGHT TETRA see *Hemigrammus erythrozonus*

Gnathonemus Mormyridae ⊕
– macrolepidotus 30cm. (12in.)
An elongated slightly compressed fish from east Africa. A slight protrusion of the chin gives an almost dolphin-like appearance. The body is grey with a blue back. **81**
– petersi ELEPHANT-NOSE 23cm. (9in.)
It has a similarly shaped body to *G. macrolepidotus* but with

Elephant-nose, *Gnathonemus petersi.*

a marked extension of the chin producing a 'trunk' which has some function in food gathering under natural conditions. The colour is variable, ranging through brown to a blue green, and it has two white vertical bars, the anterior one joining the dorsal and anal fin making an irregular diamond pattern on the body. The tail is small and forked.

It is often motionless in the tank but can produce sudden movement. It has not bred in captivity.

GOATFISH see *Mullidae, Parupensis*

Gobiidae
Various members of this family inhabit salt, brackish and fresh water. They are widely distributed throughout both tropical and temperate regions.

The most interesting feature of this family is the formation of a ventral sucker by the united pelvic fins. This enables the fish to cling onto solid objects, presumably while their large mobile eyes survey the scene. They have two dorsal fins, the first spinous and the second soft. Members of the family are usually smaller than 15cm. in length.

Though excellent aquarium inhabitants they are said to be fin nippers. They like shallow water at temperatures around 25°C. although they are reputed to withstand variation from 20–32°C. In addition many species can live in fresh or brackish water. They are carnivorous and should be fed daphnia or tubifex.

Many are territorial, keeping themselves to themselves in a little patch of water which they defend against all comers.

As spawning approaches the male brightens his hue while the female darkens. A small flower pot in shallow water is all a female goby needs for a 'nest'. She enters the pot and turns on her back and the eggs are then laid onto the upper inner surface of the pot. In comes her mate who then fertilizes his mate's upside down eggs. After several repetitions, the female's usefulness at an end, she is chased from her brood by the male and lying on his back he fans the eggs until they hatch about one week later. Fry should be fed infusoria. See *Brachygobius, Evorthodus, Gobiosoma, Lythrypnus, Paragobiodon, Ptereleotris, Stigmatogobius.*

Gobiasoma Gobiidae Ψ
– ***oceanops*** NEON GOBY   5cm. (2in.)
A lovely marine fish from Florida and Yucatan. It is small, black-bodied with a blue horizontal line along the body. They accept most live food, but in nature they clean other fish of parasites for food. Is being bred more regularly in captivity.

Gobio Cyprinidae ⊕
– ***gobio*** GUDGEON   18cm. (7in.)
A lovely streamlined fish with a yellow green body and a series of dark patches down the lateral line. It has two barbels hanging down on either side of its mouth. It is found in Europe and Asia. They live in small shoals and prefer clear water with sandy or gravel bottoms. Gudgeon live on small crustaceans and other live food. Breeding takes place in early summer when up to 800 eggs are normally laid.

It makes a very good scavenger in the aquarium, and is superior to the catfish in this respect.

GOBY see *Brachygobius, Dormitator, Gobiasoma, Gobius, Lythrypnus, Oxyeleotris, Paragobiodon, Periophthalmus*
GOGGLE-EYE see *Boleophthalmus boddaerti*
GOLDEAR KILLY see *Fundulus chrysotus*
GOLDEN
  ACARA see *Nannacara anomola*
  ANGELFISH see *Centropyge heraldi*
  BARB see *Barbus gelius, Barbus schuberti*
  BUTTERFLYFISH see *Chaetodon auriga*
  CHANCHITO see *Cichlasoma aureum*
  CICHLID, LAKE NYASA see *Pseudotropheus auratus*
  KILLY see *Fundulus chrysotus*
  MYLOSSOMA see *Mylossoma aureum*
  ORFE see *Leuciscus idus*
  PENCILFISH see *Nannostomus aripirangensis*
  RUDD see *Scardinus erythrophthalmus*
GOLDEN-EYED CICHLID see *Nannacara anomala*
GOLDEN-STRIPED SOAPFISH see *Grammistes sexlineatus*
GOLDFINCH, WATER see *Pristella riddlei*
GOLDFISH
  see *Carassius auratus*
  WILD see *Carassius carassius*

Gomphosus Labridae Ψ
– ***varius*** LONGFACE, BEAKFISH, BIRDWRASSE
25cm. (10in.)
This is a small wrasse from the Indo-Pacific which exhibits

Longface or Beakfish, *Gomphosus varius.*

sexual dimorphism. The female is a pale reddish pink anteriorly with a purple back end. The male is a lime green posteriorly with a diffuse blue anterior end. It is easily recognized by its long beak or bill which is a rather large mouth with large hooked and pointed teeth.

It is far from common and not found in any large numbers so it may take patience to obtain a specimen. Once established it is a hardy species. **82**

Goodeidae TOPMINNOWS
A small rather specialized family of live bearing fish which are found only in Mexico. In place of the gonopodium, which is the organ of intromission in the live bearing Poeciliidae, the anterior few rays of the anal fin are stiffened and separated. There is considerable maternal care of the young by supplementary nourishment in the oviduct and they are considered truly viviparous fishes. See *Neotoca.*

GORGEOUS FUNDULUS see *Nothobranchius orthonotus*
GOUCHO, FIGHTING see *Cynolebias melanotaenia*
GOURAMI see *Colisa, Helostoma, Osphronemus, Sphaerichthys, Trichogaster, Trichopsis*
GOVERNMENT BREAM see *Lutjanus sebae*
Gnat larvae see under *Food*
GRACEFUL CATFISH see *Pimelodella gracilis*

Gramma Grammidae Ψ
– ***loreto*** ROYAL GRAMMA   8cm. (3in.)
A small dwarf grouper or basslet from the Caribbean. It has a violet front end and a bright daffodil yellow posterior which is lovely to look at, if a little difficult to live with. It is hardy and readily takes a variety of live food. It is a bit of an aquabatic clown.

– melacara BLACKCAP GRAMMA 10cm. (4in.)
This delightful fish lives at great depths in the Caribbean and has to be raised carefully to the surface or it will get the 'bends', the divers' nightmare. The head and dorsal fin are black and the rest of the body purple.

Grammidae GRAMMAFISH
This marine family includes the dwarf groupers and is closely related to the Serranidae. They consume live food which is caught with a rush after a long wait in some appropriate hole in a sea wall. See *Gramma*.

Grammistes Grammistidae Ψ
– sexlineatus SIX-STRIPED GROUPER, GOLDEN-STRIPED SOAPFISH ✂ 30cm. (12in.)
A marine species which is a typical grouper having six pale yellow stripes running horizontally on a dark almost black body. It comes from the Indian and Pacific oceans. It is greedy and aggressive so beware of expensive smaller fish. Prefers to live in open water. The skin slime of this species is reported to act as a defence mechanism, being distasteful to predators.

Grammistidae SOAPFISHES
Members of this family are found in the tropical Atlantic, Pacific and the Indo-Pacific. They are related to the perches and are noticeably distinguished by the slippery feel to their skin due to the large amounts of mucus which these fish secrete when excited. These large amounts of mucus produce froth in aquaria which will kill all the inhabitants. It is toxic to predatory fish and has a bitter taste. Their generous bodies are covered with small scales and the head is large. The dorsal fin contains short spines and many have anal spines. See *Grammistes*.

GRASS
    HAIR see under *Plants – Eleocharis*
    UMBRELLA HAIR see under *Plants – Eleocharis*
GREEN
    BARB see *Barbus semifasciolatus*
    CHROMIDE see *Etroplus suratensis*
    PANCHAX see *Aplocheilus blocki*
    PARROT see *Thalassoma lunare*
    PARROTFISH see *Callyodon sordidus*
    PIGMENT see under *Photosynthesis*
    PUFFER see *Tetraodon fluviatilis*
    RIVULUS see *Rivulus cylindraceus, Rivulus urophthalmus*

Green Water
This is due to excessive algal growth. Algae are present in all tanks to a greater or lesser extent. They do however flourish in alkaline water and good light. In a well balanced

aquarium they are kept under control. Sometimes however, where too much light is available they produce what is called an algal bloom. The water becomes cloudy and has an unpleasant smell. This is dangerous to fish and requires prompt action. The water should be changed and the tank cleaned and re-established, making sure in the future to reduce light and nutrients.

GREY ANGELFISH see *Pomacanthus arcuatus*
GROUPER see *Cephalopholis, Epinephelus, Grammistes,*
    Pomicrops, Pseudochromidae, Pseudochromis, Variola
GRUNT
    POLKA-DOT see *Plectorhynchus chaetodonoides*
GUDGEON
    see *Gobio gobio*
    AUSTRALIAN PURPLE-SPOTTED see *Mogurnda mogurnda*
GULARIS see *Aphyosemion*
GUNTHER'S
    CICHLID see *Pelmatochromis guentheri*
    FUNDULUS see *Nothobranchius guentheri*
GUPPY see *Poecilia reticulata*
GUYANA
    LEAFFISH see *Polycentrus schomburgki*
    CATFISH see *Corydoras melanistius*

Gymnochanda Centropomidae ⊕
– filamentosa THREADFIN GLASSFISH 5cm. (2in.)
From Malaya, one of the more recent fish to be discovered by the aquarist. It is very similar in characteristics to the genus *Chanda* and has the typical split dorsal fin. The anal and dorsal fins of the male are extended into a series of loose filaments which provide it with the specific and common names. The body is transparent but the solid parts are coloured a rich golden brown. It should be kept in slightly brackish water.

Gymnocorymbus Characidae ⊕
– ternetzi BLACK TETRA, BLACKAMOOR, BLACK WIDOW, PETTICOATFISH 8cm. (3in.)
This distinctive characin, from the Rio Negro and Rio Paraguay, is fairly popular. Characterized by its two dark vertical bars in the front half of the body and the faintly black hind end, with a pronounced and well developed anal fin; it makes an attractive display, particularly when a group are kept together. Its military approach to group movement, proceeding as it does, in rigid formations, is another attraction. It shades from green on the head to silvery at the leading edge of the dorsal fin. As these fish grow longer than 4cm., the black begins to fade and they become less appealing to the eye. They breed readily in captivity. Sexing is very difficult and depends entirely on size comparisons.

Very suitable for the community tank for they are peaceful but not to be trifled with. **83**

Gymnotidae KNIFEFISH, GYMNOTID EELS
A group of thin elongated fish which get their popular name – Knifefish – from the very long anal fin which resembles a knife blade. They are occasionally called Gymnotid Eels although they are not eels, being closely related to the characins. Perhaps the most widely known species is the Electric Eel, *Electrophorus electricus*, which is usually classified under Gymnotidae although some experts place it in a separate family, the Electrophoridae. All Knifefish of this family come from Central or South America.

The characteristic knife shape is enhanced by the small or absent dorsal fin. Occasionally the dorsal fin is represented by a few pathetic rays resembling a worn out yard brush.

They are not ideal aquarium fish being aggressive, even cannibalistic, rather large, and active at night.

Knifefish move by undulating their long anal fin and, by reversing the waves, they can go forwards or backwards with equal facility. Committed carnivores they should be fed raw meat, earthworms or fish.

Hardy, tenacious to life even at the hands of the most neglectful of aquarists, they withstand temperatures over a wide range. They are probably best kept at about 24°C.

They have not bred in captivity perhaps because of the size stunting which captivity causes. See *Gymnotus, Hypopomus*.

Gymnotus Gymnotidae ⊕
– ***carapo*** BANDED KNIFEFISH, SOUTH AMERICAN RAZORFISH
61cm. (2ft)
From South and Central America. Its beige body is barred with wide oblique dark reddish-brown markings. The pectoral fins are small, the dorsal and the tail fins are absent.

Gyrinocheilidae
A very small family of fish which contains only three species. They all come from Thailand and Cambodia. See *Gyrinocheilus*.

Gyrinocheilus Gyrinocheilidae ⊕
– ***aymonieri*** SUCKER LOACH 13–30cm. (5–12in.)
This fish, which comes from Thailand, in captivity it rarely exceeds 13cm. and at this length it is sexually mature. It is an exceptionally good eater of algae, and has a useful place in the community tank.

Its rounded slightly depressed body is elongated. The body is basically beige with dark patches and the fins are clear with occasional dots. The mouth has protruding lips and forms a sucker. Very active fish which thrive in a large well planted aquarium. **84**

H

HAIR
GRASS see under *Plants – Eleocharis*
GRASS, UMBRELLA see under *Plants – Eleocharis*
HAIR-PIN see *Trichopterus trichopterus*
HALF-AND-HALF WRASSE see *Hemigymnus melapterus*
HALF-BANDED
BARB see *Barbus semifasciolatus*
COOLIE LOACH see *Acanthophthalmus semicinctus*
PYRRHULINA see *Pyrrhulina semifasciatus*
HALF-BEAK see *Dermogenys, Exocoetidae, Hemirhamphidae*
HALIMED TUNA see *Plants – Marine*

Hardness of Water
Water is hard due to the presence of various chemical substances. Temporary hardness is due to dissolved calcium and magnesium bicarbonate. Permanent hardness results mainly from chloride and sulphate salts of calcium and magnesium. Temporary hardness is easily removed by boiling when the bicarbonates are changed to the very much less soluble carbonates. It is these deposited carbonates of temporary hard water which cause furring of kettles. Temporary hardness is also removed by adding any soluble alkaline to the water.

Permanently hard water is softened by adding soda (sodium carbonate) to it, which precipitates the soluble salts of calcium or magnesium. Another more expensive way is to distil the permanently hard water, that is to boil the water and condense the resulting steam.

Hard water can be softened for domestic use by installing a commercial water softener, but they tend to be expensive.

Hardness of water varies with the amount of substances dissolved in it. It can be soft, medium soft, hard or very hard. Several scales are used in different countries to measure the hardness of water. The simplest method is to calculate the parts of calcium carbonate dissolved in a million parts of water (ppm). However it is often customary in the UK to use Clark's degrees which is the number of grains of calcium carbonate in each Imperial gallon, and in Germany the DH measure has been devised, which is the parts of calcium oxide in each 100,000 of water.

1 Clark's degree = 143 parts of calcium carbonate per million

1 DH degree = 179 parts of calcium oxide per million

DH degrees can be converted to Clark's by multiplying by $\frac{56}{100}$.

Clark's degrees can be converted to DH degrees by multiplying by $\frac{100}{56}$.

Testing for hardness by the Schwarzenbach method is well within the competence of anybody who has studied simple chemistry at school and can very easily be learnt by others. The apparatus is available from chemical and laboratory suppliers. Take 50 ml. of the water to be tested and place it in a titration flask. To this add 2 ml. of ammonia buffer solution, and a tablet of total hardness indicator. By shaking the flask the water will become pink. A 20 ml. burette in a stand should next be filled accurately with ethylene diamine tetra acetic acid. The flask of pink coloured test water is now placed below the burette and the titrating solution run in slowly a drop at a time. The flask should be shaken after each drop. As soon as the water in the flask turns from pink to blue read the burette. The number of ml. of titrating fluid used multiplied by 20 gives the hardness of the water in parts per million.

HARLEQUIN CATFISH see *Microglanis parahybae*
HARLEQUINFISH see *Rasbora heteromorpha*
HART'S RIVULUS see *Rivulus hartii*
HASSAR, THE see *Callichthys callichthys*
HATCHETFISH see *Carnegiella, Gasteropelecidae, Gasteropelecus, Thoracocharax*
HAWAIIAN
    LIONFISH see *Pterois sphex*
    SOLDIERFISH see *Myripristis chryseres*
    TRIGGERFISH see under *Balistes bursa*
HAWKFISH see *Amblycirrhitus, Cirrhitichthys*
HEAD-AND-TAIL-LIGHT TETRA see *Hemigrammus ocellifer*
HEADSTANDER see *Anostomus, Abramites, Charax, Chilodus*

Heating
The purpose of any heating system is to control the temperature of the water to that in which the fish being kept are adapted by evolution. It is clearly important not just to heat the water but to maintain it at a reasonably constant temperature. For this latter purpose we use a thermostat which is sensitive to the temperature of the water and can be set to any required temperature. It then controls the heater which is switched on and off as required.

The commonest form of heating employed by the amateur aquarist is electrically powered. Large commercial units often use oil or solid fuel to provide heat to large numbers of tanks at a more economical rate. The electrical aquarium heater is efficient, simple and cheap to buy. It consists of a length of wire coiled around a support, the whole being placed in a tube made of heat resistant glass. The wire ends are brought out through a waterproof bung. This is laid on the bottom of the aquarium and hidden at the rear of the tank. The electricity used for an ordinary sized tank is no more than that of a moderate electric bulb and with a thermostat in the circuit the cost should be less.

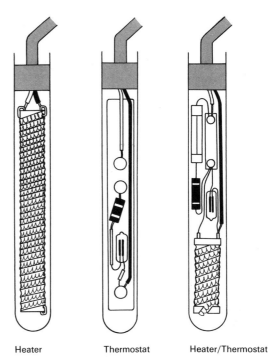

Heater   Thermostat   Heater/Thermostat

The thermostat is based on the phenomenon that metal expands when heated. In the thermostat there is a strip of metal which, when the temperature of the water cools, contracts and closes the electrical circuit, thus starting the heater. As the temperature rises the metal expands and the contact breaks, switching off the heater. The contact gap can be adjusted so that the temperature of the water only needs to fall very slightly for the thermostat to activate the circuit and start the heater. In practice the design is more complicated but this gives an outline of the basic principle.

Gas heating is used by some aquarists. There may be some reduction in cost when the enterprise is on a large scale.

Oil lamps have been used for heating but except in special circumstances, e.g. where houses have no permanent gas or electricity, they are more trouble than they are worth. See *Thermometers*.

Hearing see *Acoustico Lateralis System*
Hedge, Water see under *Plants – Dicliplis*

Helostoma Helostomatidae ⊕
– rudolfi see *H. temmincki*
– temmincki KISSING GOURAMI 30cm. (12in.)
This fish is characterized by splendid thick protruding lips which conceal a fine set of teeth. Its name comes from the habit of approaching any other fish face to face and planting a 'kiss' on its lips. This is not a prelude to mating and probably has something to do with rivalry fights. They

Kissing Gourami, *Helostoma temmincki.*

come from Thailand, the Malay Peninsula and islands of the Indonesian archipelago.

There are two colour forms. A dark greenish form with a silvery belly, light brown eyes and occasionally with horizontal bars on the side. The other form has a pinkish yellow body and dark eyes and is by some considered to be a colour variety, by others a distinct species, *H. rudolfi.* They prefer temperatures of about 24–28°C. and are mainly vegetable eaters.

Rarely breed in captivity. They lay eggs without providing a bubble nest.

Helostomatidae
A single-species family making up the group of labyrinth-fishes; the other labyrinthfish families include Anabantidae, Belontiidae, and Osphronemidae. It lives in poorly oxygenated freshwater utilizing its accessory breathing apparatus to supplement its oxygen requirements. It comes from Asia. It has long dorsal and anal fins and large lips. See *Helostoma.*

Hemichromis Cichlidae ⊕
– ***bimaculatus*** AFRICAN JEWELFISH, RED CICHLID
5cm. (2in.)
This species is from tropical Africa. Although some variation occurs with season and emotion at its best it is a lovely aquatic gem. The body is basically a rich almost bright chocolate brown turning bright red at breeding time. The belly and lower jaw are a rich ruby red. The body is scattered with blue dots giving the appearance of diamonds. The fins are transparent at the base but decorated with patterns of coloured spots, and the rays and margins are red. The operculum is particularly rich in blue spots, most

brilliant in the male – a distinguishing sexual feature.

Sadly this species is rather quarrelsome which limits its popularity. It will breed, however, providing it overcomes this aggressive tendency. It then makes a typically diligent cichlid parent. It has a wide range of temperature adaptability from 20–31°C. and breeds at the upper end of this range. **85**
– ***fasciatus*** BANDED JEWELFISH 30cm. (12in.) ✂
When adult this native of West Africa is a brassy blond with red highlights. Five or six vertical bands or patches decorate its side. A large blue spot adorns the operculum, the dorsal and tail fins are dark with red borders, and the anal fin is yellow. It grows up to 30cm. in length. During the breeding season the colours intensify and become richer while the head, anal fin and the lower lobe of the tail become red. It can be very aggressive.

Hemigrammus Characidae ⊕
– ***caudovittatus*** BUENOS AIRES TETRA 9cm. (3½in.)
This is a large characin from the River Plate. It is hardy with a very wide temperature range. The body is generally silver but tending to green above and yellowish white below. There is a black diamond mark at the base of the tail which is continuous with a faint horizontal line in front. The fins vary in colour from browny red to red.

A reasonably good community fish but may fin bite when larger or if not fed enough.

This fish breeds quite readily in captivity but the female may attack and kill the male as a reward for his attentions. Perhaps for this habit alone it should fall from the aquarist's favour.
– ***erythrozonus*** GLOWLIGHT TETRA 5cm. (2in.)
A medium-sized characin from Guyana, it has a translucent, in parts almost clear, body with a red line passing back from the eye to, but not entering the tail. There is a red blotch in the upper part of the eye. The dorsal fin alone is coloured with a red patch behind the leading edge. It is hardy, has no demanding feeding habits and can be bred in captivity. The breeding behaviour is uncharacteristic of characins. The pair locks fins in an embrace and rolls dur-ing which eggs are expelled and then fertilized by the male. Plants should be provided to catch the adhesive eggs. **86**
– ***nanus*** SILVER-TIP TETRA 5cm. (2in.)
This characin from South America is not very colourful. It needs to be specially lit from above with a dark background to bring out the beauty of its silver-tipped fins.

It readily breeds in captivity. **87**
– ***ocellifer*** HEAD-AND-TAIL-LIGHT TETRA, BEACONFISH
5cm. (2in.)
Native to the Orinoco and the Amazon Basin. The body colour varies from a translucent green dorsally to a silver belly. There is a black spot behind the operculum or gill

cover. A yellow gold line extends horizontally back from the spot to the tail fin, where it stops at a large black spot. It gets its name from the yellow glowing spots in the eye and the dorsal tail spot. The male is distinguished from the female by having a white spot towards the pointed tip of the anal fin, while the tip of the female's anal fin is rounded and spotless.

These are unusual characins in that they readily breed and most of the aquarists' demands for specimens are met from captive bred fish. For breeding the temperature should be raised to reach 26–28°C.

They have no special food requirements but thrive better with some live daphnia. **88**

– *pulcher*   PRETTY or THE GANNET TETRA   5cm. (2in.)
The Pretty Tetra comes from the upper Amazon. It has a deeper body than most characins. Its distinguishing feature is a blotch of black on the posterior part of the body which extends for somewhat less than half the body length. Above this a golden yellow line of variable distinctiveness passes the whole length of the body finishing at the head. The fins are transparent and tinted red. Not easy to breed in captivity and the young grow slowly.

– *rhodostomus*   RUMMY or RED-NOSED TETRA   4cm. (1½in.)
This attractive fish is native to the Amazon of Brazil. It has a green back, silver sides and a yellowish white belly. The head is a brilliant red and running back from the head there is a horizontal black line which grows wider as it approaches the tail. It enters the tail and, together with the black bars separated by white, gives a pied appearance to the tail.

It has only rarely been bred in captivity. Temperatures around 25°C. suit it best.

– *unilineatus*   FEATHERFIN or ONE-LINE TETRA   5cm. (2in.)
This characin comes from Trinidad and the northern part of South America.

The body is silver below gradually attaining a greenish tinge dorsally. The tail fin is brownish as is the anal fin posteriorly. It is characterized by black and white bars on the leading edge of the anal fin. In spite of the absence of any notable colour or markings it has been universally popular with aquarists for many years. Will breed fairly readily in captivity. Its feeding habits are catholic, it is also hardy and peaceful and will adapt to a wide range of temperatures, between 21–29°C.

Hemigymnus   Labridae   ✄
– *melapterus*   HALF-AND-HALF WRASSE   71cm. (28in.)
A rather large member of the family for the aquarium when adult, it is often imported when small. It comes from the Indo-Pacific. As its name implies the body colour is distinctly divided into two. The anterior half is a dirty white colour. The posterior half is a dark chocolate brown. The

caudal fin is a bright yellow. It is medium deep in the body with low, very long-based dorsal and anal fins.

Hemihaplochromis   Cichlidae   ⊕
– *multicolor*   EGYPTIAN MOUTH-BROODER   8cm. (3in.)
A native of the Nile Delta down to Tanzania, this fish is small for a cichlid.

A beautiful fish with well-defined coloration. The back is a dark purple which moves through various shades of mauve, blue and green to an almost yellow belly. The scales are edged with silver giving a sequin-like appearance. A short dark bar passes obliquely through the eye and the unpaired fins are a greeny blue speckled with pale blue-white dots.

Members of this species are popularly known as mouth brooders, although more accurately described as buccal cavity incubators, see *Cichlidae*. The female takes the eggs in her cavernous mouth and there they remain until their yolk sac is absorbed and the fry are free swimming. During this time the female does not eat and scarcely opens her mouth except to make chewing movements; these are thought to clean the eggs and to encourage water circulation, and so provide an adequate oxygen supply. Needless to say the female loses weight and looks 'all head' which to the inexperienced can appear as a diseased state. For the first few days, when just emerged from her mouth, the young keep close by and return to their oral home at the least sign of danger.

A hardy fish that withstands relatively low temperatures, it makes a suitable addition to the community tank.

Hemiodontidae
A small family of fish from Central and South America. They have a small mouth and either two teeth in the lower jaw or several very small ones. Until recently they were classified with the characins but are now classified separately mainly because of the morphology of the jaw. All members of the family have an adipose fin. They are slim, streamlined fish.

They prefer temperatures of about 24–26°C. and require great care in feeding. Very small, fine live food, such as brine shrimp, is essential, especially for the slow growing young.

At night the longitudinal stripes fade to be replaced by vertical bands. See *Characidium, Hemiodopsis*.

Hemiodopsis   Hemiodontidae
– *semitaeniatus*   20cm. (8in.)
This fish comes from Guyana and the Amazon Basin. The general body colour is metallic silver. A dark spot on the side precedes a line which extends backwards to the lower tip of the tail fin. The dark line is bordered above and below

by a thin white line. Apart from a slightly pinkish tinge to the anal and lower lobe of the tail fins, the fish is without colour. It is, however, a pleasing shape and makes an attractive addition to the community tank. Feeding is relatively easy, but it has not bred in captivity.

Hemipteronotus Labridae Ψ
– taeniurus DRAGON WRASSE 30cm. (12in.)
Behaviourally, a most interesting fish from the Indo-Pacific. It is well camouflaged to blend with its habitat of weed and moves backwards and forwards keeping time with the gentle swaying movements of the waves. It also buries itself at night so provide a thick layer of sand. It has been known by a variety of scientific names, including *Labrus taeniurus, L. hemisphaerium, Xyrichthys taeniurus* and *Novacula taeniurus.*

The basic colour of this fish, as one would expect for camouflage among seaweed, is yellow green. The body shape is broken to blend with the seaweed by a series of darker green irregular vertical lines extending onto the otherwise clear dorsal fin which extends almost the length of the body, and the anal fin which reaches forward almost to the pelvic fins. In addition there are several quite large grey patches all along the body and in particular around the eyes which are bordered with dark green.

Quite easy to keep in captivity; it readily accepts brine shrimp. **89**

Hemirhamphidae see *Exocoetidae*

Heniochus Chaetodontidae ✂
Some of the Wimplefish, *Heniochus* sp., are rather unusual in having large extensions to their fins causing confusion of classification. They closely resemble the Angelfish of the Pomacanthidae family.
– acuminatus WIMPLEFISH, FEATHERFIN, BANNERFISH 36cm. (14in.)
It has the usual compressed circular body. The pectoral fins are large and the dorsal has a very long extension of the first few rays. Its body is white with black transverse stripes and its tail fin is yellow. It is sometimes referred to as 'the poor man's Moorish Idol'.

Wimplefish, *Heniochus acuminatus.*

Quite easy to acclimatize in captivity, it readily and greedily takes all food. It is bold and forms groups of shoals in nature and comes from the Red Sea and the Indo-Pacific.

– *chrysostomus* BLACK-HEADED WIMPLEFISH, THREE-BANDED BULLFISH   23cm. (9in.)

The round compressed body has the typical elongation of the dorsal fin rays. It has a white body with black vertical bars rather similar to *H. acuminatus* but with the addition of black markings on the head. It comes from the eastern Indo-Australian archipelago and the Pacific Ocean. Rather a timid fish and a little difficult to get to feed when it first tastes captivity. Daphnia and tubifex overcome the hunger strike.

– *intermediatus* RED SEA WIMPLEFISH or BANNERFISH 25cm. (10in.)

A rather drab fish for this family, its cream body is decorated with brown vertical stripes. It comes from the Red Sea. Its claim to fame is hardiness and a ready acceptance of captivity and it takes dry food after a brief period of quarantine. This Wimplefish has the elongated rays of the dorsal fin which is common to the genus.

– *varius* HUMPHEAD BANNERFISH or SEA BULL 20cm. (8in.)

Wide ranging throughout the Indo-Pacific. Juveniles of this species are difficult to distinguish from *H. acuminatus*. The two vertical dark bands which are separate in *H. acuminatus* merge before passing onto the dorsal fin in *H. varius*. The adults are easy to identify, since they have the hump on the head which gives the species its common name. The vertical bars in adults spread inwards to merge as a dark triangle in this species, unlike *H. acuminatus*. Males possess the elongation above the eye, while the female does not. There is no elongation of the dorsal fin in adults.

They do well in captivity if provided with plenty of space, see *Establishing a Marine Aquarium*. Live food is preferred. **90**

HERRINGBONE RIVULUS see *Rivulus strigatus*

Heterandria Poecilidae ⊕
–*formosa* MOSQUITOFISH, DWARF MINNOW
♂ 2cm. (¾in.), ♀ 3cm. (c1¼in.)

From the south-eastern states of the USA this fish doesn't boast any unforgettable colour scheme. It is, however, of interest because of its very small size which gives it its popular name. It is the smallest live-bearer and nearly the smallest vertebrate. The body colour varies from an olive green to a metallic silver depending on lighting conditions. A dark irregular horizontal line runs the length of the body. The fins are clear, tinged with yellow, the dorsal having both a red and a black spot.

Their small size makes them unsuitable members of a community tank. They look too much like food to their larger companions.

Their reproduction is similar to the normal pattern for live-bearers but with an interesting modification. Instead of producing a group of young at once the young are born in pairs periodically for 2–3 weeks.

An active, interesting, if somewhat sombre, little fish.

Heteropyge xanthometapon see *Euxiphipeps xanthometapon*

Hippocampus Syngnathidae Ψ
–*erectus* syn. *H. hudsonius* GIANT or SPOTTED SEAHORSE 30cm. (12in.)

Formerly known as *H. hudsonius*, the colour of this species varies considerably with surroundings, ranging from brown through greens, yellows, and grey to black.

Some authorities designate two sub-species, a northern variety which is found anywhere from the southern coast of USA and ranges far north, and a southern type found often among sargasso weed and commonly the possessor of

Asian Seahorse, *Hippocampus kuda*.

innumerable tassels and other adornments in an attempt to camouflage itself. The southern form, also known as the Southern Giant, assumes the speckled brown and yellow coloration of sargasso weed.

Like all seahorses they are relatively slow moving and need seaweed or coral around which to wrap their prehensile tails while resting and live crustaceans for food. Failure to provide such conditions will result in an exhausted and ultimately dead seahorse. They are not good community tank candidates because, with their slow movements, they cannot compete with faster tank mates for food and are unsuitably large for most tanks.

– guttulatus EUROPEAN SEAHORSE 18cm. (7in.)
This delightful seahorse is found throughout European waters, and several subspecies have evolved. It has a rather long nose and is greyish brown dorsally, fading to irregular patches on the belly.

– hippocampus SHORT-NOSED SEAHORSE 18cm. (7in.)
A delightful inhabitant of the Mediterranean. It is a combination of black, dark and light grey thin parallel lines across the body. It lives among weed in shallow warmer water.

– hudsonius see *H. erectus*

– kuda ASIAN SEAHORSE 30cm. (12in.)
Larger than most of its kind, this delightful marine inhabitant is found over large areas of the Indo-Pacific and is the one most commonly kept in aquariums. The body is a golden yellow decorated with reddish brown lines and dots on the body and head. **91**

– zosterae DWARF SEAHORSE 5cm. (2in.)
Coming from the Caribbean and the Gulf of Mexico, these popular and delightful fish are commonly kept by marine enthusiasts. They are usually browny beige in colour but subject to wide variations depending on the environment.

Dwarf seahorses are the exception to the current marine rule and breed in captivity. The young are easily reared on baby brine shrimps.

History of Domestication

Without going deeply into the definition of a domesticated animal one can state that very few species of fish have been domesticated by man. Domestic species when used by man for food dispense with the need to spend time hunting for them. They can be bred in sufficient quantities near at hand and simply cropped when required.

Ancient civilizations, like the Egyptians, had ponds where fish were kept, if not actually bred. The Romans were great fish pond owners and influential families had salt water ponds near to the sea where the gastronomic delicacy, the Roman Moray Eel, *Muraena helaena*, could be kept for later consumption. It seems unlikely that these eels were bred in captivity. The Romans are also thought to have kept freshwater fish for food in ponds.

Archaeological evidence shows that the Carp, *Cyprinus carpio*, was a popular fish in European monasteries where it was kept in large muddy ponds and fed on waste food from the monks' tables. The Carp had, however, been kept in captivity if not actually domesticated for many centuries before it graced the abbots' tables. The Chinese were certainly breeding them before that time.

It is the Goldfish, *Carassius auratus*, which is most associated with domestication. Many varieties, some of such grotesque formation that they bear little resemblance to their forebears, have been bred for many centuries. The Chinese have done most of the breeding to produce both beauties and monstrosities. They were probably first bred as a food since the wild Goldfish, *Carassius carassius*, is far from brightly coloured, but their tenacity to life and ready breeding potential soon showed and the fancy varieties followed. Goldfish were first bred in China in the 10th century, arrived in England in the 17th century and were soon a popular curiosity.

In recent times a great variety of fish species have been kept in captivity, have bred and have been developed by aquarists into varieties. Many of these would be indistinguishable from a domestic animal, according to any definition it is possible to devise.

Histrio Antennariidae Ψ
– histrio SARGASSUMFISH 20cm. (8in.)
A fascinating fish which is found in all tropical seas of the world. It lives in the Sargassum weed which floats at the ocean surface but also occurs on coral reefs. Here it crawls among the weed using its modified pectoral fins which enable it to actually clasp the plant. Scaleless, it has a great many flaps of loose skin all over its body which are part of its camouflage. In addition it has the ability to change colour to suit its surroundings. It feeds on the rich supply of larger plankton found in amongst the weed and on fishes. It lays its eggs to form a floating platform amongst the weed. It is quite often imported for the aquarist but does not seem to be well suited to captivity and is not long lived.

Hobby Benefits

In these days of high rise apartments and concrete conurbations many people feel the need to retain some connection, however tenuous, with the world of nature. In town apartments, dogs and cats are often either unsuitable or forbidden and it is to smaller animals like cage birds, small rodents and fish that people turn. Many prefer fish to rodents or cage birds since they can be kept in conditions more closely resembling their natural habitat.

Lonely people are afforded the joy of living things in close proximity. Creatures which demand their attention and interest but without some of the ties and restrictions of larger pets. You can leave your fish for a few hours without feeling guilty.

To many, the aesthetic attraction of the hobby is reward enough. Others find mental relaxation from the peaceful silent movement. To the technically minded it provides a wealth of mechanical and electronic gadgetry.

Biologically or animal minded people here find an interest which demands as much attention and skill as the keeping of any other animal, if it is to be kept content and healthy. Successful aquarists are above all good with animals. They are sensitive to their needs and close observers of animal behaviour and no amount of technology will supplant that requirement.

HOGFISH see *Bodianus, Lachnolaimus*
HOGSNAPPER see *Lachnolaimus maximus*

Holacanthus   Chaetodontidae
– *ciliaris* QUEEN ANGELFISH   46cm (18in.)
This is a very attractive fish which is commonly imported into the USA by dealers. The body is basically a rich purple which fades to a bluish green below. The scales are edged with a deep brownish orange. The pectoral, pelvic and caudal fins are all yellow orange in colour. Blue patches decorate the head around the mouth and chin. A black patch ringed with dark blue enhances the neck, and the pectoral fins have a blue base.

This species is found from the coast of Florida to Brazil and in the Caribbean.
– *isabelita* BLUE ANGELFISH   45cm. (18in.)
A lovely fish from the Caribbean. As a youngster it shows the typical stripes of green and yellow with black, which disappear in adulthood. The adult has a greenish yellow body.
– *tricolor* ROCK BEAUTY   41cm. (16in.)
From the Caribbean, this yellow fish has a black patch that expands with age on the posterior part of the body and a red flush to the edges of the dorsal and anal fins. It suits the community tank well, before it grows too large.
– *trimaculatus* THREE-SPOT ANGELFISH   45cm. (18in.)
This fish is rather unusual in that its yellow body colour, blue mouth parts and three black head spots are established even in very young fish. It is omnivorous and comes from the Indo-Pacific region. It does not take well to captivity.
– *xanthometapon* see *Euxiphipeps xanthometapon*

Holidays
Inevitably the problem of leaving fish during holiday periods presents problems. If your absence is to be brief – a few days – then it is better to leave them without food. They will come to no harm and will not starve. Ensure that your

mechanical apparatus – heaters and filters etc. – are functioning correctly, then leave with an easy mind. It is probably better to lower the temperature of the tank a few degrees, thereby reducing the metabolic rate.

If your stay must be longer, try to enlist the help of an experienced colleague. To leave fish in the hands of novices is courting disaster. If a willing friend must be used, try to persuade the volunteer along each day for at least a week before you leave, allowing them to perform all the routine tasks under your watchful eye. Also don't forget to leave an address or telephone number where help is available in the event of an unexpected problem or emergency.

Recently a slow releasing food has become available commercially which provides adequate nutrition for some species over several weeks, clearly of value at holiday times.

Holocentridae   SOLDIERFISH or SQUIRRELFISH
A family of marine fish which have successfully colonized most of the shallow waters of the tropical seas. They are not particularly attractive in shape with spinous and soft dorsal fins and a long free anterior spine to the anal fin. They are a nocturnal family, the species of which hide during the day among the rocks and coral, and come out at night to feed on a variety of animal life including smaller fish, so beware of your community combination. They are all basically red in colour with large protruding eyes. See *Holocentrus, Myripristis.*

Holocentrus   Holocentridae   Ψ
– *ascensionis* LONG-JAW SQUIRRELFISH   60cm. (24in.)
One of the squirrelfish more popular in the USA than in Europe or the UK. It is found throughout the tropical areas of the Atlantic but is more common in the Caribbean and the Gulf of Mexico.

In nature it lives closely associated with rocky or coral reefs and its diet consists of small crustacea. Mainly nocturnal by nature.

It is bright red with white longitudinal bands running the length of the body. The dorsal lobe of the caudal fin is longer than the lower.

Although potentially a large fish it rarely reaches more than 15cm. in the aquarium.
– *diadema* CROWNED SOLDIERFISH   45cm. (18in.)
Also known as *Adioryx diadema*, this fish is from the Indo-Pacific and basically red in colour. It has a long spine on the operculum. Unsuitable as company for smaller fish which it may eat. **92**
– *rubrum* RED SQUIRRELFISH   28cm. (11in.)
From the Indo-Pacific, it is very common in the Australian and Indian waters where it spends its day hidden in rock crevices in deep water to appear only at night.

Like most members of the genus, this fish has red

coloration. There are, however, a number of horizontal stripes somewhat paler in colour. The long-based spiny dorsal fin has a dark band close to the border.

Although nocturnal in nature they switch to diurnal habits in captivity. They feed on small crustacea so do well on brine shrimp.

Hoplosternum   Callychthidae   ⊕
– ***thoracatum***   MAILED or PORT CATFISH   20cm. (8in.)
This species is widely distributed from Central America, including the islands of the Caribbean, south throughout the Amazon Basin. It varies in basic colour with distribution from a dark olive, commoner in the northern extremes of its range, to a grey brown in the south. The dorsal region is often a dark brown black while the belly is very light grey. Over the body are large and small black patches which sometimes join to form bands. The fins have dark spots.

The breeding behaviour is interesting since it requires the co-operation of several males. A group of males build a bubble nest and collectively pay court to the female. One male of the group takes a position beneath the nest and the female collects sperm from him with her suctorial mouth. She then dives to the bottom rapidly rising again to deposit eggs, which she holds in her pelvic fins, in the bubble nest. Finally she adds the sperm collected from the male. The male group take care of the young. **93**

HORA'S CLOWN LOACH see *Botia horae*
HORNWORT see under *Plants – Ceratophyllum*
HOVERCRAFT see *Tetrosomus gibbosus*
HUMBUG, BANDED see *Dascyllus aruanus*
HUMBUG DAMSELFISH see *Dascyllus aruanus, Dascyllus melanurus*
HUMPBACK HEADSTANDER see *Charax gibbosus*
HUMPBACK see *Poecilia nigrofasciata*
HUMPHEAD BANNERFISH see *Heniochus varius*
HUNCHBACK see *Poecilia nigrofasciata*
HUSSAR, BLUE-BANDED see *Lutjanus kasmira*

Hybridization
A hybrid is the result of a crossing between two different species of the same genus. This is rare in nature as geographical separation or behavioural variations between species generally prevent sexual activity. It does, however, occur and it is more common in fish than in other groups of vertebrates. Several genera of both fresh and marine fish are known to interbreed.

The offspring of such a mating may be sterile, like mules – hybrids of horse and donkey – or have some level of fertility. Hybrids show a range of characteristics, some from one parent some from the other.

Hydra see under *Unwelcome Visitors*
Hydrilla see under *Plants*
Hydrogen Ion Concentration see *pH*
Hygrophila see under *Plants*

Hyphessobrycon   Characidae   ⊕
– ***bifasciatus***   YELLOW TETRA   5cm. (2in.)
This medium-sized characin from south-eastern Brazil is of a dull yellow hue with two dark bands running vertically just behind the head. The male has a larger anal fin. It is not a very colourful fish but has the virtue of breeding readily, a characteristic more favoured by some than a colourful appearance. A hardy species, it makes a good member of a community tank.
– ***callistus***   SERPA or ROSY TETRA   4cm. (1½in.)
This medium-sized tetra comes from Paraguay. It is a delightful fish – placid, slow moving and peaceable. Its body colour tends to silver near the head, gradually turning to pinky red towards the tail. The tail, anal, pelvic and pectoral fins are a deeper red. There is a black blotch behind the head and the dorsal fin is predominantly black. The *callistus* complex has quite a variance in finnage and colour depending on locality and subspecies involved.

They are moderately difficult to breed but increasingly the hobby is being supplied with captive bred animals. A situation which all conservationists and nature lovers should applaud.
– ***eos***   DAWN TETRA   4cm. (1¾in.)
One of the smaller characins, it comes from Guyana. It is a fish of changing colour tints rather than specific markings and for this reason does not enjoy the popularity of some of its cousins. The body is a mixture of yellow, red and orange, decorated with dark spots. The fins are yellow for the most part but the tail and anal fins can become a deep orange red. The base of the tail is marked by a large dark ovoid spot, above which is a copper coloured flash.
– ***flammeus***   RED TETRA, FLAMEFISH   5cm. (2in.)
This fish is popular among aquarists. It comes from the surroundings of Rio de Janeiro. The head and belly are silvery which gradually changes into flame red towards the middle of the body. The pectorals are transparent and colourless but the pelvic, anal, tail and dorsal fins are also flame red. It is reasonably hardy, enjoys live food, and does best in temperatures around 24°C.

The anal fin of the male is larger than the female's and its ventral edge straight while the female's is curved inwards towards the body. Breeding is relatively easy providing the fishes are given plenty of room and adequate plant cover. The male and female retire to the weed where eggs are laid and fertilized in batches of about a dozen. They are slightly adhesive and will usually remain among the plants. Young hatch in just a few days depending on the temperature and do well on algae, or artificial food finely ground.

– *heterorhabdus* FLAG-STRIPED TETRA 5cm. (2in.)
The resemblance its coloured stripe has to a national flag gives rise to the apt English name of this fish. Under suitable lighting the black, yellow and red lateral stripe is striking. The general body colour is a shimmering green.

Records of breeding in captivity are rare. Males possess the characin barb on the anal fin. It enjoys live food, daphnia in particular, and survives well in any temperature between 21–26°C.

– *innesi* syn. *Paracheirodon innesi* NEON TETRA
4cm. (1¾in.)
This delightful fish can truly be described as a jewel. It comes from the border areas between Peru and Brazil. It is one of the most popular fish kept.

It is characterized by a brilliant iridescent green blue line passing backwards from the eye, and below this line at the posterior half of the body is a dazzling flash of crimson red.

Neon Tetras are notoriously difficult to breed and in spite of much effort success is rarely achieved. It is a hardy fish and peaceful by nature. It does best at temperatures close to 21°C. **94**

– *metae* syn. *H. peruvianus* LORETO TETRA 5cm. (2in.)
The upper part of this characin, which comes from Columbia and Peru, is dark green with a silvery sheen. The under part is white. Low on the side runs a wide dark horizontal band and above is a narrower copper band. The tail fin is red at the base.

Temperamentally a shy, timid fish, to date it has not bred in captivity.

– *pulchripinnis* LEMON TETRA 5cm. (2in.)
Without the jewel like quality of some of the tetras, this fish has a delicacy of colour which makes it a popular aquarium inhabitant. It comes from the Amazon. The general body colour is yellow with a somewhat translucent appearance but this is accentuated by increasing density and brilliant yellow markings on the anal and dorsal fins. A flash of red in the upper part of the eye seems almost out of character and unnecessarily gaudy. They like the water to be about 24°C.

Lemon Tetras will breed but they are ready consumers of their own eggs.

– *rosaceus* ROSY or BLACK FLAG TETRA 4cm. (1½in.)
A small to medium-sized characin the Rosy Tetra comes from Guyana.

The body colour, as one of its names suggests, is a translucent rosy pink. There is an indistinct slightly deeper red line running back from the eye and the edges of the caudal, anal and pelvic fins are outlined in deeper red. The most characteristic feature of this fish is its splendid, mainly black, and attractively shaped, dorsal fin with contrasting white lines. This fin is longer in the male, while the female's

develops a red tip. A difficult fish to breed. **95**

– *scholzei* BLACK-LINE TETRA 5cm. (2in.)
The Black-line Tetra comes from the Amazon. Males and females are difficult to distinguish. This species is one of the few characins to have bred regularly in captivity. They deposit their eggs on plants. Active fish, their carnivorous habits are fatal to young fish.

Hypopomus Rhamphichthyidae ⊕
– *artedi* SPOTTED KNIFEFISH 20cm. (8in.)
From the Guyanan regions of South America. This fish has a long eel-like, dark green body, spotted with black dots. Its dorsal fin is non-existent and the tail is absent. Does reasonably well in the aquarium.

Hypseleotris Eleotridae ⊕
– *cyprinoides* 6cm. (2½in.)
A peaceful fish which comes from Celebes. Olive green with a black horizontal band below which the fish is white. The dorsal fins afford a method of distinguishing sex since in the male they are well patterned with dots and bars.

I

Ichthyology
The scientific name for the study of fish derived from the Greek *ikhthys* – a fish, and *logia* – discourse.

Ichthyophthiriasis see *Disease*
Ich see *Disease*
Ide see *Leuciscus idus*
IDOL, MOORISH see *Zanchus cornutus*
Idus idus see *Leuciscus idus*
Illness see *Disease*

Immunization
With increasingly large and expensive collections of fish being kept by aquarists, and the difficulty of treating some diseases with medicine, immunization against certain diseases would be very useful. Attempts to date have met with only limited success.

Recent studies however, have considerably increased our knowledge of immunology in general and of immunity in fish in particular. It is to be hoped that knowledge will assist us in producing effective vaccines since prevention is always better than cure.

Most studies have been directed at fish which are farmed on a commercial scale. Salmonids have, for example, been protected against Furunculosis under experimental conditions, although some difficulties arose when attempts were made to use it on a commercial fish farm.

Infectious pancreatic necrosis, a viral infection of salmonids, has also been the subject of vaccine studies and some success can already be claimed.

Research workers examining the immune response in fish to the fungus *Saprolegnia*, which so commonly acts as a secondary infecting agent in sick fish to exacerbate the condition, have discovered information which suggests a vaccine may be a serious possibility.

From the large amount of scientific veterinary studies on fish disease it does look very hopeful that immunization against some of the more important fish diseases will become available. As this work progresses, benefits will undoubtedly accrue to the aquarist. It seems likely that most of these vaccines will be administered through the mouth, in with the food.

INDIAN
  BUTTERFLYFISH see *Chaetodon collare*
  FERN see under *Plants – Ceratopteris*
  GLASSFISH see *Chanda ranga*
Infection see *Disease*
Infusoria see under *Food*
Injections see *Immunization*
Inheritance see *Genetics*
Introduction to Tank see *Acclimatization to Tank*
ISLAND BARB see *Barbus oligolepis*

J

JACK DEMPSEY see *Cichlasoma biocellatum*
JACKS see *Anablepidae, Carangidae, Plesiapidae, Priacanthidae, Sciaenidae*
JACKKNIFEFISH see *Equetus lanceolatus*
JAPANESE
  DWARF RUSH see under *Plants – Acorus*
  LIVE-BEARING SNAIL see *Snails – Viviparus*
  MEDAKA see *Oryzias latipes*
  RICEFISH see *Oryzias latipes*
  WEATHERFISH see *Misgurnus anguillicaudatus*
JARBUA see *Therapon jarbua*
JAWFISH, YELLOWHEAD see *Opistognathus aurifrons*
JEWELFISH,
  see *Microspathodon chrysurus*
  AFRICAN see *Hemichromis bimaculatus*
  BANDED see *Hemichromis fasciatus*

JEWEL GROUPER see *Cephalopholis argus*
JIGSAW TRIGGERFISH see *Pseudobalistes fuscus*

Jordanella Cyprinodontidae ⊕
– *floridae* FLAGFISH, FLORIDA or AMERICAN FLAGFISH
5cm. (2in.) ⊕/Ψ ✂ ▥
A beautiful killy from Florida, the overall body colour is red, with red flecking in the median fins. This basic colour however is broken by large greenish blue reflective areas on the scale rows. Dark patches and coloration of varying intensity appear on the back. It is aggressive, and should only be kept with larger fish in the community tank where it spends its time near the bottom. It prefers hard alkaline water, or brackish water, at temperatures around 24°C. together with subdued lighting.

It deposits eggs in a depression on the bottom, the male having selected and defended an area of the tank for breeding. After inducing the female to deposit the eggs, the male guards the eggs and does not eat the young – unusual for a member of this family.

It is said that this species benefits from eating algae although it is largely carnivorous. **96**

Julidochromis Cichlidae ⊕
– *ornatus* JULIE 8cm. (3in.)
A very attractive fish from Lake Tanganyika in Africa. The body colour is basically a bright golden yellow. The dorsal half of the body is traversed by three thick longitudinal irregular dark brown lines, which start at the snout and pass posteriorly to the tail. The dorsal fin is very long based, starting just posterior to the operculum and extending to the tail. It is dark brown with an orange margin. The anal fin is a little deeper and moderately long based. The caudal fin is rounded.

This species will breed in captivity. A small number of eggs are laid in a rock shelter and are guarded by the female.

JULIE see *Julidochromis ornatus*
JUNIOR SWORD PLANT see under *Plants – Echinodorus*

K

KAIBI CICHLID see *Pelmatochromis pulcher*
KEYHOLE CICHLID see *Aequidens maroni*
KILLIFISH,
  see *Cyprinodontidae*
  SRI LANKAN see *Aplocheilus dayi*

KILLY see *Aplocheilus, Aphyosemion, Cubanichthys, Epiplatys, Fundulus, Lucania, Nothobranchius*
KING BUFFALOFISH see *Symphysodon discus*
KISSING GOURAMI see *Helostoma temmincki*
KITEFISH see *Monodactylus argenteus*
KNIFEFISH see *Ctenobrycon, Gymnotidae, Gymnotus, Hypopomus, Notopteridae, Notopterus, Rhamphichthyidae, Xenomystus*
KIO CARP see *Carassius hybrids*
KOOLI BARB see *Barbus vittatus*
KORAN ANGELFISH see *Pomacanthus semicirculatus*
KRIBENSIS CICHLID see *Pelmatochromis pulcher*

Kryptopterus Siluridae
– *bicirrhis* GLASS or GHOST CATFISH 10cm. (4in.)
The popular names are very descriptive indeed. This fish resembles one of those anatomical models which reveal the innermost secrets of the body. The body is truly transparent with a certain bluish hue. The organs of the body are all contained in a dark blue area close behind the head. The bony skeleton is revealed in detail. The dorsal is present as a single ray and the anal fin expansively extends the length of the body. The tail fin, again totally transparent, is forked. One pair of medium sized barbels adorn the upper jaw. Hardy, it prefers temperatures between 21–26°C. and eats live food by choice. It is an uncharacteristic catfish in that it lives not on the bottom but in the middle water of the aquarium. It comes from south-east Asia and Indonesia.

Labeo Cyprinidae ⊕
– *bicolor* RED-TAILED SHARK 13cm. (5in.)
The body of this beauty from Thailand is jet black with a velvety look. The tail is a striking and contrasting bright red. The body shape and generous dorsal fin are shark-like. Two sets of barbels adorn its protruding lips. It prefers temperatures of 25–26°C., and an alkaline pH. Eats live food, prepared food and algae. Harmlessly boisterous especially to black fish, a delight to own and watch. It is however aggressive towards members of its own species. Breeding rare.
– *frenatus* RAINBOW or RED-FINNED SHARK 8cm. (3in.)
This species from northern Thailand has a similar, if somewhat slimmer, body to its generic cousins. The body is an olive brown fading on the belly to a pale brownish yellow or even white. Black bands pass from the snout above the eye to the operculum. There is a black, roughly triangular, patch at the base of the tail. The fins are a very bright red. The male is distinguished by a black border to the anal fin.

It has become quite popular with aquarists as it is less aggressive with its own species than some members of the genus. It feeds, like *L. bicolor*, on live food and is also very fond of grazing on algae, a feature which endears it to aquarists. **97**

Glass or Ghost Catfish, *Kryptopterus bicirrhis.*

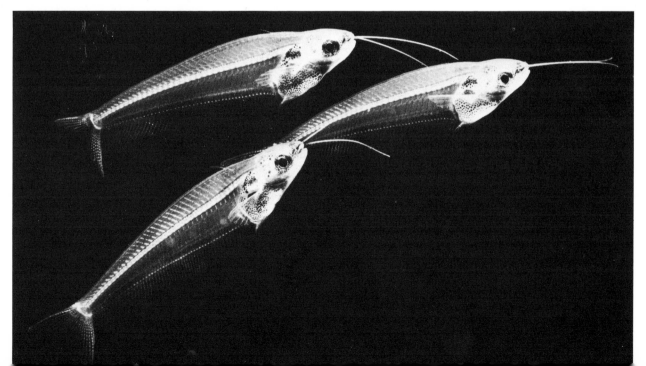

Labeotropheus Cichlidae ⊕
– ***fuelleborni*** FULLEBORN'S or NYASA CICHLID
15cm. (6in.)
A cichlid from Lake Malawi in south-eastern Africa. The males are dark sky blue with vertical bands of a slightly darker blue all along the body. The long flowing dorsal and anal fins are a mixture of blue and orange and their borders are decorated with rich orange spots. The posterior edge of the caudal fin is bordered with orange. Females may resemble the males in coloration or be a rich orange brown heavily marbled with dark blotches. This patterning and coloration extends onto the fins. The markings of both sexes are variable from one individual to the next, depending on locality of collection and selective breeding. The upper lip of both sexes is enlarged and bulbous, and well designed for consuming the algae from the rocky parts of the shores. In captivity it will also eat live food on which it thrives. See also *Nyasa Cichlids*. **98**
– ***trewavasae*** RED-FINNED NYASA CICHLID
10cm. (4in.) ✂
This exotic beauty from Lake Malawi is a bright blue in the male. The blue is not uniform but shades from a rich royal blue to a sky blue. The dorsal fin is a reddish orange. The duller female lays her eggs in a shallow pit in the sand prepared by the male. The male then fertilizes the eggs in the nest after which the female gathers her brood into her mouth to incubate the eggs for about 4 weeks. The fish are naturally vegetarian but show aggression and should be kept alone with plenty of rocky cover. See also *Nyasa Cichlids*.

Labridae WRASSES
The wrasses are a very hardy family of marine fish related closely to the Parrotfishes (Scaridae). They are widely distributed in both cold and warm water. Like the Parrot-fishes they use only their pectoral fins for locomotion and steer with their tail fin. Their teeth are sharp.

Classification of wrasses has presented ichthyologists with plenty of problems. They are polymorphic, a term applied to a species in which the males and females, young and old, adopt varied forms. In addition they can change colour with amazing speed. They may also assume some very unusual positions, curling or dangling upside down.

Some spawn in open water while others build nests in which the female deposits the eggs for the male to guard. See *Bodianus, Cheilio, Coris, Gomphosus, Hemigymnus, Hemipteronotus, Labroides, Lachnolaimus, Thalassoma*.

Labroides Labridae Ψ
– ***dimidiatus*** CLEANER WRASSE, BLUE STREAK 10cm. (4in.)
This fish from the Indo-Pacific, is of particular interest because of its behaviour. It gets its common name from its habit of cleaning the skin of other fishes of parasites and diseased tissue. This makes it a most useful member of the marine aquarium. In nature it lives in a well defined territory and fish come to its 'clinic' to be cleaned of parasites. In captivity it can be fed, and will happily accept both live and dead food.

A beautiful elongated fish with a long dorsal fin. The body colour is a mixture of blue and purple. A dark band varying in width runs from the snout through the eye to broaden on the tail and fuse with a narrower band which runs posteriorly from the base of the anal fin. A third dark band runs from the snout dorsally through the base of the dorsal fin and fades at the base of the tail. Prefers temperatures around 24°C. The colour illustration shows this fish cleaning two Badgerfishes, *Lo vulpinus*. **99**

Labrus
  hemisphaerium see *Hemipteronotus taeniurus*
  taeniurus see *Hemipteronotos taeniurus*
Labyrinth see *Acoustico Lateralis System*
LABYRINTHFISH see *Anabantidae*

Lachnolaimus Labridae Ψ
– ***maximus*** HOGSNAPPER, HOGFISH 86cm. (34in.)
A fish which is occasionally imported into the USA by dealers. The body is a mixture of brown and deep red. The mature male has a deep red patch on the neck. The first three dorsal spines are elongated and tough.

It is found in the Gulf of Mexico and the Caribbean where large specimens are sought after as food fish. It feeds on a wide variety of invertebrates, especially molluscs. Smaller specimens make reasonable inhabitants of the aquarium, but adults tend to be too large.

Lactophrys see *Acanthostracion*

Lactoria Ostraciontidae Ψ
– ***cornuta*** LONG-HORNED COWFISH 61cm. (24in.)
From the Indo-Pacific. A yellow brown or even greenish

Long-horned Cowfish, *Lactoria cornuta*.

body is flecked with brown. In addition blue spots scatter its sides. It gets its common name from the two 'horns' above the eyes and a further two pointing back below the tail.

Lagenandra see under *Plants*
Lake Malawi Cichlids see *Nyasa Cichlids*
Lake Nyasa Cichlids see *Nyasa Cichlids*
LALIUS see *Colisa lalia*
LAMP EYE see *Aplocheilichthys macrophthalmus*
LARGE CLOWNFISH KNIFEFISH see *Notopterus chitala*

Lateral Line see *Acoustico Lateralis System*
LATTICE DWARF CICHLID see *Nannacara taenia*
LATTICED BUTTERFLYFISH see *Chaetodon rafflesii*
Latimeria chalumnae see under *Classification*
LEAFFISH see *Monocirrhus, Nandidae, Polycentropsis, Polycentrus*
Learning see under *Behaviour*
LEATHERJACKET, BEAKED see *Oxymonacanthus longirostris*
LEBIA, SPANISH see *Aphanius iberus*

Lebiasinidae
A family closely related to the Characidae. They are brightly coloured freshwater fish from Central and South America. Their bodies are slim and the fins rounded. There is sometimes a small rudimentary adipose fin.

They live close to the surface in still water, feeding on insects and surface Crustacea. They lay eggs on leaves of plants near to the surface. *Copeina arnoldi* lay their eggs above the surface and keep them moist by splashing. See *Copeina, Copella, Nannostomus, Pyrrhulina.*

Lebistes reticulata see *Poecilia reticulata*
Leeches see under *Unwelcome Visitors*
LEERI see *Trichogaster leeri*
Legend see *Art and Myth*

Leiocassis Bagridae ⊕
– siamensis BUMBLE-BEE CATFISH 18cm. (7in.)
The popular name of this fish, which is found in Thailand and Cambodia, derives from the attractive arrangement of vertical white bands which contrast with the black body. White eye patches, a white collar, white waist belt, white tail band and white tail lobes produce a stunning effect. It has oral barbels. Like some other catfishes it can grunt and will seek shelter from light during the day.

Good natured, it eats anything, is peaceful, and prefers to bask in temperatures around 24°C. in soft, slightly acid water.

LEMON
BLUE SURGEONFISH see *Acanthurus leucosternon*

TETRA see *Hyphessobrycon pulchripinnis*
LEOPARD, BLUE see *Corydoras paleatus*
LEOPARD
CATFISH see *Corydoras julii*
EEL see *Acanthophthalmus kuhlii*
SCAT see *Scatophagus argus*

Lepidosiren Lepidosirenidae
– paradoxa SOUTH AMERICAN LUNGFISH 1·25m. (50in.)
Native to the swamps of central South America. It has an elongated body with continuous dorsal and anal fins. It is mottled grey brown in colour. The male makes a burrow in the mud at the beginning of the rainy season, in which the eggs are laid. They are protected by the male. The young cling to plants, using an adhesive secreted by a gland.

Lepidosirenidae LUNGFISH
Related to the Ceratodontidae, this family has developed a form of lung which enables members to utilize the oxygen in the air as well as that dissolved in water. The paired lungs are an extension of the alimentary canal, as found in primitive amphibians. It may be that amphibians evolved from a group of fish with a similar type of air breathing apparatus to lungfish. That is not to say that amphibians evolved from lungfish. These are simply a primitive type of fish which are now, and have been for millions of years, well adapted to their environment and have therefore not died out or had to change. See *Periophthalmidae*.

The only member of the family is found in South America. In nature they are found in muddy water which dries up completely in the dry season. In order to survive the drought they surround themselves in a protective hole or nest and, using their lung, breathe air. With the wet season they can return to the water. An alternative adaptation to dry seasons which allows the species but not the individual to survive is found in the annual Killifish (Cyprinodontidae). See *Lepidosiren*.

Leporinus Anostomidae
– arcus 30cm. (12in.)
This species is found quite widely distributed in South America. It has the slender, rather elongated body of the genus. The mouth is small with few teeth. A typical headstander, it often adopts the almost vertical position for which they are famed.

These fish prefer gently flowing streams with gravel bottoms. They are non-aggressive and live on plants. They do well in captivity but tend to grow rather too large for the average aquarium.

The basic body colour is a yellow ochre. The fins are red or orange. Five dark brown horizontal stripes are present on the flanks. **100**

–fasciatus BLACK-BANDED LEPORINUS 30cm. (12in.)
From South America, this fish is somewhat sluggish in the
tank but be forewarned, its hidden talent is jumping, so
keep the tank covered. It swims with its head down. The
body colour is yellow and there are several wide vertical
bands of black which increase in number with age like the
rings on a tortoise. Young fish have five bands, adults up to
10. Each new band is produced by the division of an
established one.

It is long for a community tank, but is easy to feed and
harmless to other fish. Enjoys temperatures anywhere
between 21–26°C.

Leptolucania Cyprinodontidae
– ommata 4cm. (1½in.)
From the swamp lands of Florida and Georgia, this small
fish is peaceful to the point of shyness and is quite suitable
for the community tank. The male has a pale yellow brown
body with a broad horizontal band from the snout to the
dark spot at the base of the tail fin. A few vertical bands are
also present. The dorsal fin is reddish yellow with a blue
margin while the anal has a black margin to a yellow fin.
The female is distinguished by the duller colour and the
rounded outline of the dorsal and anal fins as opposed to
those of the male which are spread out.

A plant spawner. The fry emerge in 10–20 days at 24°C.
and, being very small, they must be fed infusoria for a few
days before being given brine shrimp.

Leuciscus Cyprinidae
– idus syn. *Idus idus* IDE, ORFE 61cm. (24in.)
A lovely streamlined fish which has a silvery body with hints
of yellow. The tail, anal and pelvic fins are mauve. It rarely
exceeds 30/40cm. in the aquarium. Orfe are common
throughout northern Europe where they usually live in
lakes and rivers but they will adapt to brackish waters.
Young feed mainly on snails and crustacea while the adults
also prey on fish.

Breeding in early spring and summer the female lays up to
100,000 eggs on stones on the bottom.

The Golden Orfe, a variety well known to cold water
aquarists, is hardy and adaptable.

This is not particularly suitable for tank life, doing better
in an outdoor pond.

Lighting

Artificial lighting gives the aquarist accurate control of
illumination and improves the aesthetic appearance of the
tank. Just enough light will help to keep the plants and the
fish healthy and prevent excessive algal growth. Plants
which have no light turn yellow, those with too little become
pale and wilt.

For artificial light to be effective it must be positioned
immediately above and within a few inches of the water
surface. Canopies with reflectors are commercially available
and very suitable.

Trial and error will eventually indicate the exact amount
of illumination required for your particular tank in its
particular position. However, as a rough guide one should
aim to illuminate the tank for 8–12 hours each day, and one
should adjust the wattage of the bulb according to tank size.
A 55 litre tank requires approximately 30 watts for 12
hours, 137 litres 72 watts, and 230 litres 90 watts. Artificial
illumination should be reduced if some daylight falls on the
tank. For those of you living in hot climates remember that
electric light bulbs emit heat as well.

An interesting development in lighting has recently been
introduced into the hobby. A fluorescent tube emitting only
certain light wavelengths has become popular. Like some
of the better sunglasses it improves colour, removing
unpleasant tones and glare. Scientifically, however, criticism
has been levelled at its use and many experts prefer to use
one of the tubes with an incandescent light simultaneously.

Providing they are used with moderation, coloured bulbs
can produce some pleasing effects in the aquarium. The
tendency among some aquarists, particularly those with a
commercial interest, to promote psychedelic extravaganzas
using rotating colour filters, alternate flashes of variable
colour and other equally gaudy illuminative efforts is to be
deplored. What the poor fish must feel I hate to think. See
Plants, Positioning the Aquarium, Algae.

Limia see under *Marine Invertebrates*
Limia
  melanogaster see *Poecilia melanogaster*
  nigrofasciata see *Poecilia nigrofasciata*
  vittata see *Poecilia vittata*
Limnaea see under *Snails*
Limnophila see under *Plants*
LINEATUS see *Aplocheilus lineatus*
LIONFISH see *Dendrochirus, Pterois*
LIONHEAD see *Carassius auratus*
LIVE-BEARING
  SNAIL, JAPANESE see *Snails – Viviparus*
  TOOTH CARPS see *Poeciliidae*

Lo Siganidae Ψ
– vulpinus BADGERFISH, FOXFACE 20cm. (8in.)
A lovely member of an otherwise rather dull family, native
of the Pacific. The body is yellow. The head has dark
markings reminiscent of a badger, although the marks go
round rather than straight back. Difficult to settle into
captivity but once it accepts its new abode it is easy to feed.
101, also in **99**.

LOACH see *Acanthophthalmus, Botia, Cobitidae, Gyrinocheilus, Sorubim*

Lobster, Spine see under *Marine Invertebrates*

Locomotion

Water is a more difficult substance to penetrate than air since it is a denser medium. It is essential that fish which have to move in water adopt a shape which offers the least resistance. The fusiform or cigar shape, which the vast majority of fast moving fish and sea mammals favour, allows maximum speed in water. Each part of the body merges smoothly with the others, as does the head with the body and the body with the tail. The scales which cover the body are smooth and offer little resistance.

There are many variations on the basic shape. Gross variations to this ideal contour are generally at the expense of speed and are therefore usually accompanied by improvements in camouflage, better armour, or behaviour modifications to protect the fish against attack from predators.

Movement of fish is achieved in three ways. The most important makes use of the primitive muscle blocks which are arranged in segments throughout the length of the fish. By contracting these in sequence the fish body is thrown into an 'S' shape and the movement of the tail against the water propels the fish forwards. The body itself is braced against the water at the same time to prevent sideways movement. This method of propulsion is the most important in most fishes which have adopted the classical shape.

In addition, most fish use their fins to some extent during movement either alone when swimming slowly or in conjunction with the method described above, while some species which have departed from the classical body shape

Shaded areas on body indicate muscle contraction.

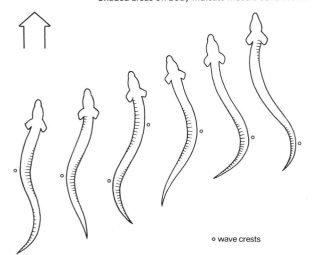

○ wave crests

like Bowfins, Filefish, and Rays use fins almost exclusively. The tail fin is moved by the muscles of the tail. Median fins can produce slow forward movement of the body by a wave-like motion controlled by their musculature or in some other fish, like Puffers or Porcupinefish, by waving the fin from side to side.

Paired fins in many fish are used for stability but in others they are organs of propulsion. In Rays, where the pectoral fins are well developed, wave like motions are again employed. In other fish the fins are small and flapped to obtain movement. Many of the marine Damselfishes use their pectorals in a rowing action, pulling the fins forward with the thin edge cutting the water and then turning them to present the maximum surface and pulling them back. Pectoral fins are used by many fish for stopping.

Finally the expulsion of water through the gills acts to varying degrees in propelling fish but is of less significance than the previous methods. It is often used most effectively when the fish moves from a standing start, particularly when frightened or pursuing prey. Flyingfishes, Mudskippers, Eels, and Seahorses use very specialized forms of locomotion for which the appropriate anatomy has been evolved. See also *Fins, Muscles.*

LONG-BODIED CATFISH see *Farlowella acus*
LONG-HORNED COWFISH see *Lactoria cornuta*
LONG-JAW SQUIRRELFISH see *Holocentrus ascensionis*
LONG-NOSED
   BUTTERFLYFISH, COPPER BANDED see *Chelmon rostratus*
   BUTTERFLY, YELLOW see *Forcipiger longirostris*

Longevity

Few fish in the wild are thought to live longer than 25–30 years. In general, as the body size of the fish decreases so does the length of life and many of the smaller fish, including those kept as pets, live for less than 4 years. Exceptions to this rule exist.

Old age in fish is recognized by a slowing of the growth rate, loss of reproductive ability; of those offspring which are produced, in later life, a greater number are abnormal. Old fish slow down and show changes in their behaviour patterns. There may be a tendency to become overweight or positively fat.

LONGFACE see *Gomphosus varius*
LONGFIN, PERUVIAN see *Pterolebias peruensis*
LONGFIN BATFISH see *Platax teira*
LORETO TETRA see *Hyphessobrycon metae*

Loricaria Loricariidae ⊕
– parva WHIPTAIL, VIEJA 10cm. (4in.)
A native of Brazil. The long head is flattened and an

elongated body tapers from the dorsal fin to the tail. The tail fin has an elongated dorsal ray. Dark patches and bands adorn the yellow brown body.

The male protects the eggs and cleans them with his mouth but little is known of the Whiptails' breeding habits.

Loricariidae
Closely related to the family Callichthyidae, members of this family come from Central and South America. They are covered in short spines which arise from bony plates that protect the back and sides. The flattened head is exposed on the undersurface, as is the belly, having either no protection or small scales. The mouth on the underside of the head takes the form of a sucker. An adipose fin, when present, is supported by a spine.

Peaceful fish which are omnivorous scavengers concentrating on algae. They make suitable fish for the community tank. Best suited to temperatues around 24°C. Most species do not breed in captivity.

Their one disadvantage is a tendency to disturb the bottom of the tank creating cloudy water. See *Ancistrus, Farlowella, Loricaria, Otocinclus, Plecostomus.*

Louse,
see under *Unwelcome Visitors*
Water Hog see under *Food*

Lucania syn *Chriopeops* Cyprinodontidae ⊕
– *goodei* BLUE-FIN KILLY 5cm. (2in.) ⊙
A lovely fish from Florida. Its slender body is a basic brownish green in the male shading to a pale silver green belly. A dark line extends horizontally the length of the body and the tail fin is streaked with red. The dorsal and anal fins are an opaline blue with black brown bases and dark margins, and these fins are held spread showing their beauty. The female is duller with clear fins.

A peaceful fish, it does well in the community tank, at temperatures ranging from 21–26°C., where it swims usually in the upper third of the tank. It is a plant spawner, laying eggs which hatch in 10–20 days. Prefers well lit conditions.

Ludwigia see under *Plants*
Lumbricus see under *Food*
LUNAR-TAILED ROCK COD see *Variola louti*
LUNGFISH see *Ceratodontidae, Lepidosiren, Lepidosirenidae, Neoceratodus, Protopteridae, Protopterus*

Lutjanidae SNAPPERS
A widely distributed family of marine fish common in tropical coastal waters. They are predators. *Lutjanus* is the

genus commonly kept in aquariums. Moderately sized, hardy and very suitable for marine aquariums. See *Lutjanus.*

Lutjanus Lutjanidae Ψ
– *decussatus* CROSS-BANDED SNAPPER 30cm. (12in.)
An attractive, if unflamboyant, snapper from the Indo-Pacific. A light grey body with brownish stripes.
– *kasmira* ARABIAN SNAPPER, TANDA-TANDA, BLUE BANDED SEA PERCH, BLUE-BANDED HUSSAR 35cm. (14in.) ✂
A somewhat aggressive fish among its own kind from the Red Sea and Indo-Pacific, though it lives in large shoals. The yellowish brown body varies in colour intensity. Several blue horizontal stripes edged with brown are permanent fixtures. The hind end of the body has dark spots.
– *sebae* EMPEROR SNAPPER, RED SNAPPER, GOVERNMENT BREAM 100cm. (3ft 3½in.)
A very attractive shape enhances the colour markings of this fish. From the mouth there is a steep rise to the dorsal fin. It is white with deep red vertical bands. The bands are dark, almost black in the young fish. Comes from the Indian and Pacific Oceans. Hardy and easy to feed in captivity.

Lymphocystis see under *Disease*
LYRETAIL see *Aphyosemion*
LYRETAIL MOLLY, ALBINO see *Poecilia formosa*

Lythrypnus Gobiidae Ψ
– *dalli* CATALINA GOBY 8cm. (3in.)
A small, marine member of the goby family and which comes from off the California coast. It is a beautiful fish with a red body transected vertically by blue bands. It will eat most live foods. It prefers water on the cool side for most tropical species. Attempt to include this in a marine tank if you have one.

M

Macrognathus Mastacembelidae
– *aculeatus* SPINY EEL 30cm. (12in.)
This is a nocturnal fish of the river mouths of India and south-east Asia. It spends its day buried in the mud, with only its head protruding. At night it emerges, and swims slowly over the bottom to hunt for its prey. It is carnivorous.

A fish of variable colour, it has a long slender body with a large nose. The dorsal fin is long with spines anteriorly and a soft dorsal fin behind. The anal fin is also long but the tail fin is rather small.

Spiny Eel, *Macrognathus aculeatus*.

In captivity it prefers temperatures around 26°C. Will readily consume earthworms. Rarely kept by aquarists. **102**

Macropodus Belontiidae ⊕
– chinensis ROUND-TAILED or CHINESE PARADISEFISH 8cm. (3in.)
A native of eastern China and Korea. Similar if less colourful than *M. opercularis*, it has an olive brown body with dark vertical bands. The dorsal fin is spotted. The male is always more colourful but when breeding he darkens and develops light spots. Prefers temperatures around 18°C.
– concolor 9cm. (3½in.)
A close relative of *M. opercularis*, and thought by some authorities to be a captive-bred variant but it differs in being less aggressive and not quite so adaptable to temperature changes.
cupanus SPIKE-TAILED PARADISEFISH 7·5cm. (3in.)
A native of India and Sri Lanka, this peaceful fish is distinguished by its pointed tail. The central portion is red while the upper and lower margins are bordered with turquoise. Turquoise, too, tips the dorsal and anal fins.
– cupanus dayi DAY'S or BROWN SPIKE-TAILED PARADISEFISH 8cm. (3in.)
A sub-species, native only of India, it has larger fins and is better coloured, with dark horizontal bands running from snout to tail. The dorsal fin is dark, the anal has a dark base with a red point and a blue border. The tail is rounded but with several of the central rays elongated.

– opercularis PARADISEFISH, MACROPODUS
9cm. (3in.) ✂

Sadly, this hardy beauty from the Orient is extremely savage and has no place in the community tank. A brick coloured body is broken by irregular vertical, blue bands. The head is peppered with black spots and a large spot adorns the operculum. The anal and dorsal fins are drawn out to points and are grey, yellow or blue, speckled black. The brick red tail is decorated with white spots and flecks and the dorsal and ventral extremities are elongated.

It comes from south China, Korea, Taiwan and Vietnam. In its natural habitat it has to withstand freezing but is best kept at temperatures around 16°C. A bubble nest builder.
103

MADAGASCAR RAINBOWFISH see *Bedotia geayi*
MADRAS KILLY see *Aplocheilus blocki*
MAILED CATFISH see *Hoplosternum thoracatum*

Maintaining the Marine Aquarium

It is a good deal harder to maintain an aquarium of any kind than to set one up. Common sense and care however, with a little luck, should ensure that your tank stays in good order.

The amount of time spent in maintenance depends on the system and equipment you have adopted. Attempt to keep things simple. For example, change the water frequently – up to a quarter of the total volume every 2–3 weeks – rather than using an ultra-violetized, power-filtered, protein-skimmed, ozonized and sterilized diluted marine computer. No amount of gadgetry can be sure of monitoring and correcting build ups or depletions of substances in a small domestic system. Small amounts of toxic metals in solution, for example, which are not dealt with by the filtering system, will build up eventually to fatal proportions. Water changing prevents this.

Soon after the aquarium is established and the first fish have been introduced there will be a build up of metabolized protein waste – ammonia, nitrite and nitrate. Initially the more toxic ammonia and nitrite will be dominant but as the bacteria are established which converts them to nitrate, they will gradually disappear. Some of the hardier species of damselfish will withstand this period.

Once the system has matured and other fish are established simple checks should be made to ensure the system runs smoothly.

For many marine fish, algae constitute a large proportion of the diet. Adequate lighting, water conditions and pH are essential for algal development. Algae are part of the biological cycle which converts nitrates into protein. This in turn is reused by the fish when algae are eaten. In addition algae make use of carbon dioxide dissolved in the water and produce oxygen during photosynthesis. Lighting should be maintained and adjusted to encourage a good but not excessive algal growth. An excess of algae – an algal bloom – results in death of the algae with putrefaction which adds toxins to the water which will then kill the fish. A correct balance must be maintained.

Although animals can adapt to changes of temperature, see *Adaptability*, they are not able to adjust to rapid change, or excessive heat or cold. Routine temperature checks are essential to monitor the successful functioning of the heater and thermostat. Most marine tropical tanks are kept successfully at about 21°C.

A tank of warm marine water standing in a room loses water by evaporation. It does not at the same time lose the salts. Therefore, as water evaporates there is an increased concentration of salts and the specific gravity changes. Specific gravity measures the density of water at a specific temperature compared to an equal column of pure water or, put another way, it measures the amount of substances dissolved in the water. It is not the same as salinity since anything dissolved will alter the specific gravity, whether it is a pint of milk or a pound of sugar. Only variation in the salts will alter the salinity. It is, however, a reasonable assumption to make, that any change of specific gravity will be due to changes of salinity or temperature.

The instrument used for measuring specific gravity is a hydrometer. Don't buy a cheap one. It is worth spending a little more money on a sound and tested instrument. Make sure it, and the water surface, are clean before use. Specific gravity is expressed as compared to pure water which is given the value 1·0. Thus sea water is denser than pure water by the ratio 1·000:1·027. Specific gravity of such water is usually written 1027. This figure is far from constant in the world's seas and can vary considerably with temperature change as well as the amount of dissolved salts. Most fish can adapt to slow changes of density without adverse effect. In fact some are not bothered by rapid changes. Marine fish have remained in water with specific gravities as varied as 1019 to 1031. Generally, one will be safe if one tops up the level of the tank with fresh water regularly and when partial or total water changes are made the same standard solution is always used whether it is natural sea water or a commercially available synthetic.

Marine water usually has an alkaline pH around pH 8·3, see *pH*. It is essential that the water is alkaline since it encourages the growth of useful micro-organisms such as algae. Again natural oceans vary considerably in their pH from pH 7·8 to pH 8·6. Test kits suitable for salt water are commercially available. Although it is rarely necessary the water can be made more acid by adding phosphoric acid or more alkaline with sodium bicarbonate.

The tank should be kept clean. The excessive build up of

algae may be corrected by reducing light, and heavy growths on rocks and gravel removed by cleaning the gravel and scrubbing the rocks. Filtration cannot be expected to deal with all waste. It certainly does not dispense with the siphon or dip tube for removal of waste food and faeces. The front of the glass is best cleaned with a sponge or cloth to which the algae will attach, rather than a scraper. If a scraper is used siphon the scraped algae afterwards or the algae will die and cause putrefaction.

Feed little and often, never more than the fish will eat within a few minutes. Be observant. Watch for dead fish and remove them. Look at and smell the water regularly and above all watch the fish because they are good indicators of tank conditions. Make all changes slowly. Partial water changes should be regular and frequent. Maintain and clean filters regularly and rejuvenate the charcoal by baking in the oven. Always have enough salt water ready for a complete change in an emergency; these can be sudden and to save the fish prompt action is essential. There will be no time to make it up and leave it for a few days to mature.

MAJESTIC ANGELFISH see *Euxiphipops navarchus*
MALABAR KILLY see *Aplocheilus lineatus*

Malapteruridae
This family of catfish has only one living representative, the Electric Catfish, *Malapterurus electricus* from Africa.

Malapterurus Malapteruridae ⊕
– *electricus* ELECTRIC CATFISH 117cm. (46in.)
The Electric Catfish comes from tropical Africa. The rather elongated, slug like body is grotesquely adorned with white oral barbels. A grey body is sparsely dotted with dark spots. Two dark bars one straight, one semi-circular adorn the tail fin. It has no dorsal fin but an adipose fin is present. Its ability to generate electricity is used for offensive or defensive behaviour.

MALAY ANGELFISH see *Monodactylus argenteus*
MALAYAN
  AIRSHIPFISH see *Sphaerichthys osphronemoides*
  BETTA see *Betta pugnax*
  GOURAMI see *Sphaerichthys osphronemoides*
  POND SNAILS see under *Snails – Melania*
Management see *Welfare*
MANDARINFISH see *Synchiropus splendidus*
MARBLED
  CICHLID see *Astronotus ocellatus*
  GOBY see *Oxyeleotris marmoratus*
  HATCHETFISH see *Carnegiella strigata*
  HEADSTANDER see *Abramites microcephalus*
  RIVULUS see *Rivulus ocellatus*

Marcusenius Mormyridae ⊕
– *isidori* 10cm. (4in.)
This species comes from the N le Delta. It is similar to, but rather more stocky than, its generic cousin *M. longianalis*. It has a stubby body with a rounded mouth and face.
– *longianalis* 15cm. (6in.)
From the River Niger, this fish resembles a reddish cigar. It has a short, blunt nose. Fits well into a community tank but has not bred in captivity.

MARINE
  Aquariums see *Establishing a Tropical Marine Aquarium*
  BETTA see *Calloplesiops altivelis*

Marine Invertebrates
Many marine aquarists like to adorn their tanks with living creatures, other than fish, which are found in the general habitat of a coral reef. There is no doubt that many add that extra touch to the general display, intrigue the viewer and test the competence of aquarists, for many of these invertebrates are more difficult than marine fish to keep successfully, though some are easier. Certainly if one's concept of an aquarium is to try to reproduce a balanced ecology, as found in nature, then it must include some invertebrates. Remember that many of these creatures are particularly sensitive to copper in solution, and since this is commonly used as a cure for Oodinium disease – be careful. Invertebrates include all animals without backbones.
Annelids. The group of creatures known as annelid worms include the common earthworm *(Lumbricus)* and tubifex, well known to aquarists. Some members of this group of animals are suitable for inclusion in the marine aquarium. The most attractive and interesting belong to the families Sabellidae and Serpulidae. These are commonly known as tubeworms from their habit of building themselves a tube which projects up from the bottom. From this tube they extrude an attractive crown of delicate and beautiful feather like tentacles which trap the microscopic organisms on which the worms feed. These will be withdrawn if the worm is in any way disturbed.
Coelenterates. Surprisingly, these attractive anemones are animals and not plants. When open these creatures extend their tentacles which are armed with a formidable fringe of poisoned arrows, deadly to small creatures although for some crustaceans and fish species a symbiotic relationship with an anemone is essential. The hydra of freshwater fame are also coelenterates. Some of the larger coelenterates, like the Portuguese Men-of-War and other jellyfish are none too pleasant for man if he is stung.

In view of the stinging and paralysing power of these creatures some of which can capture and consume fish up to 13cm. (5in.) long they are of questionable value to put in with expensive marine fish but should be included in the invertebrate tank. Some species of the genera *Discosoma* and *Radianthus* are, however, kept successfully in community tanks.

Corals are also members of the Coelenterata. Live members can be successfully kept in the marine aquarium but it is very difficult, and is probably best left until considerable experience has been gained with the marine system. They need good clean clear water, plenty of oxygen and a good deal of light.

Crustacea. To this group belong the crabs and shrimps. Hermit crabs which belong to the family Paguridae are amusing members for the community tank. Their characteristic feature is the poorly protected rear end. In order to protect their vital parts they tuck them into empty snail shells which they drag around until they have outgrown them, when new shells must be found. Scientific studies of hermit crabs have made use of transparent plastic replicas of snail shells enabling students to make detailed observations. Hermit crabs are good scavengers and the most successful are the tropical species.

The well known Caribbean Prawn or Coral Shrimp, *Stenopus hispidus,* makes a very attractive addition to the community tank, so long as only one is kept; they are far from sociable among their own kind. They should be provided with adequate cave space in which to hide. Up to 10cm. (4in.) long, they have a lovely red and white ring coloration with attractive long white antennae. They eat the normal live food including tubifex.

Other crustacea like swimming crabs (Portunidae), lobsters, particularly the Spiny Lobster from the Caribbean, *Panulirus argus,* and salt water crayfish are occasionally kept with varying degrees of success.

Echinoderms. A large group including the starfish and the sea urchins. Sadly, many of them, including the most attractive, do not do well in the community tank. A few starfish will adapt to captivity and are occasionally offered by dealers.

Sea urchins of the genus *Centrechinus* do seem to do well. They should be fed on mashed crustacea meat.

Molluscs. To this group of primitive animals belong the snails and slugs of our gardens. The snails belong to the sub-group known as univalves, while others, the cockles and mussels, are bi-valves having two shells which are hinged.

Of the snails suitable for the marine community tank one should include members of the genus *Murex,* the cowries, *Cypraea,* and the worm snails, *Vermetus,* which live in tubes and catch their prey with long threads of sticky mucus.

Of the bi-valves the scallops of the genus *Lima* are worth watching making their sudden dash through the water after slamming the two halves of their shell together. However they are difficult to keep as they feed on plankton.

Sponges. This group of very primitive animals congregate together but are scarcely organized into any form of division of labour. Each component cell does everything for itself and merely lives in close proximity to its own kind.

Small sponges will tolerate life in an aquarium providing it is well aerated. They consume microscopic particles of organic matter. They are however difficult to keep in community tanks.

The marine invertebrate is a field which has scarcely been touched by the aquarists. It is really worthy of the attention of a few dedicated marine enthusiasts prepared to specialize and make detailed studies of this wide and fascinating group of animals. Undoubtedly the sea has a great number of living treasures which could be harnessed to enrich our marine community tanks.

MAROON ANEMONEFISH see *Premnas biaculeatus*
Marsilea see under *Plants*

Mastacembelidae   SPINY EELS
This family is not closely related to the true eels. They are elongated freshwater fish of the Old World. Characteristically they have numerous spines along the back, in front of the dorsal fin which is placed well back. The anal fins are elongated and the tail fin small and rounded. See *Macrognathus.*

MEDAKA, JAPANESE see *Oryzias latipes*

Megalamphodus   Characidae   ⊕
– megalopterus   BLACK PHANTOM TETRA   4·5cm. (1¾in.)
A fish which has enjoyed a recent rise in popularity in the USA. It comes from Brazil. This is one of the few fish where the female can claim to be as, if not more, attractive than the male. This species exhibits sexual dimorphism: the male and the female are different structurally. The female has a pink body colour with rather short fins. The male is a

Black Phantom Tetra, *Megalamphodus megalopterus.*

greyish brown with very long fins. It does well in soft acid water at temperatures between 21 and 24°C. It breeds well in captivity.

Megaprotodon Chaetodontidae
– strigangulus TRIANGULATE BUTTERFLYFISH 15cm. (6in.)
It comes from the Red Sea and the Indo-Pacific where it lives on coral reefs.

An attractive fish but difficult to keep in the marine aquarium since it does not adapt easily to substitute diets in place of its natural food of living coral.

This butterflyfish has a pale yellow body colour which changes on the fins to a bright yellow. Dark greyish black chevron stripes cover the body. The tail is black with a yellow border, and a crescent shaped black patch extends from the dorsal to the tail fin. A thin black line, visible in the illustration, can be seen around the anal fin. **104**

MEINKENS RASBORA see *Rasbora meinkeni*
Melania see under *Snails*

Melanotaenia Melanotaeniidae ⊕
– fluviatilis AUSTRALIAN PINK-TAILED or CRIMSON-SPOTTED RAINBOWFISH 13cm. (5in.)
As the name implies the body colour is composed of a number of colours. In this species the dominant theme is blue green with yellow stripes. The tail, anal and second dorsal fins are tinged with pinky brown.

Like all members of the genus, they do well in the community tank where they delight their human observers with active displays of elegant movement, naturally enhanced by their colour.

Given adequate space, suitable water and temperatures around 24°C., these fish spawn readily. The eggs are attached to plants and usually ignored by the parents. One spawning will produce up to 400 fry.
– maccullochi AUSTRALIAN BLACK-LINED RAINBOWFISH 10cm. (4in.)
Very similar remarks apply to this fish as to *M. fluviatilis*. It has a pinkish brown body with several thin dark brown horizontal lines.

Melanotaeniidae RAINBOWFISH
A family of freshwater fishes mainly from Australia and New Guinea but with representatives also in Madagascar. They are mostly deep-bodied fish and quite colourful. Until recently they were classified with the Atherinidae to which family they are closely related. See *Melanotaenia*.

Melichthys Balistidae ⊕
– indicus BLACK TRIGGERFISH 25cm. (10in.)
A black body is faintly decorated with green lines about the

eyes. The dorsal and anal fins have white bases. It comes from the Red Sea and Indo-Pacific and eats crustacea. In captivity it can be induced to turn to more easily obtained nourishment.
– vidua PINK-TAILED TRIGGERFISH 30cm. (12in.)
A deep blue body, almost navy, and a pink tail. The dorsal and anal fins have white borders. This is one of the more peaceful members of the family. It comes from the Indo-Pacific. **105**

Mendel see under *Genetics*
MERRY WIDOW see *Phallichthys amates*

Mesogonistius Centrarchidae
– chaetodon BLACK-BANDED SUNFISH 8cm. (3in.)
Deeper-bodied fish than its family cousin *Elassoma evergladei*. The general body colour is silver with several

Black-banded Sunfish, *Mesogonistius chaetodon*.

vertical bars. It is restricted to the Delaware Basin in the US. Prefers soft acid water, at about 24°C. in which it has been frequently induced to breed by Europeans.

METALLIC MINNOW see *Notropis hypselopterus*

Metynnis Characidae ⊕
DOLLARFISH
There is some confusion about fish species within this genus. Several different species have been described, for example *M. maculatus*, but they may all belong to the same species and be merely local variations. I therefore do not propose to distinguish species. *Metynnis* come from the Orinoco, and the Amazon. The body is compressed to form a disc. Characteristically the adipose fin is enlarged. Fairly large with an aggressive appearance resembling piranhas, they in fact live well with other fish and make no special dietry demands but do considerable damage to plants. Silver in body colour, they are adorned with a variety of dark markings which disappear with age. Rarely breed in captivity. Temperatures of 21–27°C. suit them well. **106**

MEXICAN
ASTYANAX see *Astyanax mexicanus*
TETRA see *Astyanax mexicanus*
Micranthemum see under *Plants*

Microgeophagus Cichlidae ⊕
– ***ramirezi*** BUTTERFLY DWARF CICHLID, RAM 5cm. (2in.)

Butterfly Dwarf Cichlid, *Microgeophagus ramirezi*.

Another true dwarf beauty native of Venezuela. The colour varies, as with all cichlids. The anterior half is a basic grey brown but with bright yellow highlights. A dark vertical V-shaped bar passing through the red eye adds drama to the head. Turquoise blue spots posteriorly provide a stunning contrast to the anterior half of the body, and extend onto the unpaired fins which are bordered with orange.

Small, free from aggression and easily bred, they are popular cichlids with most aquarists.

This species is often known as *Apistogramma ramirezi*, but is distinguished from that genus by variations in reproductive and breeding behaviour. **107**

Microglanis Pimelodidae ⊕
– ***parahybae*** HARLEQUIN CATFISH 8cm. (3in.)
This fish always looks confident, a rather unusual feature of a catfish. With a brown body and large dark patches along the back. Dark bands enhance the dorsal, adipose and tail fins.

It comes from Brazil, Argentina and Paraguay. **108**

Microspathodon Pomacentridae ✂
– ***chrysurus*** JEWELFISH, YELLOW-TAILED DAMSELFISH
15cm. (6in.)
A very attractive damselfish from the Caribbean. The body is a deep purple, highlighted by small bright blue spots. The tail of the young fish is a creamy white. As the fish reaches maturity the blue spots fade a little and the tail becomes a bright yellow. Popular, particularly in the USA but is a little aggressive.

Migration see under *Behaviour*

Mimagoniates Characidae ⊕
– ***microlepis*** BLUE TETRA 7cm. (3in.)
Blue Tetra are medium-sized characins and are natives of south-eastern Brazil. They have a reputation for being difficult to keep, partly because of their susceptibility to the disease 'Ich'. They should for this reason be kept in water between 25–26°C. This species has a wide dark blue band running horizontally from the eye backwards, above which is a thin yellow line. The body is more silver grey than blue. The anal and dorsal fins have blue outer edges.

Breeds occasionally in captivity.

MINNOW see *Belonesex, Cyprinodon, Fundulus, Heterandria, Notropsis, Phoxinopsis, Phoxinus, Tanichthys*
MINSTREL PUFFERFISH see *Canthigaster valentini*

Mirolabrichthys Serranidae Ψ
– ***tuka*** PURPLE QUEEN 13cm. (5in.)
This fish has the added advantage of being smaller in length

than some members of the family. It is a pale reddish orange on the body with a distinctive cream throat. It comes from the Pacific.

Misgurnus Cobitidae
– *anguillicaudatus* JAPANESE WEATHERFISH 20cm. (8in.)
An eel-like body which grows in its native waters of Japan and China to 20cm. Has a wide range of adaptability to temperature change coping with anything from 5°C. to about 27°C. quite happily. Grey body with dark blotches on the side.

An amenable fish, it does have the unfortunate habit of creating a 'pea souper' fog during its scavenging activities.

Mochocidae UPSIDE-DOWN CATFISHES
Commonly known as the upside-down catfishes, from its behavioural habit of swimming upside-down. The reason for such an outlook on life is hard to explain. It is represented to the aquarist by one genus. See *Synodontis*.

Moenkhausia Characidae ⊕
– *oligolepis* GLASS TETRA 10cm. (4in.) ✄
This fish, which comes from Guyana and the Amazon Basin, derives its attraction not from colour so much as its textural appearance. It has a silver grey body which shades lighter towards the under belly. A large spot at the root of the tail is a useful distinguishing mark, as is the golden spot in the adipose fin. The black edging to the scales creates the texture mentioned above. One of the larger characins, it is an unsuitable community fish as it tends to be aggressive.

Not easily bred in captivity; spawning is encouraged by temperatures approaching 24°C. Has catholic tastes in food but enjoys minced raw flesh.

– *pittieri* DIAMOND TETRA 6cm. (2½in.)
A fish native to Lake Valencia in Venezuela. It attains its beauty from fine fins, not colour. The body colour is a shimmery silver all over with overtones of green and blue in certain lights, attractive enough, but the shape of the dorsal fin complemented by the splendour of the anal and pelvic fin appendages makes this fish the beauty it is. Its only definite colour is in the iris of the eye which is bright red. It has been bred in captivity, having typical characin breeding behaviour. Males have somewhat longer and more pointed dorsal and anal fins. It mixes well in a community tank.
– *sanctae-filomenae* RED-EYED TETRA 6cm. (2½in.)
Not unlike the Glass Tetra, *M. oligolepis*, this fish from Paraguay is somewhat deeper in the body. It carries very little colour apart from a dark, often diffuse, patch at the base of the tail. It gets its popular name from the red patch on the eye. Feeding and temperature as rest of the genus.
109

Mogurnda Eleotridae ⊕
– *mogurnda* AUSTRALIAN PURPLE-SPOTTED GUDGEON, SLEEPY TROUT 8cm. (3in.) ✄
A greeny brown fish with a blue sheen from eastern Australia. The body is spotted with red, yellow and blue dots. It grows to 20cm. in nature but captivity restricts it to less than 8cm.

An aggressive fin-nipper which has no place in the community tank.

Eggs are deposited on a smooth surface and hatch in about 7 days. The male takes his paternal responsibilities seriously and fans the eggs during incubation.

Molliensia latipinna see *Poecilia latipinna*
Molluscs see under *Marine Invertebrates*
MOLLY see *Poecilia*
Monocanthidae see *Balistidae*

Monocirrhus Nandidae ⊕
– *polyacanthus* AMAZON LEAFFISH ✄
A fascinating fish from the Amazon which has so well adapted its camouflage that its common name is really descriptive. Its flat, leaf-shaped body with pointed, almost stalk-like, snout is enhanced by a habit of swimming with head down at an oblique angle among the plants. Its ability to match its colour to the environmental colour completes the perfect camouflage.

An aggressive carnivore, it feeds mainly on other fish but can be induced to take meat and earthworms in captivity where it prefers soft somewhat acid water at a temperature of about 21–22°C.

Monodactylidae FINGERFISH, SILVERFISH
A small family of fish distributed from the African coasts through the seas around India and the Malay Archipelago to Australia. They live in salt or brackish water but enter rivers to breed, so have the ability to adapt to fresh water; experience shows that although brackish water is desirable, in captivity it is not essential. They are equally suited to the marine tank.

Characteristically they are markedly compressed and have extended dorsal and anal fins reminiscent of Angelfish (*Pterophyllum*).

A large aquarium kept at temperatures of about 25–26°C. suits them best and stimulates the best colours. They are carnivorous. They look their best and seem happier in groups. See *Monodactylus*.

Monodactylus Monodactylidae Ψ Ψ/⊕
– *argenteus* FINGERFISH, SILVERFISH, MALAY ANGELFISH, PSETTUS DIAMONDFISH, MOONFISH, KITEFISH 18cm. (7in.)
Usually smaller than 18cm. in captivity. It is widely

distributed from the east coast of Africa to the Malay
Archipelago through the Indian Ocean and Red Sea.

A greenish silver fish with a metallic sheen. One dark
vertical stripe runs through its eye, and a second runs
through the posterior tip of the operculum and the base of
the pectoral fin, turning backwards vertically to run along
the anterior border of the anal fin. The unpaired fins are a
rich orange colour. **110**
– *sebae* 8–20cm. (3–8in.)
If anything, more beautiful than its generic cousin *M.*
argenteus. It has a silver body with a yellow metallic tinge.
Dark vertical bars run through the eye and through the
operculum and pectoral fin base as in *M. argenteus* but a
third runs from the tip of the dorsal fin to the tip of the anal
fin and a fourth bar runs across the base of the tail and
along the base of both dorsal and anal fins. Pale yellow
unpaired fins complete the picture. Grows to 20cm. in the
wild but captivity reduces this to half. It lives in the costal
waters of tropical West Africa. **111**

MONTEZUMA PLATY see *Xiphophorus variatus*
MOON
   ANGELFISH, PURPLE see *Pomacanthus maculosus*
   BUTTERFLY FISH see *Chaetodon lunula*
   WRASSE see *Thalassoma lunare*
MOONFISH see *Monodactylus argenteus*
MOONLIGHT GOURAMI see *Trichogaster leeri*
MOOR, TELESCOPIC-EYED see *Carassius auratus*
MOORISH IDOL see *Zanclus cornutus*
Mops see *Nylon Mops*
MORAY
   EEL see *Muraenidae*
   EEL, ZEBRA see *Echidna zebra*

Mormyridae ELEPHANTFISH
An interesting family the members of which all live in
muddy freshwater in Africa. Their distinguishing feature is
the snout region. Some have short stubby jaws while others
have an elongated chin forming a 'trunk'. All can produce
weak electric charges, reportedly used in communication
such as territorial declaration, and in navigation.

They are not the easiest fish to keep but are relatively
accommodating about conditions, preferring mature water.
Rather shy, they like well planted conditions with subdued
light. Temperatures from 25–28°C. are most appreciated.
Carnivorous bottom feeders but their diet should include
some live food. See *Gnathonemus, Marcusenius*.

MOROCCAN BARB see *Barbus callensis*

Morulius Cyprinidae
– *chrysophekadion* BLACK SHARK 45cm. (18in.)

Black Shark, *Morulius chrysophekadion*.

The only disadvantage this fish has for the home aquarium
is size; it may reach up to 30cm. in captivity. Resembling a
shark, its black colour, body shape and deportment are a
visual delight. The blunt snout is whiskered with barbels.
Easy to feed, it scavenges at the bottom of the tank and
tends to introverted behaviour. Breeding in captivity is rare.

MOSAIC GOURAMI see *Trichogaster leeri*
MOSQUITOFISH see *Gambusia, Heterandria*
MOTHER-OF-PEARL EARTHEATER see *Geophagus brasiliensis*
MOUSE BOTIA see *Botia horae*
MOUTH-BREEDING FIGHTINGFISH see *Betta brederi*
MOUTH-BROODER see *Haplochromis, Tilapia*
Movement see *Locomotion*
MOZAMBIQUE MOUTHBROODER see *Tilapia mossambica*
MUDSKIPPER see *Periophthalmidae, Periophthalmus*
Mud Worms see under *Food*
MUDHOPPER see *Boleophthalmus boddaerti*
MULLET, RED see *Mullidae*

Mullidae   RED MULLETS OR GOATFISHES
This family of marine fish is widely distributed many species being found in tropical and sub-tropical seas, although a few live in more temperate waters. They crudely resemble catfish, enhanced by the mobile barbels surrounding their small mouths. They are small active fish, and live in small shoals. They boast two quite distinct dorsal fins, a moderate anal fin and a bi-lobed or forked tail fin. They have the ability to change colour with varying environmental conditions. Hardy, easy to feed members of the marine tank. See *Parupeneus, Pseudupeneus.*

MUMMICHOG see *Fundulus heteroclitus*

Muraenidae   MORAY EELS
Moray Eels are elongated marine fish, very large when adult and far too long for the average aquarium. Small ones, however, do find their way on to the retail market. They rely on smell, taste, touch, and lateral line sensory systems when searching for food in contrast to other fish which hunt by sight. Some have hinged teeth which can fold backwards but which lock in the forward position to hold prey secure when needed. In common with some sharks, some have poisonous flesh. Their elongated bodies are thrown into waves as they creep and wind in rock crevices. See *Echidna, Rhinomuraena.*

Murex see under *Marine Invertebrates*

Muscles
The muscle arrangements of fishes are far less complicated than those found in higher vertebrates. Like all vertebrates there are three basic types, the skeletal which make up the mass of the fish's body, the smooth muscles which are found mainly in the walls of the digestive system, the blood vessels and inside the eye, and the cardiac muscle found in the heart.
   Most of the fish muscles are segmented throughout the length of the body. Each muscle block or myotome is joined to each adjoining block by connective tissue. In many fish these muscles are the main driving force in locomotion, see *Locomotion*. In the hagfishes and lampreys, Cyclostomata,

this simple arrangement is unmodified as they have no paired fins, but in the higher fish the fins are supplied by muscles derived from these muscle blocks.
   Muscles supplying the eye, jaws, gills and face also arise from these primitive muscle blocks.

MYER'S CATFISH see *Corydoras myersi*

Mylossoma   Characidae   ⊕
– argenteum   SILVER MYLOSSOMA, SILVER DOLLARFISH 20cm. (8in.)
This and its close relative *M. aureum* have very compressed bodies resembling discs. Native to the Amazon Basin, the general colour is silver with a darker greeny tinge dorsally. There is a spot on the operculum. The anal fin is red.
– aureum   GOLDEN MYLOSSOMA   15cm. (6in.)
Like its cousin *M. argenteum*, it is a native of the Amazon. The body colour is silver with a yellow golden tinge and several grey vertical lines adorn each side. The anal fin is a golden brown. The eyes are golden. This species is easily fed; a good member of the community tank and enjoys a relatively wide range of temperatures. It has not been bred in captivity.

Myriophyllum see under *Plants*

Myripristis   Holocentridae   Ψ
– chryseres   HAWAIIAN SOLDIERFISH   20cm. (8in.)
This fish is fairly large. It hides in rock crevices and old shells. From this it can be gathered that it makes a timid member of the marine community tank. The body colour is an attractive red and it has large eyes and yellow fins.
– murdjan   BLOTCH EYE   30cm. (12in.)
A red body with light red fins flashed with white tips. It grows to 30cm. and comes from the Red Sea and Indo-Pacific region, where it lives a nocturnal existence preying on invertebrates.

Mystus   Bagridae   ⊕
– tengara   PUNJAB CATFISH   18cm. (7in.)
A native of northern India particularly the Punjab. It has eight barbels surrounding the mouth and nasal region. An attractive fish which makes few demands and can be kept in the community tank. Prefers temperatures around 26°C.
– vittatus   23cm. (9in.)
A delightful aquarium fish from the south-east of Asia, with a grey body with a silver sheen and blue horizontal stripes. The under parts are white and the adipose fin is elongated. The mouth barbels are very long and exotic.

Myth see *Art and Myth*

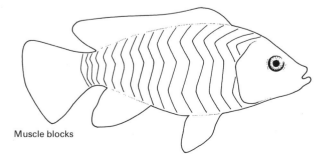
Muscle blocks

Najas see under *Plants*

Nandidae LEAFFISHES
A very small family containing a handful of genera but one which is widely scattered in the tropical regions, having members in America, Africa and Asia. They are spiny rayed fish with large mouths and appetites to match. They consume other fish with an enthusiasm which shocks most novice aquarists. They are unsuitable for any aquarium containing fish smaller than themselves. *Badis badis* is the least ferocious in temperament.

All members of the family thrive in well planted aquaria with subdued light, and plenty of live food which can include raw meat.

After spawning on the bottom, males protect the eggs. See *Monocirrhus, Polycentropsis, Polycentrus*.

Nannacara Cichlidae ⊕
– *anomala* NANNACARA, GOLDEN ACARA, GOLDEN-EYED CICHLID 8cm. (3in.)
Not exactly colourful, this dwarf cichlid from Guyana has, none the less, an attractive personality which makes it a good community tank inhabitant. It has a longer more compressed body than is typical of the cichlids. Its beauty lies in its generous fins. The large dorsal fin, rounded tail fin and elongated rather pointed anal fin combine to produce a flamboyant effect. The basically brown body has greenish highlights on the head.

The male reaches some 8cm. in length while the female is only half that size with drabber colouring.

Breeding, which is more likely at around 25–26°C. is typical for cichlids – see *Cichlidae*.
– *taenia* LATTICE DWARF CICHLID 5cm. (2in.)
A native of the Amazon Basin. The body colour is very variable being all shades of greenish brown. It gets its name from the profusion of bars, some horizontal some vertical, which traverse its body. These are seen most clearly during emotional arousal. Fins are basically clear but adopt various colour hues from time to time.

Nannaethiops Citharinidae
– *unitaeniatus* AFRICAN TETRA 8cm. (3in.)
Native to equatorial Africa from the Congo to the Nile. The back is reddish brown shading through yellow to a whitish belly. A dark horizontal stripe runs from eye to tail. A yellow line follows the dark band and in the posterior regions changes to a copper colour. The anal fin is pink as is the lower lobe of the tail fin. The upper tail lobe is deep red.

The other fins are clear. Males are smaller than females.

A happy, hardy community fish which breeds easily in captivity scattering its eggs among fine-leaved plants. The young should be fed on infusoria and later small daphnia.

Nannostomus Lebiasinidae ⊕
– *anomalus* NANNOSTOMUS 3cm. (1¼in.)
From the Amazon and also Rio Negro. The dorsal part of the body is a very dark green and the belly white. These parts are separated by a dark band running from snout to tail above which runs a golden line. The dorsal, tail and anal fins have red splashes. The male can be distinguished by the bluish points on the pelvic and anal fins.

Attractive jerky movements make it a pleasure to watch. Liberal range of temperatures from 21–26°C. Takes small particles of food both live and manufactured. Difficult to breed but when it does the eggs are scattered on the bottom.

This species is regarded by some, as a colour form of *N. beckfordi*.
– *aripirangensis* GOLDEN PENCILFISH 4cm. (1½in.)
This delightful and very beautiful fish comes from Aripiranga Island in the lower Amazon. It is very brightly coloured, with bright red pelvic fins. In the male the base of the fin assumes a red coloration. It is nowadays regarded as a colour form of *N. beckfordi*.
– *beckfordi* GOLDEN PENCILFISH 8cm. (3in.)
As the popular name suggests *N. aripirangensis* is often considered to be a colour form of this species. It comes from Guyana, the Amazon Basin and the Rio Negro.

It has the typical slender shape of the genus with a light brown dorsal coloration shading to yellow sides, red fins and a dark band runs horizontally from head to tail.

Does well in the community tank where it makes a dashing display. **112**
– *eques* TUBE-MOUTHED PENCILFISH 5cm. (2in.)
Unlike the headstanders, *Chilodus* species, these contemplate the stars. They come from the Amazon and Guyana.

A lovely golden brown body is divided horizontally by several brown lines and a wide band of black running from the head which expands finally to cover the whole of the lower lobe of the tail fin. Above the dark band is a stripe of gold. The anal fin is brown and has a blotch of red close to its base.

Poor breeders in captivity. When it does breed it lays eggs singly on leaves and guards them half heartedly. **113**
– *marginatus* DWARF PENCILFISH 4cm. (1½in.)
A small fish from the north-east of South America, this fish makes a useful contribution to the community tank or kept in large numbers it shoals well. The body colour is greeny brown with very broad dark horizontal stripes running from snout to tail. Vertical bars are seen but can disappear and reappear with surprising speed.

Breeds easily in captivity laying its eggs on the leaves of plants. Prefers temperatures around 24°C.

– *trifasciatus* THREE-STRIPED PENCILFISH 6cm. (2½in.)
A very attractive fish indeed and from the Amazon Basin, Rio Negro and Guyana. Its belly is silver grey but it is notable for the attractive horizontal bar of gold running from the eye to the tail. This is bordered by wide lines of brown. Vertical bars are seen but are transient and come and go with rapidity. The fins, with the exception of the pectorals, are all blotched with deep red. Males can be distinguished by the dots of red which run the length of the wide gold bar.

Peaceful, a happy member of the community fish tank and to which it certainly adds beauty. Sadly, not easy to breed in captivity. The eggs are adhesive and are attached to leaf ribs of plants.

– *unifasciatus* SPOT-TAIL or ONE-LINE PENCILFISH
5cm. (2in.)
A fish of slender line from the Amazon. The body colour is a pale golden brown. A broad black stripe runs from the snout through the eye broadens over the abdomen and continues into the lower lobe of the tail, where it ends in a series of red, white and black bands. The fins are pale golden yellow.

Naso Acanthuridae Ψ
– *lituratus* ORIENTAL TANG, STRIPED-FACE
UNICORNFISH 50cm. (20in.)
From the Red Sea and Indo-Pacific, this fish has a large head with a long body which tapers towards the tail. Its body is a pale turquoise dorsally, shading to dark brown or black on the belly. Yellow gold markings on the forehead streak down as tear marks, and backwards to colour the anterior part of the dorsal fin. The pectoral, pelvic, anal fins and most of the dorsal fin, are dark, dirty gold with black borders. **114**

Oriental Tang, *Naso lituratus*.

NATTERER'S
  CATFISH see *Corydoras nattereri*
  PIRANHA see *Rooseveltiella nattereri*
  PYRRHULINA see *Pyrrhulina nattereri*
NEEDLEFISH see *Farlowella acus*

Nematobrycon Characidae ⊕
– *palmeri* EMPEROR TETRA 5cm. (2in.)
This is a Columbian characin, males reaching up to 5cm. in length with the females somewhat smaller, which has rapidly gained popularity since it was introduced. It is characterized by the wide black line running from its eye to fade as it nears the tail. The median fins are accentuated by black outlines and the tail fin is particularly attractive, with an elongated tip and a long central portion. This is a particularly attractive characin which, in addition to the markings mentioned, has reddish-blue coloration with yellow-brown fins.

The male's courtship movements make use of the attractive fins which tremble before the potential mate. He later chases the female into weeds and the eggs are scattered as she emerges. Live food is claimed, by some aquarists, to promote spawnings. **115**

Neoceratodus Ceratodontidae ⊕
– *forsteri* AUSTRALIAN LUNGFISH 183cm. (6ft.)
This species can reach up to 183cm. in length in its native Australia. It is greeny brown in colour with very large well-defined scales. The anal and pectoral fins of the Australian Lungfish are reasonably well developed in contrast to those of its cousin, the African Lungfish, *Protopterus annecteus*. However, this species has a more primitive lung than *Protopterus*.

Neolebias Citharinidae ⊕
– *ansorgei* ANSORGE'S CHARACIN 4cm. (1¾in.)
A small fish from the west coast of Africa. The general body colour is yellow brown with a green sheen. Structurally males and females are similar but the male has a blue green iridescent band running horizontally along its body. There is no adipose fin.

Peaceful fish to the point of shyness. Prefers temperatures ranging from 26–28°C. Likes live food, particularly tubifex.

NEON
  GOBY see *Gobiasoma oceanops*
  TETRA see *Hyphessobrycon innesi*

Neotoca Goodeidae
– *bilineata* SKIFF, TWO-LINED NEOTOCA 5cm. (2in.)
Silver-grey, with a body shape resembling the killifishes of the family *Cyprinodontidae*. Uninspiring visually, but it

makes up for its poor appearance with its scientific interest. It differs from other live bearers in needing separate fertilization by the male for each brood. Produces up to 50 young each year in five separate broods; the parents do not consume their young.

Nepa see under *Unwelcome Visitors*

Nervous System

The nervous system, like that of other vertebrates, consists of a brain and spinal cord which make up the central control mechanisms, and the peripheral nervous system which carries information from areas in the body to the brain, and transmits instructions from the brain to the body, co-ordinating functions and movements. Closely allied to the nervous system are the endocrine and sensory systems. The latter includes the classical five senses, sight, touch, hearing, smell and taste, as well as the lateral line or pressure-sensitive system in the fish. See also *Acoustico Lateralis System, Eye, Smell, Taste.*

Nets

A large variety of nets is available. Nylon is the commonest material currently in use but muslin, being soft, is still very useful. Personal choice determines to a large extent the shape and style of the nets one uses. Most people will however need a square or oblong net with sides of 7–10cm. (3–4in.). Small rounded nets are necessary for catching fish in round transporting jars and some shaped ornamental tanks.

For very large tanks, a net approaching the surface area of the tank itself is useful. The fish can be partially restrained in this while a smaller net is used to make the final catch.

Remember that when a net is plunged into a tank it becomes a potential hazard and may carry infection to the next tank all too easily. Therefore it is preferable to have a separate net for each tank. Failing this, the net should be boiled following its use in a tank. Care and diligence in this matter may prevent a catastrophic outbreak of disease. See *Netting.*

Netting

Patience is the watchword when trapping fish. The objective is to remove the fish from the tank without damaging it or any other occupant of the tank and without uprooting the plants, stirring up the gravel or snaring the snail population.

As with handling most creatures, calm determination and respect for them will ensure success. Introduce the net quietly, position it smoothly and move it gently towards the fish. When the fish is in the net, a quick movement upwards withdraws it from the tank. Remember to enclose the net with your free hand to prevent the fish jumping out.

It is often useful in large tanks to use two nets concurrently, guiding the fish with a small net towards the larger.

Fish behave differently during netting, but experience teaches one the tricks of each species. Even individuals differ in their ability to avoid being caught, so get to know your fish. See *Nets.*

Nitella see under *Plants*
Nomaphila see under *Plants*
NORMAN'S HEADSTANDER see *Abramites microcephalus*

Nothobranchius   Cyprinodontidae   ⊕
– *guentheri*   GUNTHER'S FUNDULUS   8cm. (3in.)   ✂
This annual fish comes from East Africa, including the island of Zanzibar. The male is basically a turquoise blue colour, modified by small red areas on the scales. The fan-shaped tail is red with a black margin. The throat and belly are yellow and the large dorsal and anal fins are speckled yellow and brown, with a dark margin on the dorsal. Aggressive, it is not for the community tank. It lives on the bottom, preferring temperatures from 21–22°C. It lays its eggs in peat moss at the bottom of the tank from where the fry emerge after a dry season. Aquarists take note that a period of drying is necessary for breeding success, see *Cyprinodontidae*. **116**
– *orthonotus*   BLUE-GREEN or GORGEOUS FUNDULUS
8cm. (3in.)   ✂
Each scale of this East African cyprinodont has red and blue components. At the fore end of the fish the blue predominates while towards the tail red is the most obvious. The fan-shaped tail is brilliant brick red with small margins of dark brown. Dorsal and anal fins are reddish-yellow bordered with blue, and large pectorals are clear yellow again bordered with blue.

It is aggressive, so not for the community tank. In nature water at about 21–22°C., it lives near the bottom and lays its eggs in the mud – or sterile peat moss – after which it dies. The eggs require a dry period and can exist in desiccated conditions for several months.
– *palmquisti*   5cm. (2in.)   ✂
A dazzling fish from tropical East Africa. The male's blue body colour is modified by red patches on the scales. The tail fin is pure red and the large dorsal and anal fins are brownish yellow with dark reddish brown dots. The body is rounder than many other members of the family.

This is an annual fish which lays its eggs and buries them in the mud after the usual cyprinodont mating display by the male. After reproduction in nature, they die as the water dries up. After the months of the dry season, the eggs hatch rapidly to produce next year's fish.

The aquarist must provide appropriate conditions if he is to be successful. Mature water kept at temperatures of 21–22°C. and an appropriate bottom cover – preferably sterile peat moss – is best. The eggs must be subjected to a dry period, see *Cyprinodontidae*. Aggressive, they can live only with their own kind.

– *rachovii* FIRE KILLY 4cm. (1½in.) ✂
A small annual killy from East Africa of which the male usually displays an intensity of redness from which the species gets its name. The basic body blaze is speckled with blue dots. The dorsal, anal and tail fins are decorated with dots and bars of rich reddish brown. The female is a drab reddish orange. She is induced by the male to drop her eggs in the mud. In the drought that often ensues the parents are killed, but the eggs survive. When the rains come again, months later, they hatch within minutes.

The aquarist must accept that these fish are aggressive loners and should be kept in their own tank. They live near the bottom in which they bury their eggs. The aquarist must provide a dry season artificially for the eggs, see *Cyprinodontidae*, and small live food when the fry hatch. Temperature 21–22°C.

– *taeniopygus* RACHOW'S FUNDULUS 5cm. (2in.) ✂
This is a colourful fish from East Africa. Basically a pale blue body with a yellow orange sheen. The unpaired fins are large, rounded and mainly yellowy-orange in colour with blue margins. The tail fin has a particularly fine wide blue border with a black edging. Again, an aggressive character which should be kept with its own species. It lives on the bottom, buries its eggs and then dies as the water dries up. After the dry season, the eggs hatch with the rains to produce a new generation. Keep in mature water at temperatures around 21–22°C.

Notopteridae KNIFEFISHES
This is a small family of fish distributed in the tropical regions of both Africa and Asia. It includes two genera – *Notopterus* which are known as featherbacks because of the short-based, long dorsal fin, and *Xenomystus* in which the dorsal fin is absent. Characteristically they have a very long-based anal fin which begins just behind the pelvic fin and continues backwards, to fuse, almost indistinguishably, with the caudal fin. They have small scales which give them an eel-like texture, and small mouths with numerous teeth.

All members of the family have a connection from the swim bladder to the pharynx which enables them to breathe air. They feed on small invertebrates.

They are nocturnal fish which hide by day under rocks and vegetation close to the surface, and emerge at night to swim both forwards and backwards with equal facility by undulations of the anal fin, see *Locomotion*. See *Notopterus, Xenomystus*.

Notopterus Notopteridae ⊕
– *afer* AFRICAN FEATHERBACK 61cm. (24in.) ◍
When young, this species from central Africa, has marbled patterning all over its body made up of alternate beige and olive green markings. The fins are an opaque beige. With age this marbling merges to form a less attractive, and more uniform, greeny brown.

In the wild, they live in small groups, staying close together during the day, and hiding under vegetation. It is therefore advisable to keep at least two together in the interests of the fish's welfare. In addition, since they do not like bright lights, keep the lighting dim and provide plenty of hiding places preferably with surface plants. They are best suited to soft, acid water at temperatures around 27–28°C.

– *chitala* LARGE CLOWN KNIFEFISH 80cm. (31½in.)
This is another interesting fish which is imported from Thailand and Indonesia.

It has a dark grey dorsal region with sandy brown sides decorated with four to eight large ocellated spots starting just in front of the dorsal fin. These spots are peculiar to the Thailand population and are seldom seen on specimens from Indonesia. It is not the colour, but the method of locomotion that makes this family worth the effort, see *Notopteridae*. **117**

NOTTS KILLY see *Fundulus notti*

Notropis Cyprinidae ⊕
– *hypselopterus* METALLIC MINNOW 5cm. (2in.)
A native of the streams of Georgia and Florida. Its coppery body, darker above and with an almost yellow belly, is bisected by a metallic blue band which is bordered on either side by a golden line. The base of the dorsal fin is red shading to black. This fish prefers water temperatures between 19–22°C. with good aeration which probably excludes it from many community tanks.

Novacula taeniurus see *Hemipteronotus taeniurus*
Nuphar see under *Plants*

Nutrition
Like all animals, fish must have food which contains carbohydrates, fats and proteins. In addition, certain vitamins and minerals are essential for life and must be available. It is the art and science of good feeding to provide the correct diet for each species. While some work has been done in this field by ichthyologists, much still remains unknown. It is possible, indeed probable, that some breeding problems encountered will be resolved by correct nutrition.

Most fish develop disorders of the liver when fed a diet

high in fat. Other fish can deal with, indeed need to have, large amounts of fat in their diet.

Carbohydrates, the starches and sugars, are included in all diets. They are broken down into simple sugars for absorption.

The building bricks of proteins are the amino acids. Proteins are used for maintaining body structure and must be continually replenished in the body. Many amino acids can be manufactured by fish as they can in all animals. There are, however, certain essential amino acids which must be provided by the diet since fish are unable to manufacture them themselves. Different species differ in the amino acids they can produce themselves and it is in this field that much work needs to be done in fish nutrition.

Our knowledge of vitamin requirements in fish is very limited indeed. Natural diets provide adequate amounts of all necessary vitamins but when using artificial diets it is essential that we ensure sufficient vitamin content. Without research however this is impossible and we are forced to hope for the best when compounding diets. Work has shown for example that some species suffer when some of the **B** vitamins are excluded.

Minerals, often in minute quantities, are equally essential for survival. Again too little is known about the minerals which must be included in food for fish. See *Digestive system, Food*.

Nyasa Cichlids ⊕ ✄

In recent years aquarists have been plundering Lake Malawi, for fish to grace their tanks and they have not been unrewarded. A variety of lovely fish of medium size – up to 15cm. – have been recruited to the aquarists' freshwater army. The water of the lake is naturally of an alkaline pH, see pH, and hard, see Hardness of Water, at temperatures in the upper 24°C. Therefore, unlike most Cichlids, species from this lake need hard alkaline water in their tanks. These fish are characterized by sexual dimorphism, the male and female being of markedly different appearance. They are mouth brooders and live naturally on live food supplemented with algae and are not averse to a little fish in their meal, so do not keep them in the community tank. See *Labeotropheus, Petrotilapia, Pseudotropheus*.

Nylon Mops

These are mops made of strands of nylon tied at one end and allowed to float in a tank. They are used to help in the breeding of some types of fish, for example, characins and closely related families. Nylon can be boiled for sterilization.

OBLIQUE CHARACIN see *Thayeria obliqua*
OBSTETRICAL CATFISHES see *Aspredinidae*
OCELLATE BUTTERFLYFISH see *Parachaetodon ocellatus*
OCELLATED RIVULUS see *Rivulus ocellatus*
Odonata see *Unwelcome Visitors*

Odonus Balistidae Ψ
– niger ROYAL BLUE, BLACK, or RED-TOOTHED TRIGGERFISH, REDFANG 51cm. (20in.)
One of the less aggressive members of a family renowned for violence. If well fed, it will make a peaceful community tank member. It comes from the Pacific. Captivity considerably reduces its size. Its colour varies from turquoise to cobalt blue. It has, as is common with the family, a mouth of small dimensions but nature has given it false 'lipstick', making it appear large and fearsome.

OLIVE SURGEONFISH see *Acanthurus olivaceus*
ONE-LINE
  PENCILFISH see *Nannostomus unifasciatus*
  TETRA see *Hemigrammus unilineatus*
ONE-SPOT BARB see *Barbus terio*
ONE-SPOTTED DAMSELFISH see *Abudefduf leucozona*
OPALINE GOURAMI see *Trichogaster trichopterus sumatranus*

Opistognathidae
An interesting family of marine fish, members of which are found in both the Pacific, Indian and Atlantic oceans. Commonly called Jawfishes or Smilers, they have a relatively large jaw and a small body. Their bodies are slender, a factor of value to those species which live in burrows, which they line with shells. They enter these burrows tail first. Both dorsal and anal fins are long based. A few of the species are mouth brooders, the males carrying the eggs in their mouths. See *Opistognathus*.

Opistognathus Opistognathidae Ψ
– aurifrons YELLOWHEAD JAWFISH 8cm. (3in.)
A long bodied beauty with a blunt head, from the Caribbean. The body is pink but it shades into the blue of the dorsal, anal, and caudal fins. The dorsal is a low, long based fin. The anal fin is also low, and rounded. The caudal fin is round. The lips are tinted with yellow.

A fish much prized by those who are lucky enough to own one. They are good members of the community tank but rather aggressive to their own kind. Since they like to dig holes into which they can escape in times of danger, it is important to provide a thick layer of soft sand. A fish that settles well into the aquarium. Known to be a mouth brooder in nature. Possible to breed in captivity.

ORANDA see *Carassius auratus*
ORANGE CHROMIDE see *Etroplus maculatus*
ORANGE-SPOTTED FILEFISH see *Cantherhines pullus*
ORFE see *Leuciscus idus*
ORIENTAL
  SWEETLIP see *Plectorhynchus orientalis*
  TANG see *Naso lituratus*
ORIOLE ANGELFISH see *Centropyge bicolor*
ORNATE CLIMBING PERCH see *Ctenopoma ansorgei*

Oryzias Oryziatidae ⊕
– *latipes* JAPANESE MEDAKA, RICEFISH, COLDWATER
SAPLOCHILUS 4cm. (1½in.)
A native of Japan and not one of the most colourful fishes, but it is easy to keep, feed and breed, mixing well in community tanks. Tolerant of a very wide variety of temperatures but prefers water at about 26°C. In other words, apart from its drabness it is an ideal aquarium inmate.

  The body colour is grey-green with a hint of blue iridescence. There is also a golden variety, a result of selective breeding.

  After a spot of chasing by the male, the female lays eggs which are retained at the vent as a small egg cluster. Here they are fertilized by the male. Within a short time, the eggs are brushed off by plants as the female swims. In 10–12 days they hatch. Easy to breed but the fry are not easy to rear.

Oryziatidae
A small family of freshwater fish until recently classified with the Cyprinodontidae with which they are very closely related. They are found in rivers and marshes of Asia. They have been reclassified because anatomically they differ slightly in their mouth parts from the Cyprinodonts. See *Oryzias*.

OSCAR CICHLID see *Astronotus ocellatus*

Osmoregulation and Excretion
An understanding of osmotic pressure is necessary to appreciate the difficulties and problems experienced by fish in maintaining correct concentrations of salts in their bodies in both fresh and salt water.

  Briefly, many of the tissues of the body act as membranes, effectively barriers to salts in solution. Water, however, is able to pass through these membranes. The natural physical phenomenon of osmosis is the attempt by the water to equalize the concentrations of salts on either side of the barrier. Thus, if salt solution is on one side of the membrane

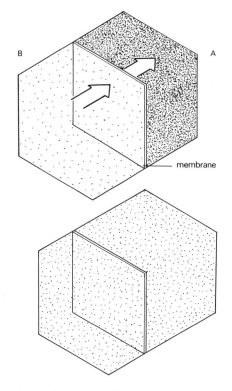

Water passes from weak to strong solution until both are of equal strength.

(side A) and water on the other (side B), water will pass from B to A in an attempt to equalize the concentrations. Similarly if a strong salt solution is on side A and only a weak solution of salt on side B, then water will pass from the weak solution to the strong solution until the solutions are at the same concentration.

  In living fish, such a situation could not be permitted or freshwater fish which have body fluids with more concentrated salts than the water in which they live would quickly become waterlogged. Marine fish which have less concentrated salts than seawater would rapidly become desiccated as the water would leave their bodies to dilute the sea. Fish, therefore, in both fresh and salt water, have to expend energy to oppose this physical tendency. It is called osmoregulation.

  In fish, the kidneys and the gills are mainly responsible for controlling the water balance in the fish. They are also responsible for disposing of the body's waste products. The gill therefore is responsible for respiration, excretion and osmoregulation.

  In freshwater teleost, or bony, fish, the kidneys are responsible for some kinds of waste products including uric acid, while the gills excrete ammonia and urea.

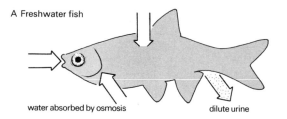

A Freshwater fish

water absorbed by osmosis

dilute urine

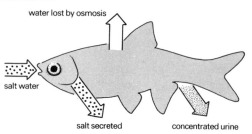

B Saltwater fish

water lost by osmosis

salt water

salt secreted

concentrated urine

Freshwater fish, as we have seen above, absorb water by osmotic pressure since their body fluids have more salt in them than fresh water. To prevent them bursting with this water, which is taken in through the membranes of the gill, mouth and skin, they have to dispose of the excess water along with the urine, which is, therefore, very watery.

Although the higher concentration of salt in the body tends to draw water in by osmosis, a second physical phenomenon – diffusion – ensures that some of the salts are paradoxically lost to the water surrounding the fish in an attempt to equalize the amount of salt in the body and the freshwater. The membranes are in fact not absolute barriers. These losses, if excessive, would be detrimental to the fish and the body has to prevent too great a loss. This task again falls to the kidneys which ensure that many of the salts passing out with the urine are reabsorbed and therefore retained by the body. The losses of salts that do take place are replenished mainly in the food and by active absorption through the gills. The important word here is active. The fish has to use energy to do this. It is not a passive physical phenomenon. We can see what a complex and dynamic problem it is which faces the fish's body if it is to live successfully in fresh water.

Marine fish are constantly losing water due to osmosis, since the salt solutions in their blood and body tissues are weaker than those of the sea. To replace this loss, the fish swallows sea water, most of which is absorbed. In addition, a great deal of water is reabsorbed as the urine passes through the kidney tissue. Unlike freshwater fish, which

produce large amounts of very dilute urine, the marine fish lose little water in that way.

Obviously the salt water swallowed to compensate for loss of water due to osmosis will contain large amounts of salts. These must be removed or the fish would soon be overburdened with excess salts. This important task is performed by special cells located both in the gills and in the mouth. It is this ability to excrete salts which allows teleost fish to live in salt water.

The question will arise in many minds as to how some fish like Salmon *(Oncorhynchus kisutch)* manage, which hatch in freshwater and migrate to salt water, returning, after an adult life in the sea, to freshwater to spawn. It is known that salmon eggs cannot live in salt water and that young salmon cannot move into salt water until they have developed the appropriate salt-secreting cells in their gills and mouth. Experimental work has also shown that adult fish like salmon, when returning to freshwater, are rapidly able to alter their osmoregulating functions and behave as freshwater fish again.

Osphronemidae

A small, single genus, family closely related to the Anabantidae and the Belontiidae. They are labyrinthfishes, having accessory breathing organs above the gills.

Breeding behaviour in this family is interesting since most are bubble nest builders. Here the male does most of the work for his brief moment of sexual pleasure. He first prepares his nest by blowing bubbles. The bubbles are 'strengthened' by the addition of an agent present in the mouth of the fish which cements the surface tension of the bubbles preventing collapse. The bubbles are often laid among floating plants which help to keep them together. Prepared now for the nuptials he entices a female to the nest, and wraps his body around her. As she sheds her eggs the male fertilizes them, and they drop to the bottom. He collects them in his mouth and blows them between the bubbles. This is repeated until she has no more eggs and then, since she is of no more use she is dismissed. Any eggs or young which drop from the nest are spat back into place. The eggs hatch in 30–40 hours depending on temperature and the young are free swimming, soon after. Not averse to a little fresh anabantid fry the male is as likely as not to eat his heirs so it is better to remove him once the hatch is complete. Under aquarium conditions it is as well to remove the female when her job is done or you may have a battered wife on your hands.

The young do well providing they are kept in constant environmental conditions. Sudden draughts causing changes in temperature can rapidly prove fatal. They should be fed on fine dry food, infusoria and algae. See *Osphronemus.*

Osphronemus Osphronemidae ⊕
– goramy GOURAMI 61cm. (24in.)
No superlatives or adjectives are needed for this monarch of
the tank. Growing up to 61cm. in length it is rarely kept by
aquarists. In its native Malay Peninsula and Indonesia, it is
prized as a food fish. A vegetarian, it grows rapidly. It
breeds in the same way as other members of the family.

In the young fish, a reddish-brown body is broken by
dark vertical bars and two spots, one near the lower base of
the tail and the second behind the operculum. Adult
gouramis are uniformly coloured. Fins are yellow brown.
Does well in temperatures of about 24°C.

Osteochilus Cyprinidae Ψ
– vittatus 26cm. (10in.)
From Indonesia, Malay, and Thailand, an all too rarely
seen fish in the aquarium. Its green back is separated from
the silver belly by an intense black band which runs
horizontally from the snout and finally fades into the caudal
fin. Short barbels adorn its mouth, transparent fins its body.
It is omnivorous. The external appearance of male and
female is identical. They have not bred in captivity. It seems
most comfortable in temperatures around 24°C.

Osteoglossidae BONY TONGUES
Exotic and colourful, elongated fishes distributed through
the tropics, in South America, Africa, south-east Asia and
Australia. They can reach over 60cm. in length. It is a
primitive freshwater family and only a few species survive.
They have useful teeth and large scales. See *Osteoglossum*.

Osteoglossum Osteoglossidae ⊕
– bicirrhosum ARAWANA 91cm. (36in.) ✂
A fish for the specialist because of its size. It is aggressive
and should be kept alone or with fish larger than itself. Its
graceful movements add greatly to its attraction. It is
elongated with a long anal fin and rather pathetic tail. Small
forward pointed barbels adorn its mouth. The colour is
changeable but centres around the greeny blue part of the
spectrum with an iridescent sheen. Lives well in captivity if
fed live food and kept in a large tank with water at about
25–26°C. **118**

Ostracion Ostraciontidae Ψ
– meleagris BLUE or SPANGLED BOXFISH 18cm. (7in.)
From the Indo-Pacific, these fish have a typical box-like
look with a head stuck on crudely at the front and the tail
behind, so that they hardly resemble fish. They are dark
bodied, deep navy blue, almost black, with white or blue
spots. Males sport red backs. Will take earthworms and

even dry food is accepted. This fish gives off a poison
when excited or dying which kills other fish. It prefers
temperatures of about 24°C. **119**
– tuberculatus BLUE-SPOTTED BOXFISH 46cm. (18in.)
Larger than *O. lentiginosum*, it has a yellow body with black
spots. It has the incredible shape of the boxfishes and is
widespread in the Red Sea and Indo-Pacific.

Ostraciontidae BOXFISHES
Slightly bizarre fish found widely distributed in warmer seas.
They have plates under the skin which give them a rigid
appearance. Pelvic fins are absent, the anal and dorsal fins are
set well back and the tail fin is simple. They are agile movers,
making great use of their fins. They feed on small live food.
See *Acanthostracion, Lactoria, Ostracion, Tetrosomus*.

Otocinclus Loricariidae ⊕
– affinis DWARF SUCKING CATFISH 4cm. (1½in.)
A small fish which is peaceful and makes a useful
community member. Feeds a great deal on algae using its
sucker-like mouth as do all members of this genus. From
south-east Brazil. A yellow-grey body with a dark
horizontal body stripe. Rarely breeds in captivity. The
fish in this genus prefer temperatures around 24°C.
– arnoldi ARNOLD'S CATFISH 6cm. (2½in.)
A small catfish from the River Plate. Its dark green body is
decorated with irregular black markings. Grey belly, clear
fins. Probably synonymous with *O. flexilis*.
– flexilis 5cm. (2in.)
Closely resembling *O. affinis*, it has a yellow body, darker
above with marbled blotching, cream below. The unpaired
fins are dotted with dark spots, on a green background. A
dark horizontal line bisects the body, running from
operculum to tail fin. It comes from the River Plate.
– vittatus 5·5cm. (2in.)
A native of southern Brazil. Dark green body with a white
belly decorated with dark irregular markings.

Oxyeleotris Eleotridae ⊕
– marmoratus MARBLED GOBY 91cm. (3ft.) ✂
An attractive but gruesome character which is found in the
Malayan peninsula and archipelago. It lies in wait to
pounce on lesser fish which it devours in its large mouth.
The brown body is beautifully marked with white irregular
patterns which provide it with its popular name. It is
adapted to any temperature between 20–30°C. Has not bred
in captivity. Size prevents it being kept by all except the
specially equipped aquarist.

Oxymonacanthus Balistidae Ψ
– longirostris EMERALD FILEFISH, BEAKED LEATHER-
JACKET 13cm. (5in.)

This is an unusual fish from the Indo-Pacific. A delightful species that lives among coral, using its well-designed snout to suck the live contents of the coral. It is a sociable species but not very well-suited to the mixed marine aquarium. It gets on well with members of its own species but being a food specialist does not live long when not fed live coral-polyps.

The basic body colour is a very beautiful leaf green. This is decorated with contrasting yellow lines which break up into lines of dots or patches on the body. The caudal fin is transparent with yellow spines, as are the long-based dorsal and anal fins, and there is a dark dot on the tail. The eye is a series of white and yellow patches. **120**

Ozonizers

A molecule of ozone contains three atoms of oxygen (O^3) instead of the more common molecule of oxygen (O^2). Ozone is a very good oxidizing agent, converting harmful substances into stable, harmless ones. It acts on the waste products of protein metabolism, but cannot convert ammonia to nitrates. It is also a powerful sterilizing agent, being particularly lethal to bacteria and other micro-organisms. Ozone is manufactured by subjecting normal oxygen or air to an electric current.

Marine ozonizers are available, which take in air from the air pump and convert the oxygen into small quantities of ozone. This may be passed into the water in the normal way through a diffuser. An ozonizer may also be used in conjunction with a protein skimmer to keep the tank clean and bright. Care needs to be taken since too much ozone in the water is lethal to animals.

P

Pachypanchax Cyprinodontidae ⊕
– playfairi PLAYFAIR'S PANCHAX 10cm. (4in.) ✂
A well known and commonly kept cyprinodont from East Africa and the Seychelles. The general body colour is greeny grey but this is much modified by horizontal rows of small reddish brown dots which extend into the tail, dorsal and anal fins. The belly is silver. A dark red edge borders the tail. The female is duller with a black patch or bar at the base of the dorsal fin.

It is an aggressive fish, which restricts its aquatic companions to the larger fish. A typical plant spawning cyprinodont. Likes the water to be 21–26°C., when it will inhabit the upper third of the available water.

PACU see *Colossoma nigripinnis*
Paintings see Art and Myth
PALEATUS CATFISH see *Corydoras paleatus*
PANCHAX see *Aplocheilus, Epiplatys, Pachypanchax*
PANTHERFISH see *Chromileptes, Pseudochromis*

Pantodon Pantodonitdae ⊕
– buchholzi BUTTERFLYFISH 10cm. (4in.)
An unusual and fascinating freshwater fish which lives close to the surface and uses its enormous pectoral fins to glide along out of the water.

The greenish body shades to a paler belly and has a bluish sheen. The fins are clear but dotted.

It is best kept in a large aquarium and its specialized feeding makes it unsuitable for the community tank. It feeds at the surface on flies and other winged insects, doubtless catching a few 'on the wing'. In captivity, it readily accepts live food and even dry food, providing it is fed from above and slowly, since once the food drops below it, it will not be taken. It prefers temperatures around 24°C. The tank should be covered.

Butterflyfish, *Pantodon buchholzi.*

Sexes are distinguished by the number of rays in the anal fin, nine in the male and 13 in the female. Butterflyfish are difficult to breed. They are egg-layers and deposit their eggs among floating plants. The eggs hatch in about a week and the young will take infusoria. They are, however, difficult to get past this stage unless adequate supplies of small flies, such as the Fruitfly, *Drosophila melanogaster*, are available. **121**

Pantodontidae
A family with only one species – *Pantodon buchholzi* – but which is closely related to the bone-tongued Osteo-glossidae. It is classified as a separate family because of

various detailed differences in its skeleton. See *Pantodon*.

PAPER SHELL see *Snails – Limnaea*

Paracanthurus Acanthuridae Ψ
– *hepatus* CLERICAL SURGEONFISH, BLUE TANG
20cm. (8in.)
From the Indo-Pacific where it reaches lengths of over
20cm., this fish is a deep rich blue with black sides. The tail
fin is a deep orange yellow edged with black. As the fish
matures the yellow colour migrates anteriorly as the blue
retreats before it.

This fish is often sold by the trade as *P. teuthis*. Young are
not difficult to acclimatize to captivity, and once this is
achieved it is an active, hardy fish and easy to feed.

Parachaetodon Chaetodontidae Ψ
– *ocellatus* OCELLATE BUTTERFLY 8cm. (3in.)
An attractive silver-bodied fish with yellow fins and four
dark bars running vertically across the body. A false 'eye' is
placed towards the posterior of the body. It comes from the

Ocellate Butterflyfish, *Parachaetodon ocellatus*.

Indo-Pacific where it is found living in groups. A rather
reluctant member of the aquarium, it will adapt if a little
care and patience are used to start it feeding.

Paracheirodon innesi see *Hyphessobrycon innesi*
PARADISEFISH see *Macropodus*

Paragobiodon Gobiidae Ψ
– *echinocephalus* PRICKLE-HEADED GOBY 4cm. (1½in.)
This species is very adaptable, and will adjust to sea or fresh
water. It is native to the Red Sea, south-east Asia, China
and the south Pacific.

Its colour varies with the water by being darker in fresh
water than in salt. Basically it is brown. The head is covered
with protrusions from which it gets its popular name.

Parasites see *Unwelcome Visitors*
Parental Behaviour see under *Behaviour*
PARROT, GREEN see *Thalassoma lunare*
PARROTFISH see *Bolbometapon, Callyodon, Scaridae*

Parupeneus Mullidae Ψ
– *pleurostigma* CARMINE or BLACKSPOT GOATFISH
61cm. (24in.)
A species from the Indo-Pacific. A scavenger in the marine
community tank. The body is reddish brown and yellow
with white additions and a distinct black spot, but it can
vary its colour to suit the environment to some extent.

PAVITA see *Cynolebias bellotti*
PEACOCK CICHLID see *Tilapia sparrmanii*
PEACOCK-EYED CICHLID see *Astronotus ocellatus*
PEARL
 DANIO see *Brachydanio albolineatus*
 GOURAMI see *Trichogaster leeri*
PEARL-SCALE BUTTERFLYFISH see *Chaetodon chrysurus*
PEARLED BUTTERFLYFISH see *Chaetodon chrysurus*
PEARLFISH see *Cynolebias*
PEARLY-SCALED ANGELFISH see *Centropyge vroliki*

Pelmatochromis Cichlidae ⊕
– *ansorgii* FIVE-SPOTTED CICHLID 9cm. (3½in.)
As do all members of the genus, this fish comes from Africa,
in this case, west Africa. Similar to other members of the
genus, it is reasonably sociable and easy on the vegetation
so it may be kept in community tanks.

The brownish grey body is tinted with mauve and red
highlights. Three horizontal lines are crossed by several
vertical bars. The green dorsal fins are peppered with
mauvish red dots, and both it and the tail fin have red
borders.

It breeds in captivity in the typical cichlid way, each egg

being attached to a flat clean surface by a filament. As are many fish, it is at its most resplendent during the mating season.

– pulcher KRIBENSIS or KAIBI CICHLID 10cm. (4in.)
This lovely fish from west Africa almost defies description. No sooner have you put pen to paper than the colours and patterns have altered like clouds in a windy sky. Their basically silver bodies vary from a pale blue to deep purple. The anal fin and belly can turn on a red blaze as fast as a light. Yellow horizontal bars appear and disappear rapidly, the dot on the operculum is positively kaleidoscopic and the fish can colour or dot its fins apparently with ease.

A peaceful, omnivorous, and active fish, which prefers temperatures from 21–26°C. For breeding, which is according to the cichlid pattern, it likes temperatures between 26–28°C. This fish is commonly sold under the name *P. kribensis*. **122**

PENCILFISH see *Nannostomus*
PENGUINFISH see *Thayeria obliqua*
PENNANT TREVALLY see *Allectis ciliaris*
PEPPERED
　CATFISH see *Corydoras paleatus*
　CORYDORAS see *Corydoras paleatus*
PERCH see *Anabas, Ctenopoma, Elassoma, Herichthys, Lutjanus, Serranus, Therapon*

Periophthalmidae MUDSKIPPERS
I am constantly amazed that such interesting, exotic and exciting creatures as mudskippers are available to the aquarist. For the student of evolution they have particular significance since here is a living example of a fish, the most primitive of vertebrates, which has managed to emerge from its ancestral aquatic environment to make a life for itself on land.

Time has proved that their method of using atmospheric oxygen, with the accessory breathing organs, was less successful than the alternative method of using lungs; it shows how nature is able to experiment to find the best design. These fish are successful, in their limited way, and are perfectly adapted to the environment in which they find themselves, the mud flats, and estuaries of Africa, India, Malay Peninsula, Indonesia and Polynesia. They spend a great deal of their time out of water moving across the mud, climbing rocks and trees during high water. In addition to their accessory breathing organs they can absorb oxygen through the skin, particularly the tail, providing it is kept moist. Observers will be rewarded with their intriguing behaviour of rolling over to moisten the eyes with their pectoral fin.

When they move they use their well developed muscular pectoral fins to drag their body along. Most of the time however they seem content just to stand and stare. When danger approaches they can make frantic dashes to safety back into the sea or under cover of the mangrove swamps.

A further adaptation to terrestrial life is the modification to their eyes. These are placed high on the head, resembling those of a frog, and are independently mobile, similar to chameleon's. If one eye sees food while the other spots an enemy the resulting psychological trauma must be intense.

For the aquarist who wants to keep these delightful fish, a large aquarium at least 91cm. long should be provided. It should be arranged so that a quarter to one third is water at a depth of 7–10cm. (3–4in.) and the rest a bank of mud. Provision must be made to prevent the mud falling into the water; this is best done by constructing an artificial water line of rocks covered in moss and fine twigs. The water should be partly salt in the proportions of half marine water, half fresh. Depending on the species some like to bury in the mud while others like to climb rocks and trees and should be provided with suitable arboreal props. As if unsure of its new environment the Mudskipper prefers to dangle its tail in the water and this position is often adopted.

They are best suited at water and air temperatures in the 26–28°C. range, and it is important that the atmosphere is humid, so keep the tank well covered at all times.

Mudskippers are carnivorous and will readily take flies, earthworms and mealworms.

Their breeding habits are interesting. They build funnel-shaped nests which reach low water in the mud. Fertilization is internal and the eggs are laid in the nest. The eggs and young are guarded by the female. See *Boleophthalmus, Periophthalmus*

Periophthalmus Periophthalmidae
– barbarus MUDSKIPPER, WALKING GOBY 15cm. (6in.)
This species is widely distributed from East Africa through Asia including Japan and China to Australia and Polynesia. It reaches 15cm. in length. The brown body is decorated with bluish dots. Both dorsal fins are blue.
– sobrinus MUDSKIPPER 15cm. (6in.)
This species is found from East Africa to the Pacific. They follow the usual behavioural patterns of the genus, spending most of their time out of the water, often burrowing in mud or in agile climbing activities.

The colour photograph shown in this book was taken in, one of its native habitats, the Seychelles, and is therefore of particular interest to those who enjoy the relationship between their hobby and ecology. **123**

Pervagor Balistidae Ψ
– spilosoma FANTAILED FILEFISH 11cm. (4½in.)
A very attractive import from the Hawaiian islands. For that reason it is more common in the USA than in Europe.

The body is bright yellow. The caudal fin is an orange
yellow with a black edge. Black spots enhance the body and
the head is covered with black longitudinal lines.

Petrotilapia Cichlidae
– *tridentiger* BLUE PETER 10cm. (4in.)
A native of Lake Malawi. This fish is a mouth brooder and
grows to 10cm. in length. It has a lovely dark blue body
traversed by several lighter blue bars. The anal fin is
decorated with yellow spots. Dines on live food and algae. It
prefers temperatures around 24°C. See *Nyasa Cichlids.*

PETTICOATFISH see *Gymnocorymbus ternetzi*
PERUVIAN LONGFIN see *Pterolebias peruensis*

pH or Hydrogen Ion Concentration
A measure of the acidity of a solution, which in our case is
the aquarium water. Physical chemists call the neutral point
pH7. Numbers below that, pH6, and pH5, for example, are
increasingly acid while numbers above pH7 are more
alkaline. The limits for fish life are between pH4·5 to pH8·5.
All school children will know that pH is measured with
litmus paper, by observing colour changes from acid red to
alkaline blue. Many other methods exist, however, and
special kits for the measurement of pH designed for
aquarists are available from dealers.

It is possible to alter the pH by adding chemicals to the
water. This is a complicated procedure and requires some
training in chemical techniques; it would, therefore, be
unwise for inexperienced aquarists to attempt it.

The need, however, to alter pH is very limited. Animals
adapt to change, see *Adaptability.* Most fish will live quite
happily in different pHs within a range, though some prefer
alkaline conditions while others do best in more acid
surroundings especially when breeding. The golden rule, as
always, is not to make sudden changes. Fish will
accommodate to small changes in pH, for example pH 7·6
to pH 8·0 but will succumb when expected to adapt
suddenly to a variation as large as pH6 to pH8. Marine
animals must be kept between pH 7·8 and pH 8·5.

Take great care when transferring newly acquired fish
from their travelling jar to the tank. Slowly add small
amounts of aquarium water to the travelling jar in order to
adjust the pH of the travelling water to the pH of the tank,
thus avoiding sudden environmental change for the fish. See
*Acclimatization to Tank, Adaptability, Hardness, Water
Quality.*

Phallichthys Poeciliidae ⊕
– *amates* MERRY WIDOW 5cm. (2in.)
The popular name is derived mainly from the dark edge to
the prominent dorsal fin of the male and, no doubt, its lively

habits. It comes from Honduras. The body colour is
brownish green shading to pale yellow on the belly. A
horizontal line extends along its side. In addition the male is
adorned with dark bars along its side. The tip of the rather
long gonopodium is turned downwards.

It breeds well at temperatures of 25–26°C., producing
some 50 offspring at a time. Take precautions as it tends to
eat its young.

PHANTOM TETRA, BLACK see *Megalamphodus megalopterus*

Phenacogrammus Characidae ⊕
– *interruptus* FEATHERTAIL or CONGO TETRA 8cm. (3in.)
This fish, which comes from Zaïre, gets its name from the
characteristic embellishment which adult males develop in
the tail. The male is larger than the female and they are
practically colourless except for a dazzling prismatic
reflection displayed when illuminated from the front and
above. The feathertail, for all its size, being one of the larger
characins, is rather shy and has a tendency to hide when not
kept in a school. It is said to prefer soft water of low pH.

PHILIPPINE TANG see *Acanthurus japonicus*

Photosynthesis
Plants, unlike animals, are able to manufacture their own
food. It is this ability which allows life, as we know it, to
exist on earth. In the presence of the green pigment
chlorophyll, which is found in all green plants, the gas
carbon dioxide combines with water to form complex food
substances, the carbohydrates and, as a bonus, in the
process releases oxygen. During the chemical reaction
energy from sunlight is essential and this energy is trapped
for later use by the plant as required.

Carbon dioxide + Water + Sun energy = Carbohydrate
+ Oxygen.
$$6CO_2 + 6H_2O + Energy = C_4H_{12}O_6 + 6O_2$$

Animals make use of this herbal ability by eating the
plants. Some animals of course eat other animals, not
plants, but since the victims, or their victims, ate plants it
can be appreciated that ultimately all animals rely on plants
to live. Photosynthesis occurs in all plants from algae to the
giant redwood trees of North America. See *Oxygen,
Plankton, Plants.*

Phoxinopsis Characidae ⊕
– *typicus* RIO MINNOW 4cm. (1½in.)
This fish comes from the district of Rio de Janeiro. The
translucent body is brownish yellow. It has a striking golden
ring surrounding the base of the tail. A stripe runs

horizontally back from the eye to the bifurcation of the tail fin. The fins are pink. There is no adipose fin so it is an atypical characin.

It is a fair community tank fish, if a little timid, but is not popular among aquarists because of its lack of distinctive colour or form.

Little is known about its breeding habits.

Phoxinus   Cyprinidae   ⊕
– phoxinus   MINNOW   12cm. (4½in.)
The minnow is found throughout Europe and northern Asia where it prefers clear, cool and running water, with gravel or sandy bottoms. It reaches 15cm. in length. Normally a rather dull greenish brown but in the breeding season – early summer – its colours become intense and red blotches develop around the mouth and gills. It lives in small shoals and feeds on minute insects, worms and fish fry.

The female lays up to 1500 eggs in mid-summer. In the aquarium it is active and makes an attractive inmate. It is better kept in small shoals and with other species.

PICASSO TRIGGERFISH see *Rhinecanthus aculeatus*
PIKE, DWARF see *Belonesox belizanus*
PIKE
  CICHLID see *Crenicichla lepidota*
  CICHLID see *Crenicichla lepidota*
  CICHLID, RING-TAILED see *Crenicichla saxatilis*
  TOP MINNOW see *Belonesox belizanus*

Pimelodella   Pimelodidae   ⊕
– gracilis   GRACEFUL CATFISH   17cm. (6½in.)   ◗
This fish from South America has a brownish green body embellished by a dark horizontal line running from the operculum to the tail. A rather splendid dorsal fin is supported by a black spine. The anal and adipose fins are also large.

It prefers mature water between 21–26°C. and either subdued lighting or a well planted tank which offers plenty of cover. As yet, no one has succeeded in breeding this species in captivity. **124**
– meeki   STRIPED CATFISH   15cm. (6in.)
This is a spectacular catfish from the Amazon region. It has recently become more readily available to the aquarist. The body is striped with horizontal bands of white and dark grey blue. The belly is pale grey or white, and the fins are translucent and colourless. Large barbels surround its mouth. **125**

Pimelodidae   CATFISHES
A family of smooth-skinned catfish from South and Central America. Their distinctive characteristics are a well developed adipose fin and barbels of enormous length, some even as long as the body itself. A peaceful family ideally suited to the community tank; they eat anything and prefer

temperatures around 24°C. See *Microglanis, Pimelodella, Sorubim.*

PINK TRIGGERFISH see *Melichthys vidua*
PINK-TAILED RAINBOWFISH, AUSTRALIAN see *Melanotaenia fluviatilis*
PINK-THROATED CATFISH see *Corydoras spilurus*
PIPEFISH see *Syngnathidae, Sygnathus*
PIRANHA see *Serrasalmus*

Plankton
Microscopic plant and animal life, in the sea and freshwater, on which all fishes ultimately depend, as plankton are the bottom of the food chain. Carnivorous fish do not eat plankton but they eat other fishes which do. Without plankton, therefore, life in the sea would be impossible. See *Photosynthesis.*

Planaria see under *Unwelcome Visitors*
Planorbis see under *Snails*

Planting
Assuming that thought has been given to the layout of the plants in the tank it is advisable to make sure that they are clean and free from dead or dying leaves and any dangerous animal life – see *Unwelcome Visitors.*

Those plants, such as *Vallisnaria*, which have roots should be laid on the surface of the water. The body of the root should then be grasped gently between thumb and forefinger, taken to the gravel and pushed into it, and the roots covered with gravel. The leafy part of the plant is then withdrawn until the crown of the root is exposed. This is important or the plant will not grow. Plants without roots, for instance cuttings, are pushed into the gravel.

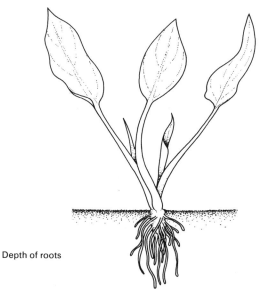

Depth of roots

Planting technique

I personally prefer planting with a planting stick; these are readily available from dealers. They are simply long sticks with a forked end, and after a little practice can be used efficiently and with speed.

Some plants do better in different soil such as a loam or clay. This need can be afforded by using planting pots. These are simply earthenware, or in these modern days, plastic pots with holes in. The chosen soil is placed in the bottom two-thirds. The top third is aquarium gravel and in this the plant is rooted. The pot is then buried in the gravel. See *Plants*.

Plants

FRESHWATER

Acorus

– *gramineus* JAPANESE DWARF RUSH up to 30cm. (1ft)
A plant with slender grass-like leaves. In nature it is found in marshy conditions but does well in the aquarium fully submerged. Several varieties exist, some of which grow to well over 30cm. (1ft), but others reach no more than 8cm. (3in.) and, being slow growing, are well suited to the foreground of the tank. A pleasing plant. The variety *A. gramineus variegatus* has yellow striped leaves.

Alternanthera

– *sessilis* 30cm. (1ft)
A very attractive plant that has recently become fashionable. Sadly, it is not very hardy and rapidly succumbs, to hard water conditions in particular. It has

long wide leaves in various tints of red, the stems being a particularly rich red. Should be considered a temporary decoration.

Anubias

– *barteri*
Like the rest of this genus it is a marshy plant from Africa. The wide, arrow-shaped, pinnate leaves are a rich shiny green and divide at the base. It prefers soft acid water and is slow growing.

– *lanceolata* WATER ASPIDISTRA 15cm. (6in.)
Somewhat resembles the much maligned Victorian drawing-room plant. The thick shiny leaves reach 15cm. in length and are carried on short thick stems. The plant has rhizomes and these may be divided for propagation and when transplanting.

– *nana* 13cm. (5in.)
Rather similar to *A. lanceolata* but is a smaller species growing only to 13cm. in height. Suitable for foreground planting.

Aponogeton

– *crispus* 61cm. (2ft)
A pleasing wispy plant from Sri Lanka, it has long thin leaves which are crinkled at the edges. It tends to adapt to the height of the aquarium but can grow as tall as 61cm. The leaves are translucent. This plant forms tubers which can be divided for transplanting.

– *fenestralis* MADAGASCAR LACE 30cm. (1ft)
Sadly, this exotic and quite unusual plant from Madagascar is difficult to grow. It demands specific conditions to thrive. The water should be running, the soil rich and the light subdued. They get their popular name from the fact that there is no body to the leaf; only the vein system exists.

– *ulvaceus* 61cm. (2ft)
A pleasing native of Madagascar which has short broad translucent leaves on a long stalk.

– *undulatus* 23cm. (9in.)
A particular favourite of mine from Sri Lanka. The long thin leaves on a single spike have attractive wavy edges.

Bacopa

– *caroliniana*
Long single stalks with numerous small rounded fleshy leaves arranged in pairs up its length. Suitable for both cold and tropical aquariums.

Blyxa

– *japonica*
A grass like plant from the continents of Asia and Australia. It is best suited to soft water, and to the middle foreground.

Cabomba

– *aquatica*
A native of Mexico it has divided leaves when submerged.

The leaves which are above water are rounded.

– caroliniana

A delightful and popular plant from the southern states of the USA. The bright green leaves are fan like and well divided into filaments. It is of value in providing hiding places for small fish and fry.

Ceratophyllum

– demersum   HORNWORT

An attractive plant with filamentous leaves and branching stems. Produces a pleasing effect against a rocky background in the middle of the tank. Can be transplanted or propagated by pushing small branches into the sand or gravel. A plant which may be left floating and in this way is useful cover in the breeding tank.

Ceratopteris

– cornuta   FLOATING FERN

A useful plant for those fish which like cover and subdued light. A thick root system hangs down into the water and offers hiding places for the fish fry.

– thalictroides   INDIAN or SUMATRA FERN, WATER SPRITE

An attractive and useful plant which grows either rooted in the sand or floating. It reproduces by sprouting new plants at the leaf edges. Leaves are more feathery when planted.

Cryptocoryne

– affinis   15cm. (6in.)

Like other members of this family it comes from south-eastern Asia. It has blue green spear-shaped leaves on long stalks. Grows to 15cm. in height. Very decorative.

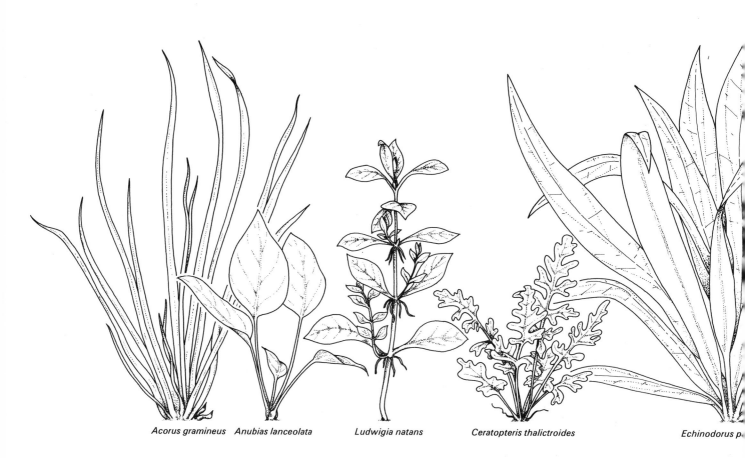

Acorus gramineus   Anubias lanceolata   Ludwigia natans   Ceratopteris thalictroides   Echinodorus p

– ciliata 60cm. (2ft)

Rather large for many aquaria growing to 60cm. in height. It has however, beautiful pale green leaves on thick stalks. Like so many of this genus it has variably shaped leaves and can tolerate relatively alkaline water or even slightly brackish water.

– griffithi 24cm. (10in.)

Pleasing dark greeny blue on topside and a brown underside to leaf. Topside sometimes flecked with reddish brown spots.

– nevillii 5–8cm. (2–3in.)

A favourite of mine for foreground planting.

– thwaitesii 18cm. (7in.)

A very attractive member of the genus with leaves varying from green to brown. It grows to 18cm. in height. Leaves vary in shape from wide oval to narrow spear shape. They have a rough surface with ragged edges.

– wendtii 8–25cm. (3–10in.)

Several forms occur depending on geographical location of origin. Colours vary from deep rich green to a form which contains more red than green. Also variable in size, anything from 8–25cm. in height.

– willisii 30cm. (1ft)

This plant enhances any aquarium. Green topside with brown underside and brown stems. The leaves are long narrow and crinkled. Grows to 30cm. in height.

Didiplis

– diandra WATER HEDGE

A useful plant where plenty of cover is required. It grows to a thick, fine leaved mass of foliage. Native to North America.

ogeton undulatus   Cabomba caroliniana   Cryptocoryne ciliata   Eleocharis acicularis   Myriophyllum hippuroides   Vallisnaria spiralis

Echinodorus

– *berteroi* CELLOPHANE PLANT

As the plant grows the pale green, thin leaves on short stems are replaced by others which are tougher and broader. It can be heavily pruned if it becomes unruly

– *brevipediceliatus* JUNIOR SWORD PLANT

A pleasing small version of *E. panuculatus* which propagates by sending out runners. Very useful for middle foreground cover.

– *grisebachii* CHAIN SWORD PLANT   10cm. (4in.)

A very useful and attractive plant which has stout broad leaves and thick stems. Providing it is allowed to send out runners it remains a diminutive 10cm.

– *paniculatus* AMAZON SWORD PLANT   46cm. (18in.)

Sometimes known as *E. intermedius*. The most popular and well known of the genus although it grows rather large. It is used by some fish for spawning on its wide, sword-shaped leaves which are held proudly on stout stems.

– *tenellus* PYGMY or DWARF SWORD PLANT

Several varieties are sold under this name. The most suitable for small aquaria are those which have a maximum height of 8cm. I like this for creating small clusters around small foreground rocks.

– *tunicatus*

This plant has broad, heart-shaped, leaves 10cm. wide, and 20cm. long on medium stems which droop in a pleasing manner and incidentally restrict its height. Again a foreground plant much favoured in my tanks.

Eleocharis

– *acicularis* HAIR GRASS   13cm. (5in.)

This is one of those delightful grass like plants which when well established provides useful cover for fish and adds much to the beauty of the aquascape. It grows to 13cm. in height and will suit cold and tropical waters.

– *vivipara* UMBRELLA HAIR GRASS   24–30cm. (10–12in.)

This attractive plant's fine hair-like stems develop buds at their tips, which themselves produce new stem growth. In their turn these new shoots produce terminal buds and further growth. The final effect is a very pleasing green canopy from which the popular name derives.

Elodea

– *densa*

Like all members of the genus this plant grows well, indeed sometimes too well, requiring a good deal of pruning. Short thin leaves grow on the stem over its entire length and are arranged in whorls. It is well suited to both tropical and cold water tanks.

Hydrilla

– *verticillata*

Small leaves grow on the stem at regular intervals over its entire length. At each leaf point, several leaves arise around the stem. Very attractive, affords good cover for fish and prefers warm water.

Hygrophila

– *guianensis* WILLOW LEAF   10cm. (4in.)

Decorative thick-stemmed plant which has wide leaves. Some species of fish like it for egg laying.

– *polysperma*

Paired pale green leaves grow on a woody stem, alternate pairs at right angles. The leaves are spatular or spoon shaped. It is rather anaemic in my opinion, but has been popular in recent years.

Lagenandra

– *lancifolia* 18–20cm. (7–8in.)

Smallish, this dark green plant makes a useful colour contrast. The leaves are spear shaped on individual stems.

– *thwaitesii*

Popular, but in my opinion, less attractive than *L. lancifolia*. Similar shaped leaves are more of a yellow green. Can grow to 4m. if not cut back.

Lemna

– *gibba* DUCKWEED

Floating plants which provide cover, shade and food for fish.

– *trisulca* THREE POINTED DUCKWEED

Short, oval, light green leaves which float just below the surface. An attractive and useful plant.

Limnophila

– *sessiliflora* AMBULIA

Whorls of feathery leaves arise along the entire length of the stem. It prefers tropical water and plenty of light as well as nutrient in the soil. It is however, slow growing and will only bush if the tips are pinched out.

Ludwigia

– *arcuata*

These are plants that in nature grow at the edge of water but they can adapt to total immersion. Stalks, from which spring the bright green narrow leaves, are fleshy. The leaves are narrow in aquariums although naturally, as a bog plant, are wider. It is propagated by seeds or cuttings. Pinching out the tip makes for a thick bushy plant.

– *natans*

A lovely broad-leaved, yellow green plant which makes a very attractive show.

– *palustris*

A rich, thick, well-formed plant with bright green young leaves which turn brown with age.

Marsilea

– *hirsuta* WATER CLOVER   ◍

Very long spindly stems give rise to a small leaf which

resembles clover. The leaves are pale green and the plant sends out long runners. Grows well and thrives in subdued lighting.

Micranthemum
– micranthemoides ⊙
An attractive small bushy plant suitable for bottom of the tropical aquarium which is well lit. The small green leaves arise along the stem's length.

Myriophyllum
– hippuroides ⊙
A very lovely feathery plant which grows well and affords good cover for small fish. It is easily propagated by simply cutting off a shoot and pushing it into the tank's soil. The submerged leaves are feather-like, though become coarser when out of water. It is suited to the heated aquarium.
– scabratum ⊙
Similar to *M. hippuroides* but even more beautiful having reddish brown or golden feathery leaves and small mauve flowers on spikes. Like its generic cousin above, it needs good light.

Najas
– flexilis
A floating plant with paired pale green leaves which have crinkled edges. An annual plant which does well in both subdued and bright light, and also grows in tropical and cold water.

Nitella
– gracilis
A fine small plant which produces dense, finely woven, olive green foliage suitable for egg layers and for fry to hide in. Grows in cold and tropical water.

Nomaphila
– stricta
Large 5cm. spear-shaped leaves arising from woody stems in pairs.

Nuphar
– japonicum
A very pleasing plant which is available in a range of colours, greens, brown, or red, depending on which variety is chosen. The leaves are large, spear-shaped with wavy edges.
– luteum
Sadly this plant is large for the average aquarium and all too soon outgrows the space. Large (20cm. across) flamboyant leaves of a rich blue green arising from a single stem.
– sagittifolium CAPE FEAR SPATTERDOCK
A lovely long-leaved plant with undulating edges, which are yellow green on single stems. Leaves up to 20cm. long.

Rotala
– indica 30cm. (1ft)
Small, attractive and functional, the long spear-shaped leaves are green in warm water and reddish brown in cold.

Sagittaria
– latifolia GIANT SAGITTARIA 45cm. (18in.)
Grass-shaped leaves which are commonly used as background plants in aquariums. They are so popular that anyone who has chanced to glance at an aquarium will have seen them. Grows in warm or cold water.
– subulata 38cm. (15in.)
Similar to *S. latifolia*, but slightly smaller. May turn reddish in bright light at lower temperatures.

Vallisnaria
– gigantea 45cm. (18in.)
If anything *Vallisnaria* are better known than *Sagittaria*. They have long grass like leaves. This species, as the name suggests, is only suitable for large aquariums and grows in cold or warm water. An attractive variety known as *V. gigantea rubrifolia* has reddish brown leaves.
– spiralis 91cm. (36in.)
The commonest oxygenating backcloth plant used by aquarists. A very lovely twisted leaved variety, *V. spiralis torta*, is an added attraction. All *Vallisnaria* are propagated by runners. They do form flowers and seeds, but seed is rarely used by aquarists to obtain these lovely plants.

MARINE PLANTS
Most marine aquarists do not have marine plants in their tanks. They are indeed rather difficult to cultivate and are probably better left until adequate experience has been gained in maintaining the marine system.

Those marine plants which are used are algae belonging to the simplest group of plants, the Thallophyta. They are closely related to the microscopic one-celled plants which grow only too well in freshwater tanks but are so essential to a balanced marine system. They are much larger than the common unicellular algae, however, and take the form, if not the complex structure, of higher plants. Algae are subdivided into green, brown, blue and red coloured forms. Several species are suitable for the marine tank providing they are given plenty of light and algal fertilizers.

Several members of the genus *Caulerpa* adapt to captivity. Tropical examples include *C. crassifolia*, *C. sertularioides* and *Halimeda tuna*.

Caulerpa species send out what are, in fact, simple underground runners and these periodically send up the flat finger like bodies of the plant.

Marine plants need not only plenty of light but a number of nutrient salts in the water.

Wickler's formula, which has proved satisfactory is:
800 ml. water
40 grams sodium phosphate ($NaHPO_4$)
40 grams calcium chloride crystals ($CaCl_2 6H_2O$)
20 grams ferric chloride ($FeCl_3$)
20 grams concentrated hydrochloric acid (HCl)

In addition nitrates both sodium and potassium are necessary where there is no animal life in the tank. With animals present the breakdown products of protein metabolism end up as nitrates and it is not necessary to add them.

Common Batfish, *Platax orbicularis*.

Platax Ephippidae Ψ
– ***orbicularis*** COMMON BATFISH 91cm. (36in.)
Widespread in the Indo-Pacific, this beauty reaches up to 91cm. in length but even more in depth. It is easy to keep, being greedy and not very fussy. Consider well before purchasing this fish as it grows large and becomes less attractive; when young it has a lovely honey yellow body and very elongated dorsal and anal fins. A very dark line passes dorso-ventrally through the eye and a second, wider reddish brown band runs parallel with the first, starting at the anterior end of the base of the dorsal fin. A further parallel band passes through the hind end of the body and the posterior parts of both the dorsal and anal fins. The tail is clear.
– ***pinnatus*** RED-FACED or PINNATUS BATFISH
76cm. (30in.) ✂
A rather aggressive fish according to some authorities. It closely resembles other batfish but has red coloration on body and fins. Frequently reluctant to start feeding in captivity and generally not as hardy as *P. orbicularis*.
– ***teira*** LONGFIN BATFISH
Similar to its cousins, but this species has even more extended dorsal and anal fins when young. Dark vertical bars transect the yellow brown fish.

PLATY see *Xiphophorus maculatus*
PLAYFAIR'S PANCHAX see *Pachypanchax playfairi*

Plecostomus Loricariidae ⊕
– ***punctatus*** BRAZILIAN SPOTTED CATFISH 30cm. (12in.)
Found in the southern parts of Brazil, this fish has established itself as a member of the aquarists' repertoire. The body is grey brown with spots and patches of various sizes. There are five, usually quite distinct, transverse bars. Between the nostrils runs a thin dark band. The belly is a pale brown to light grey. The fins are also grey brown and the dots are arranged on them in rows.

All members of this genus are fond of algae and will assist in keeping the tank sides and the larger plants free of it. It also takes a wide variety of both animal and vegetable food.

In general, a peaceful fish, but can be aggressive to a newly introduced specimen. It likes temperatures around 24°C. It may adapt to captivity better if given slightly brackish water, at least at the start of tank life. **126**
– ***rachovi*** RACHOW'S CATFISH 15cm (6in.)
A catfish which is native to Brazil. It has a grey body decorated with white spots, and is similar in shape and feeding requirements to *P. punctatus*.

Plectorhynchidae SWEETLIPS
A family which includes a variety of marine fish from the Atlantic Ocean, Red Sea and Indo-Pacific. Most of this family have a habit of snatching food while swimming in mid-water. Many have striking coloration. They live in warm shallow water where they form social groups or

shoals. They are omnivorous but all require some live food.
See *Plectorhynchus*.

Plectorhynchus Plectorhynchidae Ψ
– ***chaetodonoides*** POLKA-DOT GRUNT, CLOWN SWEETLIPS
91cm. (36in.)
From the Indo-Pacific. One common name comes, not
surprisingly, from the polka dot design on the body. It has a
brown body when young with white spots. The adult is
brown with extensive speckling. Members of this genus need
live food and thrive at temperatures between 21–26°C.
– ***gaterinoides*** YELLOW-LINED SWEETLIPS 35cm. (14in.)
A very attractive fish which ranges from the coastal waters
of Australia, the Philippines, through Indian coastal waters
to the Red Sea.
   The body is shaped like an elongated rectangle owing to
the high domed head above the eyes. The body colour is a
rich golden yellow. A wide dark brown or black band runs
from the snout and tapering at the base passes onto the
caudal fin. A second longitudinal band again starts on the
snout, broadens, runs above the previous band and ends on
the dorsal fin. A third dark band runs along the dorsal
midline. Several dark irregular lines also decorate the
tail.
   This fish has also been identified as *P. lineatus* and was
previously classified, by some authorities, in the genus
Diagramma.
   Popular with marine aquarists being hardy, adaptable to
captivity and easy to feed. They are social fish and do much
better if more than one is kept in the same tank. They feel
more secure if they have a variety of hiding places, so design
the tank decor with that in mind. They take live food of
great variety, including brine shrimps. **127**
– ***orientalis*** SEA KING, ORIENTAL SWEETLIP 60cm. (23½in.)
From the Indo-Pacific where it reaches 60cm. in length. The
young have a rich brown body which is sparsely scattered
with white or cream dots. The belly is white. Adults develop
horizontal stripes of white or cream.

Plesiopidae Roundheads Ψ
A small family of fish from the Indo-Pacific which is closely
related to the basses (Serranidae). A family characterized by
species with thick chunky and usually very dark coloured
bodies, and blunt heads with large mouths. See
Calloplesiops.

Plotosidae
A small family of elongated catfish from the Indo-Pacific
Most are marine, although some live in brackish water and
a few in freshwater. Some marine species are said to adapt
to freshwater. The body is scaleless. A first dorsal fin is
placed behind the head and the second is continuous with

the caudal and anal fins. The mouth is barbelled. Pectoral
and first dorsals carry spines which can inflict unpleasant
wounds as they are capable of injecting venom. See
Plotosus.

Plotosus Plotosidae Ψ
– ***anguillaris*** see *P. lineatus*
– ***lineatus*** BARBER EEL, SALTWATER CATFISH 30cm. (12in.)
This species is common throughout the Indo-Pacific, where
they live in large shoals when young. As the common name
suggests, the body of this fish is eel-like and elongated. Anal
and dorsal fins are continuous with, and indistinguishable
from, the pointed caudal fin. A second tall, narrow-based
dorsal fin is situated anterior to the low long-based dorsal.
The dark brownish black body is divided longitudinally by
a number of white lines which follow the contours of the
body. One starts at the eye and runs dorsally to the tail tip, a
second starts on the upper jaw and a third at the pectoral
fin. The mouth is well supplied with barbels.
   It is kept by aquarists successfully, but beware of the
spines of dorsal and pectoral fins, which inflict serious
wounds. Lives naturally in salt water, but is able to adapt to
freshwater.
   Often called *P. anguillaris* by dealers. **128**

PLUMED LYRETAIL see *Amphyosemion filamentosum*

Poecilia Poeciliidae Ψ/⊕⊙
Members of this genus come from the southern states of the
USA, Central and South America as far south as Venezuela.
They are estuarine fish and have often been found in salt
water well out to sea. It is therefore advisable to add a little
salt to their aquarium. A teaspoon of salt to every 4·5 litres
is adequate. They are relatively large fish which require
adequate space if they are to be kept successfully.
Continuous feeders, it is important that in addition to the
dried and live food, which should be given at least three
times daily, they are supplied with a good deal of vegetable
matter in the form of algae and soft-leaved plants; their
tank should therefore be placed in sunlight. In general most
species make good parents but those species, or individuals,
whose parental behaviour leaves a little to be desired should
have their young removed.
– ***formosa*** ALBINO LYRETAIL MOLLY 9cm. (3½in.)
This fish is occasionally imported from a number of areas in
Mexico, although it is probably of more interest to scientists
than to aquarists. It is a natural hybrid between *P. sphenops*
and *P. latipinna* and, as such, shows a mixture of structural
characteristics derived from both parents. Of particular
interest is that only females result from the cross and these
in turn will mate with males of either of the parent species.
   As the popular name suggests, it has no body colour,

taking highlights from the lighting. The eye is without pigment and therefore shows the red of blood vessels.

Care and management as for other *Poecilia*.It will delight the collector of curios, but not those striving for exotic colour or shape. **129**

– latipinna syn. *Mollienisia latipinna*   SAILFIN MOLLY
♀12·5cm. (5in.) ♂10cm. (4in.)
This species comes from the estuaries in the south-eastern states of USA.

It has a basic colour of rich greeny yellow fading to a yellow throat and belly. The dark and light patterning of the scales together with rows of dots give it a pleasing mosaic pattern. The splendid characteristic feature of the male is a really beautiful dorsal fin which is set on a broad base between the operculum and a point two thirds along the back. Its depth is twice that of the fish and among the light dots, which continue the mosaic effect of the body, can be seen a multitude of flashing colours.

– melanogaster syn. *Limia melanogaster*   BLUE LIMIA
♀ 6cm. (2½in.)   ♂ 4cm. (1½in.)
An underrated little fish from the islands of Jamaica and Haiti. The dark back of the female contrasts with the striking silver sides which are generously flecked with blue. A dark irregular patch is seen near the vent. The male is more attractive, having a lovely green back, shading into blue sides and belly somewhat similar to the female. A series of dark vertical bars divide the length of the body. The fins are deep rich buttercup yellow at the base shading to a clear tip.

A peaceful member of the community tank. Fifty young is the maximum produced at any one time.

– nigrofasciata syn. *Limia nigrofasciata*   HUMP or HUNCH BACK   5–7cm. (*c*.2in.)
A native of Haiti. As the male attains maturity he develops an unfortunate enlargement of the back which gives a grotesque appearance, but to clothe his problem he dons a splendid dorsal appendage. To the yellow bordered black based fin he adds several vertical body bands.

–reticulata syn. *Lebister reticulata*   GUPPY   ♀
6cm. (2½in.)
Hardy fish which come from many parts of northern South America, they are found in streams and pools of very variable physical standards, their temperature range is from 10°C. up to 38°C. They can withstand a variety of pH and DH values, see pH and Hardness of Water, and survive conditions of poor oxygenation. The naturally found female is a plump uninteresting 'tiddler'. Twice the size of her gorgeous mate, she has a dark green back with silver sides and belly. Her fins are clear. The male is a beautiful fish with seemingly no two specimens alike. The colours, dots, bars and lines combine with an equal variety of fin form to make a species of unending pleasure. It has the added advantage

of being both inexpensive and readily available.

Aquarists using selective breeding techniques have extended what nature began. Strains exist today which, breeding true, are magnificent. Enthusiasts have been so overwhelmed by this fish that fan clubs have been formed whose members spend their leisure hours trying to improve perfection. In general they attempt to stabilize the type of fin and then to create colour patterns on the basic shape. A very wide variety of types exist, from the fantail and veiltail to the double sword. Females too have been embellished and given a touch of colour, and even more striking, a little flamboyance of fin.

Once the difficult task of establishing a new variety is attained, the breeding is easy. Female guppies are very prolific, up to a hundred and fifty young are produced every few weeks. The hardy offspring quickly take to brine shrimp and on it grow rapidly.

Lovely fish, hardy and peaceful, they are good members of a community tank; easy to breed and challenging to the serious breeder, since new varieties are constantly possible. A veiltail variety is illustrated. **130**

– sphenops   SHORT-FINNED MOLLY   10cm. (4in.)
Widely distributed over the range for the genus, it is one of the smallest of the mollies. The body colour is olive green with a wide variety of black patches, bars and dots. The dorsal fin is less flamboyant than many of its cousins being rather round in shape.

Aquarists have, using selective breeding techniques, developed over many generations a number of colour variations. The commonest and most well known is undoubtedly the Black or Midnight Molly. Black varieties of *P. latipinna* and *P. velifera* have been developed and, in turn, by crossing these, stable true breeding varieties are now established. The black strain of *P. velifera* was crossed with *P. latipinna* to get the Molly known to aquarists as the Perma Black Molly. The Liberty Molly with blue body and red fins is derived from *P. sphenops,* while the Pearl Molly is a development of *P. latipinna.*

– velifera   GIANT SAILFIN MOLLY   18cm. (6½in.)
Beautiful, magnificent, and inevitably, rare, this lovely fish comes from the Yucatan regions of Central America. It grows to 18cm. in length and the male has a truly enormous dorsal fin. The colour and patterning reflects those of *P. latipinna*. The throat is an outstanding golden yellow. The young are about 1cm. long at birth and rapidly grow with good conditions. The dorsal fin of the male rarely develops much before a year old. **131**

– vittata syn. *Limia vittata*   CUBAN LIMIA
♀11cm. (4½in.)   ♂5cm. (2in.)
Needless to say, a native of Cuba. Females of the species attain lengths of up to 11cm. whilst males reach only half that size. The male has an olive back with a blue sheen on

A pair of Giant Sailfin Mollies, *Poecilia velifera*.

Cuban Limia, *Poecilia vittata*.

the sides shading to a yellow belly, and is speckled with a number of irregular dark dots on the sides and fins. Females are similarly marked but, in some cases, less well endowed with spots. The fins are clear but with a yellow tinge.

An undistinguished fish, it is an enthusiastic and prolific breeder. It accepts any food and is friendly.

Poeciliidae   LIVE-BEARING TOOTH CARPS
This family, now well known to aquarists the world over, produces live young. All members of the family are found in Central and South America and the West Indies. Somewhat resembling the Cyprinodontidae (Killifishes) in external form they may be easily distinguished since the male has the anal fin modified to form a gonopodium which is used during internal fertilization of the female. As the male reaches maturity, the hitherto slightly pointed anal fin elongates to form a shaft, which points backwards during normal activities.

The male approaches the female for mating with his fins displayed and trembling, and swims close-by. Mating takes only a second, then the male leaves, having no part in the rearing of the young.

The eggs descend from the ovary (egg-producing organ) and lie in the tube which eventually carries the young to the outside. There the eggs lie, awaiting fertilization by the male. Placental mammals form a special organ – the placenta – which is sponge-like, full of blood and attached to the wall of the womb, corresponding to the egg tube of the fish, see Reproductive System, and the embryo obtains food and oxygen from the mother's blood. Live-bearing fish embryos, on the other hand, are eggs like all other fish. They have the food they require during their development within the egg. The mother merely protects them in her body

instead of laying them and then taking them into her mouth for protection like mouth-brooders, see *Cichlidae*, or simply guarding them in a nest, or leaving them to take their chances, see *Cyprinodontidae*. This clearly has advantages and is undoubtedly an evolutionary advance. See *Evolution*.

The eggs hatch out, like other fish, a variable time after fertilization depending on the temperature, and similarly the young vary in the time it takes to emerge from the mother, but it is usually between 3–12 weeks. They are born bent double but quickly straighten out.

As a result of this revolutionary modification, live-bearing, which is more effective in protecting the young until they are better able to survive, the vast numbers of eggs and potential young produced by egg-layers are unnecessary. It is rare to find live-bearers having more than one hundred or so young and it is often a much smaller number than that.

The parents are liable to consume their young, so separation of some sort is necessary. The most natural method is simply to provide a large, well planted tank which affords the young plenty of cover. A second method is to place the ripe expectant female in a small trap which itself resides in a larger tank. The principle is that once born, the young fry escape to the outer tank away from their mother. Several types of trap have been produced – see *Traps*. Surprisingly, the former method is favoured by commercial breeders. The female can be put in the tank well in advance of her confinement which reduces any risk of damage during handling.

The young live-bearers, being well advanced, can straight away take small daphnia, brine shrimp or even some of the commercially-marketed foods. The secret of feeding is little and often, and this means at least six times each day.

Be careful not to handle ripe females, or if they must be handled, do so with extreme care, or the young will be expelled from her abused body too early, before the yolk-sacs have been absorbed. If this happens, they are unlikely to survive and her efforts and your time will have been wasted. Remove males after mating or they will consume their offspring.

A point worth noting is that from one fertilization, several broods can be produced since some sperm is retained by the female for subsequent broods. It is a serious point to note for aquarists undertaking special breeding programmes.

This basic pattern applies to most members of the family. There are some modifications, notably in the genus *Poecilia* which are included under the appropriate headings. See *Allopoecilia, Belonesox, Gambusia, Girardinus, Heterandria, Phallichthys, Poecilia, Xiphophorus*.

POINTED-HEAD EARTHEATER see *Geophagus acuticeps*

POISONING see under *Disease*
POLKA-DOT GRUNT see *Plectorhynchus chaetodonoides*

Polycentropsis Nandidae ⊕
– *abbreviata* AFRICAN LEAFFISH 9cm. (3½in.)
Less leaf-like than *Monocirrhus polyacanthus,* this fish is
found in West Africa. It has the ability to change hue
rapidly but bases its colour scheme on dark greens, light
greens, browns and black.

Females are not easily distinguishable, but carry less
distinct markings than the males. This species is unusual for
the family in being a bubble nest builder. The male blows
his bubbles among floating plants. The female laboriously
lays one egg at a time on the plants among the bubbles until
up to two hundred eggs are produced. The male is very
liable to attack her when egg-laying is complete, so the
female should be removed from the tank. In tanks at
breeding temperatures, between 25–26°C., the young hatch
in 48 hours. They are relatively simple to rear on small live
food such as daphnia. The male should be removed.

Polycentrus Nandidae ⊕
– *schomburgki* GUYANA or SCHOMBURGH'S LEAFFISH
9cm. (3½in.) ◫
This leaffish from South America and Trinidad is also less
leaf-shaped than its cousin *Monocirrhus polyacanthus* but
has a flattened body with brown, black and silver grey
markings, and the ability to swim head down at an angle to
resemble a floating leaf. The transparent latter half of the
dorsal and anal fins produce a strange cut-off appearance.

Sexing these fish is difficult but the male is somewhat
darker. They are not easy to breed. Soft, slightly acid water
in a darkened well-planted large aquarium at temperatures
around 27°C. provide the most conducive conditions. The
female lays eggs in a dark, well hidden spot and the male
fans the eggs, which hatch in four to five days at breeding
temperatures. Females should be removed after laying, and
the male when the fry appear.

Pomacanthus Chaetodontidae Ψ
– *annularis* BLUE RING ANGELFISH 60cm. (23½in.)
A lovely fish which comes from the Indian and Pacific
Oceans. Its dark brown body is divided by angled blue
marks. The blue is vivid and metallic, almost fluorescent. It
has a blue ring above and slightly behind the eye. Takes
some time to acclimatize to captivity but eventually achieves
its true glory.
– *arcuatus* BLACK or GREY ANGELFISH 51cm. (20in.)
One of the less colourful members of this family but
nonetheless attractive. It has a silver grey body with black
dots on each scale. It comes from the Caribbean and
western tropical Atlantic Ocean. Not the easiest fish to rear

and keep due to its adaptation difficulties.
– *imperator* EMPEROR ANGELFISH 30cm. (12in.)
When young, this fish has a dazzling blue body with white
markings and, as such, is really lovely, but it is outshone by
its parents which are a kaleidoscopic mixture of yellows,
greens, whites and blues. Not easily acclimatized to captive
feeding when mature. It comes from the Red Sea and Indo-
Pacific and western Indian Ocean, and rarely grows larger
than 30cm.
– *maculosus* PURPLE MOON ANGELFISH 30cm. (12in.)
From the Red Sea, this fish has a lovely purple body which
is transected by a broad irregular bar of yellow. The yellow
is repeated in the tail. A hardy species. **132**
– *paru* FRENCH ANGELFISH 40cm. (16in.)
As a young fish, this native of the Caribbean and tropical
Atlantic has a black body and yellow vertical body lines
which continue into the dorsal and anal fins, similar to
P. arcuatus. With age the bars disappear to be replaced by
a lace-like pattern. In addition, older fish have elongated
dorsal and anal fins. It can reach 40cm. in length.
– *semicirculatus* KORAN or ZEBRA ANGELFISH
38cm. (15in.)
Young Korans are electric blue with white lines. These
patterns change dramatically as they mature. They take on
formations reminiscent, so it is said, of Arabic writing on
the caudal fin.

Pomacentridae DAMSELFISHES
To a large extent, confusion still reigns about the classification of this marine family. Indeed some authorities
divide it into two families. Amphiprionidae and
Abudefdufidae. They are very closely related to the
Cichlidae, having only two nostrils. They have a similar
anatomical structure to the cichlids and behave in a similar
aggressive manner. In addition, their reproductive
mechanisms and behaviour are closely similar to cichlids,
the parents assuming some responsibility for their offspring.

They live in shallow tropical water where rocks and reefs
offer plenty of hiding places for escape when danger
threatens, and are very active and attractive fish. For the
marine enthusiast, they have many advantages, being small,
active, hardy, very decorative, and easy to feed. They have
the added challenge to the aquarist of spawning in captivity.
The problem of getting the young to accept food has not yet
been overcome and the fry usually fail to survive. In time
this difficulty will no doubt be solved. See *Abudefduf,
Amphiprion, Chromis, Dascyllus, Eupomacentrus,
Microspathodon, Pomacentrus, Premnas.*

Pomacentrus Pomacentridae Ψ
– *coeruleus* ELECTRIC BLUE DAMSELFISH 10cm. (4in.) ✄
A small fish from the Pacific which has a streamlined body

coloured a delicate milky-blue. The eyes are very dark but a small vague line passes through each eye. Somewhat aggressive but lives in small groups quite happily. Likes rocky cover.

– melanochir BLUE DEVIL, SAFFRON BLUE DAMSELFISH 8cm. (3in.) ✂
A small fish from the Indo-Pacific. It has a lovely sky-blue body and a rich golden yellow tail. Very aggressive with its own kind, so provide plenty of space and a great deal of rocky cover, or just keep one. **133**

POMPADOUR see *Symphysodon discus*
POMPANOS see *Alectis, Anablepidae, Carangidae,*
   Plestiopidae, Priacanthidae, Sciaenidae
POND
   SNAIL, COMMON see *Snails-Limnea*
   SNAIL, MALAYAN see under *Snails-Melania*
POP-EYE see *Disease*
PORCUPINEFISH see *Diodon, Diodontidae*
PORT see *Aequidens portalegrensis*

Positioning the Aquarium
Positioning the aquarium indoors is not quite the simple task it may at first appear. There must be enough light falling on the tank to allow plants to grow well but not so much as to produce excessive algal growth. Some fish need a fair amount of light while others are happy with subdued illumination. Fierce summer heat intensified through glass should be avoided since it could cause the temperature to rise above acceptable limits. For this reason a window facing south is unacceptable. The tank must be in a position that is aesthetic to the observers, but must not be in cooling draughts which may cause rapid fluctuations in temperature. Finally the tank must be placed where it will not be knocked since glass under pressure will not withstand too much abuse before it cracks.

   The simplest way of solving many of the problems is to use artificial illumination which gives the aquarist complete control and flexibility over the light in the tank. See *Lighting*.

POWDER BLUE GROUPER see *Epinephelus flavocaeruleus*

Power Filters
Power filters are basically similar in their function to standard filter systems, except that water is turned over at much greater rates. They are of little value to the average aquarist with moderate tanks but useful when large tanks are being used.

POX DISEASE see under *Disease*
PRAWN, CARIBBEAN see under *Marine Invertebrates*

Premnas Pomacentridae Ψ
– biaculeatus MAROON ANEMONEFISH 15cm. (6in.) ✂
From the Indo-Pacific and Australia, this fish is closely related to the clownfishes, but can be distinguished by the sharp protrusions which are situated below the eye. These are used in combat and are never out of action for long as this is an aggressive fish which attacks all comers, especially its own kind. Its deep wine body is adorned with three white vertical bands. It is easy to keep and feed, appreciates the presence of an anemone although this is not essential, and likes temperatures around 24°C.

PRETTY
   DAMSELFISH see *Dascyllus marginatus*
   TETRA see *Hemigrammus pulcher*

Priacanthidae Ψ
A family of moderate size which are mainly tropical or subtropical in habitat. Characteristically they have large prominent eyes. The body is deep and very many are red in colour, probably related to the nocturnal habits of many species. The fins are supported by strong spines and the pelvic fin has a flap of skin between it and the body. See *Priacanthus*.

Pricanthus Priacanthidae Ψ
– arenatus BIGEYE, CATALUFA 41cm. (16in.)
A delightful fish which is more common in the USA than in the UK or Europe. The body is red with silver grey highlights to the sides and belly. The pelvic fins are black.

   This species comes from the tropical Atlantic and the Caribbean where it lives in social groups, often closely associated with rocky reefs.

PRICKLE-HEADED GOBY see *Paragobiodon echinocephalus*

Prionobrama Characidae ⊕
– filigera TRANSLUCENT BLOODFIN 6cm. (2½in.)
This fish closely resembles *Aphyocharax rubripinnis*, but has distinctive beauty of its own. The body is a translucent blue with a narrow green stripe extending horizontally from operculum to tail. The tail fin is red with hyaline margins. The leading ray of the anal fin is porcelain white. It comes from the Rio Madeira in Brazil.

   A peaceful fish and of moderate size, it suits the community tank well and eats most food.

   The male is distinguished from the female by having a somewhat extended pectoral fin and longer first rays of his anal fin.

   It breeds in captivity scattering eggs among plants from where they hatch in about two days. The young need very tiny infusoria.

Pristella Characidae
– riddlei PRISTELLA, X-RAY FISH, WATER GOLDFINCH
4cm. (1½in.)
This fish comes from the north east of South America. Not
the most colourful of fishes, undoubtedly its attraction lies
in the shape, posture and contrasting black and white
markings of its dorsal and anal fins. The fins are large and
held well from the body which is darkish green above and,
in the latter half of the body, with a light, almost
transparent belly. There is a dark line running horizontally
which is picked out above in the posterior half of the body
by a parallel yellow line. The tail fin is a delicate reddish
pink. It is a good member of the community tank where it
helps to accentuate the colours of brighter fish. It requires a
high proportion of live food in its diet and temperatures
between 24–26°C. Sexing is relatively simple. Viewed
against a bright light, the body cavity can be seen within the
living body and is pointed in males, more rounded in
females. Matched pairs breed but only with difficulty.
Plenty of weed with not too deep water, about 10–15cm.,
and a high temperature of 26°C. Parents tend to eat young
so must be removed. **134**

Prochilodus Curimatidae ⊕
– insignis SERGEANT CHARACIN, FLAG-TAILED
PROCHILODUS 15cm. (6in.)
A native of the Amazon, this fish reaches some 15cm. in
captivity. The body is a silver grey. It is noticeable because
of its striped tail and anal fins. The dark horizontal stripes
in the tail are separated by white, the base colour.

It has a sucking mouth similar in appearance to that of
the Kissing Gourami, *Helostoma temminckii,* with which it
feeds in the mud of the river bottom. It consumes algae and,
in captivity, boiled spinach. Not aggressive but jumps high,
so keep the tank covered.
– taeniurus SILVER PROCHILODUS 15cm. (6in.)
This native Amazonian has a dark green body shading to a
yellow undercarriage. The posterior half of the fish is
divided by a horizontal line which commences below the
dorsal fin and extends as far as the tail. The dorsal fin has a
large dark spot. The tail fin has horizontal bands of black
with dark tips to the lobes and the pelvic fins are blood red.

Promicrops Serranidae Ψ
– lanceolatus TIGER or QUEENSLAND GROUPER
3m. (9ft 10in.) ✂
Although it grows very large indeed, young ones can be
kept in captivity in normal-sized tanks, but outgrow them
quickly. The black body is decorated with yellow patches in
the juveniles. Comes from the Indo-Pacific region. At full
size, they are the terror of divers, so beware. Requires live
food. This fish does not breed in captivity.

Protein Skimmers or **Protein Foam Removers**
Basically these work by frothing the water with a stream of
fine bubbles. The dissolved impurities, resulting from
protein breakdown of waste products, respond by making a
stable foam which rises to the surface from where it can be
periodically removed. Rarely necessary except in very large
aquaria. Water changes are simpler, easier to manage, and
far less expensive. See *Management of the Marine
Aquarium.*

Protopteridae AFRICAN LUNGFISH
This family, together with Ceratodontidae and
Lepidosirenidae, makes up the lungfishes. They have a pair
of lungs lying below but communicating with the
oesophagus. Like other lungfish they bury themselves in
burrows in the mud during the dry season. The male guards
the eggs which are laid in burrows. The young have external
gills which later disappear. See *Protopterus.*

Protopterus Protopteridae ⊕
– annectens AFRICAN LUNGFISH 91cm. (3ft)
Rarely kept by aquarists because of its size, it is
nevertheless an interesting fish with an elongated brown
body and an almost white belly, peppered with dark dots.
The pectoral and pelvic fins have been modified to form thin
worm-like extensions which are moved in a circular motion.
Not only can it survive dry conditions by using air, but it
must get air even when in water and will drown if not able to
surface.

A hardy aquarium inmate, providing it is kept in clean
water anywhere between 20–31°C. It is carnivorous,
normally eating small fish but will take raw meat in
captivity.

PSETTUS DIAMONDFISH see *Monodactylus argenteus*

Pseudobalistes Balistidae Ψ
– fuscus JIGSAW or BLUE-LINED TRIGGERFISH
50cm. (20in.)
This fish from the Pacific Ocean grows to 50cm. in length.
Its orange body is patterned with blue lines. A dark patch
separates the eyes, marks the base of the dorsal fin and the
tail. It can vary this colour, actually becoming black with
anger. It naturally feeds on crustacea and shelled echinoderms, and likes temperatures around 24°C.

Pseudochromidae DWARF GROUPERS, DOTTYBACKS
A small family of marine fish closely related to *Serranidae.*
They are active little fish with small anal and dorsal fins
each with only three spines. They, like Serranidae, tend to
lie in wait for their prey, hiding in small holes in rocks or
coral. See *Pseudochromis.*

Pseudochromis Pseudochromidae Ψ
– ***flavescens*** YELLOW DWARF GROUPER 8cm. (3in.)
A small fish from the Indo-Pacific which is coloured a bright yellow, and a very attractive aquarium fish. Members of the genus eat live food and prefer temperatures around 24°C.
– ***gutmanni*** DWARF FLAG GROUPER 10cm. (4in.)
This small grouper comes from the Red Sea. It is a colourful mixture of purple and yellow with white markings and is a useful and pleasing fish for the marine aquarist.
– ***punctatus*** DWARF PANTHERFISH 10cm. (4in.)
Rather a colourless fish from the Indo-Pacific. It is black with grey spots, hardy and takes most live food. In addition to its dullness of hue, it is somewhat large for the family.

Pseudocorynopoma Characidae ⊕
– ***doriae*** DRAGONFISH 8cm. (3in.)
One of the larger characins native to Paraguay and the south-eastern regions of Brazil. This is a truly lovely fish, but only for those prepared to accommodate specialist tanks, since they require a lot of open uncluttered water. This is one of the species where the male has most of the glamour. The body shades from dark green above to a silvery blue on the belly. The fins are faintly yellow with a red tip to the dorsal and a black tip to the tail. The male owes its glory to the splendour and extravagance of its dorsal, anal and pelvic fins which are much enlarged. The same fins on the female are simply functional.

The male's breeding display is attractive to watch and in keeping with his beauty. He dances around the female making characteristic trembling movements and adopting postures of unbelievable complexity. During the dance the male manages to pass a sperm packet to the female which somehow ends up in her reproductive tract. The female then lays a few eggs to be followed by a succession of pretty dances. The aquarist keen on breeding should arrange for only a depth of 20cm. of water and with large stones or glass marbles on the floor to protect the eggs from being eaten by the parents. The parents should be removed and the tank freed of feathery plants or algae before the young hatch or they will become entangled.

Pseudotropheus Cichlidae ⊕
– ***auratus*** NYASA GOLDEN CICHLID 10cm. (4in.) ✂
Males are a yellowish-gold colour but adopt blue-black body coloration in the breeding season. The females are a

Nyasa Golden Cichlids, *Pseudotropheus auratus.*

beautiful orange-brown with two wide dark longitudinal stripes, bordered with silver. The dorsal fin in the male is orange and in the female dark brown or black. They are aggressive by nature and action, so be warned. Keep them with plenty of hiding places. The female broods the eggs in her mouth for four weeks, after having them fertilized in a shallow nest in the sand prepared by the male. See also *Nyasa Cichlids*. **135**

– *zebra*   NYASA ZEBRA   10cm. (4in.)   ✂
A lovely, almost fluorescent, blue body is decorated with narrow dark-blue vertical bars. The male carries some bright yellow dots on the anal fin which are outlined with black. Its beauty is skin deep, being an aggressive fish which should be kept only with its own species. The female keeps fertilized eggs in her mouth for several weeks. See also *Nyasa Cichlids*. **136**

Pseudupeneus   Mullidae   Ψ
– *indicus*   46cm. (18in.)
A very attractive scavenger with a pale red body scattered with deep wine coloured dots. The head and back are gold. It develops green metallic sheens under certain conditions. The underparts are red, as are the fins. A large dark body

Nyasa Zebras, *Pseudotropheus zebra*.

spot is placed close to the tail. This species comes from the Indo-Pacific.

Ptereleotris   Gobiidae   Ψ
– *splendidum*   FIREFISH   10cm. (4in.)
This magnificent fish from the Indo-Pacific is likely to attain great popularity as supplies increase. The pale pink anterior shades into a blaze of fiery red on the posterior part of the elongated body. Dorsal and anal fins are long-based and take the fire colour, giving the impression that the whole hind end of the body is ablaze. There is an elongated dorsal filament matching the long pelvic fins which add to the illusion.

Behaviourally an interesting fish. It lives in burrows which it builds in the sand. Needless to say, aquarists are well advised to accommodate that need by ensuring a thick layer of fine sand. It also likes plenty of rocky hiding places. Takes brine shrimps quite happily in captivity. **137**

Pterois   Scorpaenidae   Ψ
– *antennata*   SPOTFIN LIONFISH   23cm. (9in.)
This species very closely resembles *P. volitans*. It has a rather more spiney appearance and the face is largely free of decoration being basically white.

Spotfin Lionfish, *Pterois antennata*.

From the Indian Ocean, throughout the China Sea, the Philippines and Polynesia, Spotfins are social fish and are found in pairs or groups in nature on reefs in shallow water. Normally quite retiring creatures, but they will attack if provocation is excessive.

In captivity they are quite adaptable. The same conditions should be provided as for *P. volitans*. Take great care for the dorsal spines are venomous. **138**

– radiata   WHITE FINNED or REGAL LIONFISH, TIGERFISH
20cm. (8in.)
Another member of this genus from the Indo-Pacific and
the Red Sea. Usually settle well in captivity and are very
hardy. Their appetite is something to be wondered at. If
carefully handled they make reasonable members of a
community tank.

This species has a short compressed body, a white face
and thin lines which pass vertically across the body. It is
perhaps the most prickly of all the genus. As it ages the
body colour darkens.

– sphex   HAWAIIAN LIONFISH   25cm. (10in.)
Unfortunately a rare import to the UK, although it is quite
common in the US. Similar in appearance and in
temperament to other members of the genus, it is a much
prized exhibit in any community tank. It comes from
around the island of Hawaii.

– volitans   ROYAL LIONFISH, TURKEYFISH, RED FIREFISH,
BUTTERFLYFISH, BUTTERFLYCOD   38cm. (15in.)
A gorgeous extravaganza of red and white stripes combined
with a positive superfluity of long dangling tassels. It is the
pride, or envy, of every marine aquarist, but is not common
and, therefore expensive. It comes from the Red Sea and the
Pacific and Indian oceans. When frightened, it spreads its
fins otherwise it is a slow and graceful mover.

Carnivorous, preferring small fish but will take raw meat
in captivity. Likes temperatures around 27–28°C. Not the
most suitable member for a marine community tank. Be
careful to avoid the venomous dorsal spines.

Pterolebias   Cyprinodontidae   ⊕
– longipinnis   8cm. (3in.)   ✂ ◉
From Brazil. The male is reddish brown with occasional
dark patches on its sides and red fins which are embellished
with a few well placed dots. The colourful male fins are
ostentatious, contrasting with the functionally conventional
structure of the dull brown female's.

Endowed with an aggressive personality, the species must
be maintained in social ostracism. It lives close to the
bottom, where it buries its eggs in the mud. Normally
preferring shade and temperatures of 21–22°C., it spawns
better in higher temperatures, which should be raised to
between 25–28°C. for breeding. Being an annual, its eggs
are designed to withstand the dry period, so make sure they
get one – see *Cyprinodontidae.*

– peruensis   PERUVIAN LONGFIN   9cm. (3½in.)
A rather discrete colouring enhances the beautiful shape of
the Peruvian Longfin. Basically the male has a yellow
brown body, vertically transversed by a number of bars of
darker grey brown. The barring extends into the unpaired
fins. In addition, a series of yellow dots embellish the
attractive tailfin. The female is grey brown, faintly

barred and not as attractive as the male.

Breeding habits are similar to *P. longipinnis,* but it is
difficult to induce it to accept a parental role in captivity.

Pterophyllum   Cichlidae   ⊕
ANGELFISH   15cm. (6in.)
Although some ichthyologists, whose interest lies in
classification (taxonomy), have designated at least three
species of angelfish (*P. altum, P. dumerilii* and *P. scalare*)
other authorities consider them to be only sub-species
of *P. scalare,* created by geographical or geological
separation.

Even people whose contact with tropical aquaria is
restricted perhaps, to a fleeting glance while sitting in a
dentist's waiting room, will be familiar with this popular
and undoubtedly lovely fish. Its shape is very atypical of the
cichlid pattern, being depressed laterally to form an almost
circular disc. The dorsal and anal fins are elongated and
point backwards. The tail fin is lyre-shaped with extremely
elongated angles and the rays of the pelvic fins show
extreme lengthening. The silver grey body is traversed by
dark bars, the most posterior of which extends into the
dorsal and anal fins. A second is midway along the body
while a third passes through the eye. The base of the tail fin
is also marked by a dark bar. For a reason yet to be
explained by ichthyologists, the depth of colour of the bars
can vary very rapidly, being black one minute and virtually
invisible the next. Several colour variations have been
developed, following mutations of normal stock. Notable
among these are the Lattice and Black Angels which have
become extremely popular in recent years, although I
personally prefer the original coloration. Depending on the
subspecies or variety they can reach from 10–15cm. in
length and from dorsal fin tips to anal fin tips, a good deal
more in depth.

Unlike many other members of this family, angelfish
make good members of an aquarium tank providing it is
kept at temperatures of about 24°C.

The identification of sexes in angels is notoriously
difficult. Many foolproof systems have failed me. In general,
the committed breeder, particularly the novice, is advised to
let the fish decide by putting several fish in a large tank and
leaving them to it. Pairing is until death, and the best age for
pairing and spawning is when a year old.

Their breeding behaviour is similar to the cichlid pattern
but with some small modifications. The eggs are deposited
on flat surfaces including the leaves of plants, so some stout
herbage should be provided in the form of Giant Vallisneria
Vallisneria gigantea, or the Amazon Sword Plant,
Echinodorus intermediens. Some breeders prefer to subdue
the lights. Many aquarists consider the pH to be important
and slightly acid pH 6·8 is often recommended. Breeding

Angelfish, *Pterophyllum* spp.

temperatures of 26–30°C. are most successful, stimulating spawning. After the eggs are laid, they are fertilized by the male. The young are not transferred by the parents but stay adhering to the surface when hatched for 24–30 hours, thrashing their tails violently. The parents periodically take the young fry into their mouths, perform a few gentle chewing movements and spit them back unceremoniously onto the leaf.

The fish may be induced to spawn onto a flat piece of slate, or glass rod which is then removed to an incubation tank, with water of the same chemical construction and temperature. Cleanliness is very important in fish egg rearing, to avoid the risk of fungal infections. Water agitation caused by an aerator is an excellent substitute for the parental fans. The yolk sacs absorbed, feed the young fry on newly hatched brine shrimp.

When you first see the young, don't be surprised at the lack of resemblance to adult angelfish. By the time they are a month old, the adult form will be taking shape.

PUFFER see *Canthigaster, Tetraodon*
PUFFERFISH see *Canthigaster, Tetraodon, Tetraodontidae*
PULLER, BLUE see *Chromis caeruleus*
Pumps see under *Aeration*
PUNJAB CATFISH see *Mystus tengara*
PURPLE
   FIREBALL see *Centropyge fisheri*
   MOON ANGELFISH see *Pomacanthus maculosus*
   QUEEN see *Mirolabrichthys tuka*
   WRASSE, ROSE see *Mirolabrichthys tuka*
PURPLE-HEADED BART see *Barbus nigrofasciatus*
PURPLE-SPOTTED GUDGEON, AUSTRALIAN see *Mogurnda mogurnda*
PUSSY MINNOW see *Cyprinodon variegatus*
PYGMY
   BART see *Barbus phutunio*
   CATFISH see *Corydoras hastatus*
   LIONFISH see *Dendrochirus brachypterus*
   PERCH see *Elassoma evergladei*
   RASBORA see *Rasbora maculata*
   SUNFISH see *Elassoma evergladei*
   SWORD PLANT see under *Plants – Lagenandra*

Pygoplites Chaetodontidae
– *diacanthus* REGAL ANGELFISH 25cm. (10in.)
A species popular in the USA as an aquarium fish. It has a yellow brown body with blue bands crossing it, each of which is bordered with black. The operculum is edged with blue. Young fish have a dark spot on the dorsal fin which is lost as the fish matures, while the number of blue bands begins to increase.

It comes from the Indo-Pacific and the Red Sea. It is very difficult to keep in captivity due to its food preferences. In nature it seems to feed almost exclusively on sponges. Most of the mature specimens die after a few months. Young specimens may become accustomed to aquarium food more easily.

PYJAMA
   CARDINAL see *Apogon nematopterus*
   SURGEONFISH see *Acanthurus lineatus*

Pyrrhulina Lebiasinidae ⊕
– *laeta* HALF-BANDED PYRRHULINA 8cm. (3in.)
This pyrrhulina from the Amazon Basin and Guyana follows the pattern of the genus. A dark brown body above, grading through lighter brown to a whitish belly. A line extends back from the snout continuing as a wide band to a point below the dorsal fin. The fins are brownish with a dark patch on the dorsal.
– *nattereri* NATTERER'S PYRRHULINA 5cm. (2in.)
From northern South America this, like all pyrrhulinas, is a small fish, very similar in appearance to others of the genus. There is no adipose fin. Hardy fish, they are good members of a community tank and easy to feed. A temperature range of 24–27°C. suits it best.

The general body colour of this species is browny yellow. A dark brown band runs horizontally the length of the body. Several rows of dark brown red spots run parallel to the band. The fins are generally clear while the dorsal is adorned with a black spot. The male has a pointed dorsal fin and an enlarged lobe to the tail.
– *rachoviana* RACHOW'S PYRRHULINA 5cm. (2in.)
Native to Argentina, body colour is dark brown along the spine, shading to light brown and white on the belly. A dark line commencing at the snout continues, after passing the operculum, as a jagged line to the tail. There is an orange line above. The fins are greenish and the dorsal has a black spot. In the male, there is a red edging to the anal and pelvic fins. It has wide tolerance to temperature conditions.

This is the one member of the genus to breed readily in captivity. Approximately a hundred eggs are deposited on a leaf and these are protected and fanned by the male using his fins. The eggs hatch in a day and the young fall to the bottom from where they emerge to swim free later. Remove both parents when eggs hatch.
– *vittata* STRIPED PYRRHULINA 7cm. (3in.)
An inhabitant of the Amazon basin, this fish is brown with a pinkish white belly. A line from the snout widens to a band behind the operculum and continues backwards to the anal fin. There are three patches of dark brown or black spots on the side. The fins are reddish brown and the dorsal fin has a black spot bordered by red. It reaches some 7cm. in length.

QUEEN, PURPLE see *Miralabrichthys tuka*
QUEEN
    ANGELFISH see *Holocanthus ciliaris*
    TRIGGERFISH see *Balistes vetula*
QUEENSLAND GROUPER see *Promicrops lanceolatus*

RABBITFISH see *Siganidae*
RACHOW'S
    CATFISH see *Plecostomus rachovi*
    FUNDULUS see *Nothobranchius taeniopygus*
    PYRRHULINA see *Pyrrhulina rachoviana*
    RIVULUS see *Rivulus sentensis*
Radianthus see under *Marine Invertebrates*
RAINBOW
    BUTTERFLYFISH see *Chaetodon trifasciatus*
    SHARK see *Labeo frenatus*
RAINBOWFISH see *Bedotia, Melanotaenia, Melanotaeniidae,*
    Telmatherina, Thalassoma
RAM see *Microgeophagus ramirezi*
RAMSHORN see under *Snails – Planorbis*

Rasbora Cyprinidae ⊕
This genus of fish are worthy of special note. Popular
aquarium fish, those kept by aquarists all come from south-
east Asia, from India to Borneo, where they live in streams
of acid and neutral water. Community fish, they swim in
large shoals. Their eggs are found attached to the underside
of broad-leaved plants.

They take to captivity with ease, living for years, little
troubled by disease. Rasboras are easy to feed being
omnivorous but require a fair proportion of live food in the
diet. They make colourful, peaceful and hardy inhabitants
of the community tank.

Sadly these delightful fish are all notoriously difficult to
breed in captivity. To date the reasons for this have not
been established. It may be the physical or chemical
contents of the water – it is known they like acid water with
plenty of iron – or something to do with the social group
size in which they naturally live. Sexing is difficult and is at
best, guesswork.

– argyrotaenia SILVER RASBORA 10cm. (4in.) ⊕/Ψ
A native of the Malay Peninsula, Java and Borneo, it can

adapt to brackish water and is sometimes found in such an
environment naturally.

A silvery fish with yellowish sides, a silvery band runs
from the snout to the tail. Lives best at temperatures in the
23–25°C. range.

– daniconius SLENDER RASBORA 10cm. (4in.)
From Thailand, Burma, India and Sri Lanka. The back is
olive green shading to a whitish belly. It has a horizontal
band of blue, bordered by gold lines. The fins have a golden
tinge.

– dorsiocellata macrophthalma EYE-SPOT RASBORA
3·5cm. (1½in.)
Native to the Malay Peninsula. Not a colourful species, the
body is a pale brown with green tints. It does, however, have
a distinctive black patch on the dorsal fin which is
surrounded by white. Easily bred in captivity.

– einthoveni BRILLIANT or EINTHOVEN'S RASBORA
9cm. (3½in.)
This fish comes from Thailand and the Malayan region of
Asia. An attractive golden brown body is divided by a dark
band running from snout to tail. The scales are edged with
dark brown.

Males can be distinguished by the wider and more
pronounced, dark horizontal band and the purplish hue
compared to the green of the female. It lives happily in
captivity at temperatures in the 23–26°C. range.

– elegans YELLOW or ELEGANT RASBORA 13cm. (5in.)
One of the larger rasboras, the Elegant Rasbora is peaceful
and lives happily at temperatures between 21–27°C. A
rather dull yellowish grey in colour, it is distinguished from
other species in the genus by a large ovoid blotch below the
dorsal and a second spot at the base of the tail fin. There is a
hint of red in the dorsal fin. The female has a fainter central
spot and a clear anal fin as opposed to the brownish tint in
the male. It is not a good breeder but has liberal tastes in
food.

A fish which is plentiful in the streams and rivers of
Borneo, Sumatra and the Malay Peninsula.

– heteromorpha HARLEQUINFISH, RED RASBORA
5cm. (2in.)
Such an attractive fish that it is often known as 'The
Rasbora'. A delightful fish from Thailand, east Sumatra
and the Malay Peninsula it characteristically has a dark
triangle, the base of which lies vertically below the dorsal fin
and the apex extending to the base of the tail. A very good
fish for the aquarist being active, distinctive and relatively
small. In my opinion it looks most attractive when kept in
shoals in a tank reserved for this species alone.

Males can be distinguished by the density of a gold line
which runs along the dorsal side of the triangle and less
dependably by a curving forward of the lower angle of the
triangle. Not easily bred in captivity. This may be due to the

fact that in nature they live in shoals and this may well be a factor in success. During spawning the male swims above the female while she, turning upside down, rubs herself against the undersides of leaves. The male then curves around during a brief quivering interlude and fertilizes the eggs as she deposits them. This is repeated for several hours. **139**

– maculata   SPOTTED or PYGMY RASBORA   3cm. (1in.)
Owes one of its popular names to its diminutive size and the other to its colourful array of spots. It comes from the Malay Peninsula. With a dark background and illumination from the front the body colour is reddish shading to an orange yellow belly. There is a dark spot on the side of the body behind the operculum, and one at the base of the tail fin. At the base of the anal fin one dot denotes a male and two a female. The fins carry a reddish tinge as well as small red patches.

A delightful fish, looks well in groups or in the community tank. It is small, slender in form, with well held fins.

Not easy to breed, both sexes show a deepening of body colour in the breeding season. It prefers soft water and an acid pH and temperatures around 25–26°C. for breeding. The female lays her eggs on the undersides of leaves rather like *R. heteromorpha*.

– meinkeni   MEINKEN'S RASBORA   7cm. (3in.)
Undistinguished in colour, shape or form, this rasbora

comes from Sumatra. The body is a greeny brown with yellower belly. A black line divides the monotony horizontally. Dorsal and tail fins incline to a reddish tinge. It requires no more than 24°C. and is said to breed readily which, if true, always seems typical of the less coveted species.

– pauciperforata   RED-STRIPED RASBORA   8cm. (3in.)
This fish comes from the Malay Peninsula and Sumatra. The body colour is greenish silver white, shading from dark back to a light belly. Its most distinctive feature is the horizontal line, basically a golden line bordered below by black and above by a reddish brown.

It is fairly shy by nature since it has successfully kept its breeding habits from the eyes of man. Enjoys temperatures between 21–26°C. and occasional live food. **140**

– taeniata   BLACK-STRIPED RASBORA   8cm. (3in.)
Brown body, dark line, dull gold sparingly used with mostly clear fins is an adequate enough description. The male has a small flash of orange at the base of the tail fin. This is one of the few rasboras that breeds easily in captivity. Comes from the Malay Peninsula and Sumatra.

Seemingly the only feature which distinguishes it is its susceptibility to Ichthyophthirius infection when environmental temperatures drop below 21°C.

– trilineata   SCISSORTAIL   15cm. (6in.)
One of my favourite rasboras. Its beauty lies not in its

Scissor-tails, *Rasbora trilineata*.

colour but in its shape, posture and the very distinctive tail markings. The body is basically silver with a greenish hue. A dark horizontal line runs from the region of the pectoral fins to a spot on the tail and into the caudal fin. A second line starts just anterior to the anal fin and runs backwards to the lower lobe of the caudal. On each lobe of the caudal fin is an orange mark, behind which is a black patch before the finality of the clear tips. In nature it grows to 15cm. but rarely gets beyond 8cm. in captivity, at which size it will breed, but not easily. The colour exaggerates the tail closing movement, common to many fishes, and from this action it gets its common name. It comes from the Malay Peninsula, Sumatra and Java. **141**

RAZORFISH see *Centriscidae, Gymnotus*
RED
    AND WHITE PARROTFISH see *Bolbometapon bicolor*
    CICHLID see *Hemichromis bimaculatus*
    FIREFISH see *Pterois volitans*
    MULLET see *Mullidae*
    PIRANHA see *Rooseveltiella nattereri*
    RAMSHORN see under *Snails – Planorbis*
    RASBORA see *Rasbora heteromorpha*
    RIVULUS see *Rivulus urophthalmus*
    SEA WIMPLEFISH see *Heniochus intermediatus*
    SEA BUTTERFLYFISH see *Chaetodon larvatus*
    SEA PICASSOFISH see *Rhinecanthus assasi*
    SNAIL AUSTRALIAN see under *Snails – Bulinus*
    SNAPPER see *Lutjanus sebae*
    SQUIRRELFISH see *Holocentrus rubrum*
    SURGEONFISH see *Acanthurus achilles*
    TANG see *Odonus niger*
    TETRA see *Hyphessobrycon flammeus*
RED-BREASTED CICHLID see *Cichlasoma meeki*
RED-EYED TETRA see *Moenkhausia sanctae-filomenae*
RED-FACED BATFISH see *Platax pinnatus*
RED-FINNED
    CICHLID see *Geophagus brasiliensis*
    NYASA CICHLID see *Labeotropheus trewavasae*
    SHARK see *Labeo frenatus*
    TETRA see *Aphyocharax rubripinnis*
RED-NOSED TETRA see *Hemigrammus rhodostomus*
RED-SPOTTED
    COPEINA see *Copeina guttata*
    HAWKFISH see *Amblycirrhitus pinos*
RED-STRIPED
    BUTTERFLYFISH see *Chaetodon lunula*
    RASBORA see *Rasbora pauciperforata*
RED-TAILED SHARK see *Labeo bicolor*
RED-TOOTHED TRIGGERFISH see *Odonus niger*
REDFIN see *Scardinus erythrophthalmus*
REDJAW KILLY see *Epiplatys dageti monroviae*

REGAL ANGELFISH see *Pygoplites diacanthus*
Reproductive Behaviour see under *Behaviour*

Reproductive System
Fish have in the course of time evolved a wide variety of reproductive systems. The bony fish (Osteichthyes) have a fascinating array of reproductive armoury. The more primitive kinds lay eggs which are fertilized externally. The more recently evolved teleosts, or bony, have been very inventive. Some are live-bearers, some produce astounding numbers of offspring and some have developed complex breeding behaviour.

The male system comprises a testis, where sperms are produced, and a series of ducts which carry the sperm to the exterior, either to be shed into the water at mating or, in some species, inserted into the female. In addition the testis contains tissue which produces the hormones which give the male its sexual characteristics such as a special shape, fin development or sexual colours in those species where male and female are different to look at.

In the female, eggs are produced in the ovary. These are again passed to the exterior by a series of tubes. Different species produce different numbers of eggs. In those species where the parents protect the young, and in live-bearers where the mother keeps the eggs in her body for a period, the number of young produced is relatively small since the survival rate of the young is higher. Where eggs are scattered, large numbers of eggs are the rule as many will perish long before they reach maturity.

Most fish have breeding seasons. They do not breed continuously. These seasons generally coincide with suitable environmental conditions for the survival of the young.

Fish which practise external fertilization, simply shedding eggs and sperms into the water, have developed intricate behaviour patterns. These ensure that the acts are synchronized and that male and female are in close proximity; the survival time of the sperms and eggs is very short unless fertilization occurs.

Internal fertilization varies, from the mother simply retaining the eggs in her body but the young getting their nourishment from the egg yolk, or like mammals where the mother's blood and the young fishes' blood are in complex union. In the latter the mother supplies the food through the embryonic fish's gestation period – the period inside the mother. To effect internal fertilization the males have developed special organs. In the live bearing Poeciliidae, the anal fins are modified to form a tube like organ, the gonopodium. This may be a true tube or in some species grooves through which the sperms pass.

The Poeciliidae have the simple arrangement for retaining young. The eggs have a large amount of yolk from which the embryonic fish obtain their nourishment. No complex relationships between the developing offspring and their mothers exist. It is in other families that this 'placenta' like arrangement similar to that seen in mammals exists. See *Breeding,* and family descriptions.

Research

In the past 10 years fish have become firmly established along with rats, mice, and guinea pigs, as laboratory animals. They are now used for a very wide range of studies including disease, genetics, behaviour, and perhaps, most important of all, in the identification of polluted or poisoned water. There is no doubt that the hobby aquarist's knowledge, gained by trial, error and bitter experience has been of immense value to scientists who want to study fish in the laboratory.

Respiration

Fish, like land animals, cannot live without a ready and plentiful supply of oxygen. Oxygen is necessary for the combustion of food material within the body cells to provide energy. The resulting carbon dioxide must be voided since it is harmful to animal life. Respiration is the process by which this is achieved. Land animals have evolved lungs. Fish use gills but may in addition have other accessory breathing organs. In all cases it is essential that the oxygen, whether in air or dissolved in water, comes into close contact with the body's blood to allow the exchange to take place; oxygen to be absorbed, carbon dioxide released.

Land animals take air through the nose and mouth and it passes into the lungs which are simply two sacks with a greatly folded lining, to increase the surface area, which is well supplied with blood. Here oxygen is absorbed and

carbon dioxide released. The air leaving the lungs is low in oxygen, high in carbon dioxide. In fish, water containing dissolved oxygen is taken into the mouth. From there it is passed through the internal gill slits in the sides of the pharynx, which is behind the mouth and in front of the gullet or oesophagus. Passing through the slits the water meets the gill filaments attached to the gill arches. The filaments are extremely well supplied with blood and like the lungs have increased their surface area by being much folded. Flowing across these filaments the water comes into extremely close contact with the minute blood vessels separated by only thin membranes. Here the exchange occurs, the blood coming to the gills, low in oxygen from the body, absorbs oxygen and discharges its high content of carbon dioxide. The water now passes to the outside of the fish either through the external gill slits in the sharks and its relatives or, in the bony fishes, first into a common chamber formed by the operculum and then out via the common opercular opening.

Now it is obvious that since the mouth and pharynx share the common function of taking in both food and oxygen, problems could arise. Land animals solve the difficulty by closing the entrance to the lungs with a flap when eating. No such flap is provided for fish. Fish which prey on other fish and consume very large pieces are in little danger since the internal gill slits are not large enough to be blocked by them. However those fish which consume very small animals and plants are in danger of losing these food items again through the gills; also the food would create problems in the gills by gumming up the works and detracting from their efficiency as respiratory organs. To avoid this the internal gill slits are protected by gill rakers. These are

Water flow and removal of oxygen by the gills.

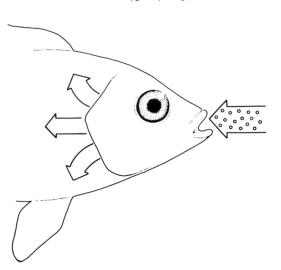

Detail of gills

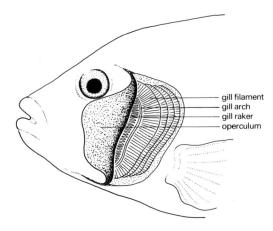

gill filament
gill arch
gill raker
operculum

attached to the inner margin of the gill arch and they usually interlock with the other gill rakers providing a fine mesh sieve to strain the water before it passes over the gill filaments. The development and complexity of the gill rakers depends on the size of the food particles eaten by the fish. In fish, which eat large chunks, they are rudimentary. In plankton-eaters some have long slender rakers resembling bristles, while filter feeders have very complex branched rakers resembling fine muslin which collects the smallest plankton.

When most fish are taken out of water the gill filaments collapse. The exposed surface for the exchange of gases is therefore markedly reduced and the essential film of water is absent. Fish which do survive out of water have developed special mechanisms for survival. Some are able to trap water in the gill chambers to keep the filaments bathed. Eels can breath through their skin. The mudskipper, perhaps the most remarkable of land-exploring fish, can keep its gill chamber filled with water and has developed an extremely good blood supply to its mouth, which allows some additional exchange. Even so the mudskipper must constantly recharge its batteries from pools.

Some of the loaches and catfish gulp air at the surface and this is passed to the intestine where, just behind the stomach, there is a pouch well supplied with blood which absorbs oxygen from the air.

Several other methods of using air to obtain oxygen have been developed by various fish. These are known as accessory breathing organs and again take the form of pouches well supplied with blood in which the gas exchange is achieved. Many fish, well known to the aquarist, fall into this category including the gouramis, *Osphronemus*, paradisefish, *Macropodus*, and the Siamese fightingfish, *Betta*. In Climbing Perch, *Anabas testudineus*, these pouches lie one on each side of the head above the gills. In the snakeheads, *Ophiocephalidae*, they are a simple pair of pouches arising from the pharynx. Some of the catfish have also developed modifications of these accessory breathing organs. Accessory organs are found exclusively in fresh-water species, or marine species inhabiting inter-tidal areas.

Comparison of the respiratory systems of land and water living vertebrates is fascinating since it was the most difficult problem which the animal kingdom had to overcome in its conquest of the land. See also: *Gas bladder, Oxygen.*

RETICULATED

CORYDORAS see *Corydoras reticulatus*
DAMSELFISH see *Dascyllus reticulatus*

Rhamphichthyidae KNIFEFISHES
A family closely related to the Gymnotidae. It is found in freshwater streams in South America. The upper jaw is

longer than the lower. They, like Gymnotidae, have a very long-based anal fin.

They possess poor eyesight, are nocturnal, and orientate themselves by using electrical charges. See *Hypopomus.*

Rhinecanthus Balistidae Ψ
– *aculeatus* PICASSO or BLACK-BARRED TRIGGERFISH
30cm. (12in.)
The white body is decorated with a pattern of yellow, black and brown stripes which reminded somebody of Picasso's abstract works. This fish was thus named. It comes from the Indo-Pacific. Very easy to feed on small crustacea.
– *assasi* RED SEA PICASSO FISH, ASSASI TRIGGER
25cm. (10in.)
A lovely and exotically decorated fish resembling a work of art by the great Spanish painter after whom it takes its name. It come from the Red Sea and is timid by nature.

It requires careful handling, a generous amount of space and plenty of rocky cover. This species is often listed as *Balistes bursa.*
– *rectangulus* BELTED TRIGGERFISH 20cm. (8in.)
A grey white body with yellow markings around the head. It has white stripes on its sides interspaced with yellow. A dark band runs from the eye to the anal fin. There is a triangular black patch on the caudal peduncle. It comes from the Indo-Pacific.

Rhinomuraena Muraenidae
– *ambonensis* BLUE RIBBON EEL 102cm. (41in.)
Ribbon Eels are found in Indonesia and the Philippines. This fish is typically eel-like to look at, being very elongated. In addition the body is considerably compressed giving it the ribbon like appearance of its common name. It is a very attractive fish with a dark greyish blue body and a bright yellow dorsal fin which runs almost the length of the body. One pair of nostrils is elongated into tubular projections and the tips spread into fan-like appendages. The mouth is also surrounded by thin projections reminiscent of barbels which doubtless have a very similar function.

An interesting and attractive marine fish to keep. It is however, better to have experience of the easier marine species before attempting to husband it. It can be difficult to feed and may need encouraging, when first purchased, with fresh live food. In addition, it is not averse, once started, to eating your small exhibits, so keep it with larger fish.

It has the unfortunate eel habit of leaving the tank when it will rapidly dehydrate and die, so covers must be provided. **142.**

Rhodeus Cyprinidae ⊕
– *amarus* BITTERLING 9cm. (3½in.)
A small chunky coldwater fish which is found throughout

northern Europe and Asia. Normally greyish silvery brown, but during the breeding season the male adopts a variety of brilliant blues, violets and greens to attract his mate. The female develops a red ovipositor from which she lays her eggs in the gills of a freshwater mussel. The eggs spend up to 20 days under mussel protection. The young stay a few days in the mussel living on their yolk sacs and then leave their host without harming it.

It is easily kept in tanks where it breeds readily, as long as a freshwater mussel is provided. Since its breeding habits are so fascinating it makes an interesting addition to the cold water collection.

RIBBON EEL, BLUE see *Rhinomuraena ambonensis*
RICEFISH, JAPANESE see *Oryzias latipes*
RING-TAILED PIKE CICHLID see *Crenicichla lepidota*
RIO
    GRANDE PERCH see *Cichlasoma cyanoguttatum*
    MINNOW see *Phoxinopsis typicus*

Rivulus Cyprinodontidae ⊕
– cylindraceus GREEN, BROWN or CUBAN RIVULUS
    5cm. (2in.)
A typical rivulus from Cuba the male is greeny brown with an emphasis on the brown. The body is dotted with a variety of coloured dots and the inevitable horizontal line of

red brown hue runs from snout to tail. A blue flash peeps behind the gill cover. The throat and belly are flesh coloured, sometimes pinker. Dorsal and caudal fins are greenish blue with dark edging to the dorsal and central borders of the caudal. The anal fin has an orange wedge from the anterior border. The female is distinguished by the dark brownish black rivulus spot, which the male lacks, just anterior to the caudal fin dorsally, which is black on a lighter patch. The female's fins are pale orange.

Like other members of the genus this fish spends a great deal of its time motionless near the surface of the water. It can however jump with incredible ease, and should therefore be kept in tanks which are well covered. It is able to exist out of water for some considerable time without ill effect. In fact it can travel overland by flopping and wriggling and is found in ponds and pools in unexpected places.

It is generally peaceful but is best restricted to community tanks with larger inhabitants. It prefers temperatures from 21–26°C. A plant spawner, typical, as are most of the genus, of the Cyprinodontidae. The young hatch in 10–20 days and should be fed infusoria for about a week after which they can take brine shrimps and small daphnia.
–hartii HART'S RIVULUS 10cm. (4in.)
An attractively shaped fish from Trinidad, east Columbia and Venezuela. Body colour grey green with horizontal

Hart's Rivulus, *Rivulus harti.*

rows of red dots. The fins are yellow including the caudal which has black markings. The female is less beautiful, a common distinguishing characteristic in fish, and does not have such a distinct rivulus spot as some of its generic cousins.

One of the larger members of this family and a peaceful fish best kept with larger colleagues. It prefers hard alkaline water at temperatures from 21–26°C. Breeding habits are typical of the family (see *Cyprinodontidae*).

– *ocellatus*   MARBLED or OCELLATED RIVULUS   5cm. (2in.)
A fish which is found in the south-eastern region of Brazil.

The general body colour of the male is a yellow green. The side has 8–10 reticulated dark patches from which it gets its common name. A dark patch at the base of the caudal fin is to be distinguished from the ocellated rivulus spot of the female which is also present. The fins are yellow with black margins to the medians.

A friendly fish which is happy to live at peace with other species in the community tank. It breeds with enthusiasm for beginner and seasoned aquarist alike. Prefers temperatures around 24°C.

– *santensis*   RACHOW'S RIVULUS   8cm. (3in.)
This fish comes from Brazil. The very dark back shades to brownish yellow sides which carry lines of red dots and a yellow belly. The dorsal fin is edged with white, the anal with black and the caudal, fin has a white upper margin and a black lower. The female is paler but carries a spot at the base of the tail fin. Breeding as rest of the genus.

– *strigatus*   HERRINGBONE RIVULUS   4cm. (1½in.)
Native to the Amazon the bluish green body of the male is attractively marked with red V-shaped bars running backwards from the head. The red throat fades to an orange belly. The caudal fin continues the body's markings, as does the dorsal. The female is duller without the distinct marks of the male. A really wonderful fish which, as so often is the case, is reflected by it being a difficult breeder with narrow environmental demands. Temperatures around 26°C. are recommended for maintenance and higher still for breeding. It is more active than many of its generic cousins, another characteristic which will endear it to aquarists.

– *tenuis*   SLENDER RIVULUS   8cm. (3in.)
An attractively shaped native of south Mexico. Its blue sides are adorned with irregular rows of deep red dots. The blue anal fin has a red margin while the deep red caudal fin is edged with black. The female's markings are irregular, unpatterned and dull. She carries the rivulus spot at the base of the tail fin.

– *urophthalmus*   RED or GREEN RIVULUS   6cm. (2½in.)
The common names may cause a raised eyebrow or two. The problem is there are colour varieties which add confusion to classification. The usual colour form, the Green Rivulus, has a greenish body with red dots in horizontal rows while, the so-called Red Rivulus has a yellow body colour with red dots, which also adorn the yellow fins. The rivulus spot cannot usually be seen.

This species is from the Amazon and Guyana. Reasonably easy for the beginner to manage in the well lit community tank where it lives a rather sluggish existence near the surface, but don't be fooled, it can perform leaps of unbelievable speed and agility. It likes temperatures ranging from 21–24°C. A plant breeder whose eggs hatch in some 10–20 days. The fry eat brine shrimp with enthusiasm.

ROCK
   BEAUTY see *Holocanthus tricolor*
   COD see *Cephalopholis argus*
   COD, LUNAR-TAILED see under *Variola louti*

Rooseveltiella   Characidae   ⊕
– *nattereri*   RED or NATTERER'S PIRANHA   ✂
30cm. (12in.)
This is another of the delights of the aquatic world so beloved of fiction writers. All they say about the Piranha's teeth and their readiness to use them is however true, so be warned.

The body is a lovely steely blue with yellow overtones and the throat and belly are a deep orange. In common with the

Red or Natterer's Piranha, *Rooseveltiella nattereri.*

family pattern the anal and dorsal fins are set well posterior and the adipose fin is present.

In captivity they will breed, but are certainly not community fish as they are extremely aggressive. Those who feel the need to keep them usually keep them alone and ply them with flesh of all kinds. Also do well in larger shoals of their own kind. **143**

ROSE PURPLE WRASSE see *Mirolabrichthys tuka*
ROSY
    BARB see *Barbus conchonius*
    TETRA see *Hyphessobrycon rosaceus*
ROT, GILL see *Disease*
Rotala see under *Plants*
ROUND WORMS see under *Disease*
ROUND-TAILED PARADISEFISH see *Macropodus chinensis*
ROYAL
    BLUE TRIGGERFISH see *Odonus niger*
    GRAMMA see *Gramma loreto*
    LIONFISH see *Pterois volitans*
    SURGEONFISH see *Acanthurus sohal*
RUBROSTIGMA see *Aplocheilus lineatus*
RUBY BARB, BLACK see *Barbus nigrofasciatus*
RUDD see *Scardinius erythrophthalmus*
RUMMY TETRA see *Hemigrammus rhodostomus*
RUSH, JAPANESE DWARF see under *Plants – Acorus*
RUST DISEASE see under *Disease*

S

SADDLE CICHLID see *Aequidens tetramerus*
SADDLEBACK
    CLOWNFISH see *Amphiprion polymnus*
    WRASSE see *Coris formosa*
SAFFRON BLUE DAMSELFISH see *Pomacentrus melanochir*
Sagittaria see under *Plants*
SAILFIN
    CHARACIN see *Crenuchus spilurus*
    MOLLY see *Poecilia velifera*
    MOLLY, GIANT see *Poecilia velifera*
    TANG see *Zebrasoma veliferum*
SALTWATER CATFISH see *Plotosus lineatus*
SANDFISH, BELTED see *Serranthus subligarius*
SAPLOCHILUS, COLDWATER see *Oryzias latipes*
SARGASSUMFISH see *Histrio histrio*
SCADS see *Anablepidae, Cirangidae, Plesiopidae, Priacanthidae, Sciaenidae*
SCALES see under *Skin*
SCALE DISEASE see under *Disease*

Scardinius Cyprinidae ⊕
– *erythrophthalmus* RUDD, GOLDEN RUDD, RED-FIN
30cm. (12in.)

From Europe and Asia these fish live in shoals among the water plants of lakes and large ponds, where they grow to 30cm. in length. They are chunky, greenish silver fish with red tail, anal and pelvic fins and the cornea of the eye has a red coloration. Rudd take insects but are largely vegetarian.

They breed from spring to summer laying up to 100,000 eggs. Several males spawn with one female.

It makes an attractive and active inhabitant of the tank when small, although it is usual to move it to an outdoor pool when it gets larger.

Scaridae PARROTFISHES
A very pleasing family of widely distributed tropical marine fish with longish bodies. They get their common name from the beak-like formation which results from a fusion of the teeth. With the beak they are able to bite off and eat coral. They also eat weed and food of animal origin. Parrotfishes are very difficult to keep in an aquarium for long periods because of their food preferences. These fishes should not be imported for the aquarium hobby. See *Bolbometapon, Callyodon*.

SCAT see *Scatophagidae, Scatophagus*

Scatophagidae SCATS
All members of this family inhabit brackish waters in river estuaries from coastal areas of the Indian Ocean the Malay Archipelago and Australia. They are scavengers and are, therefore, easily fed in captivity. Their bodies are very compressed and present a disc like shape. They can be kept in marine or fresh water; the latter preferably alkaline and hard, but prefer brackish conditions, at temperatures around 21–26°C. See *Scatophagus*.

Scatophagus Scatophagidae Ψ/⊕
– *argus* LEOPARD or TIGER SCAT, SPOTTED BUTTERFISH
25cm. (10in.)
A species which normally inhabits brackish or salt water in the Indo-Pacific but can survive in fresh water. In nature it grows to 30cm. in length but captivity usually reduces this to a mere 13–25cm. It is disc shaped and all the various colour forms are attractive and suitable for the community tank being peaceable and sociable. They prefer temperatures of 22–25°C.

The colour variety known as the Leopard Scat has a metallic yellow body with dark spots and bronze anal and dorsal fins. Tiger Scats, which are more favoured by aquarists, have bright red additional colourings on the dorsal, anal and sometimes pelvic fins, and on the head. The posterior dorsal fin, and the anal and caudal fins are golden. **144**

Leopard or Tiger Scat, *Scatophagus argus*.

Scent see *Smell*

Schilbeidae   SCHILBEID CATFISHES
A family closely related to the Siluridae. It has a higher
content of fat in the body than other fish living in a
similar environment. This is probably due to its ability to
metabolize the available foods. It is commonly represented
by only one species to the aquarist. See *Eutropiellus*.

SCHOOLING see under *Behaviour*

SCHOMBURGH'S LEAFFISH see *Polycentrus schomburgki*
SCHUBERT'S BART see *Barbus schuberti*
SCHULTZ'S CORYDORAS see *Corydoras schultzei*
SCHWANFELD'S BARB see *Barbus schwanefeldi*
SCHWARZENBACH METHOD see under *Hardness of Water*

Sciaenidae   CROAKERS and DRUMS
A large, mostly marine, family of which only a very few are
kept in aquaria. All have a very complex gas bladder which
is used to increase the volume of the noises made. They

make use of their noise apparatus in the breeding season, and to communicate in the dark. Once established in the aquarium, however they rarely call.

The family is distinguished by its 2 dorsal fins. The first is short based, while the second is long based with a large number of rays. Anal fins are small. Barbels are present on some members of the family. See *Equetus*.

SCISSORTAIL see *Rasbora trilineata*

Scorpaenidae   SCORPION FISHES
Members of this marine family are not usually kept by the aquarist. It is a large family, well distributed in tropical and temporate seas. Members of the family have glands at the base of their fin spines which discharge poison through ducts in the spines when these are depressed. People have died from the stings of certain species, so beware of handling these wolves in sheeps' clothing. They do not adapt to fresh water. See *Dendrochinus, Pterois*.

SCORPION, WATER see under *Unwelcome Visitors*

Scrapers
Algae both green and brown will always be present to a greater or lesser extent in the aquarium. Where this settles on the glass front it clouds the view of the tank. Periodically it is necessary to remove this growth from the front and for this various types of scraper are available on the market. Some are designed to hold a razor blade, others are made of plastic. However, to avoid scratching the glass, wiping with a piece of cloth is preferable to scraping.

Scraper

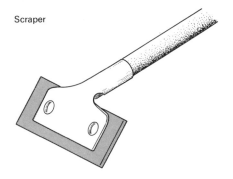

SCRAWLED COWFISH see *Acanthostracion quadricornis*
SEA
   BASS see Serranidae
   PERCH, BANDED see *Serranus scriba*
   PERCH, BLUE-BANDED see *Lutjanus kasmira*
SEAHORSES see *Hippocampus, Syngnathidae*

SEAKING see *Plectorhynchus orientalis*
SEDATE CICHLID see *Cichlasoma severum*
SELECTIVE BREEDING see *Breeding*
Sensory System see *Acoustico Lateralis System*
SERGEANT
   CHARACIN see *Prochilodus insignis*
   MAJOR DAMSELFISH see *Abudefduf saxatilis*
SERPA TETRA see *Hyphessobrycon callistus*

Serranidae   SEA BASS
A family of marine fish which are mostly found in tropical waters. They lie stationary and hidden to pounce on unsuspecting prey. They have large appetites and large mouths with powerful teeth to satisfy them. Aggressive, not suited to a community tank, but they are hardy. See *Cephalopholis, Chromileptes, Epinephelus, Mirolabrichthys, Promicrops, Serranthus, Serranus, Variola*.

Serranthus   Serranidae   Ψ
– subligarius   BELTED SANDFISH   15cm. (6in.)
Lives in the regions off Florida and neighbouring states in the USA. Dark reddish green body with pale yellow decoration near the head. It grows to 15cm. in length. Interesting, in that it is an hermaphrodite, and it forms shoals to spawn. An hermaphrodite has both male and female sexual apparatus present in the same individual. Usually, although self-fertilization may be possible it rarely occurs. Thus the shoaling is necessary to exchange eggs and sperm.

Serranus   Serranidae   Ψ
– scriba   BANDED SEA PERCH   ✂   25cm. (10in.)
A pleasant, but not exciting fish from the Mediterranean and Black Sea, and the eastern coastal waters of the Atlantic from Europe to the southern parts of Africa.

It has a beige body with a marbled decoration to the ventral part of the head. There are several irregular single and double bands running vertically all along the length of the body. The fins are grey and opaque and the dorsal has some extension of the vertical bands onto its broad base. A variable blue diffuse patch covers an area anterior to the anal fin.

It is found living a solitary territorial life among rocks. Its food consists of crustacea and small fish. Does not mix well with members of its own species.

Serrasalmus   Characidae   ⊕✂
To this genus belong the piranhas, perhaps the most written about fish in modern literature. Their reputation is well founded and, as every schoolboy knows, you get your herd of cattle across the river in which the piranhas live by

putting in an old or diseased animal first to draw them away, then while they are devouring the unfortunate beast you slip the others across upstream. Their mouths are well endowed with interlocking sets of teeth that tear the flesh off and quickly reduce a victim to a skeleton. Piranhas are native to Paraguay, the Amazon and the Guyanas where they live in shoals.

They are without doubt a fish for the specialist. In captivity they should be kept singly or in a large school in large tanks or they will eat each other. They require careful handling, or, preferably, no handling at all. Needless to say, they live on raw meat.

– *rhombeus*   SPOTTED PIRANHA   36cm. (14in.)
Native to Guyana and the Amazon Basin, this terror of the shallows has a general body colour of green broken by a silver sheen. In addition dark spots adorn the green, and the tail fin has a black edging.

– *spilopleura*   DARK-BANDED PIRANHA   25cm. (10in.)
The body shape is ovoid with a prominent dorsal and elongated anal fin. The body colour is browny yellow dorsally with a red belly and anal fin. Silvery spots break up the colour. The anal fin is bordered with black. The caudal fin is delineated with black. It is native to Brazil and reaches some 25cm. in length. Temperatures around 24°C. are preferable. Has bred in captivity.

Setting Plants see *Planting*
Setting-up a Tank see under *Establishing a Tropical Freshwater Tank*
SHARK see *Balantiocheilus, Labeo, Morulius*
SHARPNOSE PUFFER see *Canthigaster rostrata*
SHARP-NOSED PUFFER see *Canthigaster margaritatus*
SHEEPSHEAD, FRESHWATER see *Cichlasoma cyanoguttatum*
SHEEPSHEAD MINNOW see *Cyprinodon variegatus*
SHELTER-SEEKING BEHAVIOUR see under *Behaviour*
SHORT-FINNED MOLLY see *Poecilia sphenops*
SHORT-NOSED SEAHORSE see *Hippocampus hippocampus*
SHOVEL-NOSED CATFISH see *Sorubim lima*

Showing
A great deal of time and effort is devoted to showing animals, subjecting them to situations and manipulations which they must, at times, find uncomfortable, either physically or psychologically.

In order to prepare a fish for a show it must be removed from its tank where it feels secure and placed in a strange smaller tank, bare, without plants or hiding places. True, it is given the best food because only live food will get it to a peak of condition, but this is given at irregular intervals in order that the fish is constantly on the alert, some would say in a perpetual state of frustration, for that treasured moment when the judge appears. Also it must be positioned

in that part of the house where constant human movement occurs in order that it gets used to crowds and does not dash about in fear.

Show standards are available for many animals, including fish. A group of people, sometimes with little understanding of biological requirements, sit in committee to establish a list of physical attributes which they find pleasing, for example, large dorsal fins, small caudal fins, big heads, pop eyes and so on, without a thought for the animal's welfare or physical needs. These standards reflect the ever changing whim of fashion and are rarely based on the evolutionary principle of adaptation to the environment. Thus we see, in all animals which have come under man's manipulation, breeds and varieties which would succumb in any environment one would call natural.

On what do judges base their decisions? In theory the winner will be the fish which most closely approximates the standard set for that species. Very often the exhibitors' fish are so closely matched that the judge must sometimes flip a mental coin.

If anyone is keen on showing fish let me advise them to contact their national aquarist society and from them obtain a set of rules and conditions. It is then advisable to go to a few shows before beginning. Try to talk to other exhibitors and learn your way about. Usually you will find them helpful to the novice.

Fish are shown in pairs, commonly in standard clear sided tanks without decoration but there are classes for decorated tanks.

SHRIMPS
   see under *Marine Invertebrates*
   BRINE see under *Food*
   FRESHWATER see under *Food*
SHRIMPFISH see *Aeoliscus, Centriscidae*
SHUBUNKIN see *Carassius auratus*
SIAMESE FIGHTINGFISH see *Betta splendens*

Siganidae   RABBITFISH, SPINEFEET
Medium sized active and attractive fish make up this marine family. Fins have sharp venomous spines. They live in groups and are vegetarian, consuming large quantities of algae. See *Lo, Siganus.*

Siganus   Siganidae   Ψ
– *vermiculatus*   VERMICULATED SPINEFOOT   46cm. (18in.)
This fish comes from the Indian and Pacific Oceans where it reaches a length of 46cm. Its large body is decorated with a complicated brown flexuous pattern resembling a maze. The background is a pale beige. The dorsal and anal fins are long-based reaching, but not joining, the tail fin.

Siluridae EURASIAN CATFISH
Catfishes of the Old World, including two species found in
Europe, the majority of which are freshwater species. Until
recent taxonomic research, many catfish were included in
this family. Members of the family have long barbels,
usually a small dorsal fin, which is sometimes absent
altogether, and an elongated anal fin. There are no scales.
See *Kryptopterus*.

Sight see *Eye*
SILVER
    DOLLARFISH see *Mylossoma argenteum*
    HATCHETFISH see *Gasteropelecus levis, Thoracocharax*
    securis
    KNIFEFISH see *Ctenobrycon spilurus*
    MYLOSSOMA see *Mylossoma argenteum*
    PROCHILODUS see *Prochilodus taeniurus*
    RASBORA see *Rasbora argyrotaenia*
    TETRA see *Ctenobrycon spilurus*
SILVER-BELLIED CLIMBING PERCH see *Ctenopoma*
    argentoventer
SILVER-TIP TETRA see *Hemigrammus erythrozonus*
SILVERFISH see *Monodatylidae, Monodactylus*
SILVERSIDES see *Atherinidae*
SIX-BARRED ANGELFISH see *Euxiphipops sexstriatus*
SIX-BANDED
    BARD see *Barbus hexazona*
    PANCHAX see *Epiplatys sexfasciatus*
SIX-BARRED DISTICHODUS see *Distichodus sexfasciatus*
SIX-STRIPED GROUPER see *Grammistes sexlineatus*

Skeleton
Fishes developed the vertebrate body pattern from which
evolved amphibians, reptiles, birds and mammals.

Skeletons have several important functions. They provide
the rigidity essential for larger animals, offer protection to
some of the more delicate organs, particularly the brain,
spinal cord and lungs, and allow anchorage against which
muscles can pull.

Fish skeletons are made up of three main parts, the skull,
the backbone (vertebral column) and the fin skeleton. Many
variations and modifications have evolved in fish skeletons,
the most notable being their substance. In the sharks and
rays the skeleton consists of cartilage while the higher fish
have skeletons made of bone. The basic pattern is, however,
common to all.

The skull consists of the case, which encloses and protects
the brain, the jaws, and the gill supports or arches.

Lamprey's and Hagfishes are the surviving forms of a
very primitive type of fish. They have no bony support to
their mouth which is simple and takes the form of a sucker.

In all other fish there is an upper and lower jaw which has
evolved from what was originally, in primitive fish, the
second gill arch, the first having disappeared during
evolution. Likewise the third gill arch has changed its
original function and now provides skeletal support for the
tongue. The remaining arches (4–8) retain their original
function and support the gills.

The backbone or vertebral column runs from the base of
the skull, as a segmented cartilaginous or bony rod to the
tail. It is the main axis of the body and protects the delicate
spinal cord which runs through the series of neural arches
formed by the vertebrae.

Fishes have two types of ribs, dorsal (above) and ventral
(below). Ventral ribs are only found in the bony fishes.
Dorsal ribs, often known as the intermuscular (between the
muscles) bones, are found in many bony fishes including
herrings, pikes and carp.

Skeleton of bony fish

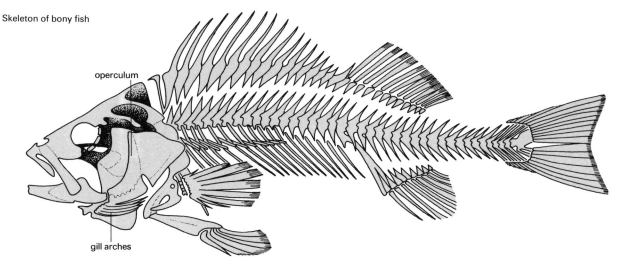

operculum

gill arches

Both median and paired fins are supported by the skeleton. In the dorsal and anal fins of bony fish this support usually consists of a three-bone structure articulating with the fin ray.

In sharks and primitive bony fish the backbone is bent up to form the caudal or tail fin of the type known as heterocercal. Characteristic of most higher bony fish is the homocercal tail fin. Appearing externally symmetrical, the homocercal tail fin is an extreme modification of the more primitive heterocercal model; the backbone turns up as before but is foreshortened. Parts of the last few vertebrae are greatly expanded into plates of bone which in turn support the caudal fin rays. See *Gills, Fins*.

SKIFF see *Neotoca bilineata*
Skimmers see *Protein skimmers*

Skin

The skin which covers the body acts as the wrapping to the fish frame and keeps it all together, so to speak. Its main function is protection. To aid this there are large numbers of horny cells, and a great many mucous cells which produce the thick slimy mucus which covers the fish skin and has several important functions. It acts as a lubricant, reducing friction as the body moves through the water, and it affords protection against infectious organisms, from parasites to viruses. In addition it plays a part in the osmotic movement of water which occurs, in part, through the skin, see *Osmoregulation*. It probably slows the osmotic movement down, assisting the fish in maintaining correct concentrations of salt. In addition the skin of some species contains poison glands, luminous or phosphorescent organs, pigment cells giving the fish colour, and in some fishes is of considerable assistance in respiration.

Arising from the skin in many fish are the bony scales. These come from the under layer of skin, the dermis. The scales improve the skin's ability to protect the fish and provide external support.

One of the most interesting uses of scales is in ageing fish. Scales grow throughout the fish's life. In cooler waters which have seasonal variations in temperature the scales grow at different rates, rather like the wood of trees or the shells of tortoises. These growth differences produce rings which can be counted to indicate the age of fish. In tropical waters where the water temperature is constant these rings do not occur.

Scales can also be used in classifying groups of fish and are much used in fossil studies of extinct fish. They cannot, however, be used to separate very closely related species.

SKIN FLUKES see under *Disease*
SKIN SPOTS see under *Disease*

SLAMET, SPRAYING see *Copella arnoldi*
SLEEPER see *Dormitator, Eleotridae*
SLEEPY TROUT see *Mogurnda mogurnda*
SLENDER
   RASBORA see *Rasbora daniconius*
   RIVULUS see *Rivulus tenuis*
SLIMY SKIN see under *Disease*

Smell

The methods of smelling used by fishes are very variable. In sharks two small pits are situated on the lower surface of the snout. Each pit has one opening, but is divided by a small flap of skin into an intake and outlet hole. A current of water containing the dissolved smelly substances passes in and out of the sac and a nerve transmits information about the smell to the brain. In teleost fish, the pits are placed near the top of the head and each pit has two quite distinct openings. The inlet is in front and the outlet behind it. Thus a stream of water, which will contain any dissolved smells, passes in and out as the fish swims. Various methods are used for directing the current through the pits. Some fish are equipped with fine hair like structures which have a wave like motion resembling the ripple of ripe corn blowing in a breeze. Others are controlled by the surrounding bony structures.

Fish vary considerably in their reliance on smell. Some, like the sharks, have a well developed sense of smell. Others, Serranids for example, place more importance on sight.

SMOOTH ARMOURED CATFISH see Callichthyidae
SNAKEHEAD see *Channa*, Channidae, *Ophicephalus*
SNAKESSKIN GOURAMI see *Trichagaster pectoralis*

Snails

Snails in the aquarium are a very controversial subject. Some aquarists value them for their scavenging behaviour which is thought to help maintain an ecologically balanced aquarium. They are beneficial in eating and breaking down uneaten food into harmless sediment which is useful for plant nutrition. They assist in keeping the algae growth on the glass of the aquarium under control. Conversely some do considerable damage to plants; they produce their own faecal sediment and their scavenging and algae clearance activities are only partially successful. They certainly do not replace the need to clean the aquarium periodically.

For those who like to have snails in their aquarium, 10–30 snails, depending on the size of the tank and the species chosen, will be adequate. Few species of snail do so well that they become a problem, since most snails spawn and young snails fall victim to the fishes.

Ampullaria Apple Snails 3cm. ($1\frac{1}{2}$in.)
Several different species belonging to this genus have been

used by aquarists. They are popularly known as apple snails. Large 'four horned' snails, they come from Central and South America and with one exception, *A. cuprina*, are voracious plant eaters and therefore unsuitable for most aquariums. *Ampullaria cuprina,* known as the Mystery Snail does not eat plants, has larger young not so readily consumed by carnivorous fish and is a reasonably efficient scavenger. It can be easily distinguished from the other apple snails having a tall spine and shallower channels around its turns. Apple snails lay their eggs out of water but just above its surface. As the young hatch they fall back below the surface to start their aquatic life.

Other members of the genus *Ampullaria* with which the Mystery Snail can be confused are *A. canaliculata, A. gigas* and *A. paludosa.*

Bulinus australianus   AUSTRALIAN RED SNAIL
2·65cm. (1¼in.)
This is a colour variety of the common Australian snail. It is very attractive and enjoys considerable popularity among snailaphiles. It does little damage to plants.

Limnaea auricularia   PAPER SHELL   2cm. (¾in.)
This has an attractive yellow shell decorated with brown patches. It is found in northern temperate zones of Europe and is useful for cold water collections.

Limnaea stagnalis   COMMON POND SNAIL   5cm. (2in.)
The greyish shell of this common beauty is streamlined. They reach up to 5cm. (2in.) in length. This snail lays its eggs in an elongated mass of jelly and the young, when they hatch out, are just about visible to the naked eye.

Common Pond Snails are useful in clearing Hydra from tanks.

Melania tuberculata   MALAYAN POND SNAIL   1·5cm.
Small conically shaped snails which rarely exceed 1cm. in length. They are useful scavengers. Nocturnal by nature, they bury themselves deep into gravel during the day. However this snail can create problems by over producing their own kind.

Planorbis albus   WHITE RAMSHORN   5–7mm.
A species of the group commonly known as Ramshorns. They are useful members of the aquarium being active and efficient scavengers and algae removers. In addition they are easy on the plant life.

Planorbis corneus   RED RAMSHORN   1cm.
This species is suitable for tropical aquaria. The flattened shell is usually black, but colour variants occur. They lay eggs enclosed in jelly throughout the year. Although their presence is of value in the community tank they do enjoy a good meal of fish eggs so should on no account be introduced to the breeding tanks.

Viviparus malleatus   JAPANESE LIVE-BEARING SNAIL
5cm. (2in.)
A large snail from south-eastern Asia that prefers cold water. It produces live fully formed young. Leaves the plants alone.

SNAPPER see *Lutjanidae, Lutjanus*
SOAPFISH see *Grammistes, Grammistidae*
SOLDIERFISH see *Holocentridae, Holocentrus, Myripristes*

Sorubim   Pimelodidae   ⊕
– **lima**   SPATULA LOACH, CUCHARON, SHOVEL-NOSED CATFISH   20cm. (8in.)

Above: Common Pond Snail, *Limnea stagnalis,* surfacing for air.

Right: Red Ramshorn Snail, *Planorbis corneus,* feeding on frogbit.

An unusually sleek and streamlined fish from South America, it is silver grey on the body with a wide dark band running from its snout into the caudal fin where it branches into each lobe. The dorsal fin is narrow, long, pointed and rapier-like.

Its compressed head reminds one of a loach which gives it one of its common names although it is, needless to say, not a loach. It has three pairs of barbels. It only grows to some 20cm. in captivity, but over 60cm. in nature. It eats small fish. Prefers temperatures of about 24°C.

Sphaerichthys Belontiidae ⊕
– *osphronemoides* CHOCOLATE or MALAYAN GOURAMI, MALAYAN AIRSHIPFISH 6cm. (2½in.)

A small chocolate coloured fish with several vertical beige stripes crossing the head and body. The fins are likewise chocolate.

A native of Sumatra and the Malay Peninsula it prefers mature acid water and temperatures around 26°C. It eats live food. The male incubates the eggs in his mouth.

Stands

Aquarists are notoriously ingenious at siting their aquaria in a living room, setting them in false walls to give pleasing effects. The tank can be placed on any piece of furniture, wood or metal, strong enough to hold it.

However, stands are produced commercially, made of angle iron, specifically for the purpose of supporting the tank. They are strong but ugly. Some attempts are made to modify their ugliness by decorating them with wrought iron, but in my opinion, even after this, they remain strong but ugly.

Stevardia Characidae ⊕
– *riisei* SWORDTAIL CHARACIN 7cm. (3in.)

A very attractive fish, native to Venezuela, Trinidad and Columbia, it is an unusual characin in not having an adipose fin. The body colour is silver but it is the fins of the male which attracts the fish to aquarists. These fins are longer and more splendid than those of the female and the lower lobe of the tail fin gives the species its common name. In addition the male has a fine extension of the operculum which extends backwards to the posterior edge of the dorsal fin where it flattens to a small plate.

It will live contentedly in a community tank at a wide range of temperature, and eats most food.

Mating is interesting since it is an internal fertilizer. The male swims round the female extending one of the operculum plates and anal fin towards her. Forty eggs are later deposited on the underside of plant leaves. These incubate in two or three days at 24°C. Sometimes classified as *Corynopoma riisei*.

STICKLEBACK see *Apeltes, Gasterosteidae, Gasterosteus*

Stigmatogobius Gobiidae ⊕
– *sadanundio* SPOTTED GOBY 8cm. (3in.)
A medium-sized goby from the Philippines, Indonesia and south-east Asia. The body is grey with black dots and patches. The spinous dorsal fin has a white border to a black base.

STRIPED
    ANOSTOMUS see *Anostomus anostomus*
    BARB see *Barbus lineatus*
    BURRFISH see *Chilomycterus schoepfi*
    CATFISH see *Pimelodella meeki*
    ·CICHLID see *Cichlasoma severum*
    CLIMBING PERCH see *Ctenopoma fasciolatum*
    FLYING BARB see *Esomus malayensis*
    HATCHETFISH see *Carnegiella strigata*
    HEADSTANDER see *Anostomus anostomus*
    LOACH see *Acanthophthalmus kuhli*
    PANCHAX see *Epiplatys fasciolatus*
    PUFFERFISH see *Tetraodon steindachneri*
    PYRRHULINA see *Pyrrhulina vittata*
STRIPED-FACE UNICORNFISH see *Naso lituratus*
SUCKER LOACH see *Gyrinocheilus aymonieri*
SUCKING CATFISH, DWARF see *Otocinctus affinis*
SUMATRA FERN see under *Plants – Ceratopteris*
SUNFISH see *Centrarchidae, Elassoma*
SUNSHOWER BUTTERFLYFISH see *Chaetodon kleini*
SURGEONFISH see *Acanthuridae, Acanthurus, Paracanthurus, Zebrasoma*
SWAMP BARB see *Barbus chola*
SWORD
    PLANT, AMAZON see under *Plants – Lagenandra*
    PLANTS, CHAIN see under *Plants – Echinodorus*
    PLANT, DWARF see under *Plants – Lagenandra*
    PLANT, JUNIOR see under *Plants – Echinodorus*
    PLANTS, PYGMY see under *Plants – Lagenandra*
SWORDTAIL see *Xiphophorus helleri*
SWORDTAIL CHARACIN see *Corynopoma riisei*
SWEETLIPS see *Gaterin, Plectorhynchidae, Plectorhynchus*
Swim Bladder see *Gas Bladder*

Surgery
The problems involved in operating on fish are indeed great.

In many of the small aquarium fish the problem of sheer size is daunting. In addition the scaley skin and the mucus covering create difficulties. In spite of these, quite complicated surgery can, and has been performed.

A special V-shaped table is used to hold the fish in position. The head must be tilted downwards to allow the gills to be submerged in water containing anaesthetic or a special device assembled to produce a stream of anaesthetic water flowing through the mouth and over the gills.

The techniques required for fish surgery are identical with those used in normal veterinary practice and present no problems to the experienced surgeon.

Symphysodon Cichlidae ⊕
– *discus* DISCUS, POMPADOUR, KING BUFFALOFISH
15cm. (6in.) ◍
Closely related to the angelfish (*Pterophyllum* sp.) it lacks the lovely fin development but makes up for it in an extravaganza of body colour. Like the angel it has a disc-shaped body with the dorsal and anal fins following closely the contour of the body. The caudal fin is clear.

Classification of this fish remains a problem for the taxonomists. Some consider that there are two species, *S. aequifasciata* which comes in a variety of colours including brown, red, blue, yellow and multicoloured, and the one above named, *S. discus*, which is said to always have blue and red wavy lines over the body. However when one hears from the taxonomists that their classification is further confused by natural interspecific breeding one becomes more than a little sceptical of their abilities to unravel the discus story. In addition environmental conditions like pH, dissolved salts and temperature can change body colour.

The fish comes from the Amazon and the Rio Negro where it lives in soft acid water in temperatures around 30–31°C. They have small mouths for cichlids and this should be remembered when deciding on the type of live food to offer. Glass worms and daphnia are quite suitable, or meat scraped with a knife into a jelly-like consistency makes an excellent substitute.

The Discus aquarium should be as large as possible, at least 20 gallons. The water should be soft, acid and at temperatures around 30–31°C. The light should be dim and cover plentiful, with plenty of hard smooth rock and large leafy plants suitable for the water conditions. The tank should be well filtered and care taken to keep all debris to a minimum by regular syphoning.

When the Discus was being assembled no concession was made to the problems which future aquarists would face trying to sex the beasts. They are identical to look at. The only way to sort them out is to let them pair off from a group of young Discus. Having established a pair transfer them to their large breeding tank with great care to avoid sudden variation to which this species is particularly sensitive. The water should be absolutely clear, of low pH. (See *pH*) and very soft. Temperatures approaching 30°C. are ideal. Offer good live food.

The eggs are laid on vertical surfaces, after a little mild cleaning activity, and they hatch in a few days. Parents spend a good deal of time cleaning both eggs and fry.

The unique factor in breeding Discus, and quite the most fascinating, is the food substances secreted by the skin on which the young feed for the first four weeks of life. Particularly interesting is the fact that both parents secrete the substance. A study of the hormone control of this secretion would prove worthwhile, since most foods secreted, like milk in mammals or pigeon milk in the crops of pigeons, are under female hormone control and are not usually produced by both sexes. After the first week of life the young will take freshly hatched brine shrimps to supplement the skin food. The secretion from the skin lasts for about four weeks, after which the parents can be removed. Plenty of space should be available for the young so the 100-strong brood will probably have to be split.

The skin food has not been synthesized in the laboratory. The parents must therefore do their own rearing which will please the purist.

A delightful and fascinating cichlid worth all the bother it causes its many aquarist devotees. **145**

Synchiropus Callionymidae Ψ
– splendidus MANDARINFISH 8cm. (3in.)
The Mandarinfish is found on the coral reefs in Indo-Australian waters where it adopts bottom living behaviour and conceals itself well under the coral. Without doubt this is one of the most striking of marine fish. The body is a marbled combination of blue, green and orange irregular patches, divided by the dark borders. In addition some of the patches take a bluer coloration on the fins, and over the operculum there is a bright blue patch decorated with bright yellow spots. The females are drab.

Little is known of its habits, but it is said to secrete a poisonous and noxious fluid from the skin. Not surprisingly, the animal is prized by aquarists, although it is not uncommon. It feeds on live food. **146**

Syngnathidae SEAHORSES, PIPEFISH
The best description I have heard of Seahorses includes the information that, like a mythical Greek monster, it has a horse's head, a monkey's tail, a kangaroo's pouch and a chameleon's eyes. Like the chameleon too, it has evolved the ability to change colour to approximate its surroundings, as a means of camouflage and to escape capture by predators. Unlike other fish it always swims in an upright position.

Structurally it is interesting having both a normal piscine internal skeleton and, in addition, large interlocking plates forming an external armour. It swims, albeit rather slowly, by vibrating its dorsal fin, and controls roll and drift by mobilizing its pectoral fins which are situated on either side of its head. In addition this anatomical curiosity has gills markedly different from any other known fish. They are rather more like small shaving brushes than the conventional filaments on gill arches.

Following a brief courtship display, there is a briefer embrace, and the female places her ovipositor into the male's brood pouch and lays the ripe eggs. The male fertilizes the eggs within the pouch, and begins his parental vigil. The female then abdicates all responsibility.

The period of incubation varies with the species, being from 10–45 days, and the number of young can be as few as 10 or as many as 200. When hatched these tiny replicas of their parents are extruded from the pouch either singly or in batches. Immediately they emerge they zoom to the surface aided by expulsive pressure from the male. This action is essentially to fill the gas bladder with air. They should be separated from their parent and placed in a separate tank or he will eat them. Freshly hatched brine shrimp is the main food. Feed, like so many small animals, a little and often.

Adults feed on marine crustacea, worms and small fish. In captivity they do well on shrimps of the genus *Gammarus* and the worm *Chironomus* (Blood Worm). They will eat surplus live-bearer fry like young guppies.

Seahorses should be kept alone or with a few selected companion species like pipefishes and a few of the marine gobies (Gobiidae) in well filtered aerated water. The reason is that being so slow at swimming they are not able to get to the food if other quicker species are present and since they are relatively non-aggressive they are victims of fin nippers and bullying species. They must be supplied with plants around which they can wind their tails in order to rest.

There are some 60 species of seahorse but classification has presented problems to the taxonomist. The reason for confusion stems from their ability not only to change body colour, but also their ability to change the external structure of the body. Those individuals which live in dense seaweed develop an array of protuberances in an attempt to approximate to the weed and thereby achieve invisibility. If removed from this environment they lose these knobs and bobs; other specimens, less fussily adorned from sparser areas, if placed in weed adopt them. There are only a few species of seahorse commonly kept in captivity, *Hippocampus erectus*, *H. hudsonius*, *H. kuda* and *H. zostarae*.

Pipefishes are no more than seahorses subjected to an evolutionary rack, that is they are straightened out seahorses. Most of the facts relating to seahorses are equally true of pipefishes. See *Hippocampus, Syngnathus*.

Syngnathus Syngnathidae   Ψ
–fuscus PIPEFISH   15cm. (6in.)
The natural history of pipefishes closely resembles that of
seahorses. They may be kept in aquariums with seahorses.
They take live food but like seahorses cannot compete with
faster fish when it comes to catching it.

They have a basically yellowish brown body with darker
brown lines running from the snout, along the elongated
body, to the caudal fin.

Synodontis Mochocidae   ⊕
– angelicus   20cm. (8in.)   ◍
One of the naked catfishes of Africa it is nocturnal, hiding in
an upright position among natural cover. Dark grey brown
body coloration is enhanced by yellow-white spots. It is
barbelled and grows to 20cm. The fins are barred
transversely. Prefers temperatures from 21–24°C. and lives

happily in a community tank with subdued lighting.
– nigriventris   UPSIDE-DOWN CATFISH   9cm. (3½in.)
This is the commonest member of the family kept in
captivity. It is native to the River Congo and its numerous
tributaries. Since its mouth is ventral one would anticipate
that it is adapted to feeding on the bottom, but it has the
unusual facility of swimming upside-down which at a stroke
turns it into a surface feeder. The usual pattern of
camouflage – dark back and light belly – is also reversed to
confuse its predators. It is grey with dark spots. The dorsal,
caudal, anal and pectoral fins are yellow brown with dark
spots. It has six barbels.

Breeds fairly easily in captivity. **147**

Syphons
A syphon is the aquarist's vacuum cleaner. The principle is
simple, a tube is filled with water and one end placed in the

Upside-down Catfish, *Synodontis nigriventris*.

tank. The other end is led to a receptacle placed below the level of the tank. Water will continue to flow from the tank to the receptacle. Personally, I prefer to have a short piece of glass tube attached to a long piece of rubber or flexible plastic tube. This is filled with water from the tap. With one finger over each end the glass tube is placed in the tank and the other allowed to hand into the receptacle. Water flows from the tank, so one simply runs the glass end over the gravel surface to remove fish faeces and the other deposits known as mulm. Syphoning stops when the end is removed from the tank. It will of course be necessary to top up the level of the water after syphoning.

'T' BARB see *Barbus lateristriga*
TAIL-LIGHT FILEFISH see *Cantherines pullus*
TALKINGFISH see *Acanthodoras spinosissimus*
TANDA-TANDA see *Lutjanus kasmira*
TANGS see *Acanthuridae, Acanthurus, Naso, Odonus,
    Paracanthuras, Zebrasoma*

Tanichthys Cyprinidae ⊕
– albonubes   WHITE CLOUD MOUNTAIN MINNOW
4cm. (1½in.)
White Cloud Mountain Minnows are, for me, the perfect kind of aquarium fish. Small, sleek, active, colourful almost beyond description, attractive in shoals and willing to breed in captivity.

They are so popular and common in dealers' tanks that anybody who has even glanced in tropical aquariums must be so familiar with this little water jewel that description is almost superfluous. For completeness, however, its body colour is browny yellow with a thin dark line running horizontally, above which is a band of yellow. The dorsal fin is clear yellow at the base with a red tip. The other fins are also marked with red.

Coming from the White Cloud Mountains near Canton in China this fish has a wide range of temperature tolerance, anywhere from 7–30°C. They breed easily, preferring temperatures around 22°C. The male chases the female who scatters the eggs. They are not voracious egg consumers but it is better to use a trap or provide plenty of plant cover. Fry should be fed on infusoria and dried food powdered finely. Young fish at the age of three months are even more attractive than the adults, having a dazzling blue green band running horizontally from eye to tail.
148

Tanks

The basic equipment for the aquarist is a container in which to place the water in which to keep the fish. Large numbers of children have been introduced to the hobby through the doubtful auspices of the glass goldfish globe. This is unfortunate since this container is unsuitable in many respects. It is too small for almost any fish let alone the goldfish, and it is therefore basically unkind to keep a fish in it. It is rarely large enough to provide suitable cover in the form of plants and rocks, forcing fish to live in a constant state of unease particularly if the family cat keeps too close a watch. Finally, and perhaps most important, the surface area at the top of a goldfish bowl is very small compared to the volume of water. Fish can only survive by passing water, in which there is dissolved oxygen, over their gills see *Respiration*. It is thus essential that the water is kept well oxygenated. Since water gets a large amount of its dissolved oxygen at the surface it is clear that the greater the area the quicker will be the replenishment of oxygen.

The tank must therefore be designed to have as large a surface area as possible. To achieve this the length and width must be large relative to depth. Perhaps the commonest size of tank in use by the aquarist is 60 × 30 × 30cm. (24 × 12 × 12in.). This combines large surface area to volume and a reasonable size. It should be pointed out that it is best to buy as large a tank as your pocket or your room will accommodate since, as one's enthusiasm grows, so do one's horizons, and a small tank will all too quickly become filled.

FRESHWATER
Several types of aquarium construction are suitable for freshwater species:
Metal and glass. The traditional and indeed most satisfactory construction, certainly for larger tanks, are those made of an angle iron frame and plates of glass, the glass being secured in place with putty thus ensuring a waterproof joint. The angle iron should be painted with lead free paint. In spite of this, some rusting will occur, but for many years now it has been possible to buy frames made of stainless steel. These have the advantage of not rusting, requiring no painting, and maintaining a clean appearance.
Plastic. More recently moulded plastic tanks have been produced. They have the advantage of light weight, no joints, and therefore no leaks, and cheapness. There is the disadvantage, that the surface becomes scratched during cleaning which reduces visibility, but if care is taken this can be kept to a minimum. Without doubt, for smaller tanks I think these are excellent value and I am currently using them for several purposes.
Wood. This has been used to make aquariums. It does, however, have the disadvantage of warping and being

porous to water. If a wooden finish is preferred to improve appearance, it is better to face a metal frame with wood than use all wood construction.

MARINE
Salt water is considerably more corrosive than fresh water. It attacks metal surfaces creating toxic substances which are then dissolved in the water and may poison any fish.
Metal and glass. Unless special precautions are taken to protect the metal this is quite unsuitable for marine aquariums. Even stainless steel succumbs. They can be used, however, if the metal is protected by a coating of plastic.
Glass. A glass tank can be constructed by bonding the plate glass of sides and bottom with silicone rubber adhesive.
Plastic. Tanks made of plastic are ideal for the small marine aquarium. They have the disadvantage of being soft and, therefore, can be scratched during cleaning.

TAPE WORMS see under *Disease*
TARGETFISH see *Therapon jarbua*

Taste
In land animals we are accustomed to the sense of taste being located in the mouth. Here the taste buds detect flavour and transmit the information to the brain. Fish have no such limitations. Many fish have the sense of taste located in the throat and gills as well as the mouth, and others have taste buds all over the surface of the body including, in some cases, the barbels.

Taxonomy see *Classification*
TEAK CLOWNFISH see *Amphiprion melanopus*
TEAR-DROP BUTTERFLYFISH see *Chaetodon falcula*
TELESCOPIC-EYED MOOR see *Carassius auratus*

Telmatherina Atherinidae ⊕
– *ladigesi* CELEBES RAINBOWFISH 8cm. (3in.)
A native of Celebes. The body colour is a dull yellowish brown. A pale blue horizontal body line starts below the dorsal fin and continues to the tail. The first rays of the second dorsal and anal fins are extended. The caudal fin is tinged with blue. Has less enthusiasm for breeding than other members of the family but persistence by the aquarist will be rewarded. Like other members of the family, they prefer some salt in their water.

Temperature
A good deal of nonsense is written and talked about this important subject. As with all things about an animal's environment there are no absolute rules. Animals can adapt, within certain limitations, to a variable range of conditions. Most fish can adjust quite happily to

temperature changes ranging over 5–8°C., providing they are not sudden. Natural water, to which fish have become adapted over many hundreds of thousands, indeed millions, of years is rarely of constant temperature. It may change from day to night, season to season, and even hour to hour, as with fish living in shallow rock pools which are exposed to intense heat during low tide and quite sudden and dramatic changes when the tide rises. Similarly goldfish in shallow ornamental garden ponds can exist during the winter at very low temperatures indeed and then in the following summer may be required to contend with near tropical temperatures. In the aquarium itself water temperatures will vary between the top and bottom of the tank. I subscribe to the body of opinion which believes environmental variation is not only tolerated but positively essential for any animal's well being.

Most freshwater tropical species, for example, live happy contented lives anywhere between 21–27°C. with at least a 3° variation.

When accidents occur causing the temperature to rise or fall outside the limits of the species concerned, the golden rule is to correct the temperature SLOWLY. Raise or lower the temperature very slowly over several hours and, in most cases, providing the change has not been catastrophic, the fish will escape death or disease. See *Acclimatization to Tank, Adaptability, Heaters.*

TENCH see *Tinca tinca*
TERI BARB see *Barbus terior*
Territorial Behaviour see under *Behaviour*
TETRA see *Anoptichthys, Aphyocharax, Astyanax, Cheirodon, Ctenobrycon, Glandulocauda, Gymnocorymbus, Hemigrammus, Hyphessobrycon, Megalamphodus, Mimagoniates, Moenkhausia, Nannaethiops, Nematobrycon, Paracheirodon, Phenacogrammus*

Tetraodon Tetraodontidae ⊕/Ψ
– *cutcutia* PUFFERFISH, GLOBEFISH, BLOWFISH 8cm. (3in.)
A native of India, south-east Asia, and Malaya. The body is green with a light belly and reticulations of a brownish yellow hue. A bordered spot marks the centre of the body. The fins are grey and the tail is tipped with carmine.
– *fluviatilis* GREEN PUFFER, FRESHWATER TETRAODON 18cm. (7in.) Ψ/⊕ ✂
The body is a yellow brown but can vary to green or yellow. Irregular patterns are created with pale brown yellow lines and dots. A body spot is often seen below the dorsal fin with a second on the base of the tail. It lives from Sri Lanka to the Philippines.

They can be kept in fresh or salt water although they prefer the latter. They are also aggressive to other species and should be kept among their own kind. Hardy and easy to feed.

Movement is achieved by the rotating action of the dorsal fin which allows the fish a smooth effortless passage, punctuated with stops and starts.

– steindachneri STRIPED PUFFERFISH, FIGURE-8 PUFFER 20cm. (8in.)
This colourful pufferfish lives in freshwater in Thailand, Borneo and Sumatra. The whole of the underparts below a line running horizontally back from the mouth is white. The upperparts are a deep chocolate brown with a great variety of designs in bright orange yellow.

Does well in a community tank provided it is not overcrowded or fin biting may occur. It is well enough adapted to captivity to breed.

Mating behaviour is interesting. Several males may attach themselves by their teeth to the underside of the female's body which stimulates her to shed her eggs. **149**

Tetraodontidae PUFFERFISH
A small family which is widely distributed in the tropical and sub-tropical seas of the world. Most of this family are exclusively marine but a few will accommodate to or live in brackish or even freshwater where they make attractive inmates.

Their particular claim to fame is an ability to blow themselves up with air or water. When air is taken the belly distends to grotesque proportions and turning upside-down the fish floats at the top. This is clearly a defence mechanism; it confuses the enemy, makes the fish hard to catch as it bobs and skids about, and finally, if caught makes it difficult to swallow.

Pufferfishes have fused dentition; two front teeth above, and below one formed into a bar, which can do damage to other fish, so keep them with their own kind. They are omnivorous, not to say scavengers, and make few demands for specialized food. Their efficient teeth enable them to dispatch snails and small crustacea (shrimps etc.) and they will take earthworms.

The female lays eggs on a flat surface which are then guarded by the male. See *Canthigaster Tetraodon*.

Tetrosomus Ostraciontidae Ψ
– gibbosus HOVERCRAFT, BOXFISH, SPINY-TRUNKFISH 30cm. (12in.)
This species is from the Indo-Pacific. It has a triangular body, with spines at all three angles. Movement by pectoral fin action reproduces the gliding appearance of the hovercraft. It has a brown body with spots. Eats animal matter of all kinds. Makes a good inhabitant of the marine aquarium.

TEXAS
    CICHLID see *Herichthys cyanoguttatum*
    GAMBUSIA see *Gambusia affinis*
    KILLY see *Fundulus pallidus*

Thalassoma Labridae
– bifasciatum BLUEHEAD WRASSE 25cm. (10in.)
This is a truly lovely fish. The body is elongated and the dorsal and anal fins are long based. When young it is a pure yellow. As a mature animal it occurs in two different colour patterns. Most fully mature fish of the species have a yellow back fading to a pale cream on the belly with a dark brown spot on the anterior part of the dorsal fin. Some, however, have a greenish body, a blue head, and a large back patch dorsally; these are always adult males.

It comes from the Caribbean and off the coast of Florida where it acts as a cleaner fish to other species when young. Fishes in the yellow phase spawn in shoals. Spawning in which the large terminal male phase is involved only takes place between a single male and one female.

– lunare GREEN PARROT or MOON WRASSE, RAINBOWFISH 25cm. (10in.)
This is one of the most attractive members of this family. It is not gaudy or striking but its colour combination of rich sea green and mauve achieves a subtle beauty. The basic colour of sea green is flecked with dashes of mauve on the body. The fins are lined with distinctive variations on blue mauve and tangerine while the head has a pattern of green and mauve. The tail is only slightly forked but a clear portion gives the visual impression of a marked fork. The pectorals are a mixture of tangerine and purple.

It comes from the Indo-Pacific where it rarely exceeds 30cm. in length. It is reasonably bold, easy to feed and a useful and attractive member of the marine community tank. **150**

Thayeria Characidae ⊕
– boehlkei PENGUINFISH, OBLIQUE CHARACIN 6cm. (2½in.)
This fish comes from the Amazon Basin and gets its name from the unusual oblique position, with head upwards, which it adopts at rest. When swimming it moves horizontally.

The body colour is green, varying from dark olive green above to yellow green below. The belly is pinkish and there is a broad horizontal black stripe extending the length of the body from operculum to tail below which is a gold, iridescent line.

An excellent member of the community tank with no special requirements but can jump well so keep the aquarium covered. Will breed and the eggs are laid near the bottom of the tank and will survive if parents are removed.

Penguinfish, *Thayeria boehlkei*, in the unusual oblique attitude they adopt when at rest.

Young need green water for food at first.

Sexes are difficult to distinguish, but the female is fatter than the male.

Therapon Theraponidae Ψ
–*jarbua* JARBUA, TIGERFISH, CRESCENT PERCH, ZEBRAFISH, TARGETFISH 25cm. (10in.)
A rather rare fish to the aquarist which is a pity because it adapts well to captivity. It comes from the coastal waters of Africa, Asia to the northern coast of Australia.

It has curved black horizontal lines on a silver body. A black spot on the anterior part of the dorsal fin enhances its appearance.

The Jarbua is found in sea water but can adapt to freshwater and will live happily at temperatures around 24°C. Of doubtful value for the community tank as it becomes aggressive with age.

Theraponidae TIGERFISH
Marine spiny-rayed fish which do, on occasions, move into freshwater rivers and streams. They come from the Indo-Pacific and are closely related to Centropomidae. See *Therapon*.

Thermometers
This is an essential piece of equipment for the tropical freshwater or tropical marine aquarist. The most satisfactory are those which are immersed in the water and held against the side of the tank by a sucker for ready viewing. Many thermometers produced commercially depend on mercury, which, being a liquid metal, also expands at a constant rate. Temperatures should be checked at least once a day in order to identify any fault in the heating system. Thermometers should be checked against a standard instrument since they can be several degrees out of true.

The recently developed unbreakable liquid crystal thermometers, which change colour according to the temperature, are easier to read than mercury thermometers. The new units are attached to the outside of the glass and may be read from across a room. They are also very accurate.

Thermostat see under *Heating*
THICK-LIPPED GOURAMI see *Colisa labiosa*

Thoracocharax Gasteropelecidae
– *maculatus* SPOTTED HATCHETFISH 8cm. (3in.)
Like its generic cousins this fish has an adipose fin. Its body colour is yellowish brown and the body is covered in dark spots. The fins are clear but the caudal has a dark base. It is native to the north of South America.
– *securis* SILVER HATCHETFISH 6cm. (2½in.)
Native to Brazil, this fish, as its name implies, has a silver sheen to its yellow body. It has a dark horizontal band running from head to tail. The fins are clear except the dorsal which has a dark spot near its anterior border.
– *stellatus* DISCOID HATCHETFISH 11cm. (4½in.)
The largest hatchetfish commonly kept in captivity, the Discoid Hatchetfish comes from the Amazon Basin. The body colour is brown with a silver sheen separated by a horizontal band running from head to tail. The fins are basically clear but with some dark markings.

Tiger Barbs
Several discrete species have been given this popular name which is confusing to the beginner. The problem must be resolved by identifying the species currently under investigation and classifying it according to its scientific name. The list of fish called Tiger Barbs includes: *Barbus hexazona, B. pentazona, B. tetrazona.*

THREADFIN
 see *Alectis ciliaris*
 BUTTERFLYFISH see *Chaetodon auriga*
THREE-BANDED BULLFISH see *Heniochus permutatus*
THREE-POINTED DUCKWEED see under *Plants – Lemna*
THREE-SPINED STICKLEBACK see *Gasterosteus aculeatus*
THREE-SPOT
 ANGELFISH see *Holacanthus trimaculatus*
 GOURAMI see *Trichopterus trichopterus*
THREE-SPOTTED HEADSTANDER see *Anostomus trimaculatus*
THREE-STRIPED PENCILFISH see *Nannostomus trifasciatus*
TICTO BARB see *Barbus ticto*
TIGER
 BARB see *Barbus hexazona, Barbus pentazona, Barbus tetrazona*
 BOTIA see *Botia macracanthus*

GROUPER see *Promicrops lanceolatus*
SCAT see *Scatophagus argus*
TIGERFISH see *Pterois, Therapon, Theraponidae*

Tilapia Cichlidae ⊕
– *hendelotii dolloi* CONGO MOUTHBROODER
16cm. (6½in.)
Like all members of this genus this fish comes from the continent of Africa and lives from Gabon to Zaïre in estuaries. Again like most of the other members of the genus it is a mouth brooder, see *Cichlidae*. In general they are peaceful to other fish but very hard on the plant life. They are omnivorous.
– *hendelotii macrocephala* BLACKJAW or BIG-HEADED MOUTHBROODER 15cm. (6in.)
A native of West Africa from the Ivory Coast to Nigeria. The silver body is often, but transiently, marked with black patterns. It also develops a very dark patch under its throat. The unpaired fins in certain emotional states are blushed with red.
 In this species the male cares for the young, although with less diligence than might be hoped for.
– *mossambica* MOZAMBIQUE MOUTHBROODER
36cm. (14in.)
This fish is green with an irregular pattern of large blobs scattered on its side. Breeding males have a white throat and a red top to the caudal fin. It comes from East Africa.
 It is a mouthbrooder in which the female performs the parental duties. A greedy fish for both animal and plant food. It prefers temperatures of about 24°C.
– *sparrmanii* PEACOCK CICHLID 18cm. (7in.) ✂
This fish lives from southern Africa to Zaïre. The body colour varies from reddish brown to green and shades to a variety of light blue or golden brown. Each scale has a light golden spot. What appears as a combination of a horizontal body line and vertical bars gives the side a patchy appearance, which is liable to change, depending on environmental and emotional conditions. The unpaired fins are broken with red.
 Preferring temperatures from 20–26°C. this fish is rather pugnacious and is best kept with its own kind. Relatively easy to spawn but shows rather more tendency than most cichlids to consume its young. The Peacock Cichlid is not a mouth-brooder as are many species of *Tilapia*.

Tinca Cyprinidae ⊕
– *tinca* TENCH 61cm. (24in.)
This fish has a dumpy body with a shortened head. It has a variable colour from yellow brown to blackish green. Found in Europe and Asia in slow moving, weedy lakes, it is adaptable to a wide range of water conditions including brackish water. It is carnivorous. The female lays up to

500,000 eggs in May to July attaching them to plants. In nature adults hibernate in bottom mud and this is reflected when kept in the aquarium by a marked decrease in activity during the winter.

The golden variety are commonly kept by aquarists. Younger fish can be kept in a tank although as they grow larger it is necessary to move them to an outdoor pool.

TOMATO CLOWNFISH see *Amphiprion ephippium*
TOOTHCARP see *Cyprinodontidae Poeciliidae*
TOPMINNOWS see *Goodeidae*

Toxotes   Toxotidae   ⊕/Ψ
–jaculator   ARCHERFISH   24cm. (9½in.)
An attractive fish, it has a low domed back with a contrastingly generous sweeping curve to the belly. The silver blue body has a greenish sheen and dark vertical wedges break the line of the body.

They are natives of Sri Lanka, India, south and south-east Asia, Malaya, the Indo-Australian Archipelago and the Philippines, where they live in brackish water supplying their gastronomic needs by employing the shooting technique described under the family heading. Their victims can be more than 1½m. (5ft) away and still be hit.

In captivity they do best in brackish water, at temperatures in the 25–28°C. range. Space is a requisite of success. Should be kept with fish of their own or of smaller size as they are rather timid. They have not bred in captivity. **151**

Toxotidae   ARCHERFISHES
A small but fascinating family of fishes native to brackish and fresh waters of northern Australia, New Guinea, the East Indies, south-east Asia and India.

Their common name comes from their method of catching their food. They feed on land insects. These are caught when the insects alight on plants above the water surface. Rapidly fired water droplets from the fish's mouth, aimed with great accuracy, continue until the victim is washed from his perch and falls to meet his fate. The most interesting facet of the whole procedure is that the fish is as accurate with its eyes under water as with them above. Now for any reader who has a knowledge of the physics of light, it will be obvious that when under water his aim must be adjusted for the refraction of light which takes place between the two media, namely air and water. When the eyes are out of water this adjustment is unnecessary. How the fish achieves this remains a mystery of nature. The fish is assisted by eyes which are set back on the head and by the ability to move its eyes in most directions. Special structures in the mouth enable the fish to spit.

In the wild a high proportion of this species' food derives from land insects, but they will take normal aquarium food

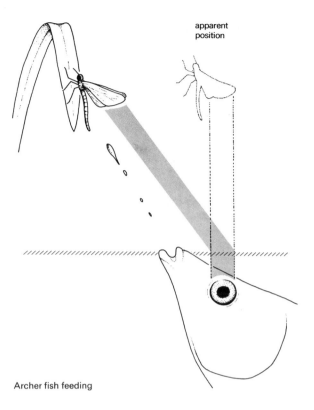

apparent
position

Archer fish feeding

of animal origin in the aquarium. See *Toxotes*.

Toys
The purpose of the aquarium is to use the products of nature to create a pleasing and interesting focus for the eye. Like gardeners, the aquarist arranges naturally occurring objects and sets them out in a way he finds attractive. Tastes obviously differ and some people find plastic effigies of wrecked galleons, divers and flooded castles agreeable in an aquarium. Plastic push-out backgrounds are also attractive to some.

All that needs to be said is that for those who can live with them, they exist in profusion, and your dealer will be only too happy to take your money. Most toys are made of plastic, but care should be taken to ensure that they have no sharp or jagged edges.

Transportation
The increase in air transport capacity has meant that fish can be carried over long distances in comparative safety. The plastic industry has facilitated this growth by providing large unbreakable plastic tanks, strong plastic bags, and cheap, heat insulating material.

Ideally, fish should be maintained in conditions for transport similar to those in which they normally live. Such conditions rarely exist, however, but the air transport industry has devised ingenious ways of protecting their piscine passengers in flight.

If possible fish should be transported in the water to which they are accustomed. Where this is not practicable the fish should be slowly acclimatized to the new conditions. It is quite common to withhold food from fish for two or three days before they travel and a similar period after arrival.

Quite large numbers of fish are transported in well insulated tanks which are provided with an air supply. Providing the journey is no more than a few hours such conditions are satisfactory. In recent years it has become common to transport fish in small amounts of water in sealed polythene bags. Before sealing, oxygen is pumped in under pressure. Naturally these will be either placed in a thermostatically controlled environment or insulated against heat loss.

In some species, notably salmonids, it is common practice to chill the fish to very low temperatures and place them in a polythene bag with a small amount of water before filling the bag with oxygen and finally sealing. This reduces the metabolic rate – the rate at which body activity takes place – and thereby reduces the amount of dangerous ammonia excreted by the fish.

In recent years the practice of anaesthetizing fish during transport over long distances has grown in popularity. Many different anaesthetic agents have been used with varying degrees of success. Anaesthetics slow down metabolic rates, reduce the stress of travel and, according to their advocates, reduce losses. This method also increases the number of fish that can be put into a container for travelling.

The careful and safe transportation of fish is important both for humanitarian reasons and as an adjunct to conservation.

Training see *Behaviour*
TRANSLUCENT BLOODFIN see *Prinobrama filiger*
Trapping Fish see *Netting*

Traps
Some breeders of live-bearing fish are keen on using traps. The ripe female is placed in a trap. She cannot escape but her tiny offspring can, and therefore avoid any cannibalistic tendencies the mother might have.

Personally I do not like the principle of traps, but there is a great variety of types commercially available. In general they are made of plastic with escape hatches for young in the form of holes or slits.

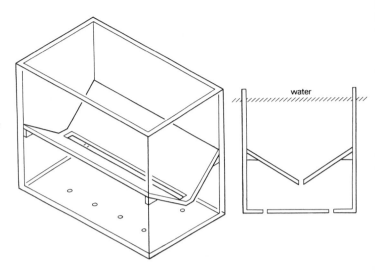

water

Breeding trap

TREVALLY, PENNANT see *Alectis ciliaris*
TRI-COLOR SHARK see *Balantiocheilus melanopterus*
TRIANGLE CICHLID see *Uaru amphiacanthoides*
TRIANGULATE BUTTERFLYFISH see *Megaprotodon strigangulus*

Trichogaster Belontiidae ⊕
– *leeri* LEERI, PEARL or MOSAIC GOURAMI 11cm. (4½in.)
A lovely peaceful fish which is native to the Malay Peninsula, Thailand, Sumatra and Borneo. A beautiful olive green body with a golden metallic sheen is patterned with small light patches which gives a mosaic effect. A dark line extends horizontally from the snout through the eye fading before it reaches the caudal fin where lies a dark spot. The unpaired fins continue the body colour and mosaic pattern in a more open form. The throat and breast are a bright orange which extends to the elongated pelvics and into the anterior half of the anal fin.

It prefers temperatures around 21–22°C. and is omnivorous. A bubble nest builder. **152**
– *microlepsis* MOONLIGHT GOURAMI 15cm. (6in.)
A native of Thailand and Cambodia. This fish is more slender and streamlined than most gouramis. It has uniform colouring resembling a cold clear night with a full moon. Males are distinguished by their red modified pelvic fins which are elongated. **153**
– *pectoralis* SNAKESKIN GOURAMI 24cm. (9½in.)
A native of Thailand and the Malay Peninsula, this fish has little to offer over the other members of the genus except that it is easily bred and very hardy.

A bluish green fish with an irregular horizontal line from snout to caudal fin and dark bars running obliquely across the body. Fins golden. It rarely exceeds 18cm. in captivity. It is a typical bubble nest builder.

– *trichopterus* TWO-SPOT, GANTER'S or THREE-SPOT GOURAMI, HAIR-PIN 15cm (6in.)

A two-spot becomes a three-spot by adding a black eye. The body colour is a broken blue. The fins are pale yellow and the dorsal and anal fins have orange dots and an orange border.

Native to Burma, Thailand, the Malay Peninsula and Indonesia. The male has a pointed dorsal fin which distinguishes him from the female.

Breeds readily, making a bubble nest. **154**

– *trichopterus sumatranus* OPALINE or BLUE GOURAMI 12cm. (4½in.)

A subspecies of *T. trichopterus*, which is darker, has no spots but faint dark patches and is similar. This is a popular fish and more commonly kept than *T. trichopterus*.

Trichopsis Belontiidae

– *pumilus* SPARKLING or CROAKING DWARF GOURAMI 4cm. (1½in.)

A charming little fish from Vietnam, Thailand and Sumatra. The body is a basic dirty green. A wide dark bar runs horizontally along the body. Blue dots forming a broken line often appear above and below the dark lateral bar and there is a blue flash behind the eye. The fins are transparent and delicate with a yellowish brown tinge. The dorsal fin is narrow-based and long with a backward slope, while the anal fin is broad-based and round.

Preferring soft water with large amounts of sphagnum moss on the bottom, this fish needs temperatures from 27–30°C.

Mating occurs in captivity. The water level should be lowered and fine floating plants provided for the bubble nest. A croaking noise is audible during mating. Only a few

Sparkling or Croaking Gouramis, *Trichopsis pumilus*.

eggs are laid and these hatch in 30–40 hours depending on conditions. **155**

TRIGGERFISH see *Balistes, Balistidae, Balistapus, Balistoides, Melichthys, Odonus, Pseudobalistes, Rhinecanthus*
TRITOLO see *Characidium fasciatum*

Tropheus Cichlidae ⊕
– ***moorei*** BLUNT-HEAD CICHLID 10cm. (4in.)
More commonly imported in recent years, this fish is from Lake Tanganyika in Africa. It has a black body when young but as it gains maturity it develops into one of several colour types. Some remain a darkish brown or black but the form commonly imported by aquarists has a black body with a wide vertical orange red band passing through the dorsal fin and across the body. In captivity it settles well but likes plenty of rocky cover and dark hiding places.

Tropical Freshwater Tank see *Establishing a Tropical Tank*
TROUT, SLEEPY see *Mogurnda mogurnda*
TRUNKFISH, SPINY see *Tetrosomus gibbosus*
TUBE-MOUTHED PENCILFISH see *Nannostomus eques*
Tuberculosis see under *Disease*
Tubifex see under *Food*
TURKEYFISH see *Pterois volitans*
TWIG PUFFER see *Canthigaster cinctus*
Twin Worm Disease see under *Disease*
TWO-EYED DAMSELFISH see *Pomacentrus chrysus*
TWO-COLOURED CATFISH see *Buncocephalus bicolor*
TWO-LINED NEOTOCA see *Neotoca bilineata*
TWO-SPOT
    ASTYANAX see *Astyanax bimaculatus*
    BARB see *Barbus ticto*
    CHANCHITO see *Cichlasoma aureum*
    CICHLID see *Cichlasoma bimaculatum*
    GOURAMI see *Trichopterus trichopterus*
    TETRA see *Astyanax bimaculatus*
    WRASSE see *Coris angulata*
TWO-STRIPED KILLY see *Aphyosemion bivittatum*

U

Uaru Cichlidae ⊕
– ***amphiacanthoides*** UARU, TRIANGLE CICHLID
25cm. (10in.)
The body shape of this species is reflected in one of its common names. It is a brownish yellow colour with a large triangular patch on its side, together with two slightly

smaller patches of the same hue.

This fish, which comes from the Amazon and Guyana, enjoys some popularity as an aquarium species particularly in the USA. It will breed but not readily. It lays its eggs on the underside of a clean flat surface. The young are dark, almost black in colour. Recommended temperature range 27–28°C.; for breeding up to 30°C.

Ultra Violet Sterilizer
The principle of this machinery is based on the circulation of water around a source of ultra violet light. Ultra violet light acts as a sterilizer. The attempt to keep a tank sterile or even relatively free from living things is not only fruitless but unnatural. In nature a balance between living things of all kinds from bacteria to whales allows life to continue. This should be the aim of the biologically minded aquarist. Ultra violet sterilizers are for technocrats not biologists.

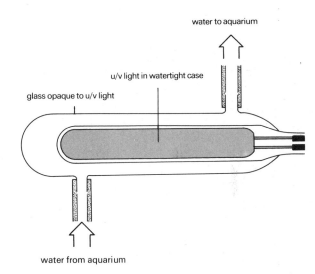

They are expensive to purchase and expensive to run. The best use is in marine aquaria to help stem an epizootic epidemic with minimal chemical therapy.

UMBRELLA HAIR GRASS see under *Plants – Eleocharis*
UNICORNFISH, STRIPE-FACED see *Naso lituratus*

Unwelcome Visitors
Most of these unwelcome visitors to the aquarium gain entry with new plants or among the live food. Fortunately they are not common.

Anchor Worms
A parasitic crustacean with a free swimming stage. It attaches to some fish notably the Goldfish, *Carassius auratus*, and tunnels in through the skin then hangs

anchored by several head appendages. To remove it, a strong sharp pull is necessary.

Argulus. Fish Louse

Occasionally attacks aquarium fish although it is more common in ponds. It is not related to true lice but is a crustacean. It attacks fish, notably Goldfish, and feeds on their blood after a suitable wound has been inflicted by its competent mouth parts. Any fish which is seen to be afflicted should be removed from the water, and the parasite induced to release its grip by applying chloroform, ether or turpentine.

Beetles

Aquatic beetles of almost any kind will attack and feed on living fish. They should therefore be removed as soon as they are spotted. One of the commonest is the Water Tiger, *Dytiscus marginalis*, which is a severe threat to fish both in the larval stage and as an adult. The beetle is very large and is easily removed. The larva grow up to 5cm. in length and are equipped with a breathing tube at the tail end. The head end has powerful and dangerous pincers which are used to attack fish. The larvae need to surface at regular intervals to breathe air but at other times hide among the weed awaiting their prey. They are collected along with live fish food like daphnia, therefore it is advisable to pour the daphnia into a shallow white bowl before feeding them to your fish. The beetle larvae will be clearly visible and can be removed by hand.

Hydra

Hydra are very primitive animals technically known as coelenterata and are closely related to Jellyfish. They have a sack-like body which is the digestive organ into which food is drawn by a number of tentacles surrounding the mouth. Each tentacle is equipped with small stinging units. When a suitable prey approaches, the tentacles, which are waving constantly, contact the victim and sting it, at the same time closing over it and drawing it to the mouth. They can reproduce either sexually or simply by budding off from the body.

Hydra are not dangerous to adult fish but they can dessimate a spawning of several hundred fish fry in a few days. They are introduced to the tank with food caught in ponds and streams. Although they are often in their extended form showing tentacles they can reduce in size to a tiny blob of jelly and be almost impossible to see. Even in the extended form they rarely exceed 6mm. in length. Although they are attached to a solid object when stationary they can move about the aquarium.

They can be cleared from an infected tank by thorough cleaning and soaking the plants in salt water. The sand should also be boiled. The snail, *Limnaea stagnalis*, will eat Hydra.

The larva of a Water Tiger, *Dytiscus marginalis* ×5.

Fish Leech, *Piscicola geometra* ×10.

Leeches

Leeches are blood-suckers and as such are not likely to kill fish. They do however remove blood and must be considered an enemy to fish. In addition most aquarists find leeches unaesthetic and prefer to keep their tanks free. They

Brown Hydra, *Hydra oligactis* ×100

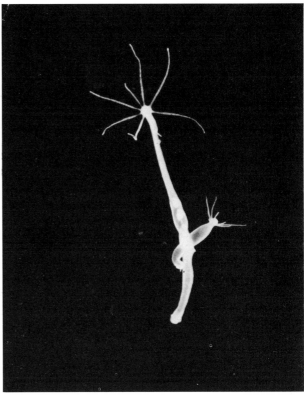

Green Hydra, *Chlorohydra viridissima* ×50.

Water Scorpion, *Nepa cinerea* ×3.

are killed by salt water and all new plants from doubtful sources should therefore be dipped in water containing 31 grams of salt per 4½ litres (1oz. per gallon) before being introduced to the tank.

Nepa cinerea. Water Scorpion
This character is introduced into the tank inadvertently with plants collected from ponds and streams. It does resemble the true Scorpion in having large legs and a pointed projection at the back. It is easy to identify and should be manually removed.

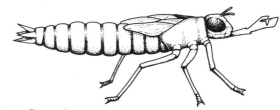

Dragon fly nymph

Odonata. Dragonfly larvae
Common inhabitants of our ponds and streams, they are equipped with formidable mouth parts well designed to inflict damage on fish. They should be removed by washing all plants before introduction. All live food caught in streams should be emptied into a shallow white dish so that these intruders can be spotted.

Planaria

These worms belong to the group known as Platyhelminthes which include the tape worms. *Planaria* are however free living, that is they are not parasites, but they do consume small fish fry and are best removed. Found in freshwater streams, they commonly live under rocks and stones or attached to plants. It is therefore advisable to wash all plants collected in water containing 31 grams (1oz.) of salt per 4½ litres (1 gall).

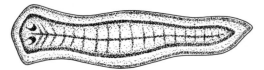

Flatworm

UPSIDE-DOWN CATFISHES see *Mochocidae, Synodontis*
URCHINS, SEA see under *Marine Invertebrates*

V

Vacation see *Holidays*
Vaccination see *Immunization*
VAGABOND BUTTERFLYFISH see *Chaetodon vagabundus*
Vallisneria see under *Plants*
VARIEGATED PLATY see *Xiphophorus variatus*

Variola   Serranidae   Ψ
– louti   CERISE GROUPER, LUNAR-TAILED ROCK COD
91cm. (3ft)
A very hardy fish from the Indo-Pacific. If anything, it is more adept at changing colour than other members of the family. Varies from bright red to brown with blue spots. The fins are bordered, at times with yellow. Certain to always look at its worst when you are showing your collection to a critical colleague. It is kept by aquarists while in its young state.

VEILTAILS see *Carassius auratus*
VELVET
  CICHLID see *Astronotus ocellatus*
  DISEASE see under *Disease*
Vernetus see under *Marine Invertebrates*
VERMICULATED SPINEFOOT see *Siganus vermiculatus*
VIEJA see *Loricaria parva*
Virus Disease see under *Disease*
Vision see *Eye*
Viviparus see under *Snails*

Vivisection

The use of animals for research purposes raises a great many doubts in many minds. How far man should be allowed to abuse the animal life on earth is a matter of philosophy. To those who object to animal experimentation there is no excuse for such activity at all. No reason justifies it. To others it is an evil necessity of which man, in his struggle for survival, must avail himself. The moral and ethical arguments on either side are complex. Fish are now being used as experimental animals and much of the technology which allows fish to be kept in laboratories results from the activities of aquarists. See *Research*.

W

WALKING
  GOBY see *Periophthalmus barbarus*
  PERCH, CLIMBING see *Anabas testudineus*
WASP GOBY see *Brachygobius doriae*

Water

Without water and its constant cycle, life, as we know it on this planet, would be impossible. The heat of the sun causes evaporation of water vapour from the sea. This in turn accumulates into clouds which, under certain conditions, drop their water content as rain. The rain, as it falls through the air, dissolves gases, notably carbon dioxide to produce very weak carbonic acid. As this percolates through the soil it dissolves substances therein to alter its composition. Water varies in different parts of the world depending on the type and amount of substance dissolved in it. Some water is very acid, some is alkaline. Some water has compounds dissolved which make it hard (see *Hardness*), some does not which is then known as 'soft'. From a practical point of view, hard water is much more difficult to lather with soap than is soft. Soft water has a slightly slippery feeling. As for fish, some prefer it hard, others like it soft.

The complete aquarist must have some knowledge of water and its constituents if he is to be successful, for correct water conditions are essential for fish welfare. Simple tests are available for measuring both the acidity (pH) and hardness and all aquarists should become familiar with their use.

Water in which fish live varies in temperature, acidity and hardness. In addition, household supplies frequently contain chloride introduced by Water Boards during the purification process and this can be deadly to fish (see

Chlorine). This can be overcome, however, quite simply by leaving the water to stand.

The question arises for the budding aquarist, 'What water do I use?' Pure water, or distilled water is unnecessary, unnatural and deadly. Fish naturally live in water which is a solvent for many substances. It would be foolish to preclude these substances. The aquarist's job is to understand the constituents and use the correct type of water for the fish to be kept. Common tap water is, in most cases, quite suitable as long as the chlorine problem is overcome.

Some aquarists prefer rain water and in country areas, where industrial fumes do not pollute the air, it is an excellent medium.

Water from ponds and streams can be quite satisfactory providing it is not polluted by industrial waste. It is as well to filter such water to remove particulate matter and pests, see *Unwelcome Visitors*.

The marine aquarist is interested in his medium – salt water. This is dealt with separately, see *Establishing the Marine Aquarium*.

WATER
    ASPIDISTRA see under *Plants – Anubias*
    CLOVER see under *Plants – Marsilea*
    FLEA see under *Food*
    GOLDFINCH see *Pristella riddlei*
    HARDNESS see *Hardness of Water*
    Hedge see under *Plants – Didiplis*
    HOG LOUSE see under *Food*
SPRITE see under *Plants – Ceratopteris*
WEATHERFISH, JAPANESE see *Misgurnus anguillicaudatus*

Welfare

The pleasure of keeping fish in aquaria is not without its responsibilities. Fish in tanks are totally dependent on the aquarist for their welfare: they don't choose to be there.

Of all species kept by man in captivity, fish can be most comfortable and suffer least, providing care is taken with management and suitable species are chosen. Some cruelties are very apparent like glass tapping and bad handling during netting but often cruelty in pet owning is not wilful but is due to ignorance. Overfeeding, failure to provide adequate hiding places for nervous species, are the kinds of things that, all too commonly, cause suffering. It is therefore the responsibility of the aquarist to be aware of the demands of the species kept and of the general principles of good management.

WHIPTAIL see *Loricaria parva*
WHITE
    CLOUD MOUNTAIN MINNOW see *Tanichthys albonubes*

LINE DANIO see *Brachydanio albolineatus*
RAMSHORN see under *Snails – Planorbis*
SPOT see under *Disease*
STAR CARDINALFISH see *Apogon lachneri*
WORM see under *Food*
WHITE-BREASTED SURGEONFISH see *Acanthurus leucosternon*
WHITE-FIN LIONFISH see *Pterois radiata*
WHITE-LINED TRIGGERFISH see *Balistes bursa*
WHITE-SPOTTED BUTTERFLYFISH see *Chaetodon kleini*
WHITE'S CYNOLEBIAS see *Cynolebias whitei*
Wickler's Formula see under *Plants – Marine*
WIDOW,
    BLACK see *Gymnocorymbus ternetzi*
    MERRY see *Phallichthys amates*
Wiedermann-Kramer Formula see under *Establishing a Tropical Marine Aquarium*
WILD GOLDFISH see *Carassius carassius*
WILLOW LEAF see under *Plants – Hygrophila*
WIMPLEFISH see *Heniochus*
WORM
    BLOOD see under *Food*
    GHOST see under *Food*
    GLASS see under *Food*
    MARINE see under *Marine Invertebrates*
    MUD see under *Food*
    ROUND see under *Disease*
    TAPE see under *Disease*
    TWIN see under *Disease*
    WHITE see under *Food*
WRASSE see *Cheilio, Coris, Hemigymnus, Hemipteronotus, Labridae, Labroides, Mirolabrichthys, Novaculichthys, Thalassoma*

X-Rays

Although X-rays are by no means commonly used in diagnosis of fish disease there is no reason why they cannot become a routine practice. Research workers have used substances opaque to X-ray to outline organs in fish in exactly similar ways to veterinary and human surgeons.

X-RAY FISH see *Pristella riddlei*

Xenomystus Notopteridae ⊕
– *nigri* AFRICAN KNIFEFISH, FALSE FEATHERBACK
20cm. (8in.)
The shape of this fish is very similar to that of members of

the genus *Notopterus*. It can be distinguished, however, by the complete absence of a dorsal fin. The body colour varies from a brownish pink to a deep brown. Sometimes thin indistinct longitudinal lines can be identified.

These fish are found in slow flowing rivers and large open ponds which contain water with sometimes low oxygen content throughout tropical Africa. Thus the advantage of breathing air becomes apparent.

Xiphophorus Poeciliidae ⊕
– helleri SWORDTAIL 13cm. (5in.) ✂
Swordtails probably need little description for those who have ever given a fleeting glance at a tropical fish tank. The wild species, however, from Mexico, Guatamala and Yucatan are far from arresting in appearance. They have basically dull green bodies with slight variations, and in the male there is a rather pathetic attempt on the part of the caudal fin to produce a sword by elongating its lower rays.

The aquarist, by careful selection of the more attractive males, and crossing them with their close generic cousins the Platys – *X. maculatus* – has produced a variety of brightly coloured swordtails. These include Green, Red, Albino, Wagtail, Black, Golden, London, and several others which delight the eye and cause one to marvel at the patience and ingenuity of their breeders. In addition those aquarists with a quenchless thirst for something different have produced a selection of swordtails with flamboyant dorsal fins known as Hi-fins.

The breeding habits relate closely to those described for the family, see *Poeciliidae*.

The Swordtail is an active fish, able to jump well, and tends to be a bully. It should only be placed in community tanks with larger fish. Gluttons, they will eat more than is good for them, unfortunately including their offspring, so take steps to protect the young by trapping them if necessary.

A pair of Swordtails, *Xiphophorus helleri*, showing the difference in shape between the male (left) and the female.

A point to be noted by those of a scientific turn of mind. Many crosses between species, known as hybrids, are, like mules in the horse family, infertile. In the case of *Xiphophorus* they are not. Therefore the unusual phenomenon is seen where crosses between *X. helleri* and *X. maculatus* are able to breed. **156**

– *maculatus* PLATY 6cm. (2½in.)
It comes as no surprise to the scientist that this fish has been reclassified to this genus from its earlier generic nomenclature of *Platypoecilis*. It makes much more sense considering the ease with which it produces fertile crosses with *X. helleri.*

The wild ancestral form of the man-made varieties comes from Central America. It has a greenish body tinged faintly with blue in certain lights. The fins are clear, the caudal having two dark spots on the tail. They are peaceful, hardy and breed easily to produce batches of over 100 young, but are rather dull.

Nothing daunted, man's ingenuity has improved on nature's gifts and, by selection and by crossing this species with *X. helleri,* has produced a large variety of extremely attractive and popular fish which have done as much as any other fish to popularize the hobby. The list of Platy's includes Red, Black, Blue, Moon, Wagtails, Yellow, Spangled, Tiger, Leopard and Bleeding Hearts. **157, 158.**

– *variatus* VARIEGATED or MONTEZUMA PLATY 6cm. (2½in.)
A native of Mexico, this fish is somewhat more slender than *X. maculatus.* The male is an olive green with a variety of coloured speckles on the side. The dorsal fin is clear with yellow tints and the tail is orange with a dark-patterned base. Some males are endowed with better looks than others and it is from these privileged individuals that the exciting colour varieties descend. Females are browny green in colour, shading to a silver belly, and with two irregular lines along the side. They are hardy, have a temperature range from 16–20°C. and breed readily.

Xyrichthys taeniurus see *Hemipterondtus taeniurus*

YELLOW
DAMSELFISH see *Eupomacentrus planifrons*
DWARF CICHLID, AMAZON see *Apistogramma pertense*
DWARF GROUPER see *Pseudochromis flavescens*
GULARIS see *Aphyosemion gulare*
LONG-NOSED BUTTERFLYFISH see *Forcipiger longirostris*

RASBORA see *Rasbora lateristriata*
SHANK CLOWNFISH see *Amphiprion akallopsisos*
TANG see *Zebrasoma flavescens*
TETRA see *Hyphessobrycon bifasciatus*
YELLOW-BACKED DAMSELFISH see *Abudefduf melanopus*
YELLOW-FACED ANGELFISH see *Euxiphipops xanthometapon*
YELLOW-LINED SWEETLIPS see *Plectorhynchus albovittatus*
YELLOW-STRIPED EMERALD TRIGGERFISH see *Balistapus undulatus*
YELLOW-TAIL
ANGELFISH see *Holocanthus xanthurus*
WRASSE see *Coris gaimardi*
YELLOW-TAILED
CLOWNFISH see *Amphiprion clarkii*
DAMSELFISH see *Microspathodon chrysurus*
YELLOWBELLY see *Girardinus falcatus*
YELLOWHEAD JAWFISH see *Opistognathus aurifrons*
Yolk, Egg see under *Food*

Moorish Idol, *Zanclus cornutus.*

Zanclus Acanthuridae Ψ
– ***canescens*** see under *Z. cornutus*
– ***cornutus*** MOORISH IDOL 25cm. (10in.)
A native of the Indo-Pacific. It has a pale yellow body with
black bands edged with blue. A very long and tapering
dorsal fin adds elegance to this beautiful fish. It likes plenty
of space and good light but even then the colour soon fades
in most hands, as it is a very difficult fish to keep in
captivity. Young fish of this species were for many years,
described as a separate species – *Z. canescens*. The young
fish has a spine at the corner of the mouth which falls off as
it approaches half the adult length. The adult gradually
develops a pair of 'horns' close to the eyes. **159**

ZEBRA
    ANGELFISH see *Pomacanthus semicirculatus*
    CHANCHITO see *Cichlasoma nigrofasciatum*
    DANIO see *Brachydanio rerio*
    KILLY see *Fundulus heteroclitus*
    LIONFISH see *Dendrochirus zebra*
    MORAY EEL see *Echidna zebra*
    SURGEONFISH see *Zebrasoma veliferum*

Zebrasoma Acanthuridae Ψ
– ***flavescens*** YELLOW TANG 18cm. (7in.)
This is a stunningly beautiful fish from the Pacific, common
around Hawaii. The bright yellow of the body and fins is
virtually unbroken, except for the dark spots of the eyes.
The dorsal fin is very high indeed and the anal fin is equally
attractive. The jaws are also rather elongated. It is easy to
keep providing it is given adequate green food
supplemented with small shrimps or other fine animal
protein.
– ***veliferum*** SAILFIN TANG, ZEBRA SURGEONFISH
30cm. (12in.)
This is one of several members of the family with a wide
distribution, ranging from the Red Sea and coastal African
waters to the Pacific. It gets its name from the very large
dorsal fin which turns the overall shape of the body from a
rather elongated tapering form into a circle. Colours vary
considerably with location. The body is basically composed
of vertical stripes of yellow or orange brown alternating
with wide bands of brown or olive green. The dorsal and
anal fins are speckled and the caudal fin is a translucent
blue. **160**

ZEBRAFISH see *Brachydanio rerio, Therapon jarbua*
Zebrasoma xanthurum see *Acanthurus xanthopterus*.

MRINAL K. DAS